THE ARCHITECTURE OF CONSTITUTIONAL AMENDMENTS

This innovative book blends constitutional theory with real-life political practice to explore the impact of codifying constitutional amendments on the operation of the constitution in relation to democracy, the rule of law and the separation of powers.

It draws from comparative, historical, political and theoretical perspectives to answer questions all constitutional designers should ask themselves:

- Should the constitution append amendments sequentially to the end of the text?
- Should it embed amendments directly into the existing text, with notations about what has been modified and how?
- Should it instead insert amendments into the text without indicating at all that any alteration has occurred?

The book examines the three major models of amendment codification – the appendative, the integrative, and the invisible models – and also shows how some jurisdictions have innovated alternative forms of amendment codification that combine elements of more than one model in a unique hybridisation driven by history, law and politics.

Constitutional designers rarely consider where in the constitution to codify amendments once they are ratified. Yet this choice is pivotal to the operation of any constitution. This groundbreaking book shows why the placement of constitutional amendments goes well beyond mere aesthetics. It influences how and whether a people remembers its past, how the constitutional text will be interpreted and by whom, and whether the constitution will be easily accessible to the governed.

A global tour of the high stakes of constitution-making, this book features 18 diverse and outstanding scholars from around the world – across Africa, America, Asia and Oceania, and Europe – raising new questions, opening our eyes to new streams of research and uncovering new possibilities for constitutional design.

The Architecture of Constitutional Amendments

History, Law, Politics

Edited by
Richard Albert

•HART•
OXFORD • LONDON • NEW YORK • NEW DELHI • SYDNEY

HART PUBLISHING

Bloomsbury Publishing Plc

Kemp House, Chawley Park, Cumnor Hill, Oxford, OX2 9PH, UK

1385 Broadway, New York, NY 10018, USA

29 Earlsfort Terrace, Dublin 2, Ireland

HART PUBLISHING, the Hart/Stag logo, BLOOMSBURY and the Diana logo are trademarks of Bloomsbury Publishing Plc

First published in Great Britain 2023

A catalogue record for this book is available from the British Library.

A catalogue record for this book is available from the Library of Congress.

ISBN: HB: 978-1-50995-908-2
ePDF: 978-1-50995-910-5
ePub: 978-1-50995-909-9

Typeset by Compuscript Ltd, Shannon

ACKNOWLEDGEMENTS

The first time I gave any thought to the codification of constitutional amendments was over 20 years ago, when I served as a research assistant to Akhil Amar, then the Southmayd Professor of Law at the Yale Law School and now a Sterling Professor of Law. One of my assignments involved research for a special lecture Professor Amar was to give at Indiana University. In his lecture – which has since been published under the title 'Architexture' (2002) 77 *Indiana Law Journal* 671 – he examined the relationship between the architecture of the United States Constitution and its legal, political and social functions. My research experience with him opened my eyes to exciting and innovative ways to read constitutions. In many ways, this book continues the fun research assignment Professor Amar gave me long ago. I thank him sincerely for the opportunity to learn under his guidance.

I thank also the many contributors to this book. When they accepted my invitation to contribute a chapter to this enterprise, we did not yet know who would publish the book. But they believed in the project and committed their time and effort to producing outstanding chapters. Fortunately, their efforts were rewarded with the opportunity to publish with Hart Publishing, our first-choice publisher for this manuscript. We are grateful to the entire team at Hart and we especially thank Kate Whetter, Rosemarie Mearns, Sarah Skinner and Jon Lloyd.

Finally, I thank my colleagues at the University of Texas at Austin. I am grateful to Trish Mair and Grace Green for their assistance in preparing this manuscript for submission. I also thank my two Deans, Ward Farnsworth and Robert Chesney, for so enthusiastically supporting my research. It is a blessing to work at this magnificent institution.

Richard Albert
Austin, Texas
18 November 2022

CONTENTS

CONTRIBUTORS

Richard Albert is the William Stamps Farish Professor in Law, Professor of Government and Director of Constitutional Studies at the University of Texas at Austin, US.

Eszter Bodnár is Associate Professor at the ELTE Eötvös Loránd University, Hungary, and Lecturer at the University of Victoria, Canada.

Catarina Santos Botelho is Professor of Constitutional Law at Porto Faculty of Law, Universidade Católica Portuguesa, Portugal.

Hui-Wen Chen is a research assistant at the School of Law, University of Warwick, UK.

Bruno Cunha is a PhD candidate at the Federal University of Pernambuco (UFPE), Brazil, and a Visiting Research Scholar at the Ohio State University Moritz College of Law, US.

Zelalem Esehtu Degifie is Assistant Professor of Comparative Public Law at Wollo University, School of Law, Ethiopia.

Masahiko Kinoshita is Professor of Constitutional Law at Kobe University, Japan.

Gert-Jan Leenknegt is Associate Professor of Constitutional Law at Tilburg University, the Netherlands.

Patricia García Majado is Assistant Professor of Constitutional Law at University of Oviedo, Spain.

Diego Moreno is Professor of Constitutional Theory at the Catholic University of Asunción, Paraguay.

Malkhaz Nakashidze is Professor of Constitutional Law and Jean Monnet Chair at the Batumi Shota Rustaveli State University, Georgia.

Jaime Olaiz-González is Professor of Constitutional Theory and International Law at Universidad Panamericana Law School, Mexico City, Mexico.

Shamshad Pasarlay is a visiting lecturer at the University of Chicago Law School, US, and a consultant at the Max Planck Foundation for International Peace and the Rule of Law.

Reijer Passchier is Assistant Professor of Constitutional Law at the Open University and Leiden University, the Netherlands

Caspar Pfrunder is a PhD candidate at the University of St Gallen, Switzerland.

Rosa Ristawati is Senior Lecturer of Constitutional Law and Comparative Constitutions at Airlangga University, Indonesia.

Radian Salman is Associate Professor of Constitutional Law at Airlangga University, Indonesia.

Sharowat Shamin is Assistant Professor of Law at the University of Dhaka, Bangladesh, and a doctoral researcher at the SOAS University of London, UK.

Arta Vorpsi is Professor of Constitutional Law at Tirana University, Albania.

Jeong-In Yun is Research Professor at the Legal Research Institute of Korea University, Republic of Korea.

CONTRIBUTORS

Richard Albert is the William Stamps Farish Professor in Law, Professor of Government and Director of Constitutional Studies at the University of Texas at Austin, US.

Eszter Bodnár is Associate Professor at the ELTE Eötvös Loránd University, Hungary, and Lecturer at the University of Victoria, Canada.

Catarina Santos Botelho is Professor of Constitutional Law at Porto Faculty of Law, Universidade Católica Portuguesa, Portugal.

Hui-Wen Chen is a research assistant at the School of Law, University of Warwick, UK.

Bruno Cunha is a PhD candidate at the Federal University of Pernambuco (UFPE), Brazil, and a Visiting Research Scholar at the Ohio State University Moritz College of Law, US.

Zelalem Esehtu Degifie is Assistant Professor of Comparative Public Law at Wollo University, School of Law, Ethiopia.

Masahiko Kinoshita is Professor of Constitutional Law at Kobe University, Japan.

Gert-Jan Leenknegt is Associate Professor of Constitutional Law at Tilburg University, the Netherlands.

Patricia García Majado is Assistant Professor of Constitutional Law at University of Oviedo, Spain.

Diego Moreno is Professor of Constitutional Theory at the Catholic University of Asunción, Paraguay.

Malkhaz Nakashidze is Professor of Constitutional Law and Jean Monnet Chair at the Batumi Shota Rustaveli State University, Georgia.

Jaime Olaiz-González is Professor of Constitutional Theory and International Law at Universidad Panamericana Law School, Mexico City, Mexico.

Shamshad Pasarlay is a visiting lecturer at the University of Chicago Law School, US, and a consultant at the Max Planck Foundation for International Peace and the Rule of Law.

Reijer Passchier is Assistant Professor of Constitutional Law at the Open University and Leiden University, the Netherlands

Caspar Pfrunder is a PhD candidate at the University of St Gallen, Switzerland.

Rosa Ristawati is Senior Lecturer of Constitutional Law and Comparative Constitutions at Airlangga University, Indonesia.

Radian Salman is Associate Professor of Constitutional Law at Airlangga University, Indonesia.

Sharowat Shamin is Assistant Professor of Law at the University of Dhaka, Bangladesh, and a doctoral researcher at the SOAS University of London, UK.

Arta Vorpsi is Professor of Constitutional Law at Tirana University, Albania.

Jeong-In Yun is Research Professor at the Legal Research Institute of Korea University, Republic of Korea.

Introduction: How Should Constitutions Codify Amendments?

RICHARD ALBERT

No constitution is perfect. All constitutions will eventually confront the need for change. That is why virtually every single written constitution in the world creates a procedure for constitutional reform.[1] These procedures offer a means to update the constitution when time and experience reveal limitations in the constitutional text.[2] Constitution-makers therefore write constitutions expecting that the text will not retain its original form and content. Yet despite creating a pathway to revise the constitutional text, constitution-makers rarely ask themselves an obvious question: how should the constitution indicate in its text that it has been amended?

There are four major models of amendment codification, and each entails significant consequences for the form and function of the constitution. These four models are often blended in innovative ways, in the end yielding hybrid models of amendment codification tied to the history, law and politics of a people or polity. In all cases, the basic elements cobbled together to build these hybrid models are derived from the four ideal types visible around the world.

Some constitutions codify constitutional amendments at the end of the constitutional text and leave all existing text unchanged. I call this the *appendative* model of amendment codification because amendments are always appended at the end of the constitutional text. Other constitutions place amendments directly into the relevant portions of the existing text of the constitution and include notations about what has changed and how. I call this the *integrative* model because amendments are integrated into the constitutional text. Still other constitutions simply rewrite the relevant portions of the amended text and leave no indication that any change has occurred. I call this the *invisible* model of amendment codification because it alters the constitutional text without highlighting what in the constitution has changed, nor how. The fourth is the *disaggregative* model, which applies to constitutions that are not codified in a single unified text. Disaggregated

[1] See Francesco Giovannoni, 'Amendment Rules in Constitutions' (2003) 115 *Public Choice* 37 at 37.

[2] For a discussion of the functions of constitutional amendment rules, see Richard Albert, 'The Expressive Function of Constitutional Amendment Rules' (2013) 59 *McGill Law Journal* 225.

constitutions exist across several distinguishable documents of equal legal significance. Under this model of amendment codification, constitutional amendments are codified as separate self-standing texts of higher law that may or may not be specially entrenched.

Amendment codification of course alters the appearance of the constitution, but it involves more than mere aesthetics. It shapes how judges will interpret the constitution, whether the text will contain obsolete rules that have been superseded in law, how easily laypersons will understand the rules the constitution sets out for basic governance, and whether the constitution will play a central role in politics as a political symbol or whether it will be limited largely to the domain of law as a legal compendium. Given the high stakes involved in the choice among models of amendment codification, we would expect constitution-makers to make this a priority when they negotiate the form and content of the new constitution prior to its promulgation. Yet the reality is that amendment codification is little more than an afterthought for constitution-makers. It is puzzling and problematic that constitutional designers do not devote time to decide – much less to discuss – how the constitutional text should record modifications to it.

The Architecture of Constitutional Amendments: History, Law, Politics draws from case studies around the world to demonstrate why constitution-makers should pay considerably more attention to amendment codification when they create new constitutions. Doing so will help them avoid predictable pitfalls in constitutional politics and could also help them foster an environment conducive to a more stable and successful lifespan for their constitution.

The overriding purpose of this book is to shine a light on a question of constitutional design that has attracted too little inquiry given its importance. As we show in this volume, so much in a country's constitutional law and politics turns on the placement of amendments in its codified constitutional text. An additional purpose of this book is to broaden the range of jurisdictions that feature in studies of comparative constitutionalism. Conventional studies of comparative constitutionalism turn to Canada, Germany, India, South Africa and a few other standard referents. In this book, we have chosen deliberately to highlight understudied jurisdictions in every region of the world in order to demonstrate just how fascinating they can be and also to encourage scholars to look beyond the usual comparators in their own studies. We have moreover assembled a group of scholars who are diverse in terms of their ideological orientation, gender identity and methodological approach. Each of us is interested in uncovering answers to the same question: what are the drivers and consequences of a country's chosen model of amendment codification?

I. Writing Rights and Wrongs

There is no better vehicle than a comparative illustration to show how and why a constitution's model of amendment codification matters. The US is fertile soil for finding contrasting examples of amendment codification within the same constitutional structure and political culture. There is variation among the 50 states in how they have chosen to codify amendments to their respective constitutions. And there is also variation in amendment codification between some state constitutions, on the one hand, and the national constitution, on the other.

One comparison is quite telling. It reveals eye-opening similarities and differences between a state constitution and the national constitution in relation to America's original sin of slavery.

When they were written long ago, the current Constitution of Alabama and the present US Constitution were both rooted deeply in racism. Ratified in 1901, the text of the Alabama Constitution leaves no doubt that its 'central purpose' was to subordinate African-Americans.[3] On the first day the Constitutional Convention met to begin drafting Alabama's new constitution, the elected president of the Convention made clear their collective objective: 'what is it that we want to do? Why, it is, within the limits imposed by the Federal Constitution, to establish white supremacy in this State'.[4] The US Constitution had been written much earlier, when enslavement was lawful. It was built in 1787 upon an infrastructure of slavery, with racist rules hidden in plain sight for all to see.[5] Today only one of these two constitutional texts has made progress in removing the hateful language of the past and reflecting modern values of inclusion and belonging. The answer is surprising: the Alabama Constitution has far surpassed the US Constitution.

Consider the current text of America's higher law. Over two centuries since its enactment, the US Constitution continues to codify its slavocratic rules on property, representation and taxation. The Three-Fifths Clause counts African Americans as less than whole persons,[6] the Fugitive Slave Clause requires the return of an enslaved person to her enslaver if she escapes to freedom,[7] the Migration and Importation Clause forbids Congress from interfering with the international trade in enslaved persons,[8] and the Census-Based Taxation Clause requires Congress to impose any direct tax on citizens only in proportion to the population of each state, a number that had been distorted by the Three-Fifths Clause. Each of these rules remains written in the US Constitution, unchanged from the day it was enacted long ago.

Of course, none of those rules retains any legal force today in relation to slavery. They have been overridden by time and change. The Thirteenth Amendment, which abolishes slavery, supersedes the Fugitive Slave Clause. The Fourteenth Amendment, which enshrines the promise of equality under law,

[3] Wayne Flynt, 'Alabama's Shame: The Historical Origins of the 1901 Constitution' (2001) 53 *Alabama Law Review* 67 at 71.

[4] *Journal of the Proceedings of the Constitutional Convention of the State of Alabama* (1901) at 9: https://archive.org/details/alabama-constitutional-convention-journal-1901/mode/2up.

[5] See Jack M Balkin, 'Does the Constitution Deserve Our Fidelity: Agreements with Hell and Other Objects of Our Faith' (1997) 65 *Fordham Law Review* 1703 at 1707.

[6] Constitution of the United States, art I, § 2, cl 3.

[7] ibid at art IV, § 2, cl 3.

[8] ibid at art I, § 9, cl 1.

nullifies the Three-Fifths Clause. And the passage of time has supplanted the Migration and Importation Clause as well as the Census-Based Taxation Clause, because both were made temporarily unamendable only until 1808. And yet although these slavocratic rules are no longer legally valid, they still appear in the written constitution. The reason why is that amendments to the US Constitution do not alter the existing constitutional text. An amendment is placed chronologically at the end of the constitutional text, leaving untouched everything that has appeared prior to its codification. That is why the US Constitution contains rules that were once in force but no longer are. This is especially problematic for rules that recall the painful memory of America's evil past.

The Constitution of Alabama was written with hateful rules of its own, but those rules have been erased. Alabamans recently engaged in an historic exercise to re-imagine their constitution. They agreed, in a series of legislative and popular votes, to rid their constitutional text of the racist rules that were once pivotal to the legal apparatus of the state. This constitutional re-imagination has produced a revised constitution that no longer shows the markings of hate. Alabama's peculiar model of amendment codification has resulted in removing the written vestiges of the state's racist constitutional beginnings.

It is worth comparing the Alabama Constitution, before and after this momentous revision.

The original text required racial segregation in education: 'Separate schools shall be provided for white and colored children, and no child of either race shall be permitted to attend a school of the other race.'[9] This text was later revised only to permit racial segregation in education: 'The legislature may authorize the parents or guardians of minors, who desire that such minors shall attend schools provided for their own race, to make election to that end.'[10] Now after the recent revision, the reference to racial segregation in education has been removed entirely.

Similarly, the original text of the Alabama Constitution – which was written after the abolition of slavery in the US – prohibited slavery, but made an exception for its use as punishment for a crime: 'That no form of slavery shall exist in this state; and there shall not be any involuntary servitude, otherwise than for the punishment of crime, of which the party shall have been duly convicted.'[11] Alabama has historically abused this exception to exploit persons who had been enslaved as well as their descendants.[12] The recent revision has eliminated the phrase 'otherwise than for the punishment of crime, of which the party shall have been duly convicted'.

[9] Constitution of Alabama at s 256 (subsequently amended).

[10] ibid (as amended in 1956).

[11] ibid at s 32.

[12] See Mike Cason, 'Alabama Constitution of 2022 Removes Repealed Laws, Racist Language' *Advance Local* (31 July 2022): https://www.al.com/news/2022/07/alabama-constitution-of-2022-removes-repealed-laws-racist-language.html.

The 1901 text of the Alabama Constitution also imposed a poll tax.[13] Alabama used poll taxes historically as a weapon in voter disenfranchisement. An editorial in the *Tuscaloosa News* once declared that 'this newspaper believes in white supremacy, and it believes that the poll tax is one of the essentials for the preservation of white supremacy'.[14] Eventually the poll tax in the original 1901 Constitution was repealed and replaced, but the constitutional text nonetheless retained this reference to poll taxes: 'All poll taxes collected in this state shall be applied to the support and furtherance of education in the respective counties where collected.'[15] The continuing codification of this constitutional rule recalled the horrors of an earlier era. But now, with the recent constitutional revision in Alabama, the poll tax language has been completely erased.

There are other instances of racist language in the original Alabama Constitution, including an outright prohibition on interracial marriage: 'The legislature shall never pass any law to authorize or legalize any marriage between any white person and a negro, or descendant of a negro.'[16] This text was later repealed by a constitutional amendment, though that amendment occurred 100 years after the enactment of the original constitution – and even then only 59 per cent of Alabamans voted to approve the amendment in a statewide constitutional referendum.[17]

The comparative point is plain. Alabama and the US have adopted different architectural strategies in their constitutional reforms. One has taken the path of renovating its old edifice, while the other has made new additions to the original building, in the process leaving untouched all of the fixtures that have been there since the beginning. The Alabama Constitution – once a document that gushed with race-based hate – has been transformed by a revision that deletes those discriminatory words. In contrast, the US Constitution continues to display the hateful language that was written into its text when it was enacted over 200 years ago.

II. The Appendative Model: A Memorial to the Past

The US Constitution is therefore something of a memorial to the past. Once a rule is added to the constitutional text, it remains codified forever, as long as the Constitution remains in force. This state of permanent codification applies both to the original rules in the founding constitutional text and to any subsequent rules that enter the text by way of a subsequent constitutional amendment. This is the essential trait of the appendative model of amendment codification.

[13] Constitution of Alabama at s 178 (subsequently amended).

[14] Alabama Advisory Committee to the US Commission on Civil Rights, Barriers to Voting in Alabama: A Report by the Alabama Advisory Committee to the United States Commission on Civil Rights (February 2020) at 2 fn 4.

[15] Constitution of Alabama at s 259.

[16] ibid at s 102 (subsequently amended).

[17] Cason (n 12).

Perhaps the past is always worth keeping in the foreground, even if it causes discomfort or sadness. For Akhil Amar, the appendative model in the US traces the 'democratizing trendline'[18] of constitutional amendments across American history, chronicling how constitutional changes have deepened democracy in steps both incremental and transformative. The mistakes of the past are not erased, or 'whitewash[ed]' in his words,[19] but rather memorialised as a reminder of how far the country has come from the days of legal exclusion, subordination and enslavement.

For Amar, there is an additional virtue of the appendative model. It doubles as a call to action for all Americans. It is invitation to ask themselves how they wish to leave a mark on their Constitution and how they wish to participate in their ongoing constitution-making project: 'The manner of adding amendments to the end reminds us that we ourselves – We, the People today – should ponder how we might leave our posterity a better document than we inherited.'[20]

Yet the appendative model raises problems of obsolescence and harmonisation. When rules old and new remain codified for as long as the constitution endures, there will inevitably be certain constitutional rules that become outdated as a result of their repeal by constitutional amendment. This gives rise to a problem of legal obsolescence. In the US, the Eighteenth Amendment has been repealed by the Twenty-First Amendment, yet the Eighteenth amendment remains codified. There is a related problem of social obsolescence. Articles I and II of the US Constitution use only the masculine pronoun in relation to congressional and presidential eligibility for election. Of course, women can lawfully run for election, and they have run for over a century since states began to drop their sex-based prohibitions. But this exclusionary gendered language may undermine social cohesion and the sense of belonging that a constitution ought to nurture among those it governs.

The problem of harmonisation is one of timing and power. The appendative model leaves to future judges the task of reconciling the meaning of the new text with the old. For example, how is the First Amendment enacted in 1791 impacted by the Fourteenth Amendment enacted in 1868? The text of the First Amendment does not tell us because, like all rules codified in the US Constitution, it is never revised, even if a subsequent amendment impacts it directly. Someone must eventually answer that question. In the US, the task of harmonisation belongs to judges at the moment a future constitutional controversy arises requiring a legal answer to the question. Under the appendative model, the passage of time combines with the power of judicial review to give judges substantial power in constitutional interpretation. In contrast, this act of reconciling the meaning of existing rules with newly inserted ones happens at a different period of time – and it is done by different political actors – under the invisible and integrative models.

[18] Akhil Reed Amar, 'Architexture' (2002) 77 *Indiana Law Journal* 671 at 686 fn 62.
[19] ibid at 687.
[20] ibid at 686.

The US Constitution is not the only constitution to use the appendative model. The Constitution of Indonesia has used this model since its enactment. In their chapter on Indonesia, Rosa Ristawati and Radian Salman trace the origins of the choice of the appendative model. Drawing from legislative debates and constitutional records, they guide readers systematically through the country's amendments to show how each has been codified. Their chapter serves concurrently as a critique of the appendative model. They explain that Indonesia publishes an unofficial version of its Constitution using the integrative model of amendment codification because this model makes it easier to understand the current state of the Constitution than the official appended version, which does not make clear what in the text remains valid and what does not. Ristawati and Salman report that the unofficial integrative version of the Indonesian Constitution is more widely used by laypersons, law professors and interestingly also by state institutions in their public campaigns. The integrative model, they conclude, is more effective for civic education and public awareness, hence the title Ristawati and Salman have given their chapter: 'The Integrative Model of Constitutional Amendment in Indonesia as Constitutional Communication'.

III. The Integrative Model: A Lawyerly Record

Under the integrative model of amendment codification, the existing text of the constitution is rewritten and accompanied by a notation indicating that it has changed. This is different from how amendment occurs under the appendative model.

To illustrate this integrative model, imagine a constitution specifies that it may be amended only by a supermajority of two-thirds in the bicameral national legislature. Now imagine that this constitution is amended to require a higher threshold of supermajority agreement, from two-thirds to three-quarters. Under the appendative model, the new threshold would appear in a new rule appended to the end of the constitutional text. The repealed two-thirds rule would remain codified in its original form, but it would be treated as superseded.

However, under the integrative model, the text of the threshold would be rewritten in the original constitution from two-thirds to three-quarters. In addition to rewriting the text, the amendment would be accompanied by some clearly identifiable notation – for instance, a footnote – indicating what had changed and how, and perhaps also providing additional information about when and why political actors had agreed to revise the constitutional text. Details like these do not appear in constitutions that use the appendative model. They are typical of the integrative model.

The explanatory details in constitutions that use the integrative model give every amendment a lawyerly record. In the Constitution of India, for instance, amendments are accompanied by bracketed texts and footnotes that specify the title of the amending law, the text that has been newly inserted into the Constitution, the text that has been replaced and the year of enactment. This makes it relatively easy to quickly assimilate what has changed in addition to where to locate further information on the origins of the amendment. But there are costs to this lawyerly record: as amendments grow more frequent, these explanatory details may clutter the constitution. Worse still, as these details multiply, they may in the end yield a text that only a lawyer can decipher.

Yet the integrative model may have an advantage over the appendative model when it comes to implementing the intent behind a constitutional amendment. While the appendative model defers the task of harmonisation, the integrative model harmonises the meaning of the new text with the old constitution at the very moment of amendment. The integrative model gives greater power in controlling constitutional meaning to the reformers responsible for amending the text because they are the ones to choose what to change in the existing constitution, and how. Their textual revision can in turn shape and constrain how courts interpret the new amendment. The same is true of the invisible model: the harmonisation occurs at the very moment of amendment.

Choosing how to harmonise the meaning of an amendment with the existing constitution at the time of the reform does not necessarily reflect a distrust of judges. For example, in his chapter on 'Amendment Codification in Switzerland: Codifying an Evolving Culture of Constitutional Pragmatism', Caspar Pfrunder uncovers a connection between the integrative model used in Switzerland and the people's ownership of their constitution. To append amendments to the original constitution might suggest a hierarchy in authority, namely that the original constitution must remain untouched because it is more authoritative than amendments, which are placed at the end of the text and rest on a different, lower basis of authority. The Swiss Constitution rejects this theory of differential authority. It allows changes to the original text. From the perspective of the Swiss Constitution, when the people amend their constitution using the integrative model of amendment codification, they do so standing on the same plane of constitutional authority as those who wrote it. The original constitution and subsequent amendments thus do not rely on different sources of legitimacy: both are expressions of the will of people, each equal to the other across time. This fosters what Pfrunder describes as a permanent dialogue among the Swiss people on what they wish for themselves and their posterity.

However, this is not to suggest that the integrative model is the perfect choice for constitution-makers. Each model of amendment codification entails risks and rewards. As Eszter Bodnár shows in her chapter on 'Codification of Constitutional Amendments as a Symbol for Transitions: A Case Study from Hungary', the act of revising the original constitutional text using the integrative model can precipitate serious constitutional questions, perhaps extending to what Bodnár describes as constitutional crises. The Hungarian case reminds us that the stakes involved in matters of constitutional form are just as high as those involved in matters of constitutional content.

IV. The Invisible Model: An Illusion of Perfection

Although the integrative model may offer the benefit of detailed notations on each amendment, it may quickly become a burden when the constitution is frequently amended. The more a constitution is amended using the integrative model, the more cluttered it can become over time. Lawyers may appreciate this degree of specificity in the constitutional record, but laypersons may find it disruptive. A much tidier model of amendment codification would dispense with the notations and simply alter the existing text of the constitution to read as though the amendment had been there all along. That is what characterises the invisible model of amendment codification. The invisible model deprioritises the paper trail that becomes embedded into constitutions under the integrative model, and instead elevates the qualities of simplicity, cleanliness and orderliness we can perceive in a constitution that is amended without much trace that it has ever been amended at all.

The Constitution of Portugal, for example, uses the invisible model. As Catarina Santos Botelho explains in her chapter on 'The Presentist Portuguese Constitution', the Constitution itself requires the text to remain unified within its original framework.[21] This therefore forecloses the appendative model as an option, and leaves open the possibility of either the invisible or integrative models. Portugal has adopted the invisible model to privilege the values of clarity and coherence over the historical virtues of record-making and knowledge-keeping the integrative model offers.

There are other reasons why a jurisdiction might choose the invisible model. In her chapter on 'The Traces of Formalism: The Spanish Invisible Model of Constitutional Codification', Patricia García Majado uncovers a theoretical alignment between Spain's chosen model of amendment codification and the Constitution's self-conscious formalist conception of itself. The formalist presuppositions of the Spanish Constitution entail an important effect: nothing in the Constitution is eternal and everything is therefore amendable, provided the relevant actors abide by the carefully delineated procedures for constitutional reform. This formalist self-understanding counsels the use of the invisible model because this model reflects the unbounded and supreme power of constitutional amendment, whose product is not to be separated from the rest of the higher law by the markings characteristic of the integrative model or the unique placement of amendments in the appendative model.

In South Korea, the standard approach to amendment codification has been the invisible model due to the peculiar way in which the Constitution is reformed. In her chapter on 'Amendment Politics in South Korea: Invisible Constitutional Replacements in 1960 and 1962', Jeong-In Yun describes a curious pattern: the

[21] See Constitution of Portugal at art 287(1).

South Korean Constitution has historically been reformed by mega-constitutional packages of constitutional amendments that effectively amount to new constitutions. Because the invisible model conceals the extent of the constitutional reforms, political actors can enact vast constitutional changes without leaving behind an easily accessible record of the extent of the reforms. And it is precisely because the model of codification has been invisible that political actors have taken liberties with the kinds of reforms they have made to the Constitution. Yun suggests that these emboldened reformers might not have attempted constitutional reforms quite as large had the operative amendment model been appendative or integrative.

There is another point worth making about the invisible model. As this book uncovers, the invisible model may simultaneously be the product of underlying social conditions just as it may exacerbate them. In the case of the Netherlands, Gert-Jan Leenknegt and Reijer Passchier suggest in 'Between Accessibility and Oblivion: Strengths and Weaknesses of the "Invisible" Dutch Constitutional Amendment Model' that the invisible model is symptomatic of what they describe as a collective forgetfulness of the country's constitutional history. Continued use of the invisible model, they caution, could ultimately compound the problem insofar as erasing older texts deprives the greater society of an historical record of the country's constitutional past. The appendative and integrative models avoid this problem.

The invisible model certainly has advantages over other models. But is it necessarily better, all things considered? It is a useful test of preference to consider which model of amendment codification to choose for a jurisdiction where the constitution has not yet been amended. This is the point of departure for Masahiko Kinoshita's chapter on 'The Form of Constitutional Amendments in Japan'. As yet unamended, the Japanese Constitution has often been the subject of amendment talk, most recently in relation to repealing or revising its founding commitment to pacifism.[22] Which amendment model is most likely to be used when the Japanese Constitution is ultimately amended, if that day ever comes? Analogising constitutional amendment to statutory amendment in current legislative practice, Kinoshita suggests that the invisible model of amendment codification is appropriate for a future amendment to the Constitution of Japan, though there are reasons to consider using either the appendative or integrative models as alternatives.

V. The Disaggregative Model: Separate Sites of Constitutional Significance

The fourth model of amendment codification is disaggregative. Under this disaggregative model, written constitutional reforms do not appear in a single codified

[22] See Richard Albert, 'Amending Constitutional Amendment Rules' (2015) 13 *International Journal of Constitutional Law* 655 at 659–61.

constitutional text; they appear instead in separate constitutional documents of equal legal significance. For instance, consider the British Constitution. Its written rules do not reside in a single constitutional text. They appear instead across several documents that are enacted as Acts of Parliament. The Bill of Rights of 1689, the Act of Settlement of 1701, the Parliament Act of 1911, the European Communities Act of 1972 and the Human Rights Act of 1998 – these are examples of legislative enactments that form part of the British Constitution, even though they exist separately as stand-alone laws.

When the British Constitution is amended by an Act of Parliament, the enactment takes the form of an ordinary statute, though its effect is anything but ordinary. The most prominent example in recent years is the European Union (Withdrawal) Act of 2018, which was the legal tool used to implement the UK's transformative constitutional exit from the EU. This Act of Parliament is not codified alongside other constitutional reforms in any single document that brings together all of the written components of the British Constitution. Instead, it appears separately – disaggregated – from other constitutional laws in the UK. As we will soon see, some constitutions discussed in this book use elements of the disaggregative model.

VI. Hybrid Models in the World

In the end, constitutional designers often pick and choose certain features from the various ideal types to build a hybrid model that best serves their own purposes. Indeed, if the chapters in this book are indicative of the broader global reality, it would appear that most constitutions in the world blend various elements from two or more of the four ideal types to create their own unique approach to codifying amendments in their higher law. This is how it should be. There is no reason why constitutional designers should feel compelled to bind themselves exclusively to any single one of the ideal types. Better to choose the path that best serves their objectives, whether that means adopting one model all the time, or one model in certain circumstances and a different model in others, or mixing and matching from the ideal types to fashion an altogether new model. The majority of the chapters in this book are evidence that hybridity is more common than not.

Some jurisdictions borrow from all four models. In Brazil, for instance, the basic mode of amendment codification is both appendative and integrative. Yet, as Bruno Cunha explains in his chapter on 'The Codification of Constitutional Amendments in Brazil: Beyond the Appendative and Integrative Models', there are specially enumerated rules that require constitutional reformers to use the disaggregative and invisible models jointly in relation to international human rights treaties and conventions adopted by the Brazilian National Congress. These constitutional amendments exist outside the four corners of Brazil's documentary Constitution and have the same legal status as amendments enacted using the appendative and integrative models.

The Republic of Georgia has likewise drawn from all four models of amendment codification. In his chapter on 'Georgia's Model of Constitutional Amendment Codification', Malkhaz Nakashidze returns to the first amendment to Georgia's modern Constitution. He connects the use of the integrative amendment model to the influence of the Soviet tradition. Yet he also gives an account of the circumstances that have required recourse to the disaggregative model of amendment codification in order to deal with amendments to the higher laws of the autonomous republics of Georgia. Nakashidze shows, in addition, why a certain set of transitional rules adopted by constitutional amendment have been codified according to the appendative model. Finally, he explains that parliamentarians have thought it useful to use the invisible model of amendment codification to publish a special consolidated edition of the constitution for public awareness. Each of these models serves its own purpose, and each model is evident in some way in the Republic of Georgia.

The same is true of Ethiopia, where all four amendment models have been used across the two levels of the federal structure of government. We learn from Zelalem Esehtu Degifie's chapter on 'The Amalgamation of Amendment Codification Models in Ethiopia: A Move Towards an Unwritten Constitution' that the Constitution of the Federal Democratic Republic of Ethiopia has been amended on two occasions. However, in neither case has the amendment been promulgated in the official constitutional text or in a separate self-standing legislative enactment; instead, they both appear in the parliamentary records alone. Degifie considers this mode of codification closest to the disaggregative model, though he proposes a more interesting formulation for how Ethiopia records its amendments: he describes it quite interestingly as a process of constitutional decodification. In contrast, in the country's 11 state constitutions, the three other major models of amendment codification have been used: appendative, integrative and invisible.

The other jurisdictions encountered in this volume are also hybrid, though not hybrids of all four models. In Taiwan, the codification of amendments fuses the appendative and invisible models. Hui-Wen Chen's chapter on 'When the Temporary Becomes Indefinite: Legitimacy, Path Dependency and Taiwan's Hybrid Approach to Constitutional Amendment Codification' lays bare the interplay between politics and the choice of which codification model to use. In Taiwan, as Chen demonstrates, the hybrid model of codification serves a useful political purpose, namely to take strategic steps towards forging a distinct constitutional identity as the people of Taiwan consider whether and how to break from the Chinese features in their documentary constitution.

Three constitutions studied in this book are hybrids of the integrative and invisible models. In Bangladesh, the main mode of codification is integrative. But, as Sharowat Shamin notes in her chapter on 'Codifying Secularism in the Bangladesh Constitution', sometimes the invisible model is used. For instance, when the same constitutional rule is amended more than once, only the most recent alteration is recorded, in the process rendering any prior change invisible.

Shamin's chapter examines this hybrid model of amendment codification in the context of the state's continuing efforts to balance competing social and political values against the backdrop of the country's founding commitment to secularism, one of the Constitution's fundamental principles.

In her chapter on the Albanian Constitution, Arta Vorpsi explains the uses of the hybrid integrative-invisible model. Her chapter on 'One Constitution, Two Models of Codification: Between Trust and Distrust Towards Constitutional Interpretations in Albania' draws from her involvement in the expert group that was responsible for writing the country's mega-constitutional package of reforms in 2016. The hybrid model has proven useful, she explains, to build political consensus behind the transformative constitutional amendments negotiated to tackle corruption in the country.

And in his chapter entitled 'Caught Between: On the Distinctive Character of Mexico's Model of Amendment Codification', Jaime Olaiz-González presents the unique Mexican experience with constitutional reform. Home to the world's most amended national constitution, Mexico has a political culture of hyper-reformism that creates peculiar challenges for managing the length, coherence and clarity of its constitutional text. He offers a descriptive and critical account of the hybrid integrative-invisible model of amendment codification, explaining both how amendments are formalised and how the process of codification does the opposite of what we expect a constitution to do: rather than making it possible for the people to grasp its meaning and objects, it erects barriers that leave the text largely impenetrable and inaccessible.

The two final chapters also involve hybrids, but of a different kind. The Constitution of Paraguay, as we learn from Diego Moreno's chapter on 'The Incorporation of Amendments in Paraguayan Constitutionalism', has not been amended frequently – only once in 30 years, in fact. But in his analysis of the larger history of constitutional reform over the decades of Paraguay's several constitutions, Moreno identifies a clear pattern in the precedents of constitutional reform: Paraguay has adopted what resembles a disaggregative model of amendment codification, despite the country's long tradition of governing under a single, unified, codified constitutional text. Moreno suggests that a more advisable model of amendment codification in Paraguay would vary the form of codification according to the nature and scope of a given constitutional reform.

Meanwhile in Afghanistan, three models have been used in the country's many constitutional lives. In 'Crafting Amendments during Political Upheaval: Amendment Models and Constitutional Stability in Afghanistan', Shamshad Pasarlay illustrates the various political and social uses of the three models as they were used in three different periods of time. The invisible model prevailed in the 1923 Constitution, the appendative model in the 1931 Constitution, and a hybrid integrative-invisible model in the 1987 Constitution. Pasarlay draws a fascinating insight from the Afghan experience with constitutional codification: the invisible approach is more likely to be used in unsteady political contexts, while the appendative model is more likely to be used in times of peace.

VII. An Agenda for Constitutional Research

We cover a lot of ground in this book, but there remains much left to explore. How do constitutions codify amendments to their text(s), and how does this matter in law and society? We offer answers in relation to many jurisdictions, some very well known, but most understudied. We invite others to follow suit with studies of their own, examining the form and consequences of constitutional amendments in the jurisdictions they know best. Perhaps their answers will complement ours. Perhaps they will complicate them. In either case, we hope only to inspire further research into the legal, political, and social consequences of choosing one form of amendment codification over another.

1

The Traces of Formalism

The Invisible Spanish Model of Constitutional Codification

PATRICIA GARCÍA MAJADO

I. Introduction

Although at first glance, amendment codification may appear to be simply a formal question, the way in which a Constitution incorporates constitutional amendments into its text has significant implications. Amendment codification deserves the attention of constitutional law scholars because it directly affects the constitution itself.

The way in which the Spanish Constitution codifies amendments has traditionally been overlooked in Spanish constitutional scholarship. There is no constitutional provision obliging amendments to be codified in any given way. There is no set form or model for doing so. Moreover, the issue was hardly discussed in the constitutional debates in 1978, nor did it attract any attention at the time of the two constitutional amendments to date, first in 1992 and then in 2011. Doctrinal studies on the subject have so far also failed to shed any light on the issue.

This is unexplored territory in Spain, yet is quite legally important. We need to interrogate the possible reasons for and consequences of the Spanish model of codifying constitutional amendments which, as I will explain below, follows the invisible model. Hence, my objective in the following pages is to demonstrate how a question of format – or what has been ingeniously called 'constitutional architexture'[1] – is based on substantive presuppositions. In other words, my aim is to explain how the fact that the 1978 Spanish Constitution follows a certain model of – invisibly – codifying amendments to the Constitution is not an accident, but rather a choice that is inherent to the Constitution's formalist conception of itself.

[1] See Akhil Reed Amar, 'Architexture' (2002) 77 *Indiana Law Review* 671.

The silence of Spanish constitutional doctrine in this respect may have something to do with this unquestioned, perfect alignment.

Bearing in mind that the two axes central to this work are formalism and invisibility – each unarguably a trait of the Spanish system – I will begin by explaining those starting points and constructing the subsequent analysis from there. I will explain why the Spanish Constitution is a merely formal Constitution and then why the Spanish model conforms to the invisible model of codifying constitutional amendments. Based on that, I will analyse how the invisible model is the best fit with this formal self-understanding of the Spanish Constitution. To that end, I will examine the strong link between invisibility and three fundamental traits of formalism that are clearly visible in the Spanish Constitution: the redundancy of repealed constitutional norms, the prohibition of implicit constitutional reforms, and the monopoly over constitutional change.

II. An Examination of the Spanish Constitution

When analysing the implications of the Spanish model of codifying constitutional amendments, it is necessary to begin by answering two questions that will guide the rest of this study. First, what type of Constitution is the Spanish Constitution? And, second, what type of codification model is used in Spain? These questions are addressed below.

A. Formalism: The Spanish Constitution as a Formal Constitution

The Spanish Constitution is the supreme law in the Spanish legal system. It stands at the top of the legal hierarchy. All other laws are therefore subordinate to it. If the Spanish Constitution is defined by its position within the legal hierarchy of the system, this means that it is not defined by the type of content it regulates, whether the subject is fundamental rights, the separation of powers or any other substantive rule. It therefore does not matter for analytical purposes whether the body of law defined as 'the Constitution' contains one kind of rule or another, or whether it is more or less democratic. As long as this body of law is at the top of the legal hierarchy, it is the Constitution. We know this to be true from constitutional provisions themselves and, fundamentally, from the clauses concerning constitutional amendment. In the Spanish Constitution, these are found in Title X.

The Spanish Constitution has no unamendable clauses. It is therefore completely amendable. There are no explicit or implicit limits to its modification. Very early on, the Constitutional Court declared that 'the Spanish Constitution, unlike the French or German, does not exclude the possibility of amending any of its clauses, nor does it place more express limits on the power of constitutional amendment than those which are strictly formal and procedural'.[2] The Court went on to highlight that there was no 'legal core that is inaccessible to the processes of constitutional amendment', such that it is entirely possible for amendments to be made that aim to modify the foundations of constitutional order as long as they are carried out within the framework of the processes for amending the Constitution, as 'following those procedures is, in every case, obligatory'.[3]

Thus, it is possible not only to change what is in the Constitution, but also to change the Constitution itself, namely its foundational elements,[4] as long as the established procedure is followed. What in other legal systems of a similar level would amount to a constitutional substitution – the modification of basic structures of the constitutional text, which is often foreclosed by ordinary constitutional amendment – is, in Spain, permitted as a complete revision of the supreme law. This must be done using a special amendment procedure in Article 168. To put it another way, the Spanish Constitution makes revolution possible through law. From this possibility, we can again deduce formalism, as it will be the constitutional rules that are approved following the legally established amendment procedures. This ensures the validity of the 'form' of the Constitution, although its content may change completely.

In Germany after the Second World War, the most important thing was to ensure human dignity – which explains the existence of unamendable clauses in the first article of the German Basic Law. However, in Spain, after the difficult years of the Franco dictatorship, the essential idea was to respect pluralism and consequently to ensure that the various – and quite different – political and ideological options could coexist under the same higher law. This explains why the constitutional framers chose the most open Constitution possible, free of unamendable clauses. As a consequence, any person would be permitted to advocate to put any concept, idea or rule in the 1978 Constitution, as long as it was achieved through legally established procedures.

That, as the Constitutional Court made clear very early on, 'is a framework of sufficiently broad coincidences so that political choices of entirely different natures fit within it'[5] such that 'there is space in our constitutional order for as many ideas as people want to put forward'.[6] With that in mind, the content of the Spanish Constitution cannot be something that remains static by law. On the contrary, the nature of the Spanish Constitution is that it must be fully subject to the possibility of change. It is here that the formal conception of Constitution

[2] STC 48/2003, 12 March (SCC: Spanish Constitutional Court).

[3] STC 103/2008, 11 September.

[4] Benito Aláez Corral, 'El procedimiento de reforma constitucional cuarenta años después' in Ramón Punset Blanco and Leonardo Álvarez (eds), *Cuarenta años de una Constitución normativa* (Cizur Menor, Thomson-Reuters Aranzadi, 2018) 641.

[5] STC 1/1981, 8 April.

[6] STC 42/2014, 25 March.

makes its presence felt. A formal Constitution is not a militant Constitution[7] – protecting certain values or political options to the detriment of others – but rather an 'amoral' Constitution.[8]

This formalism, which can be seen quite clearly in the rules on constitutional amendment, can also be seen in other rules within it. These also show that the important idea in the Spanish system is to respect procedure but not to pursue, maintain or protect substantive political options. One example is in the regulation of political parties. With regard to Organic Law 6/2002, 27 June, on political parties, the Constitutional Court explained that such parties (and groups) were able to pursue whatever ends they wished or ideas they deemed appropriate, even if they were anti-democratic. All they were prohibited from doing was pursuing those ends or expounding those ideas through *activities or behaviours* which violated the law.[9] Therefore, parties can only be prohibited or made illegal for actions that break the law and not because their ideas do not respect democratic principles. The Constitution is indifferent to political choices; it demands only that legally established procedures be followed.

In summary, the Spanish Constitution is a formalist Constitution. And, most importantly, it is what it is, not because that is how the person writing this text interprets it, but because that is how the Constitution itself is designed to be. This can be deduced from the Constitution's own provisions and from Constitutional Court interpretations over more than 40 years. It is so because of the position the Constitution occupies in the legal hierarchy, not because of the *content* it regulates.

B. Invisibility: The Invisible Model as the Spanish Model for Codifying Constitutional Amendments

In order to identify the Spanish model of codifying constitutional amendments, we must start with the only amendments that have been made to the 1978 Spanish Constitution to date: first, in 1992 and then in 2011. These are the only amendments through which we can identify the model.

Before its amendment in 1992, Article 13.2 excluded foreign nationals from the rights to political participation in Article 23, 'except in cases which may be established by treaty or by law concerning the right to vote in municipal elections,

[7] The expression 'militant democracy' (*streitbare Demokratie*) is from Karl Loewenstein, 'Militant Democracy and Fundamental Rights' (1937) 31 *American Political Science Review* 417.

[8] Richard Albert, 'America's Amoral Constitution' (2021) 70 *American University Law Review* 773. This amorality has also been highlighted in Spanish legal scholarship. See especially Javier Jiménez Campo, 'Algunos problemas de interpretación en torno al Título X de la Constitución' (1980) 7 *Revista del Departamento de Derecho Político* 81, 87–90; and Pedro de Vega, *La reforma constitucional y la problemática del poder constituyente* (Madrid, Tecnos, 1985) 157–60, who talks about 'ideological indifference'.

[9] STC 48/2003, 12 March.

and subject to the principle of reciprocity'. The amendment added the words 'and the right to be elected' following the words 'the right to vote', recognising the rights of non-nationals to both vote in and stand for office in municipal elections – in the original Spanish version, the change was from 'active "o" [or] passive suffrage to active "y" [and] passive suffrage'. The reason for the amendment was to avoid any contradiction between the Spanish Constitution and the 1992 Maastricht Treaty that was under ratification at the time. This change is the only modified wording currently in the Constitution. The other amendment, of Article 135, was much more comprehensive. The full content of the article was changed, including, fundamentally, the principle of budgetary stability and the prioritisation of paying off the public debt over any other item due to the economic crisis of the previous decade. The result of the amendment was a completely new Article 135, which became much longer than the previous one: the new Article 135 comprises six sections instead of the two sections in the old Article 135. No trace of the old text remains in the new.

In both cases, the approved constitutional amendments were inserted directly into the text, replacing the rules that had previously been there, leaving no trace of that prior text in the new text. Nor is there any indication about the modification of the text in the Constitution itself. In effect, the very constitutional amendments, once approved, established that 'article (X) will be worded as follows: …'. The Spanish Constitution therefore only contains the new text, completely disregarding the previous wording. This is precisely what we expect to see in the invisible model of amendment codification.[10]

Before proceeding to analyse this model, a word of caution is in order. The official state bulletin website (Boletín Oficial del Estado (BOE)) publishes a consolidated version of the Spanish Constitution,[11] which includes all of the modifications and indicates which sections and clauses were subject to amendment. These give an indication of precisely what has been changed and when, including a link to the amendment act itself. There is also a link that provides access to the original text – it indicates when the text was approved and until when it was in force – so that it is possible to consult the current version of the Constitution and previous versions of it. However, the fact that this is so does not determine the identity of the Spanish model of codifying constitutional amendments, as it is a function only of the BOE website. The official (non-interactive) texts include only the amended content with no additional comment – hence our classification of Spain as an example of the invisible model of codifying constitutional amendments.

Despite their material differences and the difference in time between the two constitutional amendments, they do have some things in common. First, they were both partial modifications to the Constitution which followed the simple

[10] See Richard Albert, *Constitutional Amendments: Making, Breaking and Changing Constitutions* (Oxford, Oxford University Press, 2019) 238.

[11] See Boletín Oficial del Estado, www.boe.es/buscar/act.php?id=BOE-A-1978–31229.

amendment procedure in Article 167, as they did not affect the Preliminary Part, Chapter II, Division 1 of Part I, or Part II, changes to which would have required the more rigorous, special amendment procedure of Article 168. Second, both amendments were carried out through urgent procedures with a single reading, which allowed certain procedural hurdles to be bypassed and some deadlines to be halved. This means that they were both very fast constitutional amendments. Third, both amendments were driven by Spain's membership of the EU. The first was a consequence of the ratification of the Maastricht Treaty and the second, to a large extent, was a result of the pressure of EU fiscal policy in the context of the economic crisis in the then-preceding decade.

Are these peculiarities sufficient to explain the choice of invisibly codifying constitutional amendments in Spain? The answer is no. Even if constitutional amendments had been approved regarding other topics or of other kinds, and even if the special, extended procedure of constitutional amendment Article 168 had been used, the codifying model would have been similarly invisible. This choice, as we will try to demonstrate below, is a function of these contextual questions. The choice stems instead from the structural identity of the Constitution and from the formalist understanding that the Spanish Constitution has of itself.

III. Formalism and Invisibility: Two Sides of the Same Coin

Having analysed why the Spanish Constitution is a Constitution in a formal sense and how the Spanish model is invisible, the next step is to highlight the connection between these two issues. The aim is to explain why the latter follows from the former. This will require us to examine the link between the invisible model and three profoundly formalist traits of the Spanish Constitution: the redundancy of repealed constitutional rules, the prohibition of implicit constitutional amendments, and the monopoly over constitutional change in the hands of the constitutional amendment power.

A. Invisibility and the Redundancy of Repealed Constitutional Norms

The invisible model provides the most certainty about which constitutional rules are in force: only those that are visible are effective. The text of preceding constitutional rules disappears completely following an amendment. The key aspect is that in Spain, these rules are removed, not because there is a political desire to 'leave the past behind', but rather because it makes little legal sense for a formal constitution, as we will see below, to preserve rules that are no longer in effect.

From the formal perspective, the 'past' is only a repealed rule, a rule that has lost its validity in time,[12] and therefore a rule that no longer belongs in the legal system. For formalism, it makes no sense to preserve something that is no longer in effect (whether in the constitutional text itself or in footnotes) and hence is not part of the legal system. Why, paraphrasing Jellinek, drag around 'the dead weight of repealed laws'?[13] The invisible model, then, is the model which best succeeds in demonstrating that repealed rules no longer exist because they are deleted directly. It is the best demonstration that only rules that are in force should be 'visible' because it is only those rules that exist legally. The law itself, not its history in the form of repealed law, is what matters. The constitutional preamble – which does not have legal weight – would, in any case, be the right place to refer to this historical contextualisation or to changes that have been made.[14] However, in the Spanish Constitution, the preamble has never been modified.

The fact that this is the formal perspective does not mean to say that there are no reasons for preserving rules which are no longer in effect. It only means that the reasons for doing so are strange for a formal Constitution. For example, particularly with regard to the appendative model, it has been suggested that preserving prior constitutional rules may allow the people to 'learn from their mistakes', seeing what institutions or regulations there were in the past and how they have changed over time, and how society as a whole has progressed.[15] However, talk of 'mistakes' and, in contrast, 'successes' does not fit comfortably within a formal model of a Constitution, because that would be considering the content, which could be judged as 'good' or 'bad'. The formal model only deals with the categories of valid and invalid; there are no good or bad rules, no mistakes or successes.

If preserving prior constitutional rules serves to identify mistakes and successes, it seems evident that it would also serve to identify whether amendments were forward or backward steps, democratically speaking. Once again, from a formal point of view, it is not possible to talk about 'forward steps' or 'backward steps', but rather 'valid' or 'invalid' constitutional amendments, depending on whether the amendments were made following the legally established procedures, because amendments can change the Constitution completely. The Spanish rules for constitutional amendment are not a mechanism for defending or supporting

[12] Hans Kelsen, 'Derogation', in Donald Davidson, Jaakko Hintikka, Gabriel Nuchelmans and Wesley C Salmon (eds), *Essays in Legal and Moral Philosophy* (Dordrecht, D Reidel Publishing Company, 1973) 262.

[13] Georg Jellinek, *Reforma y mutación de la Constitución* (Madrid, CEC, 1991) 13.

[14] On the constitutional preamble, with particular reference to the Spanish Constitution, see generally Javier Tajadura Tejada, *El preámbulo constitucional* (Granada, Comares, 1997).

[15] See especially Reed Amar (n 1) 685–86, who highlights that preserving the original text is a way of calling attention to 'the arch of history'; Mehrdad Payandeh, 'Constitutional Aesthetics: Appending Amendments to the United States Constitution' (2011) 25 *Brigham Young University Journal of Public Law* 87, 114; and Albert (n 10) 244, who states that said text becomes a 'living history lesson' for today's generations.

democratic ideals and values (remember, there are no unamendable clauses), but are instead a mechanism allowing society's needs and demands to be reflected in the Fundamental Law, regardless of their content.[16] The important thing is not *what* is amended, but rather *how* it is amended – hence the formal nature of the Constitution.

Therefore, because they are repealed, the only reason for preserving prior constitutional rules would be extra-legal. They would only serve to assess, based on their content, those forward or backward steps produced by the various modifications to the constitutional text. This function is irrelevant for the Spanish Constitution, which is not concerned with content, but solely with the procedures used to incorporate that content – in short, it is concerned only with the means. The invisible Spanish model is therefore the model that best highlights that the only important thing for the legal system is the rules that are in effect: 'established' law. The Spanish Constitution only shows that which legally exists.

B. Invisibility and the Prohibition of Implicit Constitutional Amendments

The Spanish Constitution contains no instructions explaining whether amendments must be explicit or whether they could also be implicit. Nothing is said about whether amendments must specify what they are amending or whether the Constitution may be implicitly modified by laws that meet the procedural requirements for constitutional amendments yet contradict the constitutional text,[17] on the understanding that the later law repeals the previous law. However, this was explicitly addressed in the 1931 Spanish Republican Constitution, which specified in Article 125 that 'the proposal shall specify the article or articles that must be removed, amended, or added'.

This question was not ignored in 1978. In a discussion about constitutional amendment, the Independent Group presented amendment 649, which proposed including a section in what was then Article 161, specifying that: 'All amendments to the Constitution shall explicitly indicate the text to be modified or added.'[18] The reasoning for this, as explained by Senator Ollero, was to avoid implicit constitutional amendments. He explained why:

> It must be a general principle that all amendments of a text mean suppressing what has been modified. Ignoring this principle will only serve to produce constitutional confusion. A much more dangerous confusion in our case when what is being introduced in this project is a constitutional justice system, one of the specific functions of which is to create explanatory legal doctrine on constitutional matters. It will be difficult to clarify

[16] See generally Benito Aláez Corral, *Los límites materiales a la reforma Constitucional de 1978* (Madrid, CEPC 2000).

[17] See Karl Loewestein, *Teoría de la Constitución* (Barcelona, Ariel, 1979) 186.

[18] *Boletín Oficial de las Cortes* no 136, 26 July 1978, 271.

> anything from a legal standpoint if the texts are contradictory … Accordingly, this is why we propose the addition of a section 4 that prevents the possibility of these implicit constitutional amendments, which may distort constitutional order and guarantees.[19]

Senator Ollero would make the same argument in the Senate session on 5 October 1978,[20] again highlighting what that prohibition would contribute to the legal security of the system. Ultimately, however, he withdrew his proposal so as not to prolong the constitutional debates or delay the approval of the Constitution. The senator's speech, noted above, clearly advocated for the prohibition of implicit constitutional amendments. However, it seems inarguable that, at the same time, he was likewise advocating for the invisible model of codifying constitutional amendments. It was not for nothing that he said 'amendments of a text mean suppressing what has been modified'. This would not happen in either an appendative model, which would simply append changes to the end of the constitutional text, or in an integrative model, where the previous text would be preserved (for example, in footnotes). This need for 'suppression' of prior constitutional rules inevitably leads to the invisible model, which is characterised by removing them completely from the constitutional text.

Although the amendment put forward by the Independent Group did not succeed at the time, the Spanish Constitution, by the formal conception it has of itself, requires constitutional amendments to be explicit. If any law adopted using the procedures or with the majorities outlined in Articles 167 and 168 were treated as a constitutional amendment,[21] it would become extremely difficult to know what the Spanish Constitution was at any given moment.[22] Some of it would be found in the text formally called the Constitution and other parts would be disseminated through various laws meeting the characteristics noted above which contradicted the constitutional text. It would be rather complicated to distinguish a constitutional amendment from a law that was simply unconstitutional.

The Spanish Constitution avoids this risk by requiring amendments to pass through a stricter procedure than is used for laws – hence the fact that laws enacted using procedures meeting the requirements for constitutional amendment cannot be treated as constitution-level laws. The Constitution is defined by the supreme position it occupies in the hierarchy of the legal system. Because of that, constitutional amendments must be presented explicitly as such in order to

[19] *Diario de Sesiones del Senado*, no 52, 8 September 1978, 2518.

[20] *Diario de Sesiones del Senado*, no 67, 5 October 1978, 3329–30.

[21] As explained by Juan Luis Requejo Pagés, 'Artículo 167' in Miguel Rodríguez-Piñero y Bravo-Ferrer and Maria Emilia Casas Baamonde (eds), *Comentarios a la Constitución Española. XL Aniversario* (Madrid, Wolters Kluwer, 2018) 187, the problem of implicit constitutional amendment may only arise from the procedure of art 167 SC. The requirements of art 168 SC are so specific (calling an election and obligatory referendum) that it is practically impossible for a law to be approved by this procedure by chance.

[22] This risk was alluded to by Loewestein (n 17) 186.

allow their identification as higher law in the Spanish system.[23] If what matters, from the formalist point of view, is the 'form' of the Constitution, only explicit modifications allow us to know what that is at any time. With that being the case, the model of constitutional amendment codification that best fits with this is no doubt the invisible model. There is no more explicit constitutional amendment than one which not only says what it will modify in the Constitution, but one which, once approved, is inserted directly into the text, replacing the old with the new. The invisible model is therefore nothing more than the almost obligatory result of constitutional amendments in Spain having to be explicit.

That being the case, if it is the amending power that explicitly decides what is to be modified and with what wording, removing what is no longer in force, and directly inserting its will into the text, we might say that in Spain, whoever amends the Constitution also 'harmonises'[24] its meaning because the amending power determines where the modification is inserted and on what terms. Eliminating uncertainty in this way about the constitutional content that is in force avoids recourse to the Constitutional Court to decide about what has really been amended.[25] The Court, in such a case, would become a 'hidden sovereign'[26] – a covert power of constitutional amendment – whose existence would undermine the monopoly of constitutional amendment power established by the Spanish Constitution. We will address this point below.

C. Invisibility and the Monopoly of Constitutional Amendment

As the Supreme Law of the Spanish legal system, all of the powers of the State, without exception, are subject to the Spanish Constitution. This has unavoidable implications for constitutional change. The Constitution cannot be the supreme

[23] Ignacio de Otto, *Derecho constitucional. Sistema de fuentes*, 12th edn (Barcelona, Ariel, 2010). In contrast, see Fernando Santaolalla López, 'Art 167', in Fernando Garrido Falla (ed), *Comentarios a la Constitución Española de 1978*, 2nd edn (Madrid, Civitas, 1985) 2405; Javier Ruipérez Alamillo, *En torno a la reforma constitucional y a la fuerza normativa de la Constitución* (Valencia, Tirant lo Blanch, 2018) 248, although these authors preferred, for legal security and clarity, that amendments be explicit. De Vega (n 8) 162 ff also believes it to be preferable 'not to resort to the bad technique of implicit constitutional amendment'.

[24] See especially Albert (n 10) 246 who has used the term 'harmonization' to refer to the act of aligning the two texts, the original and the amended.

[25] The necessary intervention in these cases of 'an arbiter of disputes over constitutional interpretation' was highlighted early on by David E Kyvig, *Explicit and Authentic Acts: Amending the US Constitution, 1776–2015* (Lawrence, University Press of Kansas, 2016) 102. The existence of greater interpretive activity, particularly in the appendative model, is also highlighted by Payandeh (n 15) 124 f and Albert (n 10) 232–33.

[26] The expression is from Otwin Massing, 'Recht als Korrelat der Macht' [1967] *Der CDUStaat* 123, who reviewed and critiqued Peter Häberle, 'La sociedad abierta de los intérpretes constitucionales: una contribución para la interpretación pluralista y procesal de la Constitución' in *Retos actuales del Estado Constitucional* (Oñati, IVAP, 1996) 29, where we took it from.

law if it can be validly amended outside of the established procedures. That would suppose the existence of powers that are not subject to it, preventing it from being supreme law. This is exactly what prevents there from being a constituent power in Spain that, as such, could act outside of the constitutional provisions for amendment. Thus, the Constitutional Court has held that:

> The unconditional primacy of the Constitution requires that all decisions of power remain, without exception, subject to the Constitution, with no spaces for the public power free from the Constitution or areas of immunity from it. In this way the democratic principle is also protected, as the guarantee of the integrity of the Constitution must be seen in turn as preservation of the respect due to the will of the people, invested in constituent power, the source of all legal-political legitimacy.[27]

Consequently, 'the supposed democratic legitimacy of a legislative body cannot oppose the unconditional primacy of the Constitution' because:

> [T]he legitimacy of acts or policies of a public power basically consist of them conforming to the Constitution and the legal system. Without conforming to the Constitution, there can be no attribution of legitimacy. In a democratic conception of power, there is no more legitimacy than that founded in the Constitution.[28]

That being the case, once the Constitution is approved, there is no distinction between the constituent power and the constitutional amendment power.[29] The former dissolves into the latter, becoming a constituted-constituent power. It is constituent in what it can change (which is anything it wishes), and it is constituted insofar as it is subject to the rules that the Constitution itself has decided to establish.[30] Not for nothing did the Constitutional Court speak of 'constitutionalised constituent power in arts 167 and 168 SC'.[31] The formal conception on which the Spanish Constitution is based therefore leads to unified powers of constitutional reform, specifically to the existence of a single power of constitutional change which can make partial or total modifications of the foundational text. All that is required is conformity to the established procedure for making these modifications.

The invisible model of codifying constitutional amendments is therefore the model that best reflects this unity born of formalism. Why is this the case? When other models of constitutional amendment's codification are used, such as the appendative or the integrative models, there are really two texts: the original – maintained in some form (in the text, in footnotes etc) – and the result of the amendment. The preservation of the two texts highlights that there are two distinct

[27] STC 42/2014, 25 March.

[28] STC 259/2015, 2 December.

[29] On this distinction, in classical terms, see the work by Emmanuel-Joseph Sieyès, *Qu'est-ce que le tiers état?* (Paris, PUF, 1982) and John Locke, *Two Treaties of Government*, Book II, ch XI (Guernsey, Guernsey Press, 1986).

[30] Raymond Carré de Malberg, *Contribution à la théorie générale de l'État*, vol II (Paris, Recueil Sirey, 1922) 497.

[31] STC 259/2015, 2 December.

powers of constitutional change, which may both act in the present: the constituent power and the constitutional amendment power.[32] In effect, it indicates what each one has done. As such, this is consistent with the idea of preserving in some way the basic constitutional design of the constituent power.[33]

In contrast, the Spanish Constitution, by directly inserting modifications into the text, removing prior rules and not having any additional reference to the modification, shows that there is only a single text, whether it is the result of the moment of constitutional creation or a subsequent moment of constitutional amendment. There are no longer two texts – the old and the new – only the latter. This is consistent with the existence of a single power of constitutional change in Spain. If, after the approval of the Spanish Constitution, the constituent power disappeared and there were only an amending power which was materially unlimited and which could therefore completely change what the first power decided, why preserve what the constituent power had created if it no longer exists and everything it did can be altered? Why, in short, differentiate between what the two powers did if only one exists in the present, and therefore only one may act in the present? The logic underlying the invisible Spanish model is therefore plain and powerful: there exists a single power of constitutional change and a single constitutional text.

Closely linked to that, the invisible model is also consistent with the existence of a single type of constitutional rules. All of the rules in the Spanish Constitution have the same legal weight because they all occupy that supreme position in the legal hierarchy, regardless of their actual content. They are therefore all equally 'constitutional'. Proof of that is that they can all be modified by the amending power. If some of them could not be amended, they could be said to be hierarchically superior to the rest but, as we have already seen, this is not the case in Spain.[34] The invisible model demonstrates, better than any other, the equal weight of the provisions of the Constitution. To put it another way, the invisible model shows that there is no distinction between the true 'Constitution' (which would be only within the reach of constituent power) and mere 'constitutional law'

[32] Payandeh (n 15) 101–05 highlights exactly the argument related to the existence of two 'sources of authority' (constituent power and amending power) as one which was argued in the First Congress of the US to choose the appendative model of codifying constitutional amendments. On this discussion in the First Congress, in which integrating the amendments in the Constitution was seen as substituting rather than reforming it, see generally Jonathan Gienapp, *The Second Creation: Fixing the American Constitution in the Founding Era* (Cambridge, MA, Belknap Press, 2018) 164 ff; Edward Hartnett, 'A "Uniform and Entire" Constitution; Or, What if Madison Had Won?' (1998) 15 *Constitutional Commentary* 251; Jason Mazzone, 'Unamendments' (2005) 90 *Iowa Law Review* 1447, 1778 ff; Price Marshall, '"A Careless Written Letter": Situating Amendments to the Federal Constitution' (1998) 51 *Arkansas Law Review* 95.

[33] This relationship between the Indian doctrine of the basic structure and the integrative model of codifying constitutional amendments that system follows has been noted by Albert (n 10) 238.

[34] However, the opposite happens with other models of codifying constitutional amendments. With regard to the appendative model, it is suggested that it allows separation to be maintained between 'the two classes of constitutional norms'. See Carlos González, 'Representational Structures through Which We the People Ratify Constitutions: The Troubling Original Understanding of the Constitutions' Ratification Clauses' (2005) 38 *University of California Davis Law Review* 1373, 1491.

(which would be susceptible to change by the amending power).[35] Consequently, the constitutional rules arising from amendments, regardless of their content, are not inferior to the original rules created by the constituent power; they are their equal. Later rules (the amendment) simply overwrite and eliminate the previous ones (the original). This complete replacement (and elimination) is a perfect demonstration of this hierarchical equality. The existence of a single type of rule (what we identify as the Constitution) produces a single power of constitutional change, and thus a single text.

In summary, the invisible model, by eliminating previous constitutional rules, is the model of codifying constitutional amendments that best shows this idea of unity underlying the Spanish Constitution. Consequently, rather than transmitting this image of preservation, as other models do, the invisible model best transmits an idea of dynamism – absolutely everything can be changed. By overwriting the text, the invisible model best echoes the 'omnipotence' of the constitutional amendment power and therefore the mutability of the Spanish constitutional system, in which there are no absolutes and everything is subject to potential change by the current generation.

IV. Conclusion

The Spanish Constitution contains no provisions on how to codify constitutional amendments, nor was this issue a subject of discussion during the constituent debates. However, this does not mean that the choice of such a model was accidental or thoughtless. As the best fit with the conception that the Spanish Constitution has of itself, the invisible model seems to have been seen as the only possible option. And in any event it has never been questioned.

Although it may not be initially apparent, formalism and invisibility maintain a close relationship in the Spanish Constitution, as two sides of the same coin. There are three main areas where this close relationship can be seen. First, the invisible model best demonstrates the invalidity of repealed constitutional norms by removing them completely from the constitutional text. A formalist constitution is reluctant to preserve rules that are no longer in effect. Second, this model aligns best with the requirement that Spanish constitutional amendments ought to be explicit. There is no reform more explicit than that which is inserted directly into the articles of the constitutional text, replacing the old with the new. Third, the invisible model best demonstrates that in Spain there is only one power of constitutional change: the derivative power of constitutional amendment. Thus, the existence of a single unified text – rather than two, as in other models such as the appendative or the integrative – shows that there is a single normative will which is, in fact, substantially unlimited. Understood in this way, invisibility is the purest expression of the sovereignty of constitutional amendment power.

[35] This classic distinction is from Carl Schmitt, *Teoría de la Constitución* (Madrid, Alianza Editorial, 2011) 57.

2

The Presentist Portuguese Constitution

CATARINA SANTOS BOTELHO

I. Introduction

For some readers, this may seem an odd topic. The relevance of the subject is not so much the aesthetics of amendment codification, but how the choice of the model might impact constitutional adjudication, the centrality of the constitution within the political arena, and even the people's connection to their constitutional text.[1] It is therefore a matter of constitutional significance that should be addressed by constitutional scholarship.

Richard Albert was undoubtedly right when he wrote that constitutional designers often fail to ask 'how and where' constitutions signal amendments.[2] Despite the notorious length of the *travaux préparatoires* of the Portuguese Constitution of 1976, there was no discussion on the codification model. Yet, that question relates to whether and how people choose to remember their past.[3] Conceptually, Albert identifies four models for codifying constitutional amendments: the appendative model (eg, the US Constitution); the integrative model (eg, the Indian Constitution); the invisible model (eg, the Irish Constitution); and the disaggregative model (eg, the British Constitution).[4]

Since its approval in 1976, the Portuguese Constitution has only been amended seven times. The last constitutional amendment took place 17 years ago. Hence, it seems that the feared amendment frenzy was replaced by amendment inertia. Although various proposals were submitted by the Parliament, they failed to overcome the formal barriers to constitutional change.

So far, Portugal has had six Constitutions (1822, 1826, 1838, 1911, 1933 and 1976). While the second one surprisingly followed an appendative model, the

[1] Richard Albert, *Constitutional Amendments: Making, Breaking, and Changing Constitutions* (Oxford, Oxford University Press, 2019) 230.

[2] ibid 229.

[3] ibid 230.

[4] ibid 229–46.

rest of them observed the invisible model. When reading the current version of the Constitution, one has the impression they are reading the original version. To learn more about possible previous versions, a search must be made on the former official versions.

This chapter starts by describing the Portuguese Constitution of 1976, which is a fully aspirational and long post-revolutionary constitutional text. It will then explore the rigid Portuguese constitutional amendment design and the respective model of codification. The Portuguese Constitution bears the lengthiest unamendable clause in the world and consecrates formal limitations to constitutional change (temporal, procedural and circumstantial). The two major consequences of the option for the invisible model are that constitutional amendments need to be explicit and that the appendative technique is rejected. Still, when compared to the classic example of amendment invisibility in Ireland, the Portuguese Constitution has some differences. I conclude with some brief observations regarding the unconscious choice of an invisible model in Portugal. Overall, when opting for an invisible model, the values of coherence and clarity outweigh the absent lesson on constitutional law history.

II. Codifying Constitution Amendments in Portugal

A. Aspirational Constitutionalism

In 1974, after nearly five decades of the right-wing authoritarian 'Estado Novo' (New State) regime, a military coup led by the Movement of Armed Forces took place.[5] The coup aimed to fast-track democratisation and decolonisation, but the overthrow of the dictatorship triggered societal polarisation between two distinct worldviews. As the pendulum swung to the left, a revolutionary path envisioned a constitutional text with authoritarian traits inspired by Marxism-Leninism such as the agrarian reform, the socialisation of the means of production, and the dictatorship of the proletariat. With another perspective in mind, the electoral path longed for a liberal and democratic constitution.[6]

[5] The dictatorship is known as 'Salazarism', although Salazar was replaced by Marcello Caetano in 1968. The political regime 'survived the "fascist era" and was not too dissimilar from the final phase of neighbouring Spain's Franco regime, despite its single party being weaker and its "limited pluralism" greater'. See Marina Costa Lobo, António Costa Pinto and Pedro Magalhães, 'The Political Institutions of Portuguese Democracy' in Sebastián Royo (ed), *Portugal in the Twenty-First Century: Politics, Society, and Economics* (Washington DC, Lexington Books, 2012) 23, 24.

[6] Andre Thomashausen, 'Die revidierte Verfassung der Republik Portugal von 1976' [1983] *Jahrbuch des öffentlichen Rechts der Gegenwart* 443; Catarina Santos Botelho, 'Is There a Middle Ground between Constitutional Patriotism and Constitutional Cosmopolitanism? The Portuguese Constitutional Court and the Use of Foreign (Case) Law' in Giuseppe Franco Ferrari (ed), *Judicial Cosmopolitanism: The Use of Foreign Law in Contemporary Constitutional Systems* (Leiden, Brill/Nijhoff, 2019) 424–25; Maria Lúcia Amaral and Ravi Afonso Pereira, 'Um tribunal como os outros. Justiça constitucional e

These were vivid times, filled with hopes and dreams, but radicalisation of political actors and military presence was also occurring.[7] The striking down of the dictatorship did not immediately and magically lead to the advent of democracy.[8] The wounds of democratic asphyxiation take time to heal. The notion of democratic transition is overly based on formal elements, such as the approval of a new constitution or a major constitutional amendment. However, democratic consolidation requires a substantive transition as well.[9]

In 1976, a new constitution was written and approved by a Constitutional Assembly. In 1975, the turnout for the election of the Constitutional Assembly was astonishing: 91.7 per cent. Since the transition to democracy, though, the turnout has been declining at a rate of 10 per cent per decade.[10]

The Portuguese Constitutional Court (PCC) was established in 1982, in the first constitutional amendment.[11] The PCC replaced the 'Council of Revolution' and marked the beginning of the end of the military presence in the political system.[12] Furthermore, the constitutional amendments of 1982 and 1989 eliminated the objective of social transformation required for a classless society, reshaped the Portuguese Constitution and made it consonant with the substantive needs of a truly democratic rule of law.[13]

The discussion of whether the 1982 and 1989 amendments qualify as a 'constitutional dismemberment' – to borrow Richard Albert's expression – is quite pertinent. Albert describes 'constitutional dismemberment' as a 'deliberate effort to transform the identity, the fundamental values or the architecture of the constitution without breaking legal continuity'.[14] Can we say that, after eliminating key

interpretação da constituição' in Maria Lúcia Amaral (ed), *Estudos em Homenagem ao Conselheiro Presidente Rui Moura Ramos* (Coimbra, Almedina, 2016) 381; and Paulo Rangel, *O Estado do Estado – Ensaios de política constitucional sobre justiça e democracia* (Lisbon, Dom Quixote, 2009) 136.

[7] Arguing that military presence was needed to secure the democratic transition, see Vasco Fernando Ferreira Rato, *Reluctant Departure: The Politics of Military Extrication in Portugal, 1977–1982* (Washington DC, Georgetown University, 2002) 302.

[8] Costa Lobo, Costa Pinto and Magalhães (n 5) 255.

[9] Francesco Biagi, *European Constitutional Courts and Transition to Democracy* (Cambridge University Press, 2020) 15.

[10] In 2015, the turnout for the parliamentary elections was 55.8 per cent. See João Cancela and Marta Vicente, *Abstenção e Participação Eleitoral em Portugal: Diagnóstico e Hipóteses de Reforma* (Cascais, Câmara Municipal de Cascais, 2019) 14.

[11] Constitutional Law no 1/82, published in Diário da República no 227, 30 September 1982, 3135–206.

[12] The Council of the Revolution operated with an advisory body: the Constitutional Commission. This Commission advised the Council of Revolution in matters related to abstract constitutional review.

[13] Constitutional Law no 1/89, published in Diário da República no 155, 8 July 1989, 2734 (2)–2734 (68). See Catarina Santos Botelho, 'Portugal: The State of Liberal Democracy' in Richard Albert, David Landau, Pietro Faraguna and Simon Drugda (eds), *2017 Global Review of Constitutional Law* (Boston, I.CONnect and the Clough Center for the Study of Constitutional Democracy at Boston College 2018) 230–34; and Nancy Bermeo, 'War and Democratization: Lessons from the Portuguese Experience' (2007) 14 *Democratization* 288, 391.

[14] Richard Albert, 'Constitutional Amendment and Dismemberment' (2018) 43(1) *Yale Journal of International Law* 1.

ideological references to socialism and mitigating the revolutionary inputs, the Portuguese Constitution remains the same?[15]

The answer is not straightforward. It is undeniable that such amendments were crucial not only for keeping the normative force of the Constitution alive, but also for securing the credentials to join the European project.[16] We can all agree that the revolutionary path was converted into a more liberal-democratic path. Yet, does this mean that the 1982 and the 1989 amendments disclosed, in fact, a camouflaged new Constitution?[17]

At first, my answer was positive.[18] But upon further reflection, I am hesitant to assert that it was a full dismemberment. If that were the case, there would have been further dismemberments in subsequent constitutional amendments related to the boosting of the EU competences.[19] Thus, maybe the concept of 'dismemberment' should be used with parsimony. Although the revolutionary narrative towards socialism was seriously diluted and the constitutional economic regulation lessened, the essential traits of the Portuguese Constitution of 1976 remained unchanged.[20] To sum up, even if the 'Janus-faced'[21] tension between the liberal and the revolutionary path disappeared, the core of the constitution remained: human dignity, liberty, equality and solidarity, the rule of law, and pluralism.[22]

Being one of the last postmodern revolutionary constitutions, the Portuguese Constitution of 1976 is clearly a *defensive* text, with singularities that set it apart from the rest of the European constitutions. As I have written elsewhere, such defensiveness can be found in several constitutional traits: 'the long unamendable clause (Article 288); the prolix catalogue of social rights, one of the widest social rights catalogue in the world and probably the widest in Europe (Articles 58 to 79);

[15] See Graziella Romeo, 'What's Wrong with Depoliticisation?' (2022) 1 *European Law Open* 168, 170.

[16] Portugal (along with Spain) acceded to the European Economic Community on 1 January 1986.

[17] Also raising this question, see Albert (n 1) 9.

[18] See Catarina Santos Botelho, 'Constitutional Narcissism on the Couch of Psychoanalysis: Constitutional Unamendability in Portugal and Spain' (2019) 21(3) *European Journal of Law Reform* 346, 361.

[19] Like the constitutional amendment of 1992 or the constitutional amendment of 2004. It is relevant to stress that the original version of the Portuguese Constitution did not mention European integration, although the main political elite was pro-European. See Francisco Pereira Coutinho and Nuno Piçarra, 'Portugal: The Impact of European Integration and the Economic Crisis on the Identity of the Constitution' in Anneli Albi and Samo Bardutzky (eds), *National Constitutions in European and Global Governance: Democracy, Rights, the Rule of Law* (The Hague, TMC Asser Press, 2019) 591, 593.

[20] Jorge Miranda, 'Introdução Geral' in Jorge Miranda and Rui Medeiros, *Constituição Portuguesa Anotada*, vol I (Coimbra, Coimbra Editora, 2010) 52; José Joaquim Gomes Canotilho and Vital Moreira, *Constituição da República Portuguesa Anotada*, vol I (Coimbra, Coimbra Editora, 2007) 29; Jose Manuel Cardoso da Costa, 'A evolução constitucional no quadro da Constituição da República de 1976' (1994) 70 *Boletim da Faculdade de Direito da Universidade de Coimbra* 389; and Rui Medeiros, *Direito Constitucional – Ensinar e Investigar* (Lisbon, Universidade Católica Editora, 2016) 31.

[21] Francisco Lucas Pires, *Teoria da Constituição de 1976 – A transição dualista* (Coimbra, FDUC, 1988) 205.

[22] Jorge Miranda, 'Valores permanentes da Constituição portuguesa' in Jorge Miranda (ed), *Nos 40 Anos da Constituição Portuguesa* (Lisbon, AAFDL, 2017) 9.

the detailed economical constitution (Articles 80 to 107); or even the semi-presidential form of government'.[23]

The constitutional design of the Portuguese Constitution is evidently aspirational. Aspirational constitutions are overly generous, they grant a vast number of fundamental rights and they may be active instruments of societal change aiming at building a more democratic and equal society.[24] The main danger of aspirational constitutionalism is the implied 'cult of constitutionalism'.[25] In this scenery, a 'quasi-religious'[26] idea of the constitution may keep it as an object of devotion and above external stimuli.

The Portuguese Constitution was influenced by foreign constitutional experiences. To name but a few, French constitutionalism influenced the Portuguese political system; the German Basic Law (1949) and the Italian Constitution (1947) inspired several norms related to the fundamental rights protection; and the impressive extent of the social rights catalogue and the consecration of an economic constitution were based on the constitutional understanding of the former Soviet Union.

The Portuguese constitutional justice model is hybrid, as it shares characteristics of the monist/Austrian model and traits of the diffused/American model of judicial review.[27] Yet, in comparison with the Italian, German and Spanish systems of judicial review, the Portuguese system has some original traits. Instead of a concentrated constitutional justice with incidental control mechanisms in the form of preliminary review, the Portuguese Constitution bestows judicial review powers upon ordinary courts as well.[28]

B. The Portuguese Amendment Design: From Amendment 'Frenzy' to Amendment Inertia

As we will see, the Portuguese design of the amendment rules is fairly rigid, especially if we combine it with the length of the Constitution, which consecrates a total of 296 articles.[29] Since its approval in 1976, the Constitution has only been amended seven times (1982, 1989, 1992, 1997, 2001, 2004 and 2005).

[23] Santos Botelho (n 18) 369.

[24] Catarina Santos Botelho, 'Aspirações constitucionais e força normativa da Constituição – Requiem pelo "conceito ocidental de Constituição"?' in Manuel Afonso Vaz et al (eds), *Jornadas nos 40 Anos da Constituição da República Portuguesa – Impacto e Evolução* (Porto, UCE-Porto, 2017) 19, 28.

[25] Richard Albert, 'The Cult of Constitutionalism' (2012) 39 *Florida State University Law Review* 373.

[26] Paul W Kahn, *Putting Liberalism in its Place* (Princeton, Princeton University Press, 2005) 287.

[27] The US influence is an indirect one. It was the first Portuguese republican Constitution (1911) that introduced the diffused model, inspired by the Brazilian Constitution (1891), which in turn was influenced by the US Constitution (1787).

[28] Article 204 states the following: 'In matters that are submitted for judgement the courts may not apply norms that contravene the provisions of the Constitution, or the principles enshrined therein.'

[29] See Pires (n 21) 157.

If, at first, scholarship dexterously clued a 'constitutional frenzy'[30] or an amendment 'in heat',[31] after 17 years of amendment inertia, we may wonder what the dreaded amendment hysteria was all about.[32] It is relevant to mention that, in the meantime, various proposals have been submitted by the Parliament, but failed to overcome the formal barriers to constitutional change.

The Portuguese amendment design is curious. At first glance, some of the traditional traits of rigid constitutions are missing. The Constitution does not distinguish ordinary and qualified procedures through the object of the amendment, nor does it require a referendum to complete the amendment process. Yet, it encloses several formal and substantive limitations (Articles 284–89).[33]

The substantive limitations are enshrined in Article 288. Throughout 14 long clauses of entrenchment, the Constitution blocks constitutional amendment on certain topics.[34] Bearing the lengthiest unamendable clause in the world justifies foreseeing some tension on the natural flow of constitutional dynamics.[35] I called this hyper-rigid[36] dysfunctionality 'constitutional narcissism'.[37]

In the similar way that psychologists recognise a 'helicopter parenting' phenomenon in our overprotective parenting generation, the founding fathers, in a messianic move, hovered over the present and future people like a helicopter.[38]

[30] Jorge Miranda, *Nos 25 Anos da Constituição da República Portuguesa de 1976* (Lisbon, AAFDL, 2001) 14.

[31] Miguel Nogueira de Brito, 'A revisão da Constituição' in José A Tavares et al (eds), *A Constituição Revista* (Lisbon, FFMS, 2011) 123.

[32] However, I recognise the pertinence of the critique that denounces an overpoliticisation of the constitutional amendment phenomenon. See, eg, António Araújo, 'A Constituição como "problema"' in Tavares et al (n 31) 135, 136; António Araújo and Miguel Nogueira de Brito, 'Argumentar e Negociar em Debates Constitucionais: A Revisão Constitucional de 1997' in Jorge Miranda (ed), *Perspetivas Constitucionais – Nos 20 Anos da Constituição de 1976* (Coimbra, Coimbra Editora, 1998) 117; Carlos Blanco de Morais, *Curso de Direito Constitucional – Teoria da Constituição em Tempo de Crise do Estado Social*, vol II (Coimbra, Coimbra Editora, 2014) 273; and José Joaquim Gomes Canotilho, 'Pela Mão de Mariana: A Propósito do Negocialismo Partidário na Revisão Constitucional' (1997) 56 *Seara Nova* 3.

[33] Arguing that previous empirical literature has not explored the distinction between substantial and procedural amendment rules, see Nuno Garoupa and Catarina Santos Botelho, 'Measuring Procedural and Substantial Amendment Rules: An Empirical Exploration' (2021) 22 *German Law Journal* 216.

[34] Nevertheless, it is worth mentioning that some norms of art 288 (former art 290) were, in fact, amended in the constitutional amendment of 1989. See Jónatas EM Machado, 'The Portuguese Constitution of 1976' in Xenophon Contiades (ed), *Engineering Constitutional Change: A Comparative Perspective on Europe, Canada and USA* (Abingdon, Routledge, 2013) 273, 286. The possibility to alter or remove procedural and substantive amendment rules still divides Portuguese literature; see Santos Botelho (n 18) 364.

[35] Michael Hein, 'Constitutional Norms for All Time? General Entrenchment Clauses in the History of European Constitutionalism' [2019] *European Journal of Law Reform* 226, 237; and Víctor Ferreres Comella, *Constitutional Courts and Democratic Values: A European Perspective* (New Haven, Yale University Press, 2009) 107.

[36] See Blanco de Morais (n 32) 268.

[37] See Santos Botelho (n 18) 346.

[38] ibid 372.

The outcome of such generational paternalism was the removal of some constitutional essentials from possible future amendments.[39]

As far as formal limitations are concerned, they can be temporal, procedural or circumstantial. Quite innovatively, and in line with Portuguese constitutional history, the current Constitution consecrates temporal limitations.[40] To begin with, the original version of the Constitution consecrated a temporal restriction on amendment. The pertinence of such a clause was highly debated in the Constituent Assembly. The idea was that to prevent the failure of the democratic transition during 'revolutionary turbulence',[41] constitutional amendments would be prohibited during the first legislature.[42] After the expiration of the temporal restriction, the constitutional amendment process began, and the amendment of 1982 was approved.

Aiming at stability, the Constitution establishes a five-year gap between two ordinary amendments.[43] No amendment process is mandatory every five years; yet, there is the possibility of amending the Constitution every five years.[44] Accordingly, Rui Medeiros refers to a five-year 'tending ban' on constitutional amendment.[45] Still, as an urgent state of affairs might arise, the Constitution also contemplates the possibility of an extraordinary amendment process.[46] Notwithstanding the abolition of the temporal limitation, in order to initiate the constitutional amendment process, an increased majority of at least four-fifths of all the Members of Parliament is required.[47]

Regarding the procedural limitations, the initiative to amend the Constitution pertains only to the Parliament.[48] No constitutional amendment may be decided by means of a referendum.[49] Moreover, the President of the Republic cannot refuse (through political veto) to enact a constitutional amendment, nor can he

[39] Albert (n 1) 146 refers to this reality as 'transformational unamendability'.

[40] For an understanding of temporal limitations in the Portuguese Constitution, see Miguel Nogueira de Brito, 'A única revisão necessária (Comentário ao artigo 284.º da Constituição da República Portuguesa)' (2003) 2(1) *Lusíada* 155. The author explains that temporal limitations were inspired by philosopher Jeremy Bentham (at 164). Few jurisdictions opted for temporal limitations. Alongside Portugal, there is the example of Greece (Constitution of 1975).

[41] See Ozan O Varol, 'The Military as the Guardian of Constitutional Democracy' (2013) 51 *Columbia Journal of Transnational Law* 547.

[42] Article 286(1) of the original version of the Constitution. See Rui Medeiros, 'Anotação ao artigo 284' in Jorge Miranda and Rui Medeiros (eds) *Constituição Portuguesa Anotada*, vol III (Lisbon, UCP Editora, 2020) 777, 779.

[43] Article 284(1) of the Constitution.

[44] Jorge Miranda, *Manual de Direito Constitucional*, vol II (Coimbra, Coimbra Editora, 2007) 192.

[45] Medeiros (n 42) 779.

[46] Nevertheless, Blanco de Morais (n 32) 272 argues that temporal limitations may be pernicious. As the extraordinary amendment procedure requires the approval of four-fifths of the Parliament, minor parties can block relevant constitutional reforms in times of crises.

[47] Article 284(2) of the Constitution.

[48] ibid art 285(1).

[49] ibid art 115(4)(a) explicitly excludes amendments to the Constitution from the scope of referenda.

request its preventive control.[50] For logistic purposes, once a draft revision of the Constitution has been submitted, 'any others have to be submitted within a time limit of thirty days'.[51] The approval of ordinary and extraordinary amendments requires a supermajority of two-thirds of the Parliament Members.[52]

Lastly, circumstantial limitations impede an amendment from happening during a state of siege or emergency, in which fundamental rights can be suspended.[53]

C. The Codification of Constitutional Amendment in Portugal

i. From the Appendative to the Invisible Model

Up to now, Portugal had adopted six Constitutions: three during the constitutional monarchy (1822, 1826 and 1838) and three after the implementation of the republic (1911, 1933 and 1976). The Constitutional Charter of 1826 followed an appendative model, while the rest of them observed the invisible model.

The first Portuguese Constitution of 1822 was a constitutional text directly inspired by the French Constitutional Charter of 1814 and concomitant with the Portuguese liberal revolution (1820). It indicated that constitutional amendments should be written in the constitutional text itself and, therefore, the constitutional text should be republished with the updates from the amendment law.[54]

To reconcile radical/progressive liberals (and later republicans) and conservatives over the issue of the royal succession, Pedro IV, King of Portugal and Emperor of Brazil, decreed the Constitutional Charter of 1826.[55] The Charter was enforced for a long time – a total of 82 years – but with several interruptions due to civil war and the approval of the Constitution of 1838.

The Charter implemented an appendative model.[56] To give an example, when the death penalty for political crimes was pioneeringly abolished, in 1852, the Additional Act stated that: 'The death penalty for political crimes is abolished … Paragraph eighteen of Article 145 of the Constitutional Charter is therefore amplified.'[57] Thus, changes to the Charter were made not directly into the constitutional text, but in additional acts separate from the original text.

[50] Respectively, ibid arts 286 (3) and 278. See Blanco de Morais (n 32) 296; and Miranda (n 44) 201. To Rui Medeiros, 'Anotação ao Artigo 286.º' in Miranda and Medeiros (n 42) 790, 796, it is important to stress that a negative judgment of the PCC can always be overridden by the requested two-thirds majority in the Parliament (art 279(2)). With a different approach, Machado (n 34) 284 recognises 'an implied constitutional power to the President to request the preventive judicial review of a constitutional amendment by the Constitutional Court and to veto it because of its unconstitutionality'.

[51] Article 285(2) of the Constitution.

[52] ibid art 286(1).

[53] ibid arts 19 and 289.

[54] Article 28 of the Constitution (1822).

[55] Paulo Ferreira da Cunha, 'Mythe et constitutionnalisme au Portugal (1778–1826). Originalité ou influence française?' (2002) XIII *Cultura Revista de História e Teoria das Ideias* 341.

[56] Article 143 of the Constitutional Charter of 1826.

[57] Article 16 of the Additional Act of 5 July 1852.

We can wonder why the appendative model was implemented in Portugal only once. It seems bizarre. Yet, I assume the reason might be related to Brazilian influence. After all, let us not forget that King Pedro IV was also Emperor of Brazil. After declaring Brazil's independence in 1822, he granted the Political Constitution of the Empire of Brazil (1824). The Portuguese Constitutional Charter of 1826 was inspired by the Brazilian constitutional experience. As the Constitution of the Empire of Brazil followed the codifying model of the US Constitution, I speculate that the US model indirectly influenced the Portuguese Constitutional Charter of 1826.

The Constitution of 1838 was of short duration (only four years) and implemented the invisible model.[58] The first republican Constitution of 1911 did not explicitly mention how constitutional amendments should be codified.[59] Still, amendment laws were subsequently approved, and they specified that the Constitution of 1911 should be republished considering the amendments.[60] The Constitution of 1933 marked the beginning of the dictatorship (which would last until 1974). Like the previous constitutional text, there was no explicit reference to amendment signalling,[61] but the amendment laws ordered the republication of the Constitution according to the amendments.[62]

There is no doubt that the current Constitution of 1976 is the clearest constitutional text so far regarding amendment codification. Article 287 states as follows:

> (New text of the Constitution)
>
> 1. Amendments to the Constitution shall be inserted in the proper place by means of the necessary replacements, eliminations, and additions.
> 2. The new text of the Constitution shall be published along with the revision law.

When Article 287 (formerly Article 289) was discussed, the Constituent Assembly did not devote much time to it. Notwithstanding the notorious length of the *travaux préparatoires* of the Portuguese Constitution and the many vivid and brilliant discussions within the Constituent Assembly, the question of the codification of constitutional amendments was, let us say, disappointing.[63] Simply put, the proposal, which had the exact wording of the current Article 287, was read to the Deputies of the Constituent Assembly.[64] The President of the Constituent Assembly asked if anyone wanted to speak. There was no request. The proposal was immediately and unanimously approved.

In Portugal, the design of the codification of constitutional amendments can be labelled as an example of the invisible model. Like the Irish Constitution, the Portuguese Constitution does not signal amendment. The constitutional text is

[58] Article 149 of the Constitution of 1838.

[59] Article 82 of the Constitution of 1911 did not refer to the codification of constitutional amendment.

[60] Article 4 of Amendment Law no 635, 28 September 1916.

[61] Article 133 of the Constitution of 1933.

[62] Article 7 of Amendment Law no 1885, 23 March 1935.

[63] See Jorge Miranda, *Da Revolução à Constituição – Memórias da Assembleia Constituinte* (Parede, Princípia, 2015).

[64] *Diário da Assembleia Constituinte* no 121, 18 March 1987, p 4018.

straightforward, fully clean and does not disclose where amendments have been codified.[65] Therefore, there are no footnotes, references or brackets that indicate changes to the text.[66]

Thus far, the Constitution has been amended seven times since its approval in 1976. For example, Article 1 of the Constitution currently declares that 'Portugal is a sovereign Republic, based on the dignity of the human person and the will of the people, and committed to building a free, just and solidary society'. Yet, the original version was quite distinct: 'Portugal is a sovereign Republic, based on the dignity of the human person and on the popular will, and committed to its transformation into a classless society.' The current wording of Article 1 derives from the 1989 constitutional amendment. When reading the present Article 1 of the Constitution, one knows nothing about the past versions of the Constitution, nor when the article was amended.

As Richard Albert humorously wrote, in the invisible model, discovering what the original version of the constitutional text once consecrated 'remains a mystery without some investigative work'.[67] To learn more about previous constitutional versions, a search must be made on the official former versions. In Portugal, constitutional amendments are published in the official journal *Diário da República*.[68] Furthermore, open online access to the previous versions is possible in multiple official pages of several constitutional organs, such as the Parliament[69] and the Constitutional Court.[70]

Yet, in practice, apart from constitutional law students and constitutional law scholars, people only read the current version of the constitutional text. The former versions are only studied in constitutional law classes, some *en passant*, others more thoroughly. If we look at the academic versions of the Portuguese Constitution that students usually purchase, the vast majority only come up with the text as amended and are republished by the last amendment. Reference is made only to the date – not the content – of the last amendment. No further information is provided.[71]

D. Comparing Two Invisible Models: The Irish and the Portuguese

There is an interesting difference between the Portuguese and the Irish constitutional amendment design. In its first pages, the Irish Constitution

[65] Albert (n 1) 230.
[66] ibid 238.
[67] ibid 239.
[68] The first series of the official journal *Diário da República* publishes all legislation and jurisdiction acts provided for in art 119(1) of the Constitution.
[69] See, in Portuguese: https://www.parlamento.pt/RevisoesConstitucionais/Paginas/default.aspx.
[70] See, in Portuguese: https://www.tribunalconstitucional.pt/tc/constituicao_.html.
[71] See, for instance, the edition of the major legal editor in Portugal: *Constituição da República Portuguesa* (Coimbra, Almedina, 2020).

signals the list of the Amending acts, while stating relatively little about each amendment. The Portuguese Constitution, in turn, displays a bit more, but only refers to the last amendment. For example, the seventh and last constitutional amendment in Portugal – Constitutional Law 1/2005[72] – starts with the following:

> The Parliament … rules the following constitutional law:
>
> Article 1
>
> The Constitution of the Portuguese Republic of 2 April 1976, as amended by Constitutional Laws No. 1/82, of September 30, 1/89, of July 8, 1/92, of November 25, 1/97, of September 20, 1/2001, of December 12, and 1/2004, of July 24, is amended in accordance with the following articles.
>
> Article 2
>
> A new Article 295 is added, with the following wording: 'Article 295 (Referendum on a European treaty) The provisions of Article 115(3) shall not affect the possibility of convening and holding a referendum on the approval of a treaty aimed at building and deepening the European Union.'
>
> Article 3
>
> Article 295 of the Constitution becomes Article 296.

After the signatures of the President and the Prime Minister, the Constitutional Law republished the former version of the Constitution with the newly added Article 295.

Therefore, apart from belonging to distinct legal families – Portugal is a civil law model and Ireland a common law model – two differences can be pointed when comparing the invisible model of the Irish Constitution with the invisible model of the Portuguese Constitution: (1) unlike the Irish model, the current official version of the Portuguese Constitution only mentions the last constitutional amendment; (2) however, it fully reveals what norms were changed/introduced/eliminated in the last constitutional amendment.

Table 1 Comparing the Irish and the Portuguese invisible models

INVISIBLE MODEL	Reference to the *dates* of the previous amendments	Disclosing the *content* of the previous amendments	Legal family
Irish Constitution	References all of them	Does not fully disclose the content	Common law
Portuguese Constitution	Only references the last one	Discloses the entire content	Civil law

[72] Published in the official legal journal *Diário da República*, I Série-A, no 155, 12 August 2005, 4642–86.

III. Conclusions: Understanding Amendment Invisibility in Portugal

As we saw, the two major consequences of the option for the invisible model are that constitutional amendments need to be explicit and that the appendative technique is rejected.[73] Within legal academia, we all acknowledge how the legal certainty principle is relevant for legal order stability. However, legal certainty and clarity about a constitutional text, which is the fundamental law of a given polity, is even more significant.[74] Therefore, there can be no tacit or implicit intention of constitutional amendment. As a legal safety measure, constitutional amendments can only occur *expressis verbis*.[75]

Regarding the second consequence, the Portuguese Constitution – as well as other constitutional texts, such as the German Basic Law[76] – expressly rejects the US model of amendment codification. In the invisible model, each constitutional amendment 'is consumed by the new constitutional text'.[77] As referred above, Article 287(1) of the Portuguese Constitution clarifies that 'amendments to the Constitution shall be inserted in the proper place'; hence, there can be no appendix or additional acts.

The Portuguese Constitution is republished with the alterations resulting from its last amendment. Yet, this new version is not a new constitution per se, not only because total constitutional amendments are not allowed,[78] but also because it is still the same constitution, just a different version.[79]

The US model, once followed by the Portuguese Constitutional Charter of 1826, was considered a dangerous option, since the appendative model does not clearly unveil what the current constitutional text is.[80] The appendative model makes the reading of the constitutional text more challenging, as the interpreter needs to differentiate the present constitutional norms from the revoked or deconstitutionalised norms.[81] Given that the revoked dispositions of the original text remain untouched, they can confuse the reader.

[73] Rui Medeiros, 'Anotação ao Artigo 287.º' in Miranda and Medeiros (n 42) 799.

[74] ibid 800.

[75] José Joaquim Gomes Canotilho, *Direito Constitucional e Teoria da Constituição* (Coimbra, Almedina, 2003) 1076. Still, several scholars recognise implicit amendments, such as the ones that resulted from the EU integration. See Armando Marques Guedes and Francisco Pereira Coutinho, 'O Processo de Integração Europeia e a Constituição Portuguesa' (2006) 115 *Nação & Defesa* 83.

[76] See Article 79(1) of the German Basic Law.

[77] José Joaquim Gomes Canotilho and Vital Moreira, *Constituição da República Portuguesa Anotada*, vol II (Coimbra, Coimbra Editora, 2010) 1006, 1007.

[78] The long unamendable clause of art 288 impedes several constitutional traits from being amended.

[79] Gomes Canotilho and Moreira (n 77) 1007.

[80] See Cristina Queiroz, *Direito Constitucional – As Instituições do Estado Democrático e Constitucional* (Coimbra, Coimbra Editora, 2009) 154.

[81] Medeiros (n 73) 799.

As Rui Medeiros points out, Article 287 consecrates 'the principle of the tendential irrelevance' of the origin of the constitutional norms.[82] The constitutional design does not seem to value whether the norms were approved in the first version or in further constitutional amendments. One can claim that the invisible model, focusing on the present moment, does not truly acknowledge the past. In the invisible model there is an 'appearance of finality' contrasting 'with the suggestion of contingency' of the integrative model.[83] Overall, that is a valid and accurate critique.[84]

Ultimately, all four codification models have virtues and flaws. The point is that some peculiarities of the Portuguese Constitution seem to advise against an appendative or integrative model. First, the long extension of the constitutional text (Article 296) makes it easier to amend the articles themselves instead of adding additional constitutional text.[85] Second, the foundations of the Portuguese Constitution are not forgotten or diminished. The Portuguese Constitution holds the longest unamendable clause in the world (Article 288), which compiles what the constitutional fathers considered the most fundamental traits of our constitutional architecture. Furthermore, the constitutional preamble, which is a non-binding historical and symbolic statement of the beginning of the democratic transition, has remained untouched.[86]

When choosing the path of the invisible model, coherence and clarity outweigh the absent lesson on constitutional law history. To sum up, and as Gomes Canotilho states, 'at a constitutional level, there can be no uncertainty'. Doubting or wavering about what is the applicable constitutional law is a 'very serious' problem.[87] Belonging to the civil law tradition, it is no wonder that the invisible models of the Portuguese and the German constitutional texts aim at securing the primacy of written constitutional law. Constitutional primacy presupposes a general and comprehensive validity of the constitution, without which it cannot stand as the fundamental legal order of the polity.[88] To conclude, and following the idea within Richard Albert's remarks, 'authority in the present moment' manifests itself on a 'powerful metaphor … here the people rule, today'.[89]

[82] ibid 801.

[83] Albert (n 1) 255.

[84] Albert (ibid 260) argues that the invisible model 'erases reminders of yesterday, denying the people a public record of where they have been'.

[85] Demonstrating the challenge of the integrative model in the long constitutional text of India, see ibid 237.

[86] The preamble of the Portuguese Constitution still consecrates the following: 'the Constituent Assembly affirms the Portuguese people's decision to open up a path towards a socialist society'. As I have written, this sentence raises pertinent questions of genuine democratic pluralism (see Catarina Santos Botelho, 'Social Rights Trapped in Enduring Misconceptions of the Social State' (2019) 1 *Rivista di Diritti Comparati* 7, 13). Therefore, as the Portuguese preamble lacks political neutrality, it should not be legally enforceable. It is a 'ceremonial-symbolic preamble' (Liav Orgad, 'The Preamble in Constitutional Interpretation' (2010) 8(4) *ICON* 714, 722).

[87] Gomes Canotilho (n 75) 1070.

[88] Horst Emke, 'Verfassungsänderung und Verfassungsdurchbrechung' [1953] 79 *Archiv des öffentlichen Rechts* 385, 396; and Konrad Hesse, *Grundzüge des Verfassungsrechts der Bundesrepublik Deutschland* (Heidelberg, CF Müller, 1999) 291.

[89] Albert (n 1) 258.

3

Caught Between

On the Distinctive Character of Mexico's Model of Amendment Codification

JAIME OLAIZ-GONZÁLEZ*

I. Introduction

For almost a century, constitutional amendment has been the order of the day in Mexico. Until 2021, the Mexican Constitution of 1917 has been amended 762 times, making it one of the most amended constitutions in the world.[1] However, this wasn't always the case. This chapter will explore how constitutional amendment became a regular and enduring practice since 1921, and how 549 reforms to the Constitution have been enacted in the past four decades, with 320 of these reforms enacted in the last 15 years alone. This staggering number of reforms has created the notion of *hyper-reformism*[2] or *amendment mania*[3] to describe the distinctive way in which Mexico's constitutional amendment practice has unfolded over the years.

* I have benefited from constructive comments on earlier versions of this chapter presented at my course of Constitutional Theory at Universidad Panamericana Law School (Mexico City) and the Advanced Research Seminar in Constitutional Change of the International Forum on the Future of Constitutionalism, organised by Professor Richard Albert. I am grateful to Francisca Pou-Giménez, Richard Albert, Hugo Ramírez, Juan Manuel Acuña, Sebastián Incháustegui and José Mario de la Garza for their helpful and enlightening comments and suggestions. I tried to address many of them here and will continue articulating this study in upcoming works. I also want to thank Grace Green for the remarkable editorial work and suggestions.

[1] Tom Ginsburg and James Melton, 'Does the Constitutional Amendment Rule Matter at All?' (2015) 13 *International Journal of Constitutional Law* 689.

[2] Francisca Pou-Giménez and Andrea Pozas-Loyo, 'The Paradox of Mexican Self-Reinforcing Hyper-reformism' in Richard Albert, Carlos Bernal and Juliano Zaiden Benvindo (eds), *Constitutional Change and Transformation in Latin America* (Oxford, Hart Publishing, 2019).

[3] Richard Albert, *Constitutional Amendments: Making, Breaking, and Changing Constitutions* (Oxford, Oxford University Press, 2019) 251.

Part of this practice has to do with the technique that has been used for more than a century and a half to amend the Constitution. Such a technique is a result of a combination of two of the four models described by Richard Albert in his distinctive theory of constitutional amendments.[4] According to Albert, there are four models of constitutional codification: the appendative, the disaggregative, the integrative and the invisible.[5] This chapter aims to demonstrate that the Mexican case utilises a peculiar combination of the integrative and the invisible models, thereby producing a complicated practice that captures the content and purpose of each amendment from a historiographic perspective along with the resulting implications in the political culture and in judicial interpretation.

II. Tracking the Past

Mexican constitutional practice did not start by leaning towards hyper-reformism. On the contrary, the first constitutions were practically unamended until each one was replaced by a new constitution.

The Constitution of 1824 was only amended in 1833 with the liberal reforms ushered in by President Gómez Farías. It was replaced consecutively by the Constitutions of 1836, 1843 and 1847 that I will group together as the *Early Constitutions*,[6] until its principles were restored in the liberal experiment of the Constitution of 1857 (the *Middle Constitution*).

The Early Constitutions endured practically unchanged in an extensive period of societal and political redefinition during which the nation fluctuated between federalism and centralism, and between enduring conservatism and emerging liberalism. These tensions were predicated in a distinctive constitutional grammar to outline the model that was expected to utter the considered judgement of the people more genuinely.[7] However, most of the time, these tensions were channelled through war and unceasing civil unrest, resulting in events such as the US invasion of 1847 and the consequent loss of substantial part of the territory, and the Reform War that eventually paved the way for the liberal Constitution of 1857.

[4] ibid 175–260.

[5] ibid 229–39.

[6] Bruce Ackerman, *We the People: Foundations* (Cambridge, MA, Belknap Press of Harvard University Press, 1991) 58–130. This classification is clearly inspired by Ackerman's distinctive narrative of constitutional moments in US history, in which he contends the existence of four regimes within the same Constitution. The outcome of each of these moments defined the early, middle and modern characters of the US Constitution.

[7] Jaime Olaiz-González, 'At the Turn of the Tide: A Framework for a Policy-Oriented Inquiry into Strategies for the Transformation of the Constitutive Process of Authoritative Decision in Mexico' (2015), https://openyls.law.yale.edu/handle/20.500.13051/17634?show=full.

The Middle Constitution introduced the amendment mechanism that has been in use since 1857. In fact, the mechanism that will be explored in more detail in the next section was replicated in the Constitution of 1917, which will be referred to henceforth as the *Modern Constitution.*

The following table provides a classification of the Early, Middle and Modern Constitutions in Mexico and their respective salient features pertaining to the amendment procedure and the number of amendments that each constitution experienced.

Table 3.1 Constitutional amendment procedures in Mexico since 1824

	Constitution	**Period**	**Type of amendment procedure**	**Number of amendments**
1	Constitution of 1824	1824–36	1. Same as in ordinary legislation. 2. Differentiated sessions of Congress to discuss and pass amendments. 3. Included unamendable provisions.	Amended with the Reforms of 1833. Replaced by the Seven Laws of 1836.
2	The Seven Laws	1836–43	1. Same as in ordinary legislation. 2. Banned amendments for seven years. 3. President had veto power over constitutional amendments.	Replaced by the Constitutional Bases of 1843.
3	Constitutional Foundations of 1843	1843–47	1. Same as in ordinary legislation. 2. First to incorporate the two-thirds congressional threshold to amend the Constitution. 3. Maintained presidential veto power.	Replaced by the Constitutive Act of 1847.
4	Constitutive Act of 1847	1847–57	1. First to introduce a special procedure for amendment. 2. Requirement of two-thirds of Congress or majority of two different and consecutive sessions of Congress. 3. Included unamendable provisions.	Not amended. Replaced by the Constitution of 1857.

(continued)

Table 3.1 ***(Continued)***

	Constitution	Period	Type of amendment procedure	Number of amendments
5	Constitution of 1857	1857–1917	1. Consolidated a special procedure for amendment requiring two-thirds of Congress and a majority of the state legislatures. 2. No restrictions to amend any constitutional provision.	Amended 73 times.
6	Constitution of 1917	1917–present	1. Replicated the same special procedure outlined in the Constitution of 1857. 2. No restrictions to amend any constitutional provision.	Amended 762 times (as of 2021).

As shown in Table 3.1, constitutional amendment was not an enduring practice before the Modern Constitution of 1917. Just consider that the Middle Constitution of 1857 was only amended 73 times over 60 years.[8] The most substantial reforms were introduced by President Lerdo de Tejada in 1873 and comprised two main goals: (1) the incorporation of the Laws of Reform that aimed at separating the Church and the state; and (2) the restoration of the Senate by reinstating a bicameral Congress.[9]

By the last quarter of the nineteenth century, most constitutional amendments focused on regulating the re-election and terms of the President and the State Governors. However, after Porfirio Díaz's reluctance to leave power after more than 30 years as President sparked the Mexican Revolution, re-election was utterly proscribed with President Madero's reform in 1911. This was the last amendment to the Constitution of 1857.[10]

In the aftermath of the Mexican Revolution of 1910, the original plan of President Carranza to summon the Constitutional Convention of 1917 was to merely amend the Middle Constitution and not to enact a new text. However, the intense deliberation of the delegates pointed to a different direction.

[8] Imer Flores, 'La Constitución de 1857 y sus reformas: A 150 años de su promulgación' in Diego Valadés and Miguel Carbonell (eds), *El proceso constituyente mexicano. A 150 años de la Constitución de 1857 y 90 de la Constitución de 1917* (Mexico City, Instituto de Investigaciones Jurídicas UNAM, 2007) 292–316, 320–24, https://archivos.juridicas.unam.mx/www/bjv/libros/5/2389/12.pdf.

[9] ibid 296–98. The original version of the Middle Constitution established a unicameral Congress as a distinctive feature of the liberal character of the Convention.

[10] ibid 299–301.

III. Framing the Mechanism

The Early Constitutions did not differentiate any special procedure to be amended. Instead, they subjected any reform to the same procedures that would change ordinary legislation. The first trace of a special procedure dates back to the Constitutive Act of 1847, in which Articles 28 and 29 outlined a threshold of two-thirds of both Houses of Congress or a majority of the different and consecutive sessions of Congress, and a majority of the state legislatures, to pass an amendment. These provisions in the Constitutive Act of 1847 evince the derivative character of the constitutional amendment mechanism in Mexico, which is clearly inspired by Article V of the US Constitution.

The Middle Constitution of 1857 changed this mechanism by eliminating the option of the consecutive sessions of Congress as agencies for constitutional amendment, and solely leaving the requirements of two-thirds of Congress, which for the first years of the Middle Constitution was unicameral, and the majority of the state legislatures to approve an amendment.[11] Article 127 established the framework to implement 73 amendments in the six decades in which the Middle Constitution was in force.

The Constitutional Convention of 1917 decided to continue with the same procedure for amendment enshrined in Article 127 of the Middle Constitution. It may be surprising that the chosen model for constitutional amendment was not discussed in the Convention and yet was unanimously approved in its 62nd Session on 25 January 1917,[12] in Article 135 of the new Constitution:

> The present Constitution may be added to or amended. No amendment or addition shall become part of the Constitution until agreed to by the Congress of the Union by a two-thirds vote of the members present and approved by a majority of the State legislatures. The Congress shall count the votes of the legislatures and make the declaration that the amendments or addition have been adopted.[13]

IV. Implementing the Model(s)

According to congressional records,[14] the practice of amendment started with the reforms of 1873 by which the integrative model was incorporated into Mexico's

[11] Constitución Federal de los Estados Unidos Mexicanos, 5 February 1857 (Mexican Constitution 1857). See https://www.diputados.gob.mx/biblioteca/bibdig/const_mex/const_1857.pdf.

[12] Patricia Galeana et al, *Diario de los Debates del Congreso Constituyente 1916–1917* (Mexico City, Instituto Nacional de Estudios Históricos de las Revoluciones de México, 2016) vol III, 447–56.

[13] Constitución Federal de los Estados Unidos Mexicanos, 5 February 1917 (Mexican Constitution 1917). See https://www.diputados.gob.mx/biblioteca/bibdig/const_mex/const_1917.pdf. See also https://www.loc.gov/exhibits/mexican-revolution-and-the-united-states/constitution-of-1917.html.

[14] Francisco Zarco, *Historia del Congreso Extraordinario Constituyente (1856–1857)* (Mexico City, El Colegio de México, 1956) 833. There is only one mention pertaining to constitutional reforms in the

constitutional-making practice. As will be explored in this section, the integrative model remained as the prevailing scheme for constitutional amendment until the early 1900s, when the invisible approach gained currency as the top model of codification combined with scant features of the integrative approach. Let us take a closer look at the legislative technique that put such a distinctive mix in motion.

A. Born Integrative

The genesis of the Mexican practice to amend the Constitution followed the integrative model of codification. According to Albert, this model is characterised by codifying constitutional amendments through integrating them 'directly to the text of the original master text constitution'.[15] He further elaborates that '[once] inserted into the existing constitution, these amendments can replace, alter, add, or delete text'.[16]

The earliest formulations of this model were the amendments to the Middle Constitution in 1873, when in Article 127, Congress passed momentous reforms regarding Church and state relations. Here is an illustration on how these amendments were *integrated* into the master text of the Constitution:

> *Art. 28.* There shall be no private nor governmental monopolies of any kind whatsoever, nor any prohibitions even under cover of protection to industry, excepting only those relating to the coinage of money, the postal service, and the privileges which, for a limited time, the law may concede to inventors or improvers of inventions.
>
> Additions of September 25, 1873.
>
> Art. 1. The church and the state are independent of each other. Congress shall not enact laws establishing or forbidding any religion.
>
> Art. 2. Marriage is a civil contract. Marriage and all other acts relating to the civil status of persons shall appertain to the exclusive jurisdiction of the civil authorities in the manner and form provided by law, and they shall have the force and validity given to them by said laws.
>
> Art. 3. No religious institutions shall acquire real estate or capital secured by mortgage on the same, except only in the case set forth in article 27 of the Constitution.
>
> Art. 4. A simple promise to tell the truth and to comply with obligations entered into, shall take the place of the religious oath with all its effects and penalties.[17]

Except for the indication of the date pertaining to the new additions to the master text of the Constitution, no further information was included to clarify the former

discussions of the Constitutional Convention, and it was made by congressmen Ponciano Arriaga and José María Mata underscoring that the constituent power resides in the people and that any constitutional amendment should require two-thirds of Congress to be approved.

[15] Albert (n 3) 236.

[16] ibid.

[17] Mexican Constitution1857, art 28.

language of Article 28, since its original language was neither replaced nor deleted. However, in the same context of the Church and state relations, an amendment to Article 27 was passed in 1901 that makes the integrative approach clearer:

> *Art. 27.* Private property shall not be taken without the consent of the owner, except for reasons of public utility, indemnification having been made. The law shall determine the authority to make the expropriation and the conditions on which it shall be carried out.
>
> *Reform of May 14, 1901.* No religious corporations and institutions of whatever character, denomination, duration or object, nor civil corporations, when under the patronage, direction or administration of the former, or of ministers of any creed shall have legal capacity to acquire title to, or administer, real property other than the buildings immediately and directly destined to the services or purposes of the said corporations and institutions. Nor shall they have legal capacity to acquire or administer loans made on such real property.
>
> Civil corporations and institutions not comprised within the above provision, may acquire and administer, in addition to the buildings mentioned, real property and loans made on such real property required for their maintenance and purposes, subject to the requisites and limitations to be established by the Federal law to be enacted by the Congress on the subject. [As amended, 14 May 1901.][18]

This amendment included a footnote, which states as follows:

> The original text was: 'No civil or religious corporations of whatever character, denomination or object, shall have legal capacity to acquire property or administer any real state property, with the sole exception of the buildings immediately or directly destined to the services or goals of the said institution.' This article, on September 25, 1873, had the following addition: 'No religious institution may acquire real state property, nor the loans made on such real property, except for the exception herein provided.'[19]

This later technique, as shown in the official text of the Middle Constitution,[20] resembled a fully fledged integrative model as portrayed by Albert when explaining the paradigmatic contemporary practice of the Indian Constitution,[21] reflecting: (1) the new text inserted into the master text; (2) an accompanying footnote presenting the old language that was replaced by the new text; and (3) the date on which the amendment took place.

This approach was faithfully followed for almost 30 years from 1873 to 1900 and seemed to maintain a clear, coherent and harmonic articulation of the Constitution as a whole. It succeeded in updating the original text of the Constitution and in reconciling it with the momentous transformations that Mexico experienced after the Reform War, the French invasion and the *Porfiriato*.[22] However, the reforms

[18] ibid art 27.
[19] 9bid.
[20] See ibid 168–70.
[21] Albert (n 3) 236–38.
[22] Roderic Ai Camp, *Mexico: What Everyone Needs to Know* (Oxford, Oxford University Press, 2011) 77–80. The *Porfiriato* is the period encompassing Porfirio Díaz's long reign over Mexican politics (1884–1911) that ended with the Mexican Revolution of 1910 and Díaz's exile.

implemented from 1901 to 1916, including the incorporation of the sacrosanct anti-re-election principle ushered in by President Madero's momentous constitutional amendment of 1911 banning re-election in Mexico for the President, the Vice-President and the State Governors, were characterised by the incorporation of the invisible model as the chief technique to codify constitutional amendments in the later years of the Middle Constitution. Here is how this amendment was worded:

> Mexican Congress, in pursuance of Article 127 of the Federal Constitution, and with the prior approval of a majority of the state legislatures, declares the amendment of Articles 78 and 109 of the Constitution, in the following terms:
>
> Article 78. The President and the Vice President will start their duties on December 1st and will be in office for six years and are banned to be reelected at any time.
>
> The President should never be elected Vice-President. The Vice-President should not be elected President for the immediately following term.
>
> Article 109. The term for the office of State Governor may not exceed six years. The prohibitions established in Article 78 for the President and the Vice-President will be equally applicable to the State Governors.
>
> Mexico, November 7, 1911.[23]

The former informative features of the integrative approach such as the old language in the form of a footnote or the date of the amendment inserted into the master text were no longer part of the amendment practice. Instead, the new language replaced the old and presidential decrees published in the Official Federal Gazette became the primary framework to formulate constitutional amendments.

B. Becoming Invisible

A keen observer of constitutional amendment design might think that the model of codification would have covered a substantial part of the debates of the constitutional convention of 1916–17. There was no such debate.

The expected discussion on the model of codification of constitutional amendments was utterly neglected and the corresponding provision in the new Constitution of 1917 – Article 135 – was merely replicated in full in Article 127 of the Middle Constitution. The mechanism for amendment originally designed in 1857 transcended the old Constitution, but the original integrative technique was ultimately replaced by a novel invisible approach initiated in the early 1900s, and gradually consolidated as the chief model of codification from the constitutional amendments enacted in 1921 to the present day.

[23] Reforms to the Mexican Constitution 1857, https://www.diputados.gob.mx/biblioteca/bibdig/const_mex/reformas-1916.pdf.

The invisible model implied the incorporation of new language into the master text of the Constitution by means of presidential decrees published in the Official Federal Gazette, describing the new grammar in all applicable provisions *without* referring to the former language that was replaced by the respective constitutional amendment.

To describe the operation of the mechanism through the invisible model of codification, I will take as an example the first amendment to Article 1. In this case, as shown below, both the original text in the Modern Constitution and the changes that this provision underwent fail to show the old language replaced by the amendment, only reflecting the new text that was incorporated into the master text of the Constitution.[24] Let's start with the first amendment to Article 1 in 2001:

> [Original language of Article 1 (in force from 1917 through 2001):]
>
> Every person in the United Mexican States shall enjoy the guarantees granted by this Constitution, which cannot be restricted or suspended except in such cases and under such conditions as are herein provided.
>
> [Amendment to Article 1 (14 August 2001):]
>
> Every person in the United Mexican States shall enjoy the guarantees granted by this Constitution, which cannot be restricted or suspended except in such cases and under such conditions as are herein provided.
>
> *Slavery is forbidden in the United Mexican States. Slaves who enter national territory from abroad shall, by this act alone, recover their freedom and enjoy the protection afforded by the laws.*
>
> *Any form of discrimination, based on ethnic or national origin, gender, age, disabilities, social status, medical conditions, religion, opinions, sexual orientation, marital status, or any other form, which violates the human dignity or seeks to annul or diminish the rights and freedoms of the people, is prohibited.*[25]

The key to fully understanding the incorporation of the invisible approach as the leading technique of codification is the use of presidential decrees as the means par excellence of enacting constitutional amendments.

This technique merely outlines the constitutional provisions affected by the amendment, to be followed by the new language in the master text of the Constitution with no further clarifications pertaining to the former language replaced by means of addition with the amendment. As regular practice, the preamble to the presidential decree outlines the type by either additions (incorporation of new text) or reforms (removal of old text),[26] and the articles affected by the amendment. The following transcription from the presidential decree pertaining to the constitutional

[24] The new language is shown in italics.

[25] For the original version, see Mexican Constitution 1917, https://www.diputados.gob.mx/biblioteca/bibdig/const_mex/const_1917.pdf. For the subsequent amendments, *see* Mexican Constitution 1917, https://www.diputados.gob.mx/LeyesBiblio/ref/cpeum_art.htm.

[26] Albert (n 3) 251.

amendment on human rights of 2011 shows in full the operation of the invisible model:

> [This Decree] *modifies* the designation of Chapter 1 of Title 1; the first and fifth paragraphs of article 1°; the second paragraph of article 3°; the first paragraph of article 11; article 15; the second paragraph of article 18; the first paragraph of article 29; the first paragraph of article 33; the fraction X of article 89; the second paragraph of article 97; the second and third paragraphs of Section B of article 102; and subsection g) of the fraction II of article 105; the *addition* of two new paragraphs, second and third, to article 1° and altering the rest in their order; a new second paragraph to article 11; a second, third, fourth, and fifth paragraphs to article 29; a new second paragraph to article 33, altering its order; and a new fifth, eighth, and eleventh paragraphs, altering the order, of Section B of article 102; all of the Political Constitution of the United Mexican States. (Emphasis added)[27]

This shows that complexity, vagueness and obscurity are the quintessential features of the Mexican adaptation of the invisible approach. Only a few can understand the cryptic nature of the way in which the amendment procedure works and is predicated. As Albert underscores when explaining the downsides of the invisible model:

> [An] enterprising reader interested in identifying where a given amendment has changed the text would have to locate two copies of the official constitution: a copy that was official immediately prior to the amendment and a copy that became official as of the day of the amendment but before any subsequent amendment, since an intervening amendment could again change the text of the amendment the reader was currently investigation without any notice.[28]

A supplementary feature of the invisible approach – in contrast to the regular additions to the text – is the derogation of constitutional provisions also by means of amendment. Again, in this case, the old text is simply deleted with no further elaboration.

Notwithstanding the enduring influence of the invisible model via replacement by addition or by deletion, there is one remaining aspect of the integrative model that has characterised the constitutional amendment practice over the last few decades. This can be appreciated in the official text of the Mexican Constitution. Again, let us take the second amendment to Article 1 to illustrate this:

> *Article 1.* In the United Mexican States, all individuals shall be entitled to the human rights granted by this Constitution and the international treaties signed by the Mexican State, as well as to the guarantees for the protection of these rights. Such human rights shall not be restricted or suspended, except for the cases and under the conditions established by this Constitution itself.
>
> Paragraph reformed DOF 10 June 2011

[27] Decree of 10 June 2011, Official Federal Gazette, http://dof.gob.mx/nota_detalle.php?codigo=5194486&fecha=10/06/2011.

[28] Albert (n 3) 239.

The provisions relating to human rights shall be interpreted according to this Constitution and the international treaties on the subject, working in favor of the broader protection of people at all times.

Paragraph added DOF 10 June 2011

All authorities, in their areas of competence, are obliged to promote, respect, protect and guarantee Human Rights, in accordance with the principles of universality, interdependence, indivisibility and progressiveness. As a consequence, the State must prevent, investigate, penalize and rectify violations to Human Rights, according to the law.

Paragraph added DOF 10 June 2011

Slavery shall be forbidden in Mexico. Every individual who is considered as a slave at a foreign country shall be freed and protected under the law by just entering the country.

Any form of discrimination, based on ethnic or national origin, gender, age, disabilities, social status, medical conditions, religion, opinions, sexual orientation, marital status, or any other form, which violates the human dignity or seeks to annul or diminish the rights and freedoms of the people, is prohibited.

Paragraph reformed DOF 4 December 2006; 10 June 2011

Article reformed DOF 14 August 2001[29]

As shown above, a small feature of the integrative model complements the invisible approach by including, in the case of additions to the master text, the date on which the amendment took effect. This is the only note informing that the provision was amended and the number of times that it has changed since 1921. Were it not for the attached clarification of the date of amendment, the Mexican case would fit entirely within the invisible model.

Consequently, the resulting combination from a strong influence of the invisible approach with a mild formulation of the integrative model has produced a distinctive mix to model the codification of constitutional amendments in Mexico.

Table 3.2 Summary of the models of amendment codification in Mexico (1873 to present)

Model of codification	Features	Constitution
Integrative.	1. New text (within the main text). 2. Old text (in a footnote). 3. Date of amendment.	1857 (from 1873 to 1900)

(continued)

[29] Mexican Constitution 1917, art 1. The official version of the Mexican Constitution today appears on the homepage of the Mexican Congress: https://www.diputados.gob.mx/LeyesBiblio/ref/cpeum.htm.

Table 3.2 ***(Continued)***

Model of codification	Features	Constitution
Invisible.	1. New text only. 2. No footnotes. 3. No date of amendment (in the main text of the Constitution). 4. Presidential decree specifies all the articles affected by the amendment.	1857 (from 1901 to 1911) 1917 (from 1921 to present)
Invisible-integrative mix	1. New text only. 2. No footnotes. 3. Presidential decree specifies all the articles affected by the amendment. 4. Informs the date of the amendment (in the official text of the Constitution).	1917 (in the official version of the Constitution, at https://www.diputados.gob.mx/LeyesBiblio/ref/cpeum.htm)

The underlying problem of the present mix is that the clarifications that approximate the invisible model besides the date of the amendment are articulated in the respective decree *and not* in the main text of the Constitution. In fact, this technique may appear closer to the disaggregative model than to the integrative approach.[30] Ultimately, this mix fails to clarify in the main text the summary of articles affected by a given amendment, making the discovery task more challenging.

Furthermore, if we take the main text of the Constitution as the exclusive framework to ascertain its respective model of amendment codification, the invisible approach dominates.[31] However, if we broaden our scope of inquiry to the presidential decrees enacting the amendments, we will then be able to discover the integrative features that shed more light on the discovery enterprise.

As we will explore in the next section, the endurance of the invisible model has created a series of challenges and problems that have resulted in a less clear, coherent and harmonic constitution.

[30] There is an influential trend to reorganise the Mexican Constitution through the implementation of the so-called Constitutional Development Law, which clearly approximates Albert's disaggregative model. See Pedro Salazar et al, *Academic Study to Reorganize and Consolidate the Mexican Constitution* (Mexico City, UNAM, 2017) Appendix, http://www2.juridicas.unam.mx/constitucion-reordenada-consolidada/files/Appendix.pdf.

[31] Nonetheless, there was an interesting shift between 2012 and 2018 in the mode in which constitutional amendments were predicated in Mexico, since the so-called *structural reforms* on elections, energy, education, antitrust, telecommunications and labour were chiefly articulated through *transitory provisions*, which in contrast to their traditional procedural character, outlined substantive features of each constitutional amendment. Altogether, these transitory provisions are a good illustration of the influence of the disaggregative model in the contemporary mode of constitutional amendment

V. A Disharmonic Constitution

As contended by Albert, harmonisation 'is a serious challenge in codifying amendments'.[32] Though not exclusive to any country, such a challenge acquires a distinctive meaning in the case of Mexico.

Albert underscores that 'the integrative and invisible models confront a related challenge unknown in the appendative and disaggregative models: the problem of incorporation. Reformers and bureaucrats operating within the first pair of models must choose where in the existing text to incorporate new rules while those within the second pair hold no such discretion. [The] task grows in complexity when even *a single amendment affects a constitution over many of its parts and rules*' (emphasis added).[33] To illustrate this, Albert chose the Mexican case as an 'exemplar of the integrative model'[34] and the challenging nature of the problem of incorporation.

Notwithstanding the fact that Albert frames the Mexican practice of constitutional amendment within the integrative model, the approach that he explains, by differentiating between *additions* and *reforms*,[35] actually describes the operation of the invisible model. In fact, Albert's account of the way in which the integrative model was downsized in Mexico evinces the mix with the invisible model described here.

It is difficult to capture the Mexican model of codification exclusively through the focal lenses of the integrative approach since both additions and reforms fail to inform the former language in the master text. Instead, they just focus on incorporating a new text (additions) or removing an old text (reforms). In either case, the model of codification merely indicates in the master text the date when the amendment took effect. At the end of the text, the official Mexican Constitution gives the date on which each provision was amended since 1921. This is the only remaining feature of the integrative model, leaving the rest of the amending practice to the invisible model.

A good example of the inconsistencies produced by this mix is the evolution of Articles 1 and 2 of the Constitution. The original text of these articles was as follows:

> *Article 1.* Every person in the United Mexican States shall enjoy the guarantees granted by this Constitution, which cannot be restricted or suspended except in such cases and under such conditions as are herein provided.

codification in Mexico. In this respect, I have benefited from the views of Francisca Pou-Giménez on this matter, who underscores that this technique deserves further analysis to ascertain whether the Mexican case portrays an additional model of codification.

[32] Albert (n 3) 233.

[33] ibid 250.

[34] ibid 251.

[35] ibid.

> *Article 2.* Slavery is forbidden in the United Mexican States. Slaves who enter national territory from abroad shall, by this act alone, recover their freedom and enjoy the protection afforded by the laws.[36]

This differentiated location in the master text remained until 2001, when a constitutional amendment merged Article 2 with Article 1 as its second paragraph. The new text of Article 1 read as follows:

> *Article 1.* Every person in the United Mexican States shall enjoy the guarantees granted by this Constitution, which cannot be restricted or suspended except in such cases and under such conditions as are herein provided.
>
> Slavery is forbidden in the United Mexican States. Slaves who enter national territory from abroad shall, by this act alone, recover their freedom and enjoy the protection afforded by the laws.[37]

The problem with this type of incorporation is that there is no record of the former status of the prohibition of slavery as an independent provision in the original master text of the Constitution. It was simply merged by means of addition in 2001, and with the constitutional amendment of 2011, it remained in Article 1, but as its fourth paragraph. In short, the invisible approach presents provisions as if they have always been there. The consequences of such a practice are obvious:

(i) An unparalleled constitution that has been altered more than 750 times and is only accessible to legal and political elites prevents the people from capturing the meaning of the constitution and its historical evolution over the last 100 years, thereby precluding common citizens to claim ownership of the Constitution.
(ii) The enduring technique that has resulted from the invisible-integrative mix has not only insulated the Constitution from the people, but has also created an incoherent, disharmonic, and disordered text that has been used by political elites more 'as a code and political platform'[38] rather than providing a basic framework for understanding society and, ultimately, civilisation.
(iii) There is also the problem of multiplicity: amending one provision may affect others within the master text, exponentially increasing the implications of the amendment in the coherence of the text. This multiplicity has resulted most of the time in contradictions within the text overlooked by law-makers when amending the Constitution that must ultimately be clarified later via interpretation by the Supreme Court.

As Albert concludes: '[The] Mexican case illustrates the risk of malfunction in the integrative model of amendment codification. It demonstrates that contemporaneous integration – as opposed to simple appending to the end of the text – does not always leave the amended constitution clear and coherent.'[39]

[36] Mexican Constitution 1917, arts 1 and 2.
[37] ibid art 1.
[38] Albert (n 3) 252.
[39] ibid 254.

Hence, what should we do to right this malfunction? Former practice may be illuminating at this point.

VI. Learning from the Middle Constitution

Historically, the amendment mechanism has been legislative centred. One of the underlying causes of Mexico's systemic hyper-reformism is the flexibility and easiness by which incumbent governing elites amend the Constitution to entrench their policies at a constitutional level and prevent their opponents from challenging such policies, since there is no judicial review of constitutional amendments in Mexico.

This practice has shown flexibility not only in the use (or abuse) of the mechanism, but also in the implemented model of codification. The current mix – characterised by the predominance of the invisible approach – evinces the relaxation of the former integrative model of the Middle Constitution. The shift from the integrative to the invisible-integrative models mix has resulted in a less sophisticated and equally less demanding technique that fails to require lawmakers to keep track of the old text replaced by the amendments. This is reflected in the poor quality that characterises the amendment practice in Mexico.

Furthermore, to the evident downsides of this mix, such as disharmony, incoherence, obscurity and the recurrence of antinomies, we must add the intangible impact of insulating the people from the Constitution, depriving them of the possibility of fully understanding the Constitution and its evolution, and the ability to collectively internalise its legitimacy and authority.

Notwithstanding this enduring practice, I contend that there is an alternative to refine and recalibrate the present mix – to enhance the integrative component by: (1) noting the replaced language in a footnote in or an appendix to the master text; (2) highlighting the new text by means of italics, brackets or parenthesis; and (3) maintaining the integrative feature of informing the date on which the amendment took effect.

In sum, this proposal aims to resume the integrative model that characterised the operational code of amendment for the Middle Constitution until 1901. This alternative may bring upon more clarity, coherence, transparency and internal logic to the master text, making the amendment procedure, ideally devised as an onerous undertaking, more sophisticated and complex. It may also help to enfranchise rank-and-file participants to feel better represented by the Constitution, which is currently monopolised by political, economic and legal elites. Ultimately, the reincorporation of the integrative model of codification may influence not only the way in which the people claim ownership over the Constitution but also the form in which judges will interpret it.

However, the reincorporation of the integrative model will not be an easy task. Although this model is a plausible alternative to most of the predicaments produced by the invisible model, the integrative mode of codification may appear inefficient if the enduring hyper-reformist practice continues. In this case, the cure may be worse than the disease. Hence, the integrative model should be considered either for a new constitution in Mexico or a radical shift of the ongoing amendment technique in the present Constitution from now on.[40]

Modelling amendments requires advanced constitutional craftsmanship. The continuous recalibration of the model of codification enhances the amendment culture and the authority of the Constitution within the polity. After more than a century of having a marginal amendment culture chiefly controlled by the political and legal elites, Mexico should challenge the enduring premises of constitutional change.

Following Albert, asking how and where to amend the Constitution is always worth exploring.[41] A good start should delve into the challenges that the present amendment culture in Mexico raises. Among others, we can observe the following:

(a) *Narrowness*: its inability to present the whole picture of amendment evolution in the master text.
(b) *Oblivion*: the inability to track and remember the past.
(c) *Erosion*: amendment-making is not always progressive or linear, and therefore there may be cases in which former prescriptions were better than present ones. However, this is not easily ascertained with the prevailing mix.
(d) *Disharmony*: as a result of hyper-reformism, the Constitution, as a whole, lacks clarity and coherence, making it 'one of the five (constitutions) most difficult in the world to interpret with any reliability'.[42]

All in all, it is worth asking the following question: have we succeeded in retaining the basic architectural design of the Constitution with the present mix? I think not. Somewhere else, I have contended that over the course of 105 years, distinctive amendments have made the present Constitution something radically different from its original form, constituting in fact a constitutional dismemberment.[43] But how can the people realise such dismemberments if the master text of the Constitution fails to capture them due to the prevailing mix of codification?

It appears that the continuing evolution of the Constitution and its underlying premises at different moments in history is an exclusive domain for lawyers, politicians, judges and lawmakers. The rest are left aside. Consequently, this is much more than a problem of design. It raises a more fundamental predicament: how can the people claim ownership over the Constitution without having the possibility

[40] I owe these reflections to the insight of Francisca Pou-Giménez and Richard Albert.
[41] Albert (n 3) 229.
[42] ibid 253.
[43] Jaime Olaiz-González, 'Derechos humanos y cambio constitucional en México: una alternativa para la mutabilidad constitucional incremental' in Hugo S Ramírez and José María Soberanes (eds), *El artículo 1° constitucional. Una teoría de los derechos humanos* (Mexico City, Instituto de Investigaciones Jurídicas UNAM, 2021) 349–82.

to capture their considered input in the master text on the rare occasions that they have signalled the need for an amendment? For the sake of present and future generations, the model of codification should be closely revised and changed in order to give credence once more to the benefits of the integrative model that Mexico followed with the Middle Constitution. If we succeed in implementing the integrative model again, we may be able to write a different constitutional narrative for upcoming generations.

4

The Incorporation of Amendments in Paraguayan Constitutionalism

DIEGO MORENO

I. Introduction: Reframing Amendment Discourse in Paraguay

Over the past few decades, constitutional amendment discourse in Paraguay has revolved around two extremes. On the one hand, numerous scholars have offered their own list of reforms to the Constitution. They have argued that the text requires different changes in order to correct imperfections and adapt it to the necessities of current times. This side of the debate has therefore focused on the several provisions that need to be modified, but it has not paid much attention to the growing field of study on constitutional change and the rich insights it has to offer.[1]

On the other hand, there have been public discussions about which of the two reform procedures specified in the Constitution must be followed to modify a specific provision, namely, the provision that prohibits presidential re-election. This particularistic approach has generated a heated, albeit limited, public debate as to which side has the 'best' interpretation on the matter. The partisanship enveloping this debate may have even created a negative public perception towards constitutional amendment in general.

Neither of these extremes has managed to capture the enormous implications that stem from the study of constitutional amendment as a field of scholarly inquiry. As a result, issues of fundamental importance have garnered much less attention. Consider, for instance, the Constitution's rules of formal change. Despite being among the Constitution's most important rules,[2] they have received little or no attention at all. This is quite striking, since the dual-track procedure established

[1] For a description of current trends, see Richard Albert, 'Introduction: The State of the Art in Constitutional Amendment' in Richard Albert, Xenophon Contiades and Alkmene Fotiadou (eds), *The Foundations and Traditions of Constitutional Amendment* (Oxford, Hart Publishing, 2017) 1–20.

[2] Richard Albert, *Constitutional Amendments: Making, Breaking, and Changing Constitutions* (Oxford, Oxford University Press, 2019) 2.

by the current 1992 Constitution for its amendment and revision has some important flaws. The Constitution of Paraguay has only been amended once in nearly 30 years, but the impact of the design of the amendment rules on constitutional rigidity and informal change has been largely ignored.

Even less has been said regarding the problem of the incorporation of constitutional amendments. It is assumed that the way in which we codify amendments into the Constitution is a simple matter with no practical consequences. This may not be much of a surprise. Since the occasions of amendment to Paraguayan fundamental laws have been scarce throughout the country's history, the codification of amendments has not come to be seen as an issue of major concern.

It is therefore quite a challenge to present a study of the relevance and implications of the codification of amendments in the Paraguayan jurisdiction. However, the way in which amendments are codified has important implications for constitutional theory and practice, as shown by an illuminating body of contemporary scholarship on comparative constitutional law.[3] It may even be linked to constitutional rigidity and amendment culture in general. There is therefore much to be gained by exploring the problem of the incorporation of constitutional amendments.

In this chapter I intend to reframe the terms of academic debate regarding constitutional amendment in Paraguay. In doing so, I will focus on the model Paraguay has followed historically when codifying its few amendments. Somewhat surprisingly, this jurisdiction has used a 'disaggregative' model for incorporating amendments, in which modifications to the Constitution have appeared scattered throughout different texts. This requires an explanation, as it is at odds with the country's tradition of a single written constitutional document. I also suggest that the 1992 Constitution's *errata* may show that an 'integrative' model could have also operated in this jurisdiction. My goal is to suggest that the Constitution needs a better amendment design, not only to partially tackle the problem of constitutional stagnation, but also to address the incorporation of amendments.

This is only the beginning of much that remains to be done in this emerging field of inquiry that poses new and fascinating questions, but I believe it is an important step forward. I shall use as a general framework Richard Albert's discussion on models for codifying constitutional amendments, as set forth in his seminal book *Constitutional Amendments*.[4] Albert offers both a valuable guide on how to deal with the codification of possible amendments to the constitution and important insights on the design of amendment rules.

The chapter shall proceed as follows. Section II offers a brief account of Paraguay's constitutions and its constitutional amendments. Section III intends to make sense of the 'disaggregative' model that has been used throughout history to codify constitutional amendments. Section IV gives an account of the *errata* to the current Constitution and describes how its informal incorporation may

[3] ibid ch 6.
[4] ibid.

resemble an integrative model in which amendments are integrated directly into the text of the original document. Sections V and VI critically assess the 1992 Constitution amendment rules and sketch proposals for their improvement, including rules regarding the codification of amendments. Section VII offers some concluding thoughts.

II. A Short History of Paraguayan Constitutions and Constitutional Amendments

Paraguay has adopted six different fundamental laws since its independence from Spain in 1811: the 1813 'Government Regulation Act'; the 1844 'Law that Establishes the Political Administration of the Republic of Paraguay and others that are included in it'; the 1870 Constitution; the 1940 Constitution; the 1967 Constitution; and the current 1992 Constitution.[5]

The 1813 Act was a brief transitional document adopted in the midst of the independence movement that began in May 1811. It established a republican form of government and was praised for leaving an important footprint in Paraguayan public law. However, the dictatorship of José Gaspar Rodríguez de Francia (1814–40) was soon to pull Paraguay off the path of constitutionalism and towards autocracy.

The 1844 Act, adopted a few years after Rodríguez de Francia's death, was inspired by Carlos Antonio López's political views for the country and how it should be governed. It came into force despite a competing proposal for a more liberal constitution. The Act established a strong presidential system that defeated any claim of a real separation of powers. It was famously criticised by Argentinian Juan B Alberdi for containing no reference at all to the word 'liberty'.[6]

The first Constitution in the liberal sense of the term came in 1870. This is so despite being adopted under military occupation, after the end of the devastating war of the Triple Alliance (1865–70), which decimated the Paraguayan population. The Constitution remained in force throughout a period of great instability in Paraguayan history until its suspension by a military coup in 1936 and its final replacement in 1940. However, this first Constitution provided the legal framework for a liberal regime in Paraguay that recognised fundamental rights and electoral democracy.

[5] There is controversy regarding which of these documents actually count as a constitution. Furthermore, some authors may offer a different list of Paraguay's fundamental public laws. For useful historical accounts, see, eg, Juan Carlos Mendonca and Daniel Mendonca, *Breve historia del constitucionalismo paraguayo* (Asunción, Intercontinental Editora, 2011); Justo J Prieto, *Constitución y Régimen Político en el Paraguay* (Asunción, El Lector, 1987) 38–51; and Luis Mariñas Otero, *Las constituciones del Paraguay* (Asunción, Centro Iberoamericano de Cooperación, 1978).

[6] Juan Bautista Alberdi, *Bases y puntos de partida para la organización política de la República Argentina* (Buenos Aires, In Octavo, 2012) 56.

The next fundamental law, the Constitution of 1940, was adopted by a presidential decree, and then submitted to a plebiscite. Its adoption did not follow the prescribed rules for constitutional reform contained in the previous 1870 Constitution, which required a convention of citizens. Furthermore, although it included some social components for the first time in Paraguayan constitutionalism, the Constitution was, in general terms, authoritarian in character.

This last trait would repeat itself in the 1967 Constitution, which replaced its predecessor. The Constitution provided the legal support for the longest military dictatorship the country has had – that of General Alfredo Stroessner, who governed with an iron fist for nearly 35 years. The regime was ousted by a military coup in 1989 that initiated a transition to democracy.

It is no surprise, then, that some authors claim that the current 1992 Constitution is the first democratic constitution in the history of the country.[7] It consolidated the transition to democracy (although an imperfect one), adopted the form of a 'social state' and recognised several social and group rights under the principle of both formal and substantive equality, namely for women, indigenous peoples, the poor and persons with disabilities. In terms of organising power, the 1992 Constitution reacted to decades of authoritarian regimes, curtailed the powers of the presidency in a way never before seen in the country's history, invigorated a bicameral Congress and provided for an independent judiciary.

Among all six fundamental laws, only three were ever amended, and only once each. In other words, Paraguay has had more fundamental laws than amendments to them.

The 1844 Act was amended in 1856 in order to enable President Carlos Antonio López to pave the way for the succession of his son, Francisco Solano López, to the presidency, although it included other provisions as well. In a pattern that was later to repeat itself, these changes were codified in a different law, thus resembling, as will be noted in the next section, a 'disaggregative' model for codifying amendments.

The 1870 Constitution – which endured for the longest period in Paraguay's history – was not amended. However, soon after its adoption, a reform project was urged by its own drafters, as well as public opinion and the government itself. In 1875, President Juan B Gill established a commission that proposed amendments. Some of the proposals were of minor scope or merely formal in nature, while others were more substantial, such as a proposal that aimed to establish restrictions for candidates running for president.[8]

The proposed amendments were eventually rejected by the lower house of Congress. Had these amendments been adopted, the issue of their constitutional

[7] Line Bareiro, 'La primera constitución democrática de la historia del Paraguay', www.cultura.gov.py/2011/05/la-primera-constitucion-democratica-de-la-historia-del-paraguay-en-1992; Bernardino Cano Radil, *Manual de derecho constitucional y político* (Asunción, Ediciones Jurídicas, 2003) 146.

[8] See Héctor F Decoud, *La Convención Nacional Constituyente y la Carta Magna de la República* (Buenos Aries, Talleres Gráficos Argentinos LJ Rosso, 1934) 379–82.

codification would surely have confronted its drafters. They may have decided to follow the same model used under the 1844 Act. However, it is open to speculation if, under the influence of the 1853 Argentinian Constitution, which served as a model for the 1870 Constitution, reformers could have followed the path of an 'invisible' model. Such was the case with the 1860 and 1866 reforms in Argentina, which were simply incorporated without any indications as to which parts of the text had been altered.[9]

Furthermore, had the amendments taken place, it is not too far-fetched to speculate that they could have altered Paraguay's cultural reluctance to constitutional amendments. The Constitution could have simply included the adaptations it needed to confront the criticisms it received.

In turn, the 1967 Constitution was amended in 1977 in order to enable the re-election of General Alfredo Stroessner as President, allowing him to consolidate his regime. As was the case in 1856, a separate document was adopted which codified this constitutional amendment.

Finally, the 1992 Constitution was amended in 2011 by the progressive government of Fernando Lugo. The amendment granted Paraguayans living abroad the right to vote. This right had been denied by the original text of the Constitution – something that was criticised on the grounds that it unfairly deprived expatriates from having a say in national political affairs. Again, following the path inaugurated in 1856, and after adhering to the constitutional reform procedures, this single-article amendment was codified in a separate document identified as 'Constitutional Amendment No 1'.[10]

III. Making Sense of the Disaggregative Model in the Paraguayan Context

If we use Albert's models as an analytical framework for codifying constitutional amendments,[11] it seems clear that Paraguay has historically not followed any of the three main models for codified constitutions. Constitutional reforms in Paraguay were not appended at the end of a master text, as is the case with the US 'appendative' model. Nor were these amendments 'integrated' into the text, as is the case of India. And nor did they replace the original text, as in the invisible model adopted by countries such as Ireland.[12]

[9] I owe this clarification to Professor Cecilia Recalde's generous explanation.

[10] The amendment had a formal flaw, as its sanction and promulgation were mandated by the Superior Tribunal for Electoral Justice, which only has the power to supervise the constitutional referendum prior to its adoption.

[11] Albert (n 2) ch 6.

[12] ibid 229–40.

It appears that the codification of amendments in Paraguay has a certain analogy with the 'disaggregative' model described by Albert. Under a disaggregative model, constitutional amendments appear scattered throughout different texts. This comes quite as a surprise, as Albert's primary examples of disaggregative models – jurisdictions such as England, Israel and Canada – all have peculiar constitutional arrangements that bear little resemblance to the Paraguayan constitutional tradition of a single, codified master text.[13] However, the reason for Paraguay's unconventional approach seems understandable from an historical perspective.

First, ordinary laws are generally amended in the same manner in which the fundamental laws of Paraguay have traditionally been amended. An ordinary law that reforms a previous ordinary law would typically be fashioned in a disaggregative way. The new law would simply state, in its title, its purpose to modify a previous law. In its text, each article of the law would go on to spell the new wording of the modified articles as well as the derogations, if any. As a result, the disaggregative method is well known in the Paraguayan legal system, albeit generally in relation to reforming ordinary laws. We must bear in mind that, after all, the 1844 Act was an ordinary law, not an entrenched constitution.[14]

Second, the formal amendments in Paraguay's constitutional past have been relatively scarce and, with the possible exception of the 1856 reform, they all had a narrow scope. After these specific changes, no other further amendments were made to the same fundamental law. There was only one single amendment for each fundamental law, despite the relative longevity of each amended constitution.

The rationale behind the method adopted could thus have had something to do with the nature, scope and exceptionality of the amendments. Incentives to incorporate specific modifications into the master text may be lower in these cases, as opposed to those dealing with more thorough or recurrent modifications of the Constitution. It seems as if the easiest thing to do is to formalise the amendment as a separate document that spells out the text and, if necessary, explains what has been modified, without going through the trouble of meddling with the original text or printing a new official edition containing the modifications.

This approach to amendment codification may also be linked to constitutional quiescence. Amendments are seen as extremely exceptional episodes. Their rare occurrence can easily be handled within the framework of the disaggregative model. On the contrary, more frequent and thorough amendments may probably press reformers to think about alternative ways of codifying amendments so as to better harmonise them with the original text.

Be that as it may, there seems to be no evidence to suggest that rules for codifying constitutional amendments were seriously considered throughout Paraguayan

[13] But see the case of Italy (ibid 235). However, the Italian Constitution expressly allows for 'constitutional laws'.

[14] Besides, the 1844 Act made references to other documents that some authors consider possessed constitutional status.

constitutional history.[15] In sections V and VI, I argue that such rules should be considered and perhaps even included in the Constitution by way of an amendment to its amendment rules. However, before doing this, I shall turn my attention to the *errata* of the 1992 Constitution.

IV. The *Errata* of the 1992 Constitution: An Experiment with the Integrative Model?

The 1992 Constitutional Convention had to discharge its duties under severe time constraints. It also faced enormous political pressure, as then-President and military strongman General Andrés Rodríguez (leader of the 1989 military coup) and his daughter were written out of the new presidential election. Rumours circulated of another military coup. The Constitution was ultimately entered into force, though without going through the promulgation process via the executive branch.

One month after the dissolution of the National Constitutional Convention, errors were found in the official printed Constitution. The former President of the Convention sent a letter to Congress with an *errata* to the Constitution. However, as some scholars have noted, the *errata* had no formal legal effect, as the Convention had already ceased to exist, and its former President – as well as the commission that compiled the *errata* – lacked legal authority to issue the document.[16] Most of the changes enumerated in the *errata* consisted of minor grammar corrections, but some were substantive. An example of the latter is Article 3, which establishes the three branches of government. The original version stated that the branches are 'separate', while the *errata* stated that they are 'independent', a modification that was especially important for a judiciary that had historically been subjugated.[17]

Since the *errata* had no legal authority, there exists no official printed version of the Constitution containing the *errata*. However, at least one private publisher started printing the Constitution with the *errata* in an edition that has even been cited in Supreme Court opinions.[18] In doing so, the publisher did not simply 'append' the *errata* at the end of the text, but actually proceeded in accordance with a model that resembles the 'integrative' model. Thus, each *erratum* has been placed

[15] For instance, in the only comprehensive textbook written on Paraguayan constitutional law for decades, despite a thorough discussion of amendments under both the US and the Argentinian Constitutions, the author makes no reference to the codification of amendments: Félix Paiva, *Estudio de la Constitución del Paraguay*, vol I (Asunción, Imprenta Nacional, 1926) 196–206.

[16] See, eg, Juan Carlos Mendonca, *Crítica al nacimiento de una Constitución* (Asunción, Editora Litocolor, 2000) 121–23.

[17] Another substantive modification is included in art 25, where the *errata* added the right to one's image.

[18] José Manuel Plano de Egea (ed), *La Constitución de la República del Paraguay con sus fundamentos* (Asunción, Editorial Latindata, 1993).

in the corresponding article containing errors. The Supreme Court did something similar some years later with its own non-official edition of the Constitution that incorporated the *errata*, in the same integrative fashion, though the Court added the *errata* in footnotes to each article.[19] These non-official editions had errors of their own but they were quite useful, as the reader could easily spot the original text and its corresponding changes.

These publications with embedded *errata* give us an idea of how an integrative model might look like in the Paraguayan jurisdiction. The integrative model does have the advantage of clearly showing where the changes are inserted. It does not require a significant task of judicial harmonisation, as the publisher does the major work of integrating the new text into the existing document. However, integration does present the problem of clutter, and it is clearly at odds with the way in which Paraguayan lawyers and other actors generally read statutes or codes, let alone their Constitution.

This discussion is not purely speculative. There is evidence that the *errata*, despite not being adopted according to legal procedures, have been incorporated into the legal system by their effective application through the judiciary, especially, through the Supreme Court and its constitutional chamber.[20] This means that the 1992 Constitution might have indeed undergone important modifications to its original text that, although lacking formal legal authority, eventually became incorporated into the Constitution through judicial application. If this is the case, then an argument could be made for codifying the *errata* and formalising their constitutional status. Rather than letting judges decide if, when or how the *errata* will become part of the Constitution, this seems a task more appropriate for a formal constitutional amendment that expresses the will of the people.

Alternatively, instead of following this integrative model, perhaps aesthetics and simplicity would suggest adopting an invisible model for incorporating minor adjustments scattered throughout the document. This is especially so with regard to merely small housekeeping changes. After all, there is no point in reminding 'the people' of its past grammatical errors.

From a different perspective, the *errata* call into question the myth of irreformability, to which we shall turn next. The *errata* intended to amend the Constitution only one month after its entry into force, correcting not only drafting mistakes, but even substantive ones, in the process demonstrating that even a brand-new Constitution may sometimes require adjustments. This, in turn, confronts us once again with the questions of whether one model of amendment codification is better than others, and why.

[19] Víctor Manuel Núñez Rodríguez (ed), *Órganos constitucionales. Constitución nacional* (Asunción, Corte Suprema de Justicia, 2007).

[20] See, eg, Ac y Sent No 222-3 [2000], CSJ (plenario); and more recently, Ac y Sent 617 [2021], CSJ (Sala Constitucional).

V. Amendment Rules in the 1992 Constitution: A Critical Assessment

The degree of obstacles imposed by the amendment procedure does not offer a complete account for measuring amendment difficulty.[21] However, it might tell part of the story as to why the 1992 Constitution has experienced only one amendment in almost 30 years. Anxieties about regression towards authoritarianism may have led the 1992 Constitutional Convention to overprotect the document, making changes very difficult in practice.

The Constitution establishes, in Articles 289 and 290, two distinct procedures: the 'amendment' procedure and the 'reform' procedure. Under both of them, the power of initiative is vested in a quarter of the members of either chamber of Congress, the President or 30,000 electors.

The 'reform' procedure requires a declaration of the necessity of a reform approved by two-thirds of members of both chambers of Congress. The next step requires calling for elections within six months to form a National Constitutional Convention, which will in turn draft the reforms or even a totally new constitution. The text sanctioned by the Convention comes into force with no need for further approvals.

The 'amendment' procedure is less onerous than the 'reform' procedure. This is so not only because it does not require assembling a special body through elections, but also because the majority required for approving the text of the amendment is less demanding than the one required in the context of a reform. It takes only an absolute majority of members of each chamber of Congress to approve the amendment. However, in this case, the Constitution does require that the amendment be submitted to a referendum within six months. Only if the referendum is successful is the text 'incorporated' into the Constitution, although the exact way to codify this incorporation is not specified.

If one looks closely at the debates of the 1992 Convention, it appears as though at some points the drafters were under the impression that the 'amendment' procedure was to be followed in cases of partial changes to the Constitution, whereas the 'reform' procedure was to be used when a totally new document was deemed necessary. However, this does not accurately reflect the adopted text.

Article 290 provides that if certain parts of the Constitution are to be modified, the 'reform' procedure should necessarily be deployed. In truth, a total revision must necessarily follow the 'reform' procedure, but both procedures can be used for bringing about partial modifications, depending on the part of the Constitution being modified. The 'reform' procedure must necessarily be followed in order to alter any provision that affects the mode of election, the composition, the duration of terms in office or the powers of any of the branches of government, as well as

[21] Albert (n 2) ch 3.

the chapters recognising the rights to life, the environment, liberty, equality and family rights.

Under the current codification, the scope of provisions that can be modified by the easier amendment procedure is severely limited. This is so not only due to the wide array of subjects that fall under Article 290, but also because, through interpretation, it could be argued that many other constitutional provisions not directly related to the mode of election, composition, attributions or others could nevertheless actually fall under the more demanding procedure.[22] This suggests an important flaw in the design of the Constitution's rules of change. It means that the more difficult procedure – devised for a total revision of the Constitution or to reform only important parts of it – could end up being the procedure required for introducing partial amendments to large swathes of the document.

Furthermore, the regulation creates inconsistencies. To provide just two examples, it leaves out of the more onerous 'reform' procedure important parts of the Constitution, such as the first three articles, where the fundamental declarations are contained. Second, it seems to imply that some rights and provisions of fundamental importance (namely political rights, social rights, the rights of indigenous peoples, provisions regarding agrarian reform, and essential clauses such as the supremacy clause and sovereignty) are less significant than other provisions, despite being perceived by many as reflecting some of the most cherished values of the 1992 Constitution.

Be that as it may, it is not surprising that, aside from the successful 2011 amendment that granted voting rights to Paraguayans living abroad,[23] only one other modification of the Constitution has had any chance of being adopted. Under the presidency of Horacio Cartes, his political allies (including part of the opposition) tried to modify the Constitution to allow for presidential re-election in 2017 using the 'amendment' procedure. Doubts arose as to the legitimacy of deploying this less demanding track, which sparked opposition that escalated into violence due to police repression, the burning down of the Congress building by protestors, and eventually the backing away of the President from the attempt.

It is no wonder that there are widespread fears of modifying the 1992 Constitution. Furthermore, the 1977 reform was passed to allow a dictator to remain in power, whereas the previous 1856 reform had sought to allow the President's son to become president. Even though different scholars and other actors have proposed modifications to the Constitution, there is a widespread concern that reforms or amendments could be used to only to the benefit of a discredited political class and against the national interest.

[22] Luis Lezcano Claude, *Derecho Constitucional. Parte Orgánica* (Asunción, Imprenta Salesiana, 2018) 669–72.

[23] Some argued that even this modification should have followed the 'reform' procedure. See Gonzalo Quintana, 'Enmienda y voto de paraguayos en el extranjero' *ABC Color* (21 May 2011).

VI. Taking Amendment (and Amendment Codification) Rules Seriously

Of course, there are arguments for and against introducing changes to the Constitution. Some of its institutions or specific provisions have proven inadequate in practice. The question is whether the current Constitution will eventually die out of impotence in the face of changing social and political realities, or whether reforms will be able to keep it in tune with the evolving necessities of time. Some of the existing concerns about constitutional change in Paraguay may be addressed with a better design of the current rules of change.

The framers apparently intended their own constitution to last for decades. Thus, one prominent drafter said the following in the 1992 Convention: 'We have heard on numerous occasions members in the Committee and in the plenary sessions express the desire that the Constitution be in force 50 or 60 years.'[24] If, however, the Constitution is meant to endure, it seems natural to allow some room for changes that will have to be made to adapt it to different circumstances.[25] A strong case could be made for amending different parts of the Constitution, and different authors and political and social actors have been offering their own 'reform list' for years.

From a different angle, pressure for reform could come from the Inter-American Court on Human Rights (IACtHR). By virtue of its current doctrine, the Court may regard some of its decisions to be incompatible with the Inter-American Convention on Human Rights. As an example, the IACtHR doctrine on same-sex marriage, as expressed in its Advisory Opinion on Gender Identity, Equality and Non-Discrimination of Same-Sex Couples,[26] is clearly at odds with Articles 49–52 of the 1992 Paraguayan Constitution.

In order to allow for future changes, it seems reasonable to consider improving the rules for constitutional change. The idea, of course, is not to make the Constitution too easily amendable or, worse, readily subject to dismemberment.[27] Instead, the objective is to improve a double-track procedure that nevertheless leaves large parts of the Constitution reformable only through the more demanding procedure, which in practice renders changes very difficult and the other procedure largely unusable.

There are several ways of designing amendment rules, and Albert's work also provides valuable insight into this task.[28] Of course, this is not the place to explore

[24] *Actas. Comisión Redactora* (R Campos Cervera), 10 April 1992, https://www.bacn.gov.py/constitucion/comision-redactora/cr-04-10-sesion-nro30.htm#Art%C3%ADculo289.

[25] Zachary Elkins, Tom Ginsburg and James Melton, *The Endurance of National Constitutions* (Cambridge, Cambridge University Press, 2009) 82 (establishing a connection between endurance and flexibility).

[26] Advisory Opinion OC-24/17, Inter-Am Ct HR (ser A) No 24 (24 November 2017).

[27] Albert (n 2) ch 2.

[28] ibid ch 5; Richard Albert, *Formas y función de la enmienda constitucional* (Bogotá, Universidad Externado, 2017) ch 3.

this complex issue thoroughly. In what follows I will sketch a few tentative thoughts that will have to be refined on a different occasion.

It must be acknowledged that the double-track procedure does offer advantages by differentiating the values we attach to different clauses. However, under a new design, each track should be better tailored, leaving the 'reform' procedure as an exceptional means for total revision and for some specific provisions that express fundamental values, as well as the amendment rules themselves.[29] The 'amendment' procedure would, of course, include a more comprehensive range of subjects.

One could even think of adding other tracks with appropriate levels of difficulty and consensus according to each subject (for instance, for fundamental rights,[30] territorial organisation, constitutional organs that are not part of any of the three branches of government, and for clauses that regulate more technical matters).[31] Some of these tracks could be made subject-specific so as to avoid fears related to 'wholesale constitutional overhaul'.[32] Others may include a more sophisticated referendum process that allows for more deliberation and a more accurate assessment of the general will. Provisions that regulate technical matters or issues of secondary importance may not require a referendum at all.

So far, this approach intends to provide a better double or multi-track procedure that does not necessarily relax all requirements for constitutional change. Nevertheless, it does provide a wider scope of rules that can be altered without resorting to the creation of a constitutional convention. The model does not necessarily guarantee more reforms, as in any case the frequency of reform will turn on the jurisdiction's constitutional culture.[33] But a better design may eventually alleviate amendment phobia and make the Paraguayan Constitution more open to change and improvement. At the same time, it may also reassure Paraguayans that their most important constitutional values will be granted the highest degree of protection against a distrusted political class.

To the extent that this is design might generate more amendments, it makes sense to consider a model for incorporating them. The disaggregative model does not seem fit for a country that codifies its fundamental law in a single, master text. Depending on the nature and scope of amendments introduced, perhaps an invisible model, coupled with a detailed summary of amendments appended at the end of the text so as to keep track of changes, would be a good choice. It would dodge the dispersion that the current disaggregative model generates, it would escape the

[29] One could say that the 'reform procedure' will be left for cases of 'dismemberment'. For a discussion on this, see Albert (n 2) 76–92.

[30] The procedure could also specify that no regressive changes may be introduced when it comes to rights, so as to ease anxieties that amendments could curtail rights.

[31] So as to avoid ambiguities, reference must be made to specific articles or parts of articles.

[32] For a discussion, see Albert (n 2) 186–88.

[33] See Tom Ginsburg and James Melton, 'Does the Constitutional Amendment Rule Matter at All? Amendment Cultures and the Challenges of Measuring Amendment Difficulty' (2015) 13(3) *International Journal of Constitutional Law* 686.

harmonisation problems posed by the appendative model, and it would avoid the clutter and intricacies of the integrative model.

It is not obvious that contemplating rules for the incorporation of amendments will end up having an impact on amendment culture in general. But it is important that 'the people' be made aware in advance of the way in which constitutional changes will come to be incorporated into their Constitution or, at the very least, that they be assured that the constitutional reformers will confront this question seriously when the time comes.

VII. Conclusion

Paraguay has had more fundamental laws than partial reforms to them. Only three formal amendments have been made to its six fundamental laws, although informal changes included in the *errata* to the current Constitution seem to have been incorporated into the legal system by the Supreme Court.

From an historical perspective, the disaggregative model for incorporating amendments has been prevalent in the Paraguayan context. Amendments have been codified as separate documents, although they were meant to be read in connection with the master text. Despite running contrary to what would be expected from a tradition that codifies its constitution in a single master text, the scarcity of formal amendments has not posed a serious problem of harmonisation, though it has rendered obsolete a few rules in the master constitutional text.

However, constitutional rigidity may pose a different kind of problem. The 1992 Constitution has proven very difficult to amend. Stagnated constitutions may have contributed not only to informal changes of dubious legitimacy, but even to regression towards authoritarianism. This was arguably the case with the liberal 1870 Constitution and the authoritarian constitutions of 1940 and 1967 that followed,[34] although departures from the previous constitutional order might have occurred regardless of the possibility of introducing amendments to the Constitution.

Nonetheless, a healthy dose of formal amendments to the Constitution may allow it to more adequately fulfil its promises of dignity, rights, equality, democracy and the rule of law, without the need for a discontinuous or even traumatic departure from the previous order. Amending the imperfect amendment rules may be an intelligent move in this direction, especially when the Constitution contains provisions regulating different issues that may prove inadequate in practice and whose modification does not justify especially onerous procedures.

In turn, making formal amendments more accessible obliges us to consider how to incorporate future amendments to the Constitution. Designers should be

[34] Justo J Prieto, 'Epílogo' in *La Constitución Paraguaya Concordada* (Asunción, Imprenta El Gráfico, 1990).

aware that there are several ways of incorporating amendments, and that each has its advantages and disadvantages. Whereas the current disaggregative model does not seem to possess any salient virtues, a hybrid approach that takes into account the nature and scope of amendments seems more promising.

Albert's discussion of the architecture of constitutional amendment rules, coupled with his models for codifying constitutional amendments, provides an invaluable guide for the future of amendments in the Paraguayan context. It opens new possibilities for intelligent constitutional design. At the same time, it allows us to see the importance of taking amendment codification seriously, reminding us that the way in which we codify our amendments has profound implications for constitutional law and practice.

5

The Codification of Constitutional Amendments in Brazil

Beyond the Appendative and Integrative Models

BRUNO CUNHA

I. Introduction

There is a debate among constitutional law scholars over whether Brazil has been living under its seventh or eighth Constitution since its independence in 1822. The debatable question lies in whether one amendment to the 1967 Constitution should be considered an entirely new constitution. Formally, it was adopted and approved as Constitutional Amendment n 1 in 1969 (CA 1/1969) by the leaders of the dictatorial military government of the time. For the majority of Brazilian scholars, CA 1/1969 is regarded not as an amendment to the constitutional regime of 1967, but as a new constitutional order.[1] The main reason for such a conclusion is that the entire text of the 1967 Constitution was replaced by the amendment. On the face of it, CA 1/1969 declared it aimed 'to edit the new text of the 1967 Constitution'. In practical terms, Article 1 of the amendment stated that 'the Constitution of 1967 becomes effective with the following wording …', and the text that followed contained significant differences from the previous one. Hence, this chapter argues that the amendment in 1969 is considered an autonomous constitutional order in Brazil. It is the seventh Brazilian Constitution (the eighth being the current Constitution of 1988).

This debate is only one among many controversies involving constitutional amendments in Brazil's 200 years of constitutional history. Since the first Brazilian Constitution of 1824, adopted during the monarchical regime, the patterns of constitutional design have been unreliable at best, which led to many controversies

[1] Virgílio Afonso da Silva, *Direito constitucional brasileiro* (São Paulo, Edusp, 2021) 74.

about their amendments, constitutional structure and validity. One of the main goals of this chapter is to describe and analyse the development of constitutional amendment rules throughout Brazil's constitutional history. The final aim is to present Brazil's current state of affairs with regard to constitutional amendments under the Constitution of 1998.

To be fair, the Brazilian Constitution of 1988 established clearer rules concerning the approval procedures of constitutional amendments than previous constitutions. Despite these new rules, the current Constitution did not establish any particular model for the codification of amendments, leading to a spike of amendments (137 in 35 years) with distinct structures, designs and codification models.

The study of constitutional changes and constitutional amendments is on the rise worldwide. As the title of this book indicates – and as Richard Albert says in one of the leading textbooks about the topic[2] – the architecture of constitutional amendments is now a major theme in comparative constitutional law, making it possible to affirm the 'emergence of comparative constitutional amendment as a distinct field of study in public law'.[3] As this distinct field emerges and grows, new approaches are established to deal with it, and new ideas are discussed to 'identify the underpinnings of constitutional change'.[4]

Although the field is on the rise, a specific theme has not been addressed in detail thus far: the codification of constitutional amendments. The main guidelines on this topic can be found in the influential work of Richard Albert regarding constitutional amendments.[5] Albert dedicates Chapter 6 of his book *Constitutional Amendments: Making, Breaking and Changing Constitutions* to the study of distinct models of codification of constitutional amendments. As he points out, two imperative questions need to be answered when the topic is the architecture and codification of constitutional amendments: 'how and where will the constitution indicate that it has been amended?'[6] However, as Albert explains, 'constitutional designers commonly defer these questions to future generations until the very moment when the reality of a ratified amendment forces lawmakers to answer them'.[7] This specific chapter seeks to address this, along with a comparative, doctrinal and historical analysis of the architecture of constitutional amendments.

Albert's descriptive theory about the models of codification of constitutional amendments is the starting point of the present analysis. From that theory, this work intends to analyse the codification of constitutional changes in Brazil since

[2] Richard Albert, 'The State of the Art in Constitutional Amendment' in Richard Albert, Xenophon Contiades and Alkmeni Fotiadou (eds), *The Foundations and Traditions of Constitutional Amendment* (Oxford, Hart Publishing, 2017).

[3] ibid 3.

[4] ibid.

[5] Richard Albert, *Constitutional Amendments: Making, Breaking and Changing Constitutions* (Oxford, Oxford University Press, 2019).

[6] ibid 229.

[7] ibid.

its first Constitution in 1824. It aims to discuss how the Brazilian constitutional practice of amendments, from 1824 until today, falls within the framework of Albert's proposed models for codifying constitutional amendments.

Starting with the debate between Roger Sherman and James Madison about the models of amendments under the US Constitution (the appendative or integrative models), the idea is to explore how Brazil has been using these models at the same time through its eight Constitutions (1824, 1891, 1934, 1937, 1946, 1967, 1969 and 1988). The chapter concludes by arguing that more than the appendative and integrative models, the Brazilian Constitution today establishes a mandatory disaggregative and invisible model for the codification of some specific amendments. At the time of writing, appendative, integrative, disaggregative and invisible models for the codification of constitutional amendments are in use in Brazil.

II. The Theoretical Foundations of Codification of Constitutional Amendments

According to Albert's theory,[8] there are four basic models for codifying constitutional amendments: the appendative, integrative, invisible and disaggregative models.

In the appendative model, 'the amendments are appended sequentially to the end of the text'.[9] Even though the constitutional norms are changed by the amendments passed, the text of the original Constitution remains untouched. In the integrative model, the 'amendments are incorporated directly into the master text of the original constitution'.[10] They appear as interwoven clauses. In this model, the external form of the original Constitution is preserved, even though its content has been altered.

The main distinction between the two basic models (appendative and integrative) can be illustrated by the famous clash during the first US Congress in 1791 between Roger Sherman and James Madison. Shortly after the adoption of the US Constitution in 1787 and the proposal of the first 10 amendments in 1789 (which ended up forming the Bill of Rights, which was approved in 1791), one of the main discussions that took place in terms of constitutional policy in the US concerned the codification of the approved amendments. The following question hovered over the first amendments to the US Constitution: should amendments be added to the original text of the Constitution, altering it, or should they compose an appendix in which the amendments would appear separately, thereby leaving the original text unchanged?

[8] ibid.
[9] ibid 230.
[10] ibid.

On one side was James Madison, from Virginia, who is considered by many to be the father of the US Constitution and who would become President of the country from 1809 to 1817. Madison believed that the best approach was to integrate the amendments into the existing body of the Constitution (the integrative model). A single constitutional text harmonised with later amendments would add an element of cohesion and 'would indicate exactly how the rights in question were to be protected'.[11] It would also bring clarity and ease the difficulties of its future interpretation.

On the other side was Roger Sherman, an influential representative from Connecticut and signer of three constitutive texts in US history[12] (the Declaration of Independence, the Articles of Confederation and the US Constitution). Sherman believed that the power of amendment contained in Article V of the US Constitution did not grant Congress the authority to change the original text of the Constitution. As Jack N Rakove said, 'Sherman objected that Congress had no right to alter the original text produced by the Convention of 1787, but could only add to it'.[13] For Sherman, the amendments should be added in the form of an appendix to the original text of the Constitution (the appendative model). Any solution to the contrary would threaten the integrity of the Constitution.

Sherman's position prevailed. After a long debate, Congress endorsed his view that 'the amendments should appear as supplemental articles, not interwoven clauses'.[14] Amendments to the US Constitution have since followed the appendative rather than the integrative model. That is why the US Constitution's text remains in its original version today. The current 27 amendments are part of a sequential appendix that must be harmonised with the original text for the application and practical operation of the Constitution.

The solutions suggested by Madison (integration) and Sherman (appendix) at the end of the eighteenth century became two basic models for the codification of constitutional amendments in several jurisdictions today. Historically, the eight Brazilian Constitutions never established the methodology for codifying constitutional amendments. Nevertheless, all Constitutions (including the current one) have used the appendative and integrative models.

According to Albert, the two lesser-known models for the codification of constitutional amendments are called the invisible and disaggregative models. In the invisible model, as the name suggests, 'the constitution does not indicate where the amendment has been codified'.[15] In this particular model, an amendment 'inserts, removes, and changes the constitutional text without any clear indication of what in the text has been altered, how it has been altered, or when

[11] Jack Rakove, *The Annotated US Constitution and Declaration of Independence* (Cambridge, MA, Harvard University Press, 2009) 60.

[12] Albert (n 5) 231.

[13] Rakove (n 11) 60.

[14] ibid 60.

[15] Albert (n 5) 230.

precisely it was altered'.[16] The reader of the constitution will face the original text with no remarks and 'no other details that could quite readily alert readers that something new may have been inserted, something old may have been removed, or that anything at all may have changed'.[17]

The disaggregative model can be described as 'a form of codification characteristic of uncodified constitutions that situate their constitutive rules and principles in different sites of constitutional importance'.[18] Within such a model, the changes in the constitution may appear in distinct documents or even through unwritten constitutional norms.[19]

The first particularity of the disaggregative model is its ability to combine features of the appendative, integrative and invisible modes.[20] The second is the fact that the model may be applied both to codified and uncodified constitutions (the British Constitution being the best example of the latter). Albert uses the Italian Constitution of 1947 as an example of the combination of different models applied to codified constitutions. The current Italian Constitution adopts both the disaggregative and the integrative models. According to Albert, the Italian Constitution is 'amendable by a special procedure authorizing the alteration of its text and it is amendable also by the adoption of separately codified constitutional laws that change the meaning of the constitution but leave the master text unchanged'.[21] This example is helpful as it bears similarities to the argument concerning the Brazilian Constitution of 1988. The current Brazilian Constitution also demands the model of separately codified constitutional laws – or 'disaggregated constitutional laws'[22] – for some specific types of constitutional amendments.

This theoretical background of the codification of constitutional amendments is fundamental to understanding the present models used by the Brazilian Constitution of 1988. The constitutional history of Brazil is a distinct yet equally significant aspect of the present analysis. In the following sections, this work surveys the history of Brazil's eight Constitutions, from the monarchical Constitution of 1824 to the current Constitution of 1988.

III. The Constitutions of Brazil and their Amendment Procedures: 1824–1969

After achieving its independence in 1822 the new Empire of Brazil needed to break its political and legal ties with Portugal. Pedro I, Emperor of Brazil, promptly

[16] ibid 238.
[17] ibid.
[18] ibid 230.
[19] ibid 234.
[20] ibid 230.
[21] ibid 235.
[22] ibid.

took the necessary measures to install a Constituent Assembly even before the Declaration of Independence of Brazil in September 1822. The Assembly had its inaugural session in May 1823. However, the political instability in the newly independent country and the clashes between its members and the Emperor led to violent disruption of the Assembly's works in November 1823. The crux of the disagreement concerned the division of powers and the relations between the executive and the legislative branches of government. As Virgílio Afonso da Silva describes it, 'the Emperor wanted more control over the legislature than the members of the Assembly were willing to grant'.[23]

Following these frictions, Pedro I ordered the army to dissolve the Constituent Assembly in an episode called 'The Night of Agony'. The imperial forces arrested opponents, who were soon deported. Immediately after the Assembly's dissolution, Pedro I appointed a new Council of State with members of his trust, who were to complete the works begun by the Constituent Assembly without further approval by another Assembly.[24] On 25 March 1824, the Constitution was finally adopted and called the 'Political Constitution of the Empire of Brazil, prepared by a Council of State and granted by Emperor D. Pedro I, on 3.25.1824'.

The authoritarian measures of the Emperor that culminated in 'The Night of Agony' abbreviated the political process leading to the Constitution of 1824. This interference in the Assembly's works created an environment of constitutional deliberations that was entirely in the hands of the Council of State's members. In light of this, there are no in-depth historical records of the debates and discussions concerning constitutional changes or amendments prior to the adoption of the Constitution of 1824.

According to Article 173 of the Constitution of 1824, the Legislative Power (called 'Assembléa Geral' and made up of two distinct Chambers: the Chamber of Deputies and the Senate) was responsible for examining whether the Political Constitution of the Empire of Brazil was being followed at the beginning of its annual sessions. The Constitution of 1824 brought in its Articles 174–77 the procedures of constitutional change (voting order, procedures and time lapses for deliberations and approval), but it did not mention any particular scheme about how the changes would be added to the Constitution after their approval.

Although the process for constitutional changes was provided in Articles 174–77, the most important provision of the Constitution regarding amendments was Article 178. In a literal translation, Article 178 stated that: 'It is only Constitutional that which concerns the limits and respective attributions of the Political Powers, the Political Rights and Individual Rights of the Citizens. Everything that is not Constitutional can be changed, without the formalities mentioned above, by the

[23] Virgílio Afonso da Silva, *The Constitution of Brazil: A Contextual Analysis* (Oxford, Hart Publishing, 2019) 15.

[24] For a detailed description of the background to the Constituent Assembly and the debates that led to the adoption of the Constitution of 1824, see Paulo Bonavides and Paes de Andrade, *História Constitucional do Brasil*, 9th edn (Brasília, OAB Editora, 2008).

ordinary Legislatures.' As Octaciano Nogueira noted, the Constitution of 1824 was inspired by English constitutionalism of the time, according to which only what concerns the powers of the state, individual rights and guarantees are considered to be a constitutional matter.[25] Thus, although the Constitution of 1824 was formally amended only once in 1834, it was completed, changed and adapted by a series of ordinary laws that dealt with matters that were not considered to be materially constitutional at the time.

There are two points still worth mentioning about the Constitution of 1824. First, contrary to what became a tradition in the following constitutions, basically the whole text of the Constitution of 1824 could be changed through amendments (the federal system, the form and regime of government, the right to vote etc). Second, the procedures for approving an amendment were quite similar to the legislative procedures of ordinary laws. According to Nogueira, the Constitution of 1824 had greater plasticity and flexibility than any other Brazilian Constitution.[26]

The only constitutional amendment passed during the 65-year period under the Constitution of 1824 followed the appendative model, as no direct changes were made to the original text of the Constitution. The amendment was approved as 'The Additional Act of 1834' and regulated the increase in the provinces' autonomy.[27] As its title mentioned, the Additional Act of 1834 'made some changes and additions to the Political Constitution of the Empire', though none became part of the original text, which remained untouched for 65 years. The Constitution of 1824 lasted until 1889, when a military coup led by Marshal Deodoro da Fonseca overthrew the monarchic regime and established the Brazilian Republic.[28]

On the same day of the coup d'etat, the new government that took power issued Decree n 1/1889, which 'provisionally proclaimed as the form of government for the Brazilian nation the Federative Republic'. According to Article 4, until the election of a Constituent Congress, the Brazilian nation would be governed by the Provisional Government of the Republic. The Constituent Congress was elected in 1890, and the new Constitution was promulgated in 1891, laying down 'the foundation of the Brazilian constitutional system that remains today: presidential and federal systems, as well as judicial review of legislation'.[29]

Article 90 of the Constitution of 1891 provided that it could be amended by the initiative of either one-quarter of any of the Houses of the National Congress (the Senate or the Chamber of Deputies) or two-thirds of the State Assemblies. Article 90, §1° inaugurated the idea of a distinct approval quorum for constitutional

[25] Octaciano Nogueira, *Constituições Brasileiras: 1824*, 3rd edn (Brasília, Senado Federal, 2012) 10.

[26] ibid 12.

[27] Waldemar Martins Ferreira, *História do Direito Constitucional Brasileiro*, 2nd edn (Rio de Janeiro, Forense, 2019) 53.

[28] For an in-depth historical analysis of the transition between the monarchical and the republican government, see Emília Viotti da Costa, *Da Monarquia à República*, 9th edn (São Paulo, Editora Unesp, 2010).

[29] Da Silva (n 23) 17.

amendments in contrast to ordinary laws in Brazil. The amendments needed a qualified quorum of two-thirds of the votes of the respective members, in three rounds of voting, in each House of the National Congress. Another novelty of the Constitution of 1891 was the establishment of unamendable rules. For example, propositions that aimed at abolishing the republican form of government, the federal system and the equality of representation among the states in the Senate could not be admitted for deliberation in Congress (Article 90, §4º).

In terms of architecture, Article 90, §3º established that an approved amendment would be 'incorporated into the Constitution, as an integral part of it'. The only amendment approved during the 40 years under the Constitution of 1891 was then incorporated into the main constitutional text. In a purely integrative fashion, the amendment approved in 1926 completely rewrote six articles of the Constitution of 1891 and maintained its original external form.

After 40 years of the Constitution of 1891, another coup d'etat, now led by Getúlio Vargas, overthrew the constitutional government in 1930. Following a loss in the presidential election of 1930, Vargas led the '1930 Revolution' with the support of discontented states, 'aiming to prevent the newly elected president, Júlio Prestes, from taking office. The goal, however, was not only to seize power as such, but to change the oligarchical power structure in Brazil'.[30] With the coup's success, Vargas was declared chief of a Provisional Government[31] in November 1930, and soon promised a new constitution for the country. The calling and election of a Constituent Assembly took almost three years. One year later, in 1934, the third Brazilian Constitution was promulgated.

The Constitution of 1934 had a short lifespan. It remained in operation for only three years. Its Article 178 inaugurated two distinct methods of formal constitutional change: constitutional amendments and constitutional revisions. On the one hand, the Constitution could be amended when the proposed changes were not aimed at modifying 'the political structure of the State and the organization of the sovereign powers within it'. On the other hand, a constitutional revision was needed when the propositions related to such themes. Following the previous Constitution, propositions that aimed at abolishing the republican form of government and the federal system could not be admitted for deliberation in Congress (Article 178, §5º).

In addition to different initiative quorums (constitutional amendments required more than half of the State Assemblies or one-quarter of the Senate or of the Chamber of Deputies, while constitutional revisions required two-fifths of any of the Houses of the National Congress or two-thirds of the State Assemblies), Article 178, §3º provided a distinct form of codification for each method of constitutional change. Amendments were to be appended to the original text, while revisions would be integrated into it. Only one constitutional change passed during the short three-year period of the Constitution of 1934. Three

[30] ibid 18.
[31] ibid.

constitutional amendments (n 1, n 2 and n 3) were approved in a single procedure in 1935 (Legislative Decree n 6/1935) and were appended to the original text of the Constitution.

On the day after the Constitution of 1934 was enacted, the same Constituent Assembly that produced it elected Getúlio Vargas for a four-year term as President (Article 1 of the Temporary Constitutional Provisions). New elections would be held in 1938, and Vargas could not seek re-election under the Constitution of 1934. With that in mind, on 10 November 1937 and 'under the pretext of fighting a communist threat, [he] suspended the 1934 Constitution and established a fascist-inspired, dictatorial rule. In the same day that he suspended the 1934 Constitution, Vargas personally granted a new Constitution'[32] to the country.

The new Constitution of 1937 provided for a strong executive power in Vargas' hands and a weak and almost non-operational legislative branch. According to Waldemar Martins Ferreira, it brought about a powerful President of the Republic as the supreme leader of the state, concentrating both the legislative and executive functions of government.[33] The procedures for amending the Constitution of 1937 reflected the executive's political dominance in constitutional practice.

First, any amendment proposed or backed by the President would be approved with a simple majority vote in both Houses of Congress (Article 174, §1º). In contrast, amendments proposed by members of Congress needed to be approved by an absolute majority of each House (Article 174, §2º). Oddly enough, the President could send back to Congress any approved amendment proposed by its members. In a second vote, this amendment would need a two-thirds majority to pass in each House (Article 174, §3º). Finally, if an amendment proposed by the President was rejected or an amendment proposed by Congress was definitively approved, the President had the power to submit it to a national plebiscite (Article 174, §4º). According to these procedures, 21 amendments were passed from 1938 until 1946, all using either the appendative or integrative models of codification.

CA 9/1945 was approved on 28 February 1945. It scheduled new general elections for the end of 1945 for both the National Congress and the presidency. On 12 November 1945, a novel constitutional amendment, CA 13/1945 established that those elected at the end of 1945 would form a Constituent Assembly with unlimited powers to approve a new constitution for the country.[34] Before the elections, Getúlio Vargas was forced by the military to resign as his dictatorial regime weakened.[35] Backed by Vargas, Eurico Gaspar Dutra was elected President of Brazil. A new Constitution was approved on 18 September 1946.

[32] ibid.

[33] Ferreira (n 27) 104–06.

[34] Lilia Moritz Schwarcz and Heloisa Murgel Starling, *Brasil: uma biografia*, 2nd edn (Rio de Janeiro, Companhia das Letras, 2018) 396.

[35] Da Silva (n 23) 19.

The Constitution of 1946 restored democratic principles and a more balanced separation of powers while maintaining the basic features of the federal republic in place since 1891.[36] Article 217 established amendment procedures that followed the general terms (including limitations) set out in the Constitution of 1934. The Constitution provided that an approved amendment 'would be annexed, with the respective serial number, to the text of the Constitution' (Article 217, §4°). Between 1950 and 1966, 21 amendments were passed under these procedures using both the appendative and integrative models of codification.

Besides 21 'regular' amendments, the Constitution of 1946 was altered by another kind of mechanism called 'Atos Institucionais' ('Institutional Acts'). These Institutional Acts were approved by the executive branch (the military government) without the participation of the National Congress. They were introduced after a military coup d'etat overthrew the democratic government of João Goulart, who was accused of being a communist by part of the population and the military.[37] As da Silva points out, 'on 1 April 1964, a military coup, strongly supported by the United States, extinguished the fragile democratic experience under the 1946 Constitution. A period of more than 20 years of authoritarianism, violence, torture, censorship and general lack of freedom began'.[38]

Between 1964 and 1966, under the Constitution of 1946, the new military government passed four Institutional Acts. They rewrote large parts of the Constitution of 1946 and eliminated the foundations of its democratic character. These Acts legitimised the new authoritarian regime and 'authorized the commanders-in-chief of the army, air force and navy to suspend basic constitutional rights for 10 years, to remove members of the Congress from office, among other things'.[39] On 7 December 1966, the military dictatorship led by President Marshal Castello Branco passed the Institutional Act n 4/1966. It called the National Congress to meet extraordinarily to discuss and vote on a new draft Constitution presented by the President. On 24 January 1967, the sixth Brazilian Constitution was approved by Congress: the Constitution of 1967.

The Constitution of 1967 presented only minor changes in the legislative procedures of constitutional amendments compared to the former Constitution of 1946. Most importantly, it broadened the list of those entitled to submit amendment proposals for deliberation in Congress, including (i) any member of Congress, (ii) the President and (iii) more than half of the State Assemblies. But the vast majority of constitutional changes made under the Constitution of 1967 were adopted by Institutional Acts. From January 1967 to October 1969, the military government passed 13 Institutional Acts, most of them involving major changes to the Constitution of 1967.

[36] See Aliomar Baleeiro and Barbosa Lima Sobrinho, *Constituições Brasileiras: 1946*, 3rd edn (Brasilia, Senado Federal, 2018).

[37] Boris Fausto, *História Concisa do Brasil*, 2nd edn (São Paulo, Edusp, 2010) 254–59.

[38] Da Silva (n 23) 19–20.

[39] ibid 20.

The primary example is the Institutional Act n 5 ('AI-5'), adopted on 13 December 1968. Its changes were so overarching in both breadth and depth that they virtually dismantled the whole constitutional order of the time. Virgílio Afonso da Silva explains in detail the reach of the Act:

> Among the 17 institutional acts issued in the first five years of the authoritarian regime, the most important – in a negative sense – was AI-5, of 13 December 1968. In that moment, exceptionalism reached its peak. AI-5 granted absolute power for the President of the Republic to close the National Congress, to declare a state of exception and federal intervention in the states, to suspend political rights and to limit the exercise of any public or private right, to remove members of the Congress from office, among other things. Moreover, no decision based on this institutional act could be challenged before the courts.[40]

With no Congress in session, many of its members removed from office, and the presidency under a military junta due to the illness of President Marshal Costa e Silva, the only constitutional amendment under the Constitution of 1967 was adopted directly by the Junta on 17 October 1969. CA 1/1969 rewrote the entire text of the Constitution of 1967, as explained in section I above, and is considered an autonomous constitutional order in Brazil: the Constitution of 1969, the seventh in Brazil's history.

The Constitution of 1969 provided an even more authoritarian framework for the military's executive power. Constitutional freedoms could be suspended easily by the executive, such as the suspension of habeas corpus, restrictions on travel and the banishment of undesired citizens.[41] In terms of amendments and its procedures, the Constitution of 1969 maintained the structure of its predecessor. The only minor change related to those entitled to propose amendments. The Constitution of 1969 could be amended by the initiative of either one-third of any of Houses of the National Congress (the Senate or the Chamber of Deputies) or the President. From 1972 to 1985, 26 amendments were passed using both the appendative and integrative models of codification.

While the military regime showed its weaknesses in the late 1970s and early 1980s, the idea of democratisation with a new constitution to replace the authoritarian regime of 1969 gained force. On 27 November 1985, CA 26/1985 was approved, which called for a Constituent Assembly to start in 1987. After more than a year and a half of debates, the Assembly approved Brazil's eighth and current Constitution on 5 October 1988: the Constitution of 1988.

IV. The Constitution of 1988: Appendix and Integration

Article 60 of the Constitution of 1988 provides all the material and formal rules about constitutional amendments. They can be proposed by one-third of

[40] Da Silva (n 23) 21.
[41] Schwarcz and Starling (n 34) 459.

the members of the Chamber of Deputies or of the Senate (at least 171 out of the 513 representatives, or 27 out of the 81 senators), by the President of the Republic or by more than half of the State Assemblies (at least 14 out of 27). The proposal shall be discussed and voted upon in each House of the National Congress in two readings. The amendment shall be considered approved if it obtains, in both readings, three-fifths of the votes of the respective members (Article 60, §2º) – that is, 308 representatives and 49 senators.

The main constitutional rules limiting or prohibiting deliberation about constitutional amendments are found in Article 60, §1º, §4º and §5º. First, §1º provides that the Constitution shall not be amended while a federal intervention, a state of defence or a state of siege is in force. Second, §4º indicates that no proposal shall be considered which is aimed at abolishing: (i) the federative form of the state; (ii) the direct, secret, universal and periodic vote; (iii) the separation of powers; or (iv) individual rights and guarantees. These provisions are considered eternity or entrenched clauses under the Brazilian Constitution of 1988. Third, §5º establishes that the matter dealt with in an amendment's proposal that is rejected or considered impaired shall not be the subject of another proposal in the same legislative session. A legislative session comprises two legislative periods, the first running from 2 February to 17 July and the second from 1 August to 22 December.

As of January 2023, there have been 137 amendments to the Brazilian Constitution of 1988: 128 regular constitutional amendments enacted through the ordinary procedure outlined in Article 60; six based on an expedited procedure of constitutional revision (revision amendments); and three arising from international human rights treaties and conventions equivalent to constitutional amendments.

The distinct procedure for the revision amendments was brought by Article 3 of the Temporary Constitutional Provisions Act, as follows: 'The revision of the Constitution shall be effected after five years as of its promulgation, by the vote of the absolute majority of the members of the National Congress in a unicameral session.' It was a temporary opportunity to revisit and revise the Constitution in its fifth anniversary with a lower quorum for approving amendments.

Though the Constitution of 1988 was silent about methods for the codifications of its amendments, both the regular amendments (128) and the revision amendments (6) followed the basic appendative and integrative models. The first three regular constitutional amendments adopted in 1992 and 1993 illustrate the two distinct models of codification both in a pure and a hybrid fashion.

First, CA 1/1992 is an example of an amendment using a pure integrative model for its codification. It made changes in one specific provision (Article 27, §2º), added two items to another (Article 29, VI and VII), and these changes are noted in the Constitution's text. Second, CA 2/1992 was codified through a pure appendative approach, as the constitutional changes were carried out based on the provisions contained only in the text of the amendment (as an appendix to the Constitution). Third, CA 3/1992 used a hybrid model. In this specific case, Articles 1 and 6 of the amendment changed the text of eight articles in the original text of the Constitution, while Articles 2, 3, 4 and 5 brought in new constitutional provisions that were added as an appendix to the Constitution.

V. Conclusion: The Constitution of 1988 and its Mandatory Disaggregation and Invisibility

Beyond the appendative and integrative models, since 2004, with the approval of CA 45/2004, the Constitution of 1988 has established a disaggregative and invisible model for the codification of some specific amendments. CA 45/2004 added the following provision to Article 5, §3º: 'The international human rights treaties and conventions which are approved in each House of the National Congress, in two rounds of voting, by three-fifths of the votes of the respective members, shall be equivalent to constitutional amendments.'

Resembling the Italian example brought by Richard Albert and cited above,[42] the international human rights treaties and conventions approved by the Brazilian National Congress under Article 5, §3º of the 1988 Constitution lead to 'separately codified constitutional laws that change the meaning of the constitution but leave the master text unchanged'.[43] These disaggregated constitutional laws will also be invisible, as the master text of the Constitution remains unchanged. There will be no integration of these treaties and conventions with the original text of the Constitution and no indication of them in the appendix of amendments. Therefore, when Article 5, §3º says that these international human rights treaties and conventions 'shall be equivalent to constitutional amendments', it establishes a mandatory disaggregative and invisible model for codifying this special kind of amendment.

International human rights treaties or conventions may be approved and adopted in Brazil by two distinct procedures: (i) by a simple majority of the votes in each House of Congress, in which case they will have a merely legal status;[44] or (ii) following the procedures of Article 5, §3º, in which case they will be equivalent to constitutional amendments. As of January 2023, there were three constitutional amendments (or equivalents) arising from international human rights treaties and conventions adopted in Brazil: (i) the Convention on the Rights of Persons with Disabilities and its Optional Protocol (New York, 2007), adopted in 2009; (ii) the Marrakesh Treaty to Facilitate Access to Published

[42] See n 21.

[43] Albert (n 5) 235.

[44] In 2008, the Supreme Federal Court of Brazil ruled that international human rights treaties approved by a single majority in each House of Congress are not equivalent to constitutional amendments, but are considered to hold a status above ordinary law ('supra-legal' status). See Federal Supreme Court, RE 466343, judgment of 3 December 2008, portal.stf.jus.br/jurisprudenciaRepercussao/tema.asp?num=60.

Works for Persons Who are Blind, Visually Impaired or Otherwise Print Disabled (Marrakesh, 2013), adopted in 2018; (iii) the Inter-American Convention against Racism, Racial Discrimination and Related Forms of Intolerance (Guatemala, 2013), adopted in 2022.

After this long journey throughout the Brazilian constitutional history of the last 200 years, it is safe to say that the codification of constitutional amendments underwent few variations from the first Constitution in 1824 until the eighth Constitution in 1988. This period was marked by an alternation between the integrative and the appendative models for the codification of constitutional amendments. Under the Constitution of 1988 and until 2004, the integrative and appendative models continued to be used as the only methods for the codification of amendments in Brazil. Finally, after the approval of Constitutional Amendment n 45 in 2004 (CA 45/2004), new amendment rules and regulations have led to a mandatory disaggregative and invisible model for the codification of some specific amendments. As of today, the appendative, integrative, disaggregative and invisible models for the codification of constitutional amendments are in use in Brazil.

6

The Form of Constitutional Amendments in Japan

MASAHIKO KINOSHITA

I. Introduction

What has been the form of constitutional amendments in Japan? Answering this question is difficult, perhaps impossible, because Japan has never experienced a 'normal' constitutional amendment. Historically, Japan has had two constitutions: the Meiji Constitution (Constitution of the Empire of Japan), which was in effect from 1890 to 1947, and the 1946 Constitution (Constitution of Japan), from 1947 to the present. The history of constitutionalism in Japan has already run for more than 130 years. Nevertheless, there have been no constitutional amendments other than the transition from the Meiji Constitution to the 1946 Constitution, which can hardly be described as a 'normal' amendment.

However, the question as to what form 'ordinary statutory amendments' (amendments to statutes enacted by the Diet, the national legislature of Japan) have taken is not so difficult to answer. Rich legislative practices have accumulated with ordinary statutory amendments. Additionally, based on such practices, it is possible to provide some answers to the question of what the form of Japanese constitutional amendments will or even should be. Hence, while the materials available for discussion are limited, this chapter explores what can be postulated regarding the form of Japanese constitutional amendments and further implications that can be drawn relying on Richard Albert's model of the form of constitutional amendments.[1]

This chapter is divided into three subsequent sections. Section II describes the form of ordinary statutory amendments. Section III addresses the form of transition from the Meiji Constitution to the 1946 Constitution. Section IV examines the form of amendments to the 1946 Constitution.

[1] See Richard Albert, *Constitutional Amendments: Making, Breaking, and Changing Constitutions* (Oxford, Oxford University Press 2019) ch 6; and the Introduction to this volume.

II. The Form of Ordinary Statutory Amendments

In Japan, ordinary statutory amendments are implemented according to sophisticated rules that have been developed by professional bureaucrats, especially in the Cabinet Legislative Bureau and the Legislative Bureaus of both houses of the Diet. The foundation of these rules is influenced by the practices of the Western European civil law systems, but these rules have some aspects that evolved uniquely in Japan. The practical techniques of making amendments to statutes appear to be the craftsmanship of bureaucrats. However, bureaucrats have published several books on their practices, from which an overview can be obtained.[2]

A. The Basic Framework

Japanese statutes consist of a title, preamble, table of contents and main body. The main body is further divided into two parts: main provisions and supplementary provisions. The main provisions are the core of the statute. In contrast, the supplementary provisions stipulate subsidiary matters: the effective date of the statute, transitional matters etc.

Changes to a statute are classified into three types: repeal-and-replace, total amendment and partial amendment. The repeal-and-replace is a method of repealing the existing statute in its entirety and enacting a new comprehensive statute. On the other hand, a total amendment is a method of amending an existing statute in its entirety without repealing it. The main provisions of both the statute implementing the repeal-and-replace and the statute implementing the total amendment are comprehensive and do not differ from those of an independently new statute which is not concerned with any changes to an existing statute. However, the statute for repeal-and-replace has the sentence '[name of old act] shall be hereby repealed' in its supplementary provisions, while the statute for total amendment has the sentence 'The entire [name of old act] shall be hereby amended' in its preamble, so that they can be distinguished by careful reading.

The partial amendment is more complex than the other two types. Statutes making partial amendments differ significantly in terms of their content from statutes making repeal-and-replace and total amendments. Japanese bureaucrats have recognized that there are potentially two possible forms of partial amendment: the *zōho* method and the *tokekomi* method. The term *zōho* means 'appendix' in English, so the *zōho* method corresponds almost exactly to Albert's appendative model.[3] In fact, the constitutional amendment model of the US Constitution

[2] See, eg, Shuzo Hayashi, *Hōrei Sakusei no Jōshiki* [*Common Practices in Law-Making*] (Tokyo, Nihonhyoronsha, 1975); Toshihiko Oshima, *Hōsei Shitsumu no Kiso Chishiki* [*Fundamental Knowledge of Legislative Affairs*], 3rd edn (Tokyo, Daiichihoki, 2011); Hosei Shitsumu Kenkyu Kai (ed), *Wāku Bukku Hōsei Shitsumu* [*Workbook on the Legislative Affairs*, 2nd edn (Tokyo, Gyosei, 2018).

[3] Albert (n 1) 230.

has been put forward as a typical example of the *zōho* method. In contrast, the term *tokekomi* corresponds to 'consolidation' or 'integration' in English. However, Japanese legal practice does not have a tradition of officially attaching footnotes to the statutes to indicate the history of amendments, so based on Albert's modelling, the *tokekomi* method falls not under the integrative model, but under the invisible model.[4] During the period of the Meiji Constitution, the Imperial Household Law, which governed the status and succession of the imperial family, was amended several times by the *zōho* method.[5] However, almost all amendments to ordinary statutes are based on the invisible model.

B. The Practical Process of Partial Amendments

This section explains the detailed method of partial amendments, using the 2018 Civil Code amendment as an example. Figure 6.1 is a schematic illustration of the partial amendment process.

Figure 6.1 The partial amendment process

Original Master Text Statute (Act No. 89 of 1896)

Title	Civil Code
Main Provisions	Article 1 • • • Article 2 • • • Article 3 • • • Article 4 The age of majority is 20 years of age. Article 5 • • •

Amendment Statute (Act No. 59 of 2018)

Title	Act Partially Amending the Civil Code
Main Provisions	The Civil Code (Act No. 89 of 1896) shall be partially revised as stated below. '20 years of age' in Article 4 shall be revised to '18 years of age'.
Supplementary Provisions	Article 1 This Act shall come into force as of 1 April 2022. Article 2 • • •

Integration

New Master Text Statute after 2022 (Change effective without publication)

Title	Civil Code
Main Provisions	Article 1 • • • Article 2 • • • Article 3 • • • Article 4 The age of majority is 18 years of age. Article 5 • • •

[4] ibid.

[5] The Addition of the Imperial House Law (11 February 1907); the Addition of the Imperial House Law (28 November 1918).

Previously, Article 4 of the Civil Code stipulated that the age of majority to perform legal acts independently was 20 years.[6] However, in 2018, the Civil Code was amended to lower it to 18 years. The title of the statute that made this amendment is 'Act Partially Amending the Civil Code'.[7]

After this title, the Act Partially Amending the Civil Code has one sentence: 'The Civil Code (Act No 89 of 1896) shall be partially revised as stated below.' This is a fixed phrase used in statutes for partial amendments, called an 'amendment statement'. Following the statement, the specific amendments to be made to existing statutes are set out; in the case of the 2018 Act Partially Amending the Civil Code, '"20 years of age" in Article 4 shall be revised to "18 years of age"'. Generally, in this way, the indication of the content of the amendment is provided by picking out only the individual words or phrases that are the target of the change. However, if there are multiple amendments to a single provision, the instructions for amendment may become complex and difficult to understand. In such cases, the entire provision could be denoted rather than the individual words to be amended.[8] In addition, it is usually difficult to understand what will be amended by reading only the amendment bill. Therefore, when an amendment bill is submitted to the Diet, a comparison table, as shown in Table 6.1 below, is attached and made public to see at a glance where changes are to be made.

Table 6.1 A comparison table of old and new articles

Amendment Bill	**Current**
Article 4 The age of majority is *18 years* of age.	Article 4 The age of majority is *20 years* of age.

At the end, the 2018 Act Partially Amending the Civil Code contains a supplementary provision that provides for the Act to take effect on 1 April 2022. Accordingly, the words of the original master text changed on that date.

Here, it is necessary to explain the 'promulgation' of statutes. In Japanese practice, a statute enacted by the Diet must be promulgated by the emperor in order to have legal effect,[9] and this is done by publishing the texts of the statutes in the Official Gazette.[10] The text printed in the Official Gazette has legal effect in lieu of the original copy of the statute passed by the Diet. These legal practices are also influenced by the Western European civil law systems, especially that of France.[11]

[6] Civil Code (Act No 89 of 1896).

[7] Act Partially Amending the Civil Code (Act No 59 of 2018).

[8] Hayashi (n 2) 87.

[9] Under the 1946 Constitution, the Emperor does not have the power to veto promulgations.

[10] See Shigenori Matsui, *The Constitution of Japan: A Contextual Analysis* (Oxford, Hart Publishing, 2011) 69 fn 5.

[11] Makoto Oishi, 'Kōfu Saikō' [Revisiting the Promulgation] in *Kempō Seido no Keisei* [*The Formation of the Constitutional System*] (Tokyo, Shinzansya, 2021) 262.

In addition, it is worth noting that in Japan, while amendment statutes are promulgated, the finished statutes that consolidate amendment statutes into existing master statutes are neither promulgated nor officially printed. In the example cited above for the change of the age of majority, the only texts that are officially available are the original Civil Code and the 2018 Act Partially Amending the Civil Code. The work of integrating amendment statutes with existing ones on paper has been done primarily by private publishers of law books.[12] Although in recent years the government has provided the texts of consolidated statutes online, these online texts, just like texts from private publishers, do not have the same legal effect as the Official Gazette.[13]

C. What is the Difference between the Appendative Model and the Invisible Model?

In Japan, the appendative model (the *zōho* model) and the invisible model (the *tokekomi* model) have long been recognised as contrasting methods of partial amendments. However, when carefully comparing the appendative model of the US Constitution with the invisible model of Japanese ordinary statutory amendments, it is not easy to find clear distinctions between the two.

In Japan, the existing provisions of a statute may be modified or repealed by an amendment act. In the same way, the US Constitution can be amended. For example, the Twenty-First Amendment explicitly abolished the Eighteenth Amendment.[14] Under the appendative model, the Eighteenth Amendment was not removed from the original master text, though it did lose its legal effect. Similarly, in Japan, there is no official creation of a new integrated master text that manifests the modification of the legal effect caused by the amendment. In other words, the appendative model of the US Constitution and the invisible model of Japan are the same in that the revision and abolition do not occur in the official text.

Perhaps the difference between the two lies in whether the implied modification of an existing provision is treated as normal or abnormal. The appendative model allows an amendment to overwrite or nullify a provision without explicitly modifying or eliminating it. For example, the Thirteenth Amendment,[15] although not explicitly stated, is deemed to have repealed the fugitive slave clause and the three-fifths compromise in the original text.[16] In Japan, when two contradictory

[12] Oshima (n 2) 171–72.

[13] For example, the Digital Agency provides a legislation data online system named 'e-Gov Law Search', available at https://elaws.e-gov.go.jp. However, the e-Gov Law Search notes that there are cases where the notation differs from that in the Official Gazette, and cautions that if what it provides differs from what was published in the Official Gazette, the Official Gazette takes precedence.

[14] US Constititon, amendment XXI; US Constititon, amendment XVIII.

[15] US Constititon, amendment XIII.

[16] Albert (n 1) 240–41.

provisions exist, the *lex posterior derogat priori* (the later law repeals the earlier one) principle is applied and the earlier provision loses its legal effect even if it is not explicitly repealed. However, the existence of contradictory provisions in Japan is often simply a legislative error. In Japanese practice, it is customary to explicitly modify and delete the previous clause at the drafting stage to avoid inconsistencies within the legal system. As a result, *lex posterior derogat priori* applies to very few cases.[17] In other words, an existing provision cannot be modified and nullified without explicit repeal, unless the inconsistency between the former and latter provisions can be regarded as a legislative error. The difference between implied modification being normal and abnormal is an important factor when considering the choice of the constitutional amendment form in Japan.

III. The Form of the Transition from the Meiji Constitution to the 1946 Constitution

A. The 1946 Constitution as a Total Amendment of the Meiji Constitution

Similar to ordinary statutory changes, three distinctions can be assumed in constitutional changes: repeal-and-replace, total amendment and partial amendment. In Japan, there has been no experience with partial amendments since the Meiji Constitution was enacted in 1889. Moreover, it is hard to say whether the change from the Meiji Constitution to the 1946 Constitution is a case of repeal-and-replace or a total amendment.

In August 1945, Japan accepted the Potsdam Declaration presented by the Allied Powers and surrendered.[18] The Potsdam Declaration provided for the 'revival and strengthening of democratic tendencies among the Japanese people' as one of the conditions of Japan's surrender. After the surrender, Japan was under the control of the Supreme Commander for the Allied Powers (SCAP), a position held by General Douglas MacArthur. On 4 October, MacArthur mentioned to Fumimaro Konoye, a key figure in the government, the need to amend the Meiji Constitution as an implementation of the stipulation in the Potsdam Declaration.[19] This triggered the establishment of the Constitution Investigation Committee (the Matsumoto Committee) to examine constitutional amendments to the Meiji Constitution.

[17] Masahiro Sakata, *Seifu no Kempō Kaishaku* [*The Constitutional Interpretation of Government*] (Tokyo, Yuhikaku, 2013) 322.

[18] For the detailed historical analysis on drafting the 1946 Constitution, see Shoichi Koseki, *The Birth of Japan's Postwar Constitution*, Ray A Moore (trans) (Boulder, Westview Press, 1997); Ray A Moore and Donald L Robinson, *Partners for Democracy: Crafting the New Japanese State under MacArthur* (Oxford, Oxford University Press, 2002).

[19] Record of Meeting of Minister of State Konoye and General MacArthur, 4 October 1945, available at https://www.ndl.go.jp/constitution/e/shiryo/01/025_1shoshi.html.

Although the proposals for amendments that the Matsumoto Committee examined were kept secret, one of the drafts, prepared by constitutional law professor Toshiyoshi Miyazawa, was acquired and revealed by the *Mainichi* newspaper on 1 February 1946.[20] The revealed draft can be categorised as a partial amendment that maintained many articles of the Meiji Constitution, and the style of writing presupposed an invisible model. On 8 February, the Japanese government submitted to MacArthur an outlined version of the final draft prepared by the Matsumoto Committee, which was also a partial amendment based on the invisible model.[21] At that time, Japanese jurists undoubtedly took for granted that constitutional amendments should be made on the basis of the invisible model, just as ordinary statutory amendments were.

MacArthur was not satisfied with the proposal and ordered his office staff to write their own amendment draft.[22] This is known as the MacArthur Draft or the GHQ Draft. Although the members who worked on the draft were American, the text of the MacArthur Draft was not designed following the appendative model like the amendments to the US Constitution. It was not even a rewriting of the Meiji Constitution, but rather the preparation of an entirely new constitution. The Japanese government accepted most of the contents of the MacArthur Draft and on 6 March 1946, it published a Japanese-language version as the Japanese Cabinet draft.[23] This became the direct draft of the 1946 Constitution.

The texts of the Meiji Constitution and the 1946 Constitution are completely different. Even the official title was changed from 'The Constitution of the Empire of Japan' to 'The Constitution of Japan'. Furthermore, while it cannot be discerned from English translations, the 1946 Constitution uses contemporary Japanese language throughout, whereas the Meiji Constitution used the classical Japanese language (*bungo*). When comparing the two constitutions, we cannot find any identical places.

However, MacArthur strongly urged that legal continuity be maintained with respect to the replacement of the Constitution.[24] Therefore, the replacement of the Meiji Constitution with the 1946 Constitution was implemented as a constitutional amendment in accordance with the amendment process under the Meiji Constitution, which was still in force at that time.

[20] Miyazawa Drafts (A), January 4, 1946, available at https://www.ndl.go.jp/constitution/e/shiryo/02/058ashoshi.html.

[21] Matsumoto Draft Submitted to GHQ, available at https://www.ndl.go.jp/constitution/e/shiryo/03/074shoshi.html.

[22] GHQ Draft, 13 February 1946, available at https://www.ndl.go.jp/constitution/e/shiryo/03/076shoshi.html.

[23] For discussion on the translation of the MacArthur draft to Japanese, see Kyoko Inoue, *MacArthur's Japanese Constitution: Linguistic and Cultural Study of its Making* (Chicago, University of Chicago Press, 1991).

[24] MacArthur's Statement on Deliberations over the Constitution Draft, 21 June 1946 (laying down a principle to be followed in consideration of the constitution: 'That the procedure followed assures complete legal continuity with the constitution of 1889 now existing'), available at https://www.ndl.go.jp/constitution/e/shiryo/04/116shoshi.html.

The 1946 Constitution was promulgated on 3 November 1946. Under the Meiji Constitution, the Ordinance for Promulgation required that constitutional amendments be prefaced by an imperial edict.[25] Accordingly, when the 1946 Constitution was promulgated, the following imperial edict was placed before the title:

> I rejoice that the foundation for the construction of a new Japan has been laid according to the will of the Japanese people, and hereby sanction and promulgate the amendments of the Imperial Japanese Constitution affected following the consultation with the Privy Council and the decision of the Imperial Diet made in accordance with Article 73 of the said Constitution.

This imperial edict stated unequivocally that the 1946 Constitution was an 'amendment' of the Meiji Constitution, and the Emperor had sanctioned it. This edict is also found in the original physical text of the 1946 Constitution and in the Official Gazette.

B. The 1946 Constitution as a New Constitution

Notwithstanding the statement in the imperial edict, there are persistent notions among Japanese constitutional academics that the 1946 Constitution is not a total amendment of the Meiji Constitution, but a completely new constitution that was established independently. Indeed, there are several reasons that make it possible to characterise the 1946 Constitution as new.

First, sentences set out in the promulgation before the title are usually not considered part of a statute.[26] Based on this general understanding, the imperial edict that precedes the title is also not part of the 1946 Constitution.[27] Hence, the statement in the edict is constitutionally meaningless. On the other hand, the preamble after the title of the 1946 Constitution begins with the following statement: 'We, the Japanese people … do proclaim that sovereign power resides with the people and do firmly establish this Constitution.'[28] This implies that the 1946 Constitution was not passed by amending the Meiji Constitution and by imperial sanction, but was newly established by the Japanese people as sovereigns. This preamble is clearly considered part of the Constitution.[29] In other words, based on the constitutionally meaningful text in the 1946 Constitution, the 1946 Constitution is a new constitution.

Second, there is a theoretical paradox in viewing the 1946 Constitution as an amendment to the Meiji Constitution. The Meiji Constitution was based on

[25] The Ordinance for Promulgation, art 3 (Imperial Order No 6, 1907).

[26] Hayashi (n 2) 67; Hosei Shitsumu Kenkyu Kai (n 2) 22.

[27] Toshiyoshi Miyazawa (supplanted by Nobuyoshi Ashibe), *Zentei Nihonkoku Kempō* [*The Constitution of Japan, Complete Edition*] (Tokyo, Nihonhyoronsha, 1978) 22.

[28] Japanese Constitution, Preamble.

[29] Nobuyoshi Ashibe (supplanted by Kazuyuki Takahashi), *Kempō* [*Constitutional Law*], 7th edn (Tokyo, Iwanamishoten, 2019) 37.

the fundamental premise that it was established by the emperor as the holder of constituent power (constitution-making power). However, the 1946 Constitution positions the Japanese people as the holders of constituent power. According to this fundamental premise of the 1946 Constitution, the Meiji Constitution is illegitimate from its foundation. Or, the amendment clause of the Meiji Constitution could not allow suicidal amendments that would deny the foundation of its own legitimacy. From the perspective of the 1946 Constitution, the Meiji Constitution is an illegitimate constitution, whereas from the perspective of the Meiji Constitution, the 1946 Constitution is an unconstitutional constitutional amendment. This creates a theoretical paradox.

The most accepted explanation of the relationship between the Meiji Constitution and the 1946 Constitution in Japanese academia is the 'August Revolution' theory advanced by Toshiyoshi Miyazawa.[30] The formal amendment to the Meiji Constitution was implemented in May 1947. However, the August Revolution theory posits that by the acceptance of the Potsdam Declaration in August 1945, a paradigm shift in the basic premise of the Constitution had occurred, changing the holder of constituent power from the emperor to the people. As an inevitable consequence of this paradigm shift, the original Meiji Constitution was transformed into a new constitution without waiting for explicit amendment. The 1946 Constitution is thus explained as an amendment to the Meiji Constitution as it was transformed in August 1945, rather than an amendment to the original Meiji Constitution enacted in 1889. This August Revolution theory acknowledges legal continuity between the transformed Meiji Constitution of 1945 and the 1946 Constitution, but does not recognise legal continuity between the original Meiji Constitution and the 1946 Constitution, meaning that the 1946 Constitution is entirely new in relation to the original Meiji Constitution.

C. The Two Dimensions of the 1946 Constitution and the Forms of Amendments

There are various views regarding the legal continuity between the Meiji Constitution and the 1946 Constitution, including the August Revolution theory. It is appropriate to view the two constitutions as having *procedural legal continuity* based on the fact that the amendment procedure was formally followed, but they are inconsistent in terms of content and paradigm, so there is no *substantive legal continuity* between them.

[30] Toshiyoshi Miyazawa, 'Nihonkoku Kempōseitei no Hōri' [The Theory on the Foundation of the Constitution of Japan] in *Kempō no Genri* [*Constitutional Principles*] (Tokyo, Iwanamishoten, 1967) 375. For discussions on the August Revolution theory, see also Yasuo Hasebe, 'The August Revolution Thesis and the Making of the Constitution of Japan' (1997) 17 *Rechtstheorie* 335; Chaihark Hahm and Sung Ho Kim, *Making We the People: Democratic Constitutional Founding in Postwar Japan and South Korea* (Cambridge, Cambridge University Press, 2015) 144–47.

Albert created the concept of 'constitutional dismemberment' as a description of a middle ground in constitutional change that is 'more than a constitutional amendment but less than a new constitution'.[31] However, in the case of the 1946 Constitution, it would be more fitting to view the constitutional amendment and the new constitution not along the same lines, but rather as existing simultaneously in two different dimensions: both as a constitutional amendment from the perspective of procedural legal continuity and as a new constitution from the perspective of substantive legal continuity.

This ambivalent nature of the formulation of the 1946 Constitution is likely related to the fate of the Constitution itself. In his reminiscences, MacArthur commented: 'The new Japanese constitution is really an amendment to the older Meiji one. I felt that by using this particular device we could ensure continuity, and continuity is important in Japan.'[32] In fact, the appearance of (procedural) legal continuity between the Meiji Constitution and the 1946 Constitution was politically and socially necessary for the smooth acceptance of the 1946 Constitution by the people of that time. The legitimacy of the 1946 Constitution has been questioned on the grounds of it being an imposed constitution, and it is easy to imagine that without the procedural legal continuity, these criticisms would have been even stronger.

Without the implicit adoption of the invisible model by the Japanese public, it might not have been possible to bring the 1946 Constitution into existence through the process of constitutional amendment. If the Meiji Constitution had undergone a series of US Constitution-style amendments, it would have been more difficult to replace it with the 1946 Constitution through the amendment process.[33] The US Constitution-style appendative model assumes that the original text remains as part of the constitution in visible form. Following this appendative model faithfully, the 1946 Constitution should have been appended after the Meiji Constitution. It would have appeared unnatural and could have given the impression that the two constitutions coexisted. Under the appendative model, only partial amendments are de facto permissible. If there had been an established custom in Japan to amend the Constitution by the appendative model, the form of amendments would need to have been changed, in addition to amending the text of the Meiji Constitution totally. Such abandonment of customary form would have been controversial and would have undermined legal continuity even more significantly.

The invisible model, on the other hand, can eliminate all remnants of the former constitution so that it is literally invisible. Thus, the invisible model renders moot the challenges that the appendative model would have faced. The choice of

[31] Albert (n 1) 85.

[32] Douglas Macarthur, *Reminiscences* (Annapolis, Naval Institute Press, 1964) 301.

[33] The Meiji Constitution could well have been amended on the appendative model, as the Imperial Household Law, which was supposed to be the same supreme law as the Meiji Constitution, had been amended by the *zōho* method.

the form of constitutional amendments, the appendative model or the invisible model, is not logically related to the question of whether and to what extent there are legal limits to constitutional amendments. However, as a political and sociological phenomenon, total amendments like the 1946 Constitution would be more likely to occur under the invisible model tradition because the invisible model allows for total amendments in the ways that the appendative model cannot.

IV. The Form of Amendments to the 1946 Constitution

A. The Amendment Clause and Its Interpretation

In the 1946 Constitution, Article 96 is the amendment clause and reads as follows:

> *Article 96*. Amendments to this Constitution shall be initiated by the Diet, through a concurring vote of two-thirds or more of all the members of each House and shall thereupon be submitted to the people for ratification, which shall require the affirmative vote of a majority of all votes cast thereon, at a special referendum or at such election as the Diet shall specify.
>
> Amendments when so ratified shall immediately be promulgated by the Emperor in the name of the people, as an integral part of this Constitution.[34]

In accordance with this amendment clause, constitutional amendments go through three stages: initiation by the Diet; referendum by the people; and promulgation by the emperor. Since the Constitution of Japan came into effect in 1947, there has never been a referendum. Although several political parties have proposed amendment drafts to the 1946 Constitution, these drafts have never been submitted to the Diet.

Article 96 says nothing directly about the form of constitutional amendments. However, the phrase 'as an integral part of this Constitution' has been viewed as having some connection to the form of constitutional amendments. This phrase is clearly derived from Article V of the US Constitution: 'Amendments … shall be valid to all Intents and Purpose, as Part of this Constitution.'[35] Early on, it was argued that the last phrase of Article 96 should be interpreted as a statement requiring the adoption of the appendative model, as in the US Constitution.[36] However, there is no inevitable relationship between that phrase and the requirement of the appendative model. Indeed, in the debates on the first amendments to

[34] Japan Constitution, art 96. During the Allied occupation, Official Gazettes, English Edition were published. The English translations of the Constitution published by the Japanese government on online sites such as https://www.japaneselawtranslation.go.jp/ja/laws/view/174 are based on what was published in Official Gazettes, English Edition.

[35] United States Constitution, art V.

[36] Kichiemon Ishikawa, 'Kempō Kaisei' [Constitutional Amendment] (1949) 67(1) *Hōgaku Kyōkai Zasshi* 84.

the US Constitution, James Madison expressly argued against the use of the appendative model.[37] Today, almost no constitutional scholar adopts the interpretation that the 1946 Constitution mandates the appendative model.

On the other hand, insofar as the traditional invisible model is followed, it is self-evident that amendments should be integrated into the original constitution. In other words, if the Constitution required the invisible model, the phrase 'as an integral part of this Constitution' would be unnecessary. Rather, it is reasonable to interpret this phrase as a provision that prepares for a situation in which the amendments exist outside of the original text of the 1946 Constitution like the amendments to the US Constitution. Thus, this phrase is meaningful in that it ensures that the amendment is not a separate constitution from the original, but is an integral and indivisible part of it, even when it exists outside the original text.[38] After all, the 1946 Constitution neither requires nor prohibits the appendative model; the choice of model is left to the political discretion of the Diet, which has the authority to initiate constitutional amendments.[39] However, as of the summer of 2022, there are no statutes that specifically prescribe the form of constitutional amendments.

B. Amendment Forms and Popular Referendums

Although thus far there are no practical examples of constitutional amendments, many constitutional scholars predict that constitutional amendments will be based on the invisible model, similar to ordinary statutory amendments.[40] In fact, the majority of constitutional amendments proposed by political parties and newspapers have been based on the invisible model; no examples have been widely circulated of proposed amendments based on the appendative model.[41]

Nevertheless, some constitutional scholars suggest that it is better to adopt the appendative model. For example, Koji Sato, one of the leading contemporary constitutional scholars, argues that 'if we are to continue to regard the Constitution of Japan as the basic normative life space in which we live, it makes sense to list and clarify transitions of changes; therefore, an appendative model is the most appropriate form.'[42]

[37] 1 Annals of Congress 735, House of Representatives, 1st Congress, 1st Session (13 August 1789). See also Edward Hartnett, 'A "Uniform and Entire" Constitution; Or, What if Madison Had Won?' (1998) 15 *Constitutional Commentary* 251; Albert (n 1) 232–33.

[38] See Hougaku Kyokai (ed), *Chūkai Nihonkoku Kempō Ge-Kan* [*Commentary on the Constitution of Japan Volume 2*] (Tokyo, Yuhikaku, 1953) 1451; Isao Sato, *Pokeet Kempō Shin-Ban Ge-Kan* [*Pocket Constitution New Edition Volume 2*] (Tokyo, Yuhikaku, 1984) 1263; Koji Sato, *Nihonkoku Kempō Ron* [*Treatise on the Constitution of Japan*], 2nd edn (Tokyo, Seibundou, 2020) 318.

[39] See Miyazawa (n 27) 785.

[40] For example, Kyokai (n 38) 1451; Shiro Kiyomiya, *Kempō I* [*Constitutional Law, Volume 1*], 3rd edn (Tokyo, Yuhikaku, 1979) 406; Isao Sato (n 38) 1263.

[41] For discussion of constitutional amendment proposal by political parties and newspapers, see Matsui (n 10) 265–70.

[42] Koji Sato (n 38) 50.

Both the appendative and the invisible models have their advantages and disadvantages, but in defining the form of constitutional amendments, it must be borne in mind that constitutional amendments will ultimately be decided by popular referendum. A referendum involves a large number of people without legal expertise.

When a constitution calls for a referendum, the form of constitutional amendments should be easier for the people to understand than amendments requiring ratification solely by representatives. As discussed in section II.C above, under the traditional Japanese invisible model, unless the deletion of a provision is expressly directed, it is largely assumed that the provision maintains its effect. In contrast, in US practice, even without an explicit directive to delete a provision, the legal effect of the provision may disappear completely. It is clear that the appendative model makes it more difficult to foresee the consequences of an amendment. Furthermore, given the lack of experience in amending the constitution through the appendative model and the usual practice of amending ordinary statutes according to the invisible model, it is possible that people could misunderstand the effect of the amendment under the appendative model in a referendum. Certainly, it is beneficial for the public to be able to review the historical transition of amendments after they have been made. However, if a constitutional amendment requires a referendum, it is more important that the people have in advance a clear understanding of what the Constitution will be after the amendment.[43]

C. Uncontrollable Amendments: Clarification or Substantial Amendments to Existing Interpretations

Even in the integrative model and the invisible model, the consequences of amendments are not always ascertainable and controllable in advance. Admittedly, under the traditional Japanese invisible model, unless a provision is explicitly deleted, typically it never loses its effect. However, even if the existing provision continues to exist, the previous interpretation may change with the addition of a new provision. The impact of the amendments on existing interpretations cannot be ascertained by a simple comparison of the wording and cannot be controllable a priori. This type of uncertainty is particularly salient in constitutional amendments that aim to clarify existing interpretations. The development of the constitutional amendment debate regarding the pacifist clause, Article 9 of the 1946 Constitution, provides a typical case study of this issue.

[43] Even if amendments are made based on the invisible model, no official text will be produced reflecting the integrated constitution. Some countries that adopt the integrative or the invisible model have constitutional provisions that explicitly stipulate that a new, complete version of the amended constitution should be promulgated – the Portuguese and Dutch Constitutions are examples of this. However, Japan has no such constitutional provision. See Portuguese Constitution, art 287(2); Dutch Constitution, art 141.

The phrase 'land, sea, and air forces, as well as other war potential, will never be maintained' in the first sentence of the second paragraph of Article 9 has been the most controversial part of the 1946 Constitution. This statement was initially read as prohibiting the maintenance of any military organisation, so conservative politicians wishing to strengthen military power have pushed for its abolition. However, although the conservative faction-based Liberal Democratic Party (LDP) has had a majority in the Diet for much of the time since its formation in 1955, it has not yet been able to achieve an amendment to Article 9.

Instead of amendment, LDP governments have adopted a strategy of legitimising rearmament through constitutional interpretation, specifically that (1) Article 9 does not deny the right to self-defence of Japan and, therefore, (2) 'the defense capabilities limited to the minimum necessary for self-defense' are not to be equated with 'war potential'.[44] Based on this interpretation, the governments have continued to justify the maintenance of the Self-Defense Forces (SDF), a military organisation formed in 1954.

This interpretation has been criticised as untenable. However, it is undeniable that this interpretation, which states that only the 'minimum necessary' force can be maintained, not only justifies the SDF but has also served an important role in restraining the expansion of Japanese military forces.

Ironically, as the SDF became more widely accepted by Japanese society, the argument for amending Article 9 weakened for a time. However, since the 2000s, advocacy for amending Article 9 has gradually strengthened once again. In 2005 and 2012, the LDP released drafts of constitutional amendments, both of which proposed deleting the second paragraph of Article 9 and adding a new provision establishing the National Defence Forces (NDF) as a new military organisation (the NDF Clause).[45]

However, there were criticisms that the deletion of the second paragraph of Article 9 and the addition of the NDF clause would lead to the creation of a larger military organisation in terms of quality and quantity than the current SDF. Due to such criticism, the amendment in that direction did not come to pass. With this background, the direction of the amendment proposed by the LDP was changed to win broader support. In 2018, the LDP proposed that Article 9 be completely sustained, including the second paragraph, but that a clause be added after Article 9 and before Article 10 as Article 9-2, which would permit the maintenance of the

[44] See Director-General of the Defence Agency Omura Seiichi, answering questions to the Diet, the 21st National Diet Session, 2 House of Representatives Budget Committee Meeting Records 1 (22 December 1954). For a detailed discussion on the interpretation and politics of art 9, see also Craig Martin, 'The Legitimacy of Informal Constitutional Amendment and the Reinterpretation of Japan's War Powers' (2016) 40 *Fordham International Law Journal* 427 (2016); Yukiko Nishikawa, *Political Sociology of Japanese Pacifism* (Abingdon, Routledge, 2019).

[45] Liberal Democratic Party, 'Shin-Kempō Sōan' [The Draft of the New Constitution] (2005), reprinted in Osamu Watanabe (ed), *Kempō Kaisei Mondai Shiryō Gekan* [*Materials on Constitutional Amendment Issues, Volume 2*] (Tokyo, Jumposha, 2015) 337; Liberal Democratic Party, 'Nihonkoku Kempō Kaisei Sōan' [The Draft of the Amendment to the Constitution of Japan] (2012), reprinted in ibid 729.

current SDF without creating the new NDF (the SDF clause).[46] The proposed wording is as follows:

> *Article 9-2.* The provisions of the preceding clause shall not preclude the implementation of necessary self-defense measures to defend our country's peace and independence and ensure the safety of the country and the people, and for that purpose, the Self-Defense Forces, with its supreme commander being the Prime Minister who is the head of the Cabinet, shall be maintained as an armed organization, as provided by law.
>
> The conduct of the Self-Defense Forces shall follow Diet approval and other control, as provided by law.[47]

In summary, there are three positions on amending Article 9:

(a) the Constitution is not amended, and the constitutionality of the SDF is affirmed through constitutional interpretation;
(b) the original Article 9 is not revised, but a new SDF clause is added as Article 9-2 after Article 9;
(c) the original Article 9, paragraph 2 is revised or deleted, and a new NDF clause is added.

Of these, (a) has been the strategy conventionally adopted by the government. In addition, the LDP's previous proposals were (c), but in recent years, in order to increase public support, the LDP has proposed (b).

The LDP explains that (b) does not change the status quo, but rather simply writes its status quo interpretation into the 1946 Constitution. However, it is not easy for the public to assess whether this LDP explanation is correct.

Unlike (c), (b) does not change the original text of Article 9. However, in this case, the target concept and language that the public should compare the proposed amendment to is not the actual existing text of the Constitution, but rather the existing interpretation of the Constitution. For example, 'minimum' is in the existing governmental interpretation, but Article 9-2, as proposed by the LDP, does not contain this word. If read as worded, the proposed Article 9-2 could eliminate the restriction that the SDF's capabilities must be minimal. In addition, one of the traditional interpretations of Article 9 includes a prohibition on the maintenance of offensive aircraft carriers, but the impact of the addition of Article 9-2 on that interpretation is also uncertain. It is difficult even for legal specialists to grasp the whole picture of existing interpretations that have accumulated over the past 70 years, and drafting all of them into written articles without adding or deleting anything would not be an easy task.

[46] Liberal Democratic Party, 'Kempō Kaisei ni kansuru Giron no Jōkyō ni tsuite' [On the State of Discussion on Constitutional Amendments] (2018), available at https://constitution.jimin.jp/document/discussion.

[47] This translation follows 'LDP to Pursue Abe-Proposed Amendment of Pacifist Constitution' *Kyodo News* (22 March 2018), available at https://english.kyodonews.net/news/2018/03/1528a70ac8a8-update1-ldp-to-pursue-abe-proposed-amendment-of-pacifist-constitution.html.

There may be an argument that even if it is difficult to convert existing interpretations into articles verbatim, problems can be alleviated to a certain extent if the proponent of the amendments ensures that the amendment is only intended to clarify the status quo interpretations. However, it is inherently impossible to completely control constitutional interpretation in advance. The LDP seems to be proposing clarification of existing interpretations through Article 9-2 as a no-risk constitutional amendment in terms of concerns about changing the status quo, but a no-risk constitutional amendment is not realistic, given that it is a modification to something that already exists.

It is true that if the existing interpretation is considered paramount, amendments to clarify existing interpretations are of great significance when, for example, the existing interpretation is in danger of being revised by governmental authorities such as a supreme court. On the other hand, the more stabilised the existing interpretation is, the greater the risk that the amendment itself will trigger a change in the status quo interpretation. This means that in the referendum, the people are required to make a careful assessment of the risks of not amending versus the risks of amending, in addition to textual and interpretive comparisons.

Importantly, the practice of adding Articles 9-2, 9-3, and so on, while keeping the original Article 9 as a historical memorial, creates the appendative model-like situation in the invisible model. While this practice has the advantage of the appendative model of commemoration, it does not fully bring out the clarity inherent in the invisible model.

V. Conclusion

In Japan, the invisible model has traditionally been adopted for ordinary statutory amendments, so this model is already familiar to the Japanese people. Moreover, in general, the invisible model enables people to predict easily at a glance what will change and what will not change. Given that the 1946 Constitution requires a referendum for its amendments, the invisible model is an appropriate form to use with constitutional amendments.

However, as the Article 9 case study shows, there are cases where even amendments based on the integrative and the invisible model are not easy for the people to understand and foresee. The clarity of amendments depends not only on the form of amendments but also on the purpose, content and writing style. Further work to analyse the relationship between the clarity of amendments and the manners of amendments is needed.

7

When the Temporary Becomes Indefinite

Legitimacy, Path Dependency and Taiwan's Hybrid Approach to Constitutional Amendment Codification

HUI-WEN CHEN

I. Introduction

For those who have had a chance to glance at Taiwan's master-text constitution, it is not hard to see that its codification of constitutional amendment falls into the appendative model in Richard Albert's quadripartite typology.[1] After all, Taiwan's working master-text constitution comprises two bodies: the 1947 Constitution of the Republic of China (hereinafter the 1947 Constitution) and a set of Additional Articles of the Constitution of the Republic of China (hereinafter the Additional Articles). However, a closer look blurs this apparent view. Where is the appendage of the amended Additional Articles 1, 2, 4, 5 and 8 – apart from a new Additional Article 12 – after Taiwan's latest and seventh round of constitutional revision in 2005?[2] Digging deeper, we still only see the 1947 Constitution – with its original scripts intact and without any integrated 'mess-up' – and the add-on Additional Articles – with no amendment sequentially and directly appended to the latter to be found – and cannot find other constitutional master texts elsewhere in Taiwan's *corpus juris*. So neither the integrative nor the disaggregative model as identified by Albert applies to the amendment of the Additional Articles, let alone Taiwan's overall master-text constitution. Is the 2005 amendment of Additional Articles 1, 2, 4, 5 and 8 rendered in the invisible model when codified? Yes, full stop.

[1] Richard Albert identifies four models for codifying constitutional amendments: appendative, integrative, invisible, and disaggregative. See Richard Albert, *Constitutional Amendments: Making, Breaking and Changing Constitutions* (Oxford, Oxford University Press, 2019) 229–40.

[2] See the synopsis of the legislative history of the Additional Articles at https://law.moj.gov.tw/ENG/LawClass/LawHistory.aspx?pcode=A0000002.

Short as this answer may be, it gives away the fact that Taiwan's codification of constitutional amendment apparently deviates from Albert's quadripartite typology by combining features of both the appendative and invisible models, resulting in a hybrid model.[3] It is appendative because the 1947 Constitution has been amended by a constitutional add-on – the Additional Articles – while its original text remains unchanged. It is invisible to the extent that in contrast to the amendment of the original provisions of the 1947 Constitution, the revision of the Additional Articles comes close to the invisible model. To make sense of how Taiwan's constitutional amendment codification settled on the appendative-invisible hybrid model, I situate the debate over how to codify constitutional amendment in the critical moments in Taiwan's constitutional development, with a focus on its democratic transition in the late 1980s followed by seven rounds of constitutional revision from 1991 to 2005.[4] In this chapter, I aim to shed light on Taiwan's *sui generis* codification model in terms of path dependency and consideration of legitimacy. First, the root of the appendative-invisible hybrid model can be traced back to the appendage of the Temporary Provisions Effective during the Period of the Communist Rebellion (hereinafter the Temporary Provisions) to the then pristine 1947 Constitution – essentially an add-on emergency constitution adopted according to the latter's provisions for constitutional amendment – in 1948 when the Chinese Civil War reached fever pitch. When the Temporary Provisions were eventually repealed in 1991 and replaced by the current Additional Articles, the practices having materialised in the former's previous amendments carried over into the latter's.

Second, the appendative-invisible hybrid model is accommodating of concerns over institutional continuity in the evolving debate over the legitimacy of the constitutional order. For the once-dominant Nationalists (also known as Kuomintang), the 1947 Constitution signifies their continuing claim of sovereignty over China. Because of this, the original body of the 1947 Constitution (including the preamble) was considered sacrosanct soon after the 1947 Constitution came into force and has since been left intact despite multiple revisions. However, the appendages (both the Temporary Provisions and the Additional Articles) do not have such symbolic significance and are thus subject to script replacement when amended – hence, the convenient but temporary solution becomes clear by combining the appendative and invisible models. While the identity of the 1947 Constitution has evolved in tandem with Taiwan's transformation from a Chinese frontier province into a new democratic island nation, the Additional Articles have been mostly amended in the same way as ordinary statutes have been invisibly amended in Taiwan. Taiwan's hybrid model of constitutional amendment codification reflects the struggle over political identity in Taiwan's winding path towards constitutional

[3] It should be noted that Albert acknowledges that the hybrid models do exist – for example, the Italian Constitution and the Canadian Constitution. See Albert (n 1) 235, 246–48.

[4] For a brief history of Taiwan's constitutional reforms since democratisation, see Jiunn-rong Yeh, *The Constitution of Taiwan: A Contextual Analysis* (Oxford, Hart Publishing, 2016) 38–48.

democracy. Though first considered a convenient but temporary solution, the appendative-invisible hybrid model has turned indefinite down the road of path dependency, betraying the Taiwanese people's equivocation on constitutional identity in face of an uncertain political future. Following the introduction, I will first trace the root of the appendative-invisible hybrid model back to Taiwan's add-on emergency constitution in section II and will then discuss its subsequent development in Taiwan's transition to democracy in section III. I will conclude with final thoughts on the hybrid model as it evolves from a temporary solution into an indefinite form in section IV.

II. Tracing the Root of the Hybrid Appendative-Invisible Model: The Temporary Provisions of 1948

Although the legal status of the Temporary Provisions has long been a bone of contention among Taiwanese constitutional scholars,[5] it is an indelible part of Taiwan's constitutional history[6] and, as will be discussed, casts a long shadow over the codification of constitutional amendment in Taiwan. To show how constitutional practices under the dictatorial Temporary Provisions resulted in Taiwan's appendative-invisible hybrid model, I will first discuss the birth of the Temporary Provisions as an appendage to the 1947 Constitution in China and will then examine its invisible amendment in Taiwan.

A. The Making of the Temporary Provisions: Settling on the Appendative Model

When Taiwan fell under the administration of the authorities of the Republic of China (ROC) on behalf of the Allies at the end of the Second World War on 25 October 1945, China was still a party-state under the Nationalist Tutelage regime, which was set to be replaced by a constitutional government proper following the making of the constitution.[7] Only on 25 December 1946 did the

[5] See, eg, Hong-hsi Lee, *Constitution and Human Rights* (Taipei, National Taiwan University Department of Law, 1985) 45–75 (in Chinese); Yeong-chin Su, *Essays on Constitution and Society* (Taipei, San Min Book, 1988) 195–210 (in Chinese); Tzong-li Hsu, *Recht und Staatsgewalt*, 2nd edn (Taipei, Angle Publishing, 1993) 401–30 (in Chinese); Jiunn-rong Yeh, *Democratic Transition and Constitutional Change* (Taipei, Angle Publishing, 2003) 114–22 (in Chinese).

[6] Tzu-Yi Lin, Ming-Sung Kuo and Hui-Wen Chen, 'Seventy Years on: The Taiwan Constitutional Court and Judicial Activism in a Changing Constitutional Landscape' (2018) 48 *Hong Kong Law Journal* 995, 1002–09; see also Chien-Chih Lin, 'Survival of the Fittest(?): The Endurance of the ROC Constitution and the Constitution of Japan' (2014) 62 *American Journal of Comparative Law* 775, 782–87.

[7] Secretariat of the National Assembly (ed), *Records of the National Assembly* (Taipei, Secretariat of the National Assembly, 1946) 7–9 (in Chinese).

Constituent National Assembly[8] – convened in Nanjing, China – accomplish its task of adopting a new 'Constitution of the Republic of China', which was promulgated on 1 January 1947 and was set to come into effect on 25 December 1947. This is how the 1947 Constitution came into being.[9]

Once the 1947 Constitution came into force, China formally moved from the Nationalist Tutelage into the era of constitutional government. However, the arrival of constitutionalism in China did not follow; instead, China at the time was already engulfed in a civil war between the Communists and the Nationalists. In response to the escalating civil war, in July 1947 – less than six months before the formal end of the Nationalist Tutelage – the Nationalist Government declared in a decree that China had entered the Period of National Mobilisation for Suppression of the Communist Rebellion (hereinafter the Period of Communist Rebellion). In the meantime, a Guideline on National Mobilisation for Suppression of the Communist Rebellion was promulgated, placing resources under the government control to fight the Communist rebellion. Therefore China, under Chiang Kai-shek's Nationalist Government, had entered a state of emergency even before the 1947 Constitution took effect.

Even so, the plan to formally end the Nationalist Tutelage with the 1947 Constitution pressed on. On 29 March 1948, the First National Assembly – which was vested with, inter alia, the power to elect and recall the President and the Vice President and to amend the Constitution[10] – convened for the first time in Nanjing.[11] Originally, the main purpose of this meeting was to elect the first President and Vice President.[12] However, in face of the intensifying civil war, the Nationalist Government decided to expand President's emergency powers. To that end, the pristine 1947 Constitution, which was then about four months old, had to be amended.[13]

Although most of the delegates agreed that it was urgent and necessary to enhance presidential power in face of the Communist rebellion, a debate arose over how to codify such amendment apart from following the procedures set out in the 1947 Constitution.[14] Should the conceived emergency constitution be

[8] It was attended by about 1,700 delegates from all Chinese provinces and other administrative regions – including 18 delegates from Taiwan – with the Communists boycotting. See ibid 326.

[9] For the making of the 1947 Constitution, see Chien-Chih Lin, 'The Birth of the Constitution of the Republic of China' in Kevin YL Tan and Michael Ng (eds), *Constitutional Foundings in Northeast Asia* (Oxford, Hart Publishing, 2021).

[10] Article 27 of the 1947 Constitution.

[11] The election of the First National Assembly was organised by the Nationalist Government and was held in November 1947 in accordance with the newly enacted 1947 Constitution.

[12] Secretariat of the National Assembly (ed), *Records of the First National Assembly, Vol One: The First Session* (Taipei, Secretariat of the National Assembly, 1961) 101 (in Chinese).

[13] A total of 13 proposed amendments were submitted by the delegates of the National Assembly, six of which met the requirements set out in art 174, para 1, subpara 1 of the 1947 Constitution. Among them, five were shelved. Only one proposed amendment concerning the Temporary Provisions was passed by the National Assembly on 18 April 1948.

[14] Article 174, para 1, subpara 1 of the 1947 Constitution.

written into the body of the 1947 Constitution? Or should it be adopted as an addendum at the end of the 1947 Constitution's original text?

As in many other civil law jurisdictions, the invisible model had been characteristic of the codification of amendments on ordinary statutes in China since its reception of modern law at the turn of the twentieth century, continuing into the current legislative practices in Taiwan. Against this backdrop, the debate over the form of constitutional amendment codification came across as a puzzle. Wouldn't it be natural for the National Assembly to directly write the new emergency power into the 1947 Constitution's body with the provisions concerned deleted, amended or replaced under the invisible model of amendment codification?

Yet the dominant Nationalists in the National Assembly chose the appendative model to codify the new emergency power instead.[15] With the Temporary Provisions appended at the end of the body of the 1947 Constitution, its original scripts were left intact. The rationale behind the deviation from the invisible model was revealed in the deliberation leading up to the adoption of the Temporary Provisions in 1948. Conscious of the expansion of presidential power at the expense of the Legislative Yuan with the adoption of the new emergency provisions, supporters of the appendative model essentially appealed to two considerations. First, the 1947 Constitution only took effect in December 1947. Changing its original scripts less than four months after it came into force would be popularly perceived as wasting the great effort in constitution-making, threatening its integrity.[16] Second, unlike the provisions of the 1947 Constitution, which were supposed to be long-lasting, the Temporary Provisions apparently denoted its temporary and transitional character.[17] It was only intended to tackle the Communist rebellion and to end the civil war. Once the rebellion was suppressed, the Temporary Provisions would come to an end as well.

Noticeably, the National Assembly only attended to its main purpose – electing the first President and Vice President – one day after its adoption of the add-on Temporary Provisions on 18 April 1948. The Temporary Provisions formally took effect on 10 May 1948. When the first constitutional ROC Government was eventually set in motion with Chiang Kai-shek sworn in as the first President under the 1947 Constitution on 20 May 1948, the original body of the Constitution had already been altered by the appendative Temporary Provisions.

B. The Amendment of the Temporary Provisions: Reverting to the Invisible Model

The Temporary Provisions did not help change the political fortunes of Chiang and his Nationalists-controlled ROC Government. Defeated by the Communists,

[15] Secretariat of the National Assembly (n 12) 219–21.
[16] ibid 220.
[17] ibid 267.

Chiang moved the seat of government to Taipei in 1949 and continued his existential struggle with the Communists under the ROC banner. In the eye of Chiang's ROC Government, the Chinese Civil War did not end with the establishment of the People's Republic of China (PRC) by Chairman Mao, and the Communist PRC was nothing but a gang of rebel bandits. The Period of Communist Rebellion continued and the Temporary Provisions remained in force.

Notably, even under the extended emergency regime,[18] Chiang and his comrades strived to maintain the façade of constitutional legitimacy and institutional continuity of the ROC Government in the Nationalist fight against Communist China.[19] To battle against his perceived lawless Communist enemy with his ostensible constitutional government, Chiang had to attend to the legality of the Temporary Provisions among other issues concerning the legitimacy of the ROC Government in Taiwan.[20] When it was adopted in 1948, the Temporary Provisions not only expanded the President's emergency power,[21] but also further provided for an ostensible sunset clause, stipulating that the President shall convoke the National Assembly to meet at an extraordinary session by 25 December 1950 to debate constitutional amendment bills and decide whether to extend or repeal the Temporary Provisions if the President had not yet declared the end of the Period of Communist Rebellion.[22] As time passed amid his continuing struggle with the Communists, it was mandatory for Chiang to convoke the National Assembly in accordance with the Temporary Provisions, barely a year after he moved the ROC Government to Taipei. However, only around 1,000 of the 3,045 members of the National Assembly were able to convene in Taipei at that time,[23] far short of the quorum. According to the 1947 Constitution, a quorate meeting of the National Assembly for the purpose of constitutional amendment required the attendance of two-thirds of its whole membership.[24] As a result, the mandated extraordinary session was never convened, throwing the Temporary Provisions into a legal limbo following the lapse of the deadline of 25 December 1950.[25]

In September 1953 the delegates of the First National Assembly who were elected in 1947 had their terms extended indefinitely.[26] Although the National

[18] A decree of regional martial law rule was declared for Taiwan in May 1949.

[19] Jiunn-rong Yeh, 'The Cult of *Fatung*: Representational Manipulation and Reconstruction in Taiwan' in Graham Hassall and Cheryl Saunders (eds), *The People's Representatives: Electoral Systems in the Asia-Pacific Region* (Sydney, Allen & Unwin, 1997).

[20] For a discussion of such constitutional issues and how they were addressed through legal manoeuvres, see Lin, Kuo and Chen (n 6) 1007–09.

[21] Paragraph 1 of the 1948 Temporary Provisions.

[22] ibid para 4.

[23] Secretariat of the National Assembly (ed), *Records of the First National Assembly, Vol Two: The Second Session* (Taipei, Secretariat of the National Assembly, 1961) 199–200 (in Chinese).

[24] Article 174, para 1, subpara 1 of the 1947 Constitution. As regards the quorum for the National Assembly when it exercises power other than constitutional amendment, it was stipulated in the Organic Law of the National Assembly passed by the Legislative Yuan.

[25] Secretariat of the National Assembly (n 23) 199–200.

[26] Since the ROC Government relocated to Taiwan in 1949, it was impossible to hold a new election for the Second National Assembly to represent constituencies in mainland China. In order to resolve the 'representational crisis', in September 1953, President Chiang conveyed to the National Assembly a

Assembly managed to meet the quorum in February 1954 and re-elect President Chiang following successive legislative manoeuvres,[27] the legal limbo in which the Temporary Provisions found themselves did not go away. The legality of the Temporary Provisions eventually came to a head when Chiang sought a third term in 1960, despite the provision for term limits in the 1947 Constitution.[28] This time, thanks to the newly reconstituted Grand Justices of the Judicial Yuan (also known as the Taiwan Constitutional Court (TCC)) with its controversial JY Interpretation No 85, the National Assembly met the constitutionally mandated quorum to pave the constitutional way for Chiang's re-election again.[29] Here resurfaced the debate over the form of codification, 12 years after it first appeared in the adoption of the Temporary Provisions in 1948.

To clear the constitutional hurdle to Chiang's third presidential term, four constitutional amendment bills were introduced in the third normal session of the National Assembly in 1960.[30] While all these bills were proposed to remove the two-term limit on presidency under Article 47 of the 1947 Constitution, there was no consensus on the form of codification. Although the majority proposed to amend Article 47 in the 1947 Constitution's body by way of changes on the appended Temporary Provisions, one proposal would directly change the text of Article 47 itself.[31] The dispute was short-lived and settled on the leader's call – of course, from Chiang himself.

After his humiliating retreat to Taiwan in 1949, Chiang had persistently emphasised the importance of preserving the symbolic *Fatung* of the 1947 Constitution.[32] As Jiunn-rong Yeh explained, *Fatung* is 'a traditional Chinese canon expression for a political claim based on the authenticity of power succession'.[33] For Chiang, the 1947 Constitution, together with the First National Assembly, the First Control Yuan and the First Legislative Yuan, embodied *Fatung* and was essential to the Nationalists-controlled ROC Government's claim to sovereignty over China. Thus, he maintained that the original body of the 1947 Constitution should be kept intact until the mainland was liberated from the Communists. Only then would the Chinese people be able to express their views on the 1947 Constitution. With his view made known to the delegates, the National Assembly rejected the

resolution adopted by the Executive Yuan to the effect that the term of the First National Assembly did not end until the convocation of the Second National Assembly, despite the constitutional provision for the election of delegates to the National Assembly every six years (ibid 1–2). As a result, delegates to the First National Assembly continued to hold office without periodic elections. Later, the Taiwan Constitutional Court rendered the infamous JY Interpretation No 31 in January 1954 and effectively extended the terms of the First Control Yuan and the First Legislative Yuan indefinitely. For the discussion on representational crisis and manipulation of representation, see Yeh (n 19).

[27] Secretariat of the National Assembly (n 23) 1–10.

[28] Article 47 of the 1947 Constitution.

[29] Lin, Kuo and Chen (n 6) 1008–09.

[30] Secretariat of the National Assembly (ed), *Records of the First National Assembly, Vol Three: The Third Session* (Taipei, Secretariat of the National Assembly, 1961) 241–42 (in Chinese).

[31] ibid 244–62.

[32] ibid 241.

[33] See Yeh (n 4) 33.

proposal to directly amend the 1947 Constitution and amended the Temporary Provisions to resolve constitutional issues on hand.[34]

By leaving the body of the 1947 Constitution unchanged, the 1960 amendment seemed to continue along the appendative path blazed by the 1948 appendage of the Temporary Provisions. Yet the 1960 amendment diverged from the appendative path because it was not appended to the end of the 1948 Temporary Provisions; instead, the revision of the 1948 Temporary Provisions reverted to the conventional invisible model. While the original body of the 1947 Constitution remained untouched, the relevant texts of the 1948 Temporary Provisions were simply rewritten with no visible indication of any change left.

It should be noted that the 1960 Temporary Provisions not only lifted the presidential term limit but also helped convert a supposedly temporary legal arrangement into an indefinite constitutional add-on by removing the ostensible sunset clause that prompted uncertainties surrounding the legality of the 1948 Temporary Provisions after 25 December 1950. Thanks to the 1960 Temporary Provisions, Chiang's time-bound emergency regime was normalised as a constitutional dictatorship. Afterwards, the Temporary Provisions further underwent three rounds of amendment under the invisible model in February and March 1966, and 1972, respectively. Reorganised and even renumbered in each round of amendment, the Temporary Provisions were essentially rewritten as if they were an entirely new legal instrument.[35]

Without delving into the details, on the one hand, the constitutional amendments by way of changes on the Temporary Provisions enlarged the executive power as well as the role of the National Assembly at the expense of the original design of separation of powers. On the other hand, the successive amendments[36] provided for token parliamentary elections[37] in Taiwan, thereby embellishing Chiang's ageing regime with its much-needed symbolic legitimacy. With the appended Temporary Provisions, the 1947 Constitution entered an extended state of 'constitutional dismemberment'[38] – despite its original body being preserved without change – while Taiwan was placed under a 'dual state' regime until the repeal of the Temporary Provisions in 1991.[39]

[34] Secretariat of the National Assembly (n 30) 280.

[35] Yeh (n 5) 121.

[36] Article 6 of the 1972 Temporary Provisions (originally article 5 of the March 1966 Temporary Provisions).

[37] According to the controversial JY Interpretation No 76 (1957), the extra-constitutional term 'Parliament' was recognised and interpreted as comprising the National Assembly, the Control Yuan and the Legislative Yuan.

[38] For the discussion of constitutional dismemberment, see Richard Albert, 'Constitutional Amendment and Dismemberment' (2018) 43 *Yale Journal of International Law* 1. Some scholars argued that the amendments of the Temporary Provisions amounted to *Verfassungsdurchbrechung* as had been developed by German constitutional scholars. See Hsu (n 5).

[39] Lin, Kuo and Chen (n 6) 1001. For the concept of a dual state, see Ernst Fraenkel, *The Dual State: A Contribution to the Theory of Dictatorship* (Oxford, Oxford University Press, 2017).

In sum, the legitimacy of Chiang's ROC Government depended on the myth that Taiwan was part of a divided China, and the 1947 Constitution was pivotal to the Nationalists' claim to *Fatung* and sovereignty over China in the historic struggle with the Communists.[40] The appendative-invisible codification of constitutional amendment by way of the add-on Temporary Provisions was instrumental to maintaining the façade legitimacy that the 1947 Constitution's original body augurs. By the add-on Temporary Provisions, the 1947 Constitution could be dismembered to suit political needs while continuing to create a constitutional myth around its preserved original body. With its own changes rendered invisible, the Temporary Provisions also erased the once-unsettling question about the legality of the 1948 appendage from public memory. How this hybrid model of constitutional amendment codification has found its second life in democratic Taiwan is the story I will tell next.

III. The Additional Articles, Institutional Continuity and Democratic Legitimacy

Formed amid the Nationalists' struggle with the Communists, the appendative-invisible hybrid model continues today – albeit not without change. To see how the inherited model of codification has been reshaped by considerations of democratic legitimacy and institutional continuity in Taiwan's transition to constitutional democracy, here I discuss its evolving development from the adoption of the Additional Articles as an appendage to the hybrid codification of the subsequent amendments of the Additional Articles in order.

A. The Making of the Additional Articles: Appendage 2.0

Despite constitutional embellishment through the Temporary Provisions, the façade of legitimacy built on institutional continuity that Chiang and his aged comrades relied upon for political survival could not last forever. It cracked in the face of 'the very long First Parliament'.[41] Even with the token parliamentary elections in Taiwan from 1969 onwards, thanks to the Temporary Provisions,[42]

[40] Yeh (n 19).

[41] Ming-Sung Kuo and Hui-Wen Chen, '"The Parliament Is Dead, Long Live the Court": Thirty Years after the Rise of the Taiwan Constitutional Court from the Ashes of Taiwan's Very Long Parliament', *International Journal of Constitutional Law Blog*, 27 June 2020, www.iconnectblog.com/2020/06/the-parliament-is-dead-long-live-the-court-thirty-years-after-the-rise-of-the-taiwan-constitutional-court-from-the-ashes-of-taiwans-very-long-parliament.

[42] Apart from the members elected in 1947 and 1948, the First Parliament was added with two distinct small cohorts of members elected in Taiwan (as well as other territories controlled by the ROC Government). The first cohort comprised the members chosen in a one-off supplemental election in 1969 and served an indefinite term together with their fellow members elected in China. The second cohort were those who had been regularly (re-)elected since 1972 under the Temporary Provisions.

the continuing operation of the First Parliament of 1948, which included the National Assembly, the Control Yuan and the Legislative Yuan, no longer embodied institutional continuity. Instead, it gradually became a source of embarrassment to the ruling Nationalists, throwing the Temporary Provisions-underpinned ROC regime into an existential crisis.[43] Hence, the First Parliament and the Temporary Provisions became the thorniest issues facing Lee Teng-hui, a native Taiwanese who succeeded President Chiang Ching-kuo – Chiang Kai-shek's son – upon his death in January 1988, even though the decree of martial law had been lifted on 15 July 1987.[44]

The constitutional crisis broke out when thousands of students held a sit-in protest for democratic reform in Taipei from 16 to 22 March 1990. Among the protestors' demands for reform were the dissolution of the National Assembly, the repeal of the Temporary Provisions and the convocation of a roundtable-like National Affairs Conference (NAC).[45] Playing the pressure for reform from the civil society and the opposition Democratic Progressive Party (DPP) against the conservative forces within his own Nationalist camp,[46] Lee first promised to hold an NAC on constitutional reform when he was formally elected President on 21 March 1990.[47] In his inaugural speech on 20 May, he further vowed to terminate the Period of Communist Rebellion and carry out constitutional reform within two years.[48] On the heels of Lee's pledge on constitutional reform, the TCC rendered JY Interpretation No 261 on 21 June to the effect that all the life-tenure members of the First Parliament must leave office by 31 December 1991 and general elections for the Second Parliament be held in due course.[49] The TCC thus helped discontinue the source of constitutional embarrassment.[50]

Notably, when and how to hold the TCC-decreed general elections when Free China was confined to Taiwan as well as some tiny islands off the coast of mainland China remained unclear. It would be up to the NAC to hammer out the called-for constitutional reform, including holding the general election as mandated in JY Interpretation No 261. Lee Teng-hui formally convened the NAC with the support of the opposition DPP on 28 June 1990.[51] Before its closure on 4 July, the NAC

Their terms were limited, corresponding to those stipulated in the 1947 Constitution. See Lin, Kuo and Chen (n 6) 1011.

[43] Yeh (n 4) 39–41.

[44] ibid 37.

[45] J Bruce Jacobs, *Democratizing Taiwan* (Leiden, Brill Academic Publishers, 2012) 74–75.

[46] ibid 72–74.

[47] ibid 74–75.

[48] ibid 75–76.

[49] Hui-Wen Chen, 'Ending the Indefinite First Parliament amid the Democratic Upsurge: An Archival Analysis of JY Interpretation No 261' in Transitional Justice Commission (ed), *The Grand Justices and Transitional Justice* (Taipei, Transitional Justice Commission, 2021) (in Chinese).

[50] Tom Ginsburg, *Judicial Review in New Democracy: Constitutional Courts in East Asia* (Cambridge, Cambridge University Press, 2003) 145–48.

[51] Several preparatory meetings had been held before the official opening of the NAC. See Records of the National Affairs Conference Editorial Team (ed), *Records of the National Affairs Conference, Vol One* (Taipei, Secretariat of the National Affairs Conference, 1990) 1–163 (in Chinese).

considered various proposals for constitutional revision among other matters. While consensus materialised on the repeal of the Temporary Provisions and the urgency of constitutional reform,[52] opinions were divided over how to carry out the required constitutional revision.[53] Should a new constitution be adopted? If not, how should the revision be codified?

For the Nationalists, all proposals for constitution-making were unacceptable. With the First Parliament set to end before long, the 1947 Constitution would then become the foremost symbol for them to continue laying claim to sovereignty over China vis-à-vis their Communist enemy. Thus, the continuation of the ROC regime was the bottom line of constitutional reform. Considering the symbolic significance of the 1947 Constitution and its legitimacy-bestowing importance in sustaining the ROC regime, the Nationalists, to no one's surprise, rejected proposals for adopting a new constitution. They further took issue with reform proposals involving rewriting the original body of the 1947 Constitution as if a rewritten body of the 1947 Constitution would compromise the 'One China' principle, moving Taiwan towards independence. To dispel the objection that another constitutional appendage reminiscent of the add-on form of the Temporary Provisions could not carry through a genuine constitutional revamp, the amendment of the US Constitution was conveniently drawn upon as an analogy for the Nationalist proposal that held the 1947 Constitution's original text to be untouchable.[54] Eventually, the appendative model emerged as the approach to codify constitutional reform required for Taiwan's transition to constitutional democracy.

It followed that Lee settled for a new constitutional appendage – the Additional Articles – without changing the 1947 Constitution's original text as the National Assembly did with the appendative Temporary Provisions in 1948. Almost five months after the NAC's closure, Lee laid out a 'one institution, two stages' proposal for a constitutional revamp in December 1990.[55] By 'one institution', he meant that the planned constitutional reform would be carried out only by the National Assembly as required by the 1947 Constitution.[56] Yet the 'two stages' element indicated that the constitutional revamp would be phased in gradually. Specifically the geriatric First National Assembly would be tasked with repealing the Temporary Provisions and adopting a limited constitutional revision before it drew to a close. In this stage, constitutional reform would include the transposition of the powers granted to the executive by the Temporary Provisions to the new constitutional appendage, and the reframing of the relationship between the ROC-administered Taiwan and the Communist PRC after the end of the Chinese Civil War with the planned termination of the Period of Communist Rebellion. Yet the most urgent reform in the first stage was to provide for the constitutional basis for holding

[52] ibid 1345.

[53] ibid 1346–51.

[54] Secretariat of the National Assembly (ed), *Records of the First National Assembly: The Second Extraordinary Session* (Taipei, Secretariat of the National Assembly, 1991) 110 (in Chinese).

[55] See Yeh (n 5) 95.

[56] Article 174, para 1, subpara 1 of the 1947 Constitution.

general elections after the closure of the First Parliament. Only in the next stage would the then democratically elected Second National Assembly take up further substantial constitutional revision to complete the constitutional reform deemed necessary for Taiwan's transition to constitutional democracy in the early 1990s. With this constitutional choreography, Lee managed to address the question of democratic legitimacy of constitutional revamp by the National Assembly without sacrificing institutional continuity.

Following the carefully crafted roadmap, the winding-down First National Assembly adopted the first batch of Additional Articles – numbered Articles 1–10 – on 22 April 1991 just before it repealed the Temporary Provisions.[57] Paralleling the Additional Articles scheduled to take effect on 1 May 1991, Lee Teng-hui declared that the Period of Communist Rebellion would conclude at the end of 30 April 1991.[58] Under the Additional Articles passed by the First National Assembly, democratic elections for delegates to the National Assembly were held in December 1991 and the Second National Assembly convened in March 1992. The Nationalists-dominated Second National Assembly passed the second batch of Additional Articles – numbered Articles 11–18 – as an appendage codified sequentially to the end of the first batch on 27 May 1992.[59] Notably, the second batch even amended some provisions in the first batch of Additional Articles without changing the text of Additional Articles in the first batch. With this appendage 2.0, Lee's choreography of democratic reform with institutional continuity was given full play.

As with the appendage of the Temporary Provisions in 1948, the Additional Articles of 1991 and 1992 were supposedly temporary responses to contemporaneous political needs. While the former was intended to suppress the Communist rebellion and eventually resulted in decades-long constitutional dictatorship, the latter was introduced to end the Chinese Civil War. As indicated in its preamble,[60] the appendage of the Additional Articles would provide for constitutional basis of Taiwan's transition to democracy until its unification with mainland China.[61] Regardless of the contrasting political needs, both took the form of constitutional add-on to preserve the 1947 Constitution's original text, only for different reasons. As discussed above, the appendage of the Temporary Provisions in 1948 reflected the ambivalence of its framers about the conceived emergency constitution in face of the then-pristine 1947 Constitution. Corresponding to the preamble to the

[57] Secretariat of the National Assembly (n 54) 132–35.

[58] ibid 151.

[59] Secretariat of the National Assembly (ed), *Records of the Second National Assembly: The (First) Extraordinary Session* (Taipei, Secretariat of the National Assembly, 1992) 464–69 (in Chinese).

[60] The Preamble to the Additional Articles states that 'to meet the requisites of the nation prior to national unification, the following articles of the ROC Constitution are added or amended to the ROC Constitution in accordance with Art 27, Para 1, Item 3 and Art 174, Item 1'.

[61] Chien-Chih Lin, 'Undemocratic Constitutional Law in Taiwan' in Brian Christopher Jones (ed), *Democracy and the Rule of Law in China's Shadow* (Oxford, Hart Publishing, 2021).

Additional Articles, the appendative form in 1991–92 was chosen to accommodate the Nationalists' longing for a unified China in the future.

In sum, paralleling the Temporary Provisions, the Additional Articles were adopted as an appendage for its supplementary and provisional nature in the preservation of the 1947 Constitution's original body. Nevertheless, for its choreographed character, the enactment of the Additional Articles was phased in, resulting in a two-part constitutional appendage: the first batch of Articles 1–10 was first appended to the 1947 Constitution and was further amended and supplemented by the appendative second batch of Articles 11–18. The *phased* appendative model of codifying constitutional amendment in the 1991–92 enactment of the Additional Articles highlighted the efforts to reconcile democratic legitimacy and institutional continuity in Taiwan's early constitutional reform.

B. The Amendment of the Additional Articles: The Culmination of the Hybrid Model

After the two-stage enactment of the appendative Additional Articles in 1991–92, Taiwan had five more rounds of constitutional revision from 1994 to 2005, including the 1999 amendment nullified by the TCC in JY Interpretation No 499.[62] The 1994–2005 revision took place through the amendment of the Additional Articles. Taken as a whole, the Additional Articles effectively rewrote the 1947 Constitution intended for China to fit with Taiwan as it continues to evolve as a democratic island nation. The Additional Articles have extensively altered the provisions for, inter alia, national elections, separation of powers, local self-government and the amendment procedures in the 1947 Constitution. As a result, the Additional Articles have instituted direct election of the President and Vice President,[63] degraded the outsize Taiwanese provincial government as a skeletal government unit,[64] abolished the National Assembly and laid down a new procedure for constitutional amendment that involves a referendum.[65] With the head of state elected by popular votes, the required approval of constitutional amendment bills passed by the Legislative Yuan through referendum, and the increasing identification of the designation Taiwan with the national authorities rather than a provincial government, the idea that Taiwan and its people exist as a subject of popular sovereignty thus grows gradually.[66] As Jiunn-rong Yeh observes, the seven-round constitutional revision period spanning about 14 years has tackled constitutional

[62] Jiunn-rong Yeh, 'Beyond Unconstitutionality: The Public Oversights of Constitutional Revision in Taiwan' in Rehan Abeyratne and Ngoc Son Bui (eds), *The Law and Politics of Unconstitutional Constitutional Amendment in Asia* (Abingdon, Routledge, 2021).

[63] 1992 and 1994 amendments of the Additional Articles.

[64] 1997 amendment of the Additional Articles.

[65] 2005 amendment of the Additional Articles.

[66] Yeh (n 4) 38–48.

issues 'in a gradual, piecemeal and incremental fashion',[67] virtually culminating in a new constitution for Taiwan.

Even so, the original body of the 1947 Constitution is preserved intact and the temporary character of the Additional Articles as suggested in its preamble remains unchanged. Seen in this light, the shadow cast by the appendage of the Temporary Provisions over the phased enactment of the Additional Articles is further extended.[68] Upon closer examination, the experience of the invisible amendment of the Temporary Provisions has played a role in the codification of the post-1992 five-round amendment of the Additional Articles. It is worth noting that the 1994 and 1997 rounds of constitutional revision were codified as the Additional Articles. Yet, unlike the appendative codification of the 1992 amendment, the 1994 and 1997 revisions further led to the reorganisation and renumbering of the entire body of the Additional Articles, evoking the experience of the amendment of the Temporary Provisions as discussed above. As the 18-provision 1991–92 Additional Articles were reorganised as the 10-provision 1994 Additional Articles, which were further reconfigured as the 11-provision 1997 Additional Articles, the Additional Articles hardly kept its own past in the present, moving in the direction of the invisible model.[69] Following the substantial change introduced by the 1997 round of revision, the subsequent three amendments of the Additional Articles reverted to the classical invisible model of amendment codification without opening itself to reorganisation or renumbering.

Taken together, the codification of the 1994–2005 five rounds of constitutional revision following the 1991–92 phased enactment of the Additional Articles has reflected the hybrid model shaping up in the amendment of the Temporary Provisions. It continues to be appendative as the original body of the 1947 Constitution was left untouched throughout a series of constitutional amendments. Living in the long shadow of the Temporary Provisions, the 1994–2005 incremental revision has seen the Additional Articles reorganised and renumbered only with the past of their own original body rendered invisible. In sum, the appendative-invisible model, rooted in constitutional dictatorship instituted by the Temporary Provisions, has continued into the codification of constitutional amendment through the Additional Articles in democratic Taiwan.

IV. Final Thoughts: What if the Temporary Becomes Indefinite?

With the root of the form of Taiwan's constitutional amendment codification as expressed in the Additional Articles uncovered, the appendative-invisible hybrid

[67] ibid 12.
[68] Yeh (n 5) 120–21.
[69] ibid 130.

model that continues with the practice resulting from the appendage of the Temporary Provisions evokes path dependency. As discussed above, the hybrid model was originally adopted to subsume constitutional amendment necessitated by Taiwan's democratic development under the Chinese identity as symbolised in the 1947 Constitution's untouchable original body. If Albert is correct in stating that the way in which a country chooses to codify constitutional amendments is 'a choice about how and whether a people choose to remember its past',[70] staying on the hybrid path blazed by the Temporary Provisions in Taiwan's constitutional amendment gives away Taiwan and its people's choice about how to remember the past – China as the indelible origin of Taiwan's constitutional identity. Or does it?

Recent polls consistently show that a distinct Taiwanese consciousness of political and constitutional identity has emerged,[71] despite the remaining Chinese character of Taiwan's constitutional master texts. The question is: why does the indigenous constitutional consciousness not blossom into a new master-text constitution that will free democratic Taiwan of the Chinese body of the 1947 Constitution and its appendage?

To achieve that goal, the Taiwanese people may break with the constitutional past of Chinese character and give themselves a new constitution. Yet, in light of the looming threat from the PRC and Taiwan's uncertain status in the international legal order,[72] such a radical 'constitutional revolution'[73] may not help much in the event. Alternatively, they may work hard to rid their constitutional master texts of the inbuilt Chinese components ranging from the 1947 Constitution's original body to the unification-leaning preamble to the Additional Articles. Remaking constitutional identity through amendment can be another way to assert constituent power.[74] However, the road to constitutional redemption through amendment has been effectively blocked since the last revision of the Additional Articles that laid down a very high threshold for constitutional amendment in 2005.[75] Despite continuing calls to update the master-text constitution from 2005 onwards, no constitutional amendment has been adopted in the past 17 years;[76] in comparison, Taiwan experienced seven rounds of constitutional revision in the 1991–2005

[70] Albert (n 1) 230.

[71] Shelley Rigger et al, 'Why is Unification so Unpopular in Taiwan? It's the PRC Political System, Not Just Culture', *Brookings*, 7 February 2022, https://www.brookings.edu/blog/order-from-chaos/2022/02/07/why-is-unification-so-unpopular-in-taiwan-its-the-prc-political-system-not-just-culture.

[72] David Dyzenhaus, 'Introduction: The Politics of Sovereignty' in Hermann Heller, *Sovereignty: A Contribution to the Theory of Public and International Law*, David Dyzenhaus (ed and trans) (Oxford, Oxford University Press, 2019) 46–47. See also Lin (n 61) 195.

[73] Gary Jacobsohn and Yaniv Roznai, *Constitutional Revolution* (New Haven, Yale University Press, 2020).

[74] ibid.

[75] Article 12 of the 2005 Additional Articles.

[76] On 25 March 2022, the Legislative Yuan passed a constitutional amendment bill to lower the voting age from 20 to 18, which failed to pass the threshold for ratification in a referendum on 26 November 2022. See the Legislative Yuan's public announcement of the amendment bill of the lowering the voting age at https://www.ly.gov.tw/Pages/Detail.aspx?nodeid=1933&pid=218245.

period at the height of democratic reform. The road of reform seems to lead nowhere.

In face of an uncertain political future, the Taiwanese people tread gingerly on the road towards their own constitutional identity. Steering away from the explosive option of constitution making, they consistently keep to the road of reform. The hybrid model that was meant to tie Taiwan's democratic development to the 1947 Constitution's Chinese body continues to be the chosen form to codify constitutional amendment. Is this evidence to path dependency under which a convenient but temporary solution becomes indefinite? The form of codification matters. Leaving the inbuilt Chinese components of the master-text constitution untouched and adhering to the appendative-invisible hybrid model path-dependently, the Taiwanese people equivocate – substantively and procedurally – on the identity question in the continuing pursuit of constitutional reform.

8

Amendment Politics in South Korea

Invisible Constitutional Replacements in 1960 and 1962

JEONG-IN YUN

I. Introduction: On Amendment Politics

Korean constitutional politics have been turbulent, with 12 years of presidential dictatorship and 25 years of military dictatorship. Through it all, the Korean Constitution has been formally amended nine times since 1948. Constitutional amendments have transformed the entire governmental structure on at least four different occasions. The last stage of constitutional transformation was the democratic transition carried out by the Ninth Amendment in 1987. To date, the Constitution has remained unamended since then.

Some scholars have indicated that the Korean practice is an unusual example wherein constitutional transformation was brought about by an amendment procedure rather than adopting a new constitution.[1] In other literature, in terms of 'amendment culture', it is said that the Korean 'common practice has been to use the amendment procedure for transformative changes that effectively replace the constitution but are nonetheless understood as amendment'.[2] Accordingly, the following questions regarding the Korean amendment practice may arise: how come even major constitutional changes were made through the amendment procedure (and how was it possible)? Are there any specific reasons that the constitutional changes were performed only through amendments? That being so, has the original 1948 Constitution really never been replaced?

[1] See, eg, David Law and Ryan Whalen, 'Constitutional Amendment versus Constitutional Replacement: An Empirical Comparison' in Xenophon Contiades and Alkmene Fotiadou (eds), *Routledge Handbook of Comparative Constitutional Change* (Abingdon, Routledge, 2021) 76; Yaniv Roznai, 'Constitutional Transformations: Hungary' in David Law (ed), *Constitutionalism in Context* (Cambridge, Cambridge University Press, 2022) 140; Ngoc Son Bui, 'Institutionalism and Comparative Constitutional Amendment' (2020) 11 *Yonsei Law Journal* 17, 31–35.

[2] See Richard Albert, *Constitutional Amendments: Making, Breaking and Changing Constitutions* (Oxford, Oxford University Press, 2019) 112.

With a formalist approach, it is hard to answer or ascertain what shaped such a practice. In reality, besides formally entrenched rules of amendment, underlying contexts such as socio-political factors, actors and contingent factors are also involved in shaping the process and contents of the formal constitutional changes. For example, the nature of the polity, the form of government and significant political events can create or greatly affect constitutional moments and shape the actual pathway.[3] In this chapter, I capture the political factors affecting the dynamics of constitutional amendment with the concept of 'amendment politics'. This concept involves exploring how formal constitutional change operates in the political context and why the amendment procedure is especially deployed. The concept indicates a sort of political pattern, strategy or modus operandi that makes use of 'constitutional amendment' in politics. Depending on the circumstances, political actors (and others involved) may manipulate the motive, process, legitimacy[4] and implementation of the constitutional amendment as part of power politics.

This chapter explores how amendment politics operated in the process of constitutionalisation of two dramatic moments in Korean constitutional history: the April Revolution in 1960 and the 16 May Coup in 1961. In addition, this chapter identifies how the codification practice affected the choice to pursue amendment, rather than replacement, of the Constitution. Although codification has indeed been an underexplored technical aspect of constitutional amendment, Richard Albert in his work[5] proposed the four codification models concerning a constitutional amendment. Based on that, this chapter identifies that the codification model has, to some extent, influenced the amending formula and thereby interplayed with amendment politics.

Section II elucidates the typology and codification models of formal constitutional changes to examine the 'constitutional transformation through amendment' cases in Korea. Sections III and IV deal with the Third and Fifth Amendments of the Korean Constitution, respectively. Each section comprises a description of the background which triggered the constitutional transformation, an examination of the specific context which allowed the amendment procedure, and an analysis of the interplay between the amending formula and the codification technique. Finally, the chapter concludes with an emphasis on *amendment politics* as a useful concept to capture specific types of amendment practices.

II. Modes and Codification of Formal Constitutional Change

What are the factors that make the reformers avail themselves of constitutional amendment rather than other means to update the constitution? This section will

[3] See also Bui (n 1) 25.

[4] See generally, Andrew Arato, *Post Sovereign Constitution Making: Learning and Legitimacy* (Oxford, Oxford University Press, 2016).

[5] See especially, Albert (n 2) ch 6.

first clarify the term 'amendment' and distinguish it from other forms of constitutional change. Second, it will look at the interplay between codification practice and the actual choice of constitutional change method.

A. Conceptual Varieties of Formal Constitutional Change

When dealing with formal constitutional change, it is a common approach and presupposition to start from the distinction between making a new constitution and amending the existing one. However, it is a question of whether the dichotomy is useful and, even so, how to clearly distinguish between them. Moreover, modes and terms of constitutional change vary across jurisdictions.[6] At any rate, constitutions change under certain labels,[7] such as 'amendment', '(partial/total) revision' or others as subcategories of constitutional change.

As an act of modifying, altering and deleting some parts of the constitutional text, 'amendment' and 'revision' are most prevalently used and compared. They are both related to something that has to be mended. In a quick glance at the recent literature, for example, Manfred Stelzer views amendment as healing or mending something broken to improve it, whereas revision is to make changes to correct something to be 'scrutinised against imperfections and flaws'.[8] However, he does not suggest a clear-cut difference between the two concepts. According to comparative cases, he assumes both are used synonymously. For example, the Swiss Constitution uses the terms 'partial revision' and 'total revision' separately, and imposes certain restrictions only on the former,[9] which seems close to an ordinary amendment in other jurisdictions. In contrast, Richard Albert sees amendment as updating or eradicating an observed fault from the text,[10] particularly as 'an effort to continue the constitution-making project', whereas revision is an 'effort to unmake the constitution by introducing an extraordinary change that is inconsistent with the fundamental presuppositions of the constitution'.[11] Thus, he distinguishes amendment from revision in qualitative terms.

[6] See generally Xenophon Contiades (ed), *Engineering Constitutional Change: A Comparative Perspective on Europe, Canada and the USA* (Abingdon, Routledge, 2012); and Dawn Oliver and Carlo Fusaro (eds), *How Constitutions Change: A Comparative Study* (Oxford, Hart Publishing, 2011).

[7] In comparative constitutional change, labels should be given special caution because of at least two reasons. First, it is attributed to linguistic confusion. Some labels in the original language could be misunderstood due to imperfect translations. Another confusion could arise when labels are arbitrarily used inconsistently with the nature of the constitutional change. The latter will be discussed in more detail in sections III and IV below.

[8] Manfred Stelzer, 'Constitutional Design through Amendment' in Xenophon Contiades and Alkmene Fotiadou (eds), *Routledge Handbook of Comparative Constitutional Change* (Abingdon, Routledge, 2021) 141–42.

[9] Swiss Constitution, arts 193 and 194.

[10] Albert (n 2) 39.

[11] Richard Albert, 'Amendment and Revision in the Unmaking of Constitutions' in David Landau and Hanna Lerner (eds), *Comparative Constitution Making* (Cheltenham, Edward Elgar Publishing, 2019) 27–46.

Concerning an extraordinary transformation, Albert further suggests a new term 'dismemberment'[12] to distinguish it from the ordinary amendment.

Beyond the mere modification of texts within the constitutional document, there exists an important and frequently used term: 'replacement'. This refers to a 'substitution' of a constitutional text by another text. As usually understood, Carlos Bernal clearly distinguishes replacement from revision,[13] and David Law and Ryan Whalen use 'replacement' to mean the making or adoption of a new constitution.[14] The latter, a view regarding constitutional replacement as synonymous with adopting a new constitution, also makes sense because most constitutions are no longer created *ex nihilo* and instead are replaced these days. This then raises a question: is every replacement exactly the same as making a new constitution also in a legal sense? Carl Schmitt might offer some useful terms such as *Verfassungsvernichtung* and *Verfassungsbeseitigung*[15] for that concern. The former refers to the abrogation of the existing constitution at the time that the constituent power changes (for example, revolution), while the latter involves the abolition of the existing constitution when governmental power is transferred to a new group (for example, in a coup) without changing the constituent power. This distinction may be considered in relation to the legitimacy and legality of the new constitution which replaced (and thus repealed) old one, and therefore could provide some insights to the case analyses given below.

In short, under the umbrella concept of constitutional change, the foregoing terms are used, which are sometimes accompanied by adjectives, without specific usage manuals or precise rules, depending on the circumstances under which constitutional change is called for. In Korea, since the enactment of the 1948 Constitution, formal constitutional changes have been made nine times: five instances of 'partial amendment' and four of 'whole amendment'. The labels attached to each constitutional change seem to be intuitively clear; however, some of them are quite problematic in form and substance. These will be examined in sections III and IV below.

B. Codification in Practice

Codification has a special meaning in the civil law tradition as one of its defining features.[16] It is not merely a restatement or compilation of rules; rather, it seeks

[12] Albert (n 2) 84.

[13] Carlos Bernal, 'Constitution-Making (without Constituent) Power: On the Conceptual Limits of the Power to Replace or Revise the Constitution' in Richard Albert, Carlos Bernal and Juliano Zaiden Benvindo (eds), *Constitutional Change and Transformation in Latin America* (Oxford, Hart Publishing, 2019) 22.

[14] Law and Whalen (n 1) 74–75.

[15] Carl Schmitt, *Verfassungslehre* (Berlin, Duncker & Humblot, 1957) 99 f.

[16] For comparative features of codification between civil and common law systems, see Jean Louis Bergel, 'Principal Features and Methods of Codification' (1988) 48 *Louisiana Law Review* 1073, 1076.

to complete a systematic construction of written rules based on internal logical coherence. While codification has been employed worldwide regardless of the legal system, the concept of codification is inherently oriented to codifying law and its amendments in a single document in a systematic manner.

In Korean legislative practice, the ordinary statutes are amended/revised in an 'absorptive' way,[17] by which the amendments – elements to be added, modified or deleted – are edited into the existing main text. However, the process is different at the constitutional level: the Constitution is amended by making a new document into which amendments are incorporated and systematically rearranged. In other words, every constitutional change generates a new document, whether or not the act is one of constitution-making or constitution-amending, and regardless of whether the change amounts to a total revision or a partial amendment. Any type of formal constitutional change replaces – in a literal sense – the old master text with the new one. In that case, the before-and-after version of each provision is not identified on the face of the document because newly added or deleted elements have been incorporated at the appropriate places across the document, without any marks. Thus, the practice of constitutional amendment in Korea takes an 'invisible codification model', as Richard Albert coined it.[18]

According to Albert's account, the invisible model of amendment codification makes it more difficult than the 'appendative' or 'integrative' models for readers to identify where and what changes have been made in the current constitutional text.[19] Nevertheless, the invisible model has an advantage in two ways: first, it is more readable as it does not retain dead or obsolete provisions; and, second, it therefore might give fewer burdens to the interpreters (and the courts) than other codification models which juxtapose old and new texts within a document.

However, there are problematic features in Korean constitutional amendment practice, namely the use of the omnibus amendment bill.[20] In Korean practice, when an amendment occurs, large packages of constitutional reforms are put to the vote as a whole for parliamentary approval and national referendum rather than requiring separate votes on each item. In this way, approval and ratification votes require accepting the entirety of the bundled packages or rejecting all. When combined with the invisible model of amendment codification, constitutional rules can be modified or deleted stealthily with no explicit indication of the changes, unless someone acknowledges or discovers it.

[17] National Assembly Legislative Counsel Office, *Pŏpche Iron gwa Silje* [*Theory and Practice of Legislative Drafting*] (Seoul, National Assembly Legislative Counsel Office, 2019) 124.

[18] See Albert (n 2) ch 6.

[19] ibid 239–40.

[20] On the problem of the omnibus amendment bill, see ibid 165–68.

III. Revolution and the Third Constitutional Amendment in 1960

In June 1960, the Constitution of the Republic of Korea was revised by the Third Amendment to transform the system of government from a presidential to a parliamentary system. The change was triggered by citizens' bloody protests, known as 'the April Revolution', which overthrew the presidential dictatorship. This constitutional transformation of government structure was achieved using the procedure of amendment.

A. The Path to the April 1960 Revolution

In order to understand the background of the 1960 constitutional change, we must go back to 1948 when the Constitution was first created. The original constitutional draft was dramatically changed just before the plenary session for deliberation, against the drafter's idea and the Constitution Drafting Committee's resolution.[21] Syngman Rhee, an old political leader and the sole presidential candidate, urged the change from a parliamentary to a presidential system,[22] and accordingly the draft could not avoid a last-minute change. Due to this abrupt change, the compromise draft included a hybrid form of government with some remnants of the parliamentary system. Nonetheless, the drafters still clung to the hope that such remnants would work as a control device over presidential power. However, after coming to power, President Rhee's regime devolved into authoritarian rule with a personified presidency. That is what prompted consideration of a constitutional amendment to restore the drafter's original idea for a parliamentary system.

In January 1950, only two years after the establishment of the inaugural government, a constitutional amendment bill was proposed, but was voted down by the Parliament. As public antipathy grew, President Rhee, who feared losing the next presidential election, mapped out the constitutional amendment in an effort to hold on to power. In the midst of the Korean War, in November 1951, the government attempted a constitutional amendment to change the method of the presidential election, but was outvoted by the Parliament. Then, Rhee's government outmanoeuvred the Parliament by mobilising the people, intimidating the political

[21] For a description of the constitution-making process in 1948, see generally Jeong-In Yun, 'Founding and/or Refounding: South Korea's 1948 Constitution' in Ngoc Son Bui and Mara Malagodi (eds), *Asian Comparative Constitutional Law, Volume 1: Constitution-Making* (Oxford, Hart Publishing, forthcoming).

[22] Dr Rhee, an unrivalled political figure at the time who had a background in independent movements and overseas activities, was obsessed with presidentialism. He threatened to campaign against the inaugural government if his proposal was not accepted.

opposition and even letting the military police arrest the shuttle bus which was full of legislators on 26 May. The amendment bill introducing a popular vote for the presidential election was submitted to the Parliament and was eventually passed by a standing vote on 4 July 1952. This was the First Constitutional Amendment in 1952. Rhee won re-election under this new electoral system.

The re-elected President Rhee and the ruling party then planned another constitutional amendment in pursuit of permanent power. The ruling party proposed an amendment bill to exempt the incumbent President from the term limit. It was put to vote in the Parliament on 27 November 1954. Lacking a quorum by one vote, it was declared to have been defeated; however, two days later, it was announced that the bill had passed according to a recalculation of the vote. This was the Second Constitutional Amendment. Rhee was re-elected in 1956, again with no term limit according to the new rule. Four years later, the Rhee government and the ruling party rigged the presidential and vice-presidential elections conducted on 15 March 1960 using various illegal means.[23] The ruling party won both elections, including Rhee, who was elected President for a fourth term.

This finally ignited anger among citizens, which had been accumulating for a long time. Students began protesting in Masan against the election, and this ultimately triggered a violent police response. On 11 April 1960, after a dead high school student – with a bullet in his eye – was discovered off the coast of Masan, enraged students and citizenry took to the streets. On 18 April, students from Korea University held rallies in the centre of Seoul, and they were attacked by government-hired thugs. The next day (19 April), students from almost all universities in Seoul, as well as students from high schools, poured onto the streets. This resulted in bloodshed, therefore, the government declared martial law. Finally, on 26 April, President Rhee backed down, making a public statement announcing his resignation. Furthermore, the Vice-President-Elect and his family killed themselves.[24] Ultimately, then, the First Republic – which lasted for 12 years – collapsed. 'The April 1960 Student Revolution' thus marked a significant democratic moment where the wrecked constitutional government – which had set off on the wrong foot in 1948 – was stopped by the people themselves.[25] This revolution ushered in the Second Republic.

[23] For example, with the aid of the civil and military police, using violence and coercion to prevent opposition candidates' registration, stuffing 40 per cent of the votes before voting began, coercing votes as a group, disturbing supervision of the ballots and so on. See Chi-Young Pak, *Political Opposition in Korea 1945–1960* (Seoul, Seoul National University Press, 1980) 195–98.

[24] During Rhee's regime, Ki-Boong Lee, the Vice-President-Elect, wielded enormous power and his family represented a corruption of the regime. Moreover, since he was actively involved in the 15 March rigged election, somehow a tragic ending for his family was inevitable.

[25] See, eg, Chin-O Yu, 'Pokpung'ŭl Tturhŭn Haksaeng Jegun ege' [To Students Who Brokethrough the Storm] (1960) 83 *Sasanggye* 58, 59: 'a democratic revolution attaining freedom with blood'; Ki-baik Lee, *A New History of Korea* (Cambridge, MA, Harvard University Press, 1984) 85: 'The April Revolution was the first in the history of Korea wherein a people armed with nothing but their bare fists succeeded in overthrowing an oppressive government.'

B. Between a New Constitution and Constitutional Amendment

Considering that revolution itself aims to radically change the constitutional order and political construction, it necessarily involves an extra-legal and radical process of change, such as abrogating the existing constitution.[26] Thus, a new constitution cannot be built on the amendment procedure codified in the previous (soon-to-be-replaced) constitution. Therefore, it is a common belief that a successful revolution should end with constitution-making[27] and, indeed, revolution often provides the impetus for the making of new constitutions.[28]

However, the constitutional reform after the April Revolution was, despite its momentous occasion, carried out within a very short period and through the existing amendment procedure. It was attributed to two distinctive features of the revolutionary context in 1960. First, the constitutional reform took the form of an 'amendment' rather than the creation of a 'new constitution'. Students – who were the central figures of the revolution – neither sought to take the power from the established politicians nor to lead in making a constitution themselves; instead, they went back to school, leaving the task to politicians.[29] Moreover, as the revolution had aimed to oust a dictator who ignored the rule of law and used violence for political means, students and citizens preferred constitutional reform through a peaceful process with respect for law and order.

Second, at the time, the transition to the parliamentary system was regarded as the cure-all for a new democratic settlement. Thus, the primary goal of the revolution was constitutional reform to change the governmental form. Based on such a consensus, there was a debate on whether to amend the Constitution *before* or *after* dissolving the existing Parliament and holding a new election.[30] The main arguments favouring the so-called *first-amendment-then-election* approach were as follows. If the election preceded the amendment, no one could guarantee successful constitutional reform by the newly formed Parliament. Under the caretaker government, the *first-dissolution-then-amendment* approach would bring about a precarious vacuum in governmental operation for a while. The existing Parliament with the majority ruling party, which became a powerless nominal majority, was

[26] Stephen Gardbaum, 'Revolutionary Constitutionalism' (2017) 15 *International Journal of Constitutional Law* 173, 177.

[27] See, eg, ibid 185; Ulrich K Preuss, 'The Politics of Constitution Making: Transforming Politics into Constitutions' (1991) 13 *Law & Policy* 107.

[28] Jon Elster, 'Forces and Mechanisms in the Constitution-Making Process' (1995) 45 *Duke Law Journal* 364, 371–72.

[29] *cf* Seon-Taek Kim, 'Hŏnbŏp kwa Hyŏngmyŏng – Simin Iphŏn Juŭi' [Constitution and Revolution – Civic Constitutionalism] (2013) 58 *Dong-A Law Review* 1, 5–8 (pointing out that repetitive patterns of 'revolution by the people, and constitution-making/amending without the people' in Korean politics have left the people as the object rather than the subject of the Constitution.).

[30] For a brief description of the debate, see Byong Gyu Lee, 'Che 2 Kongwaguk Hŏnbŏbŭi Sŏngnibe Kwanhan Yŏn'gu' [A Study on the Formation of the Constitution of the Second Republic of Korea] (2003) 34 *Journal of Studies on Korean National Movement* 167, 174–76.

expected to work more moderately, and in terms of separation of powers, it seemed better to have the existing Parliament amend the Constitution (as a constitutional legislator) and let the future parliament implement the reformed Constitution.[31] Thus, in the end, the existing Parliament, with its dissolution looming immediately after the task, was made to amend the existing Constitution in conformity with the amendment procedure.

On 26 April, the Parliament held a meeting to convene the drafting committee of a constitutional amendment. Three days later, it launched the committee composed of nine MPs as well as two constitutional scholars as expert advisers. According to the amendment procedure of the existing Constitution, an amendment bill was submitted to the Parliament on 11 May and was approved on 16 June as the Third Constitutional Amendment.[32] It was the first legal constitutional amendment since 1948.[33]

C. Invisible Constitutional Replacement and Safe Transition

The Third Amendment changed 52 constitutional provisions and 15 parts of the Constitution's supplementary rules – an enormous change to the Constitution quantitatively. And, as described above, it transformed the governmental form which reshaped the basic institutions and power mechanisms in the Constitution, which amounts to a total revision qualitatively. Yet, it was conducted through an amendment procedure. This shows that the political context at that time was decisive in choosing the method of constitutional transformation – yet also, I assume, the method of amendment codification seems relevant to such a choice.

Consider the appendative model (eg. the US Constitution) in this case. It would have been inefficient and confusing to add fundamental changes in the governmental structure to the end of the original constitutional text that frames the previous governmental structure. Or, consider the integrative model (eg. the Indian Constitution) which leaves the amendment history in the text. Such structural governmental transformation might have overcomplicated the main text. If the Korean practice adopted either of these methods, the Third Amendment might not have been conducted through an amendment procedure. Due to the invisible model, which enables the constitutional replacement under the name of

[31] See also Do-chang Kim, 'Kaejŏng Hŏnbŏbe taehan Haesŏlg'wa Bipan' [A Comment and Criticism on the Third Amendment to the Constitution of Republic of Korea, 1960] (1960) 2 *Seoul National Law Review* 1, 2–3.

[32] For the process of drafting an amendment bill, see Hee Kyung Suh, *Hankuk Hŏnchŏngsa 1948–1987* [*The Constitutional History of Korea, 1984–1987*] (Seoul, Forum, 2020) 370–82. Alongside the transition to the parliamentary system, the Third Amendment introduced some important institutions to support democratic government – for example, it established an independent constitutional court for judicial review and central election commission for observation of fair elections.

[33] Jong-Wook Moon, 'Che-i-Kongwaguk Hŏnjŏng e kwanhan Yŏn'gu' [A Study of the Constitutionalism of the Second Republic of Korea] (2005) 18 *Law Review* 47, 49.

amendment, whether big or small, the changes could have been accommodated neatly in the constitutional document. The invisible model made it possible for transformative constitutional changes to make a soft landing through the existing amendment rules, without breaking legal continuity.

IV. The Coup and the Fifth Constitutional Amendment in 1962

In May 1961, while the Second Republic was stumbling forward with a new constitutional experiment, the Korean Constitution and constitutional government faced a critical challenge. Military officers staged a coup d'etat followed by immediate suspension of the existing Constitution. The military junta enacted a new Constitution and declared an inauguration of the Third Republic. However, this large-scale work of constitution-making was again named a constitutional 'amendment'.

A. The 16 May Military Coup and the Suspension of Constitutional Government

On 16 May 1961, a military coup d'etat took place. It was no more than a year since the Second Republic operated the newly adopted parliamentary system. At dawn, groups of military officers and soldiers, led by Park Chung Hee, advanced to Seoul and quickly seized administrative buildings of governmental branches, the headquarters of the broadcasting systems and the presidential residence. At 5 am, on the KBS radio station, they announced that military forces occupied all governmental branches by organising the 'Military Revolutionary Committee' and proclaimed the 'Revolutionary Pledges'[34] to declare their action as a 'military revolution'. The Committee issued martial law throughout the country and dissolved the Parliament by issuing Committee Proclamation No 4. Three days later, the Committee was renamed 'Supreme Council for National Reconstruction' (hereinafter 'the Supreme Council'), and the military junta started henceforth.

On 6 June, the military junta promulgated the National Reconstruction Emergency Measures Act (hereinafter 'the Act') as a Supreme Council Decree No 42. According to the drafter, constitutional law professor Tae-yeon Han,[35] the Act was drafted with reference to the Enabling Act 1933 in Germany delegating

[34] The sixth article of the Pledges proclaimed that they would yield power to civilians and return to the military duties after completing the revolutionary mission. See generally Chi Young Pak, 'The Third Republic Constitution of Korea: An Analysis' (1968) 21 *Western Political Quarterly* 110, 113.

[35] Tae-yeon Han, 'Han'guk Hŏnbŏpkwa Hŏnbŏphag ŭi Hoego' [Reflection on Korean Constitution and Constitutional Jurisprudence] (2002) 8 *Constitutional Law* 9, 34–35.

all powers to Hitler. Article 24 of the Act prescribed that if any part of the existing Constitution does not comply with the Act, the Act shall have an effect, thereby giving superior effect to the Act over the Constitution. Therefore, the Act was practically understood as an interim or provisional constitution,[36] and the existing Constitution was regarded as being abolished or destructed, or at least, partly suspended by the Act.

Then, one might ask the following question: how did the military junta justify its authority to exercise superior juridical power over the existing Constitution? The military junta – like other cases of coups in the world – tried to justify its destruction of the Constitution in the name of 'revolution'.[37] It strongly claimed that the Second Republic, a product of the April Revolution, failed and resulted in social disorder. Similar self-justification was also observed in Spain and Chile, where military dictatorships lasted for several decades. In those cases, the juntas argued that the coup has a revolutionary nature, and thus the military leader has a supreme authority to ignore and destroy the existing constitutional order and create a new constitution. In such cases, a number of constitutional scholars supported the junta by theorisation of the junta's non-commissioned constituent power drawing from Carl Schmitt's account of sovereignty and constituent power.[38] The same thing happened in Korea too.

B. Between a New Constitution and Constitutional Amendment

In August 1961, the military junta announced that it would make a new constitution and hold an election to transfer the governmental power to the newly elected government. However, contrary to the official announcement, the junta was planning to create a new constitution for itself and restore strong presidentialism, with Park Chung Hee as the head of the government. On 11 July 1962, the Supreme Council officially organised the 'Constitution Deliberative Committee', which

[36] See, eg, Tae-yeon Han, *Kukkajaegŏn Bisangjoch'ibŏp* [*National Reconstruction Emergency Measures Act*] (Seoul, Bobmunsa, 1961); Il-gyŏng Pak, *Hyŏngmyŏng Jŏngbu wa Hŏnpŏp* [*Revolutionary Government and Constitution*] (Seoul, Jinmoyng Munhwasa, 1961). A judicial judgment recognised the Act as a basic law equivalent to the Constitution in effect (Supreme Court Decision 63Cho8, decided 7 November 1963).

[37] However, the coup is distinguished from the revolution in that the latter is an action by a mass of people, whereas the former is attempted by a small group of people. See, eg, Edward Luttwak, *Coup d'État: A Practical Handbook* (Cambridge, MA, Harvard University Press, 2016) 12; Jonathan M Powell and Clayton L Thyne, 'Global Instances of Coups from 1950 to 2010: A New Dataset' (2011) 48 *Journal of Peace Research* 249, 252 (specifying 'military or other elites' as a subject and emphasising illegality).

[38] For a description of both countries' cases, see generally Joel Colón-Ríos, *Constituent Power and the Law* (Oxford, Oxford University Press, 2020) 248–50; on theories developed for military dictatorship and its constitution-making power, see Renato Cristi, 'The Metaphysic of Constituent Power: Schmitt and the Genesis of Chile's 1980 Constitution' (2000) 21 *Cardozo Law Review* 1749, 1763–75.

comprised nine members from the military and 21 scholars as expert advisers, and entrusted them with drafting a new constitution.[39] The project was held in confidence within the Supreme Council building, and the discussion process and drafting details were not documented. In fact, around September 1961, the junta had unofficially assembled a team of a small number of scholars for the preliminary work for drafting and enacting a constitution, election law and party law in preparation for holding power; the members involved joined the Constitution Deliberative Committee later on.[40] Thus, the constitution-making project under the military junta was conducted with a clear goal in a secret room,[41] as if it were a military operation.

In the process, there was a debate on whether the military junta should make/adopt an entirely new constitution or merely amend the existing one. Some scholars favouring amendment argued that constitutional change should follow the amendment procedure provided in Article 98 of the then Constitution[42] as it was not explicitly repealed, and making a new constitution was inessential as the constituent power had not changed.[43] While the junta at heart favoured a new constitution to affirm a new beginning and thereby consolidate its political power,[44] it also had to think of the political and legal effects that a new constitution would bring about. In other words, on the one hand, making a new constitution that implies a legal break from the past might raise problems with a state's identity and continuity in the eyes of the international society and, on the other hand, might represent the self-confession of usurpation of the former government. The junta finally agreed to call it an 'amendment', but did not follow the existing procedure.

Despite of label of 'amendment', the junta wanted to employ an extraordinary procedure corresponding to making a new constitution. Therefore, it amended Article 9 of the Act to adopt a new constitutional amendment procedure: approval by the Supreme Council and the following national referendum. The latter was designed for gaining legitimacy by involving the constituent power. As prescribed in Article 9, the amendment bill was approved by the Supreme Council on 5 December and was confirmed by a national vote on 17 December, with 79 per cent

[39] For the organisation of the drafting body and its undisclosed process, see Ho-Dong Choi, '1962 nyŏn Hŏnbŏpsang Chŏngch'ijed oŭi Hyŏngsŏng Gwajŏng e kwanhan Koch'al' [A Study on the Constitutional Formation on Political Institutions in 1962] (2021) 50 *Public Law* 97, 104–06.

[40] ibid 103.

[41] Since the invisible codification model makes it relatively inconvenient to identify where the changes have been incorporated into the text (Albert (n 2) 239–40), if documentation of work on constitutional legislation is ignored or intentionally concealed, this may result in another level of difficulty in terms of both constitutional practice and scholarship.

[42] According to art 98 of the Constitution (last amended in 1954), the Constitution can be amended when the amendment bill is proposed by the President or one-third of either Houses, or half a million voters, and then approved by two-thirds of both Houses.

[43] For a theoretical aspect of the debate, see Dong Eun Joh, '1962 nyŏn Hŏnbŏpchejŏngnon'gwa Kaejŏngnonŭi Nonjaeng'e Taehan Yŏn'gu' [A Study on the Debate Concerning the Procedure of 1962 Constitution Formation in Korea] (2016) 49 *Chonbuk Law Review* 57, 84–90.

[44] See also ibid 57, 80.

approval among the 80 per cent of entire voters. Thus, the Fifth Amendment 1962 was accomplished. Its supplementary rules provided that the Act would become invalid at the same as this Constitution took effect.

C. Stealth Constitutional Replacement and Concealed Illegitimacy

Officially, the so-called 1962 Fifth Amendment was labelled a '*whole* amendment'. As it transformed the governing structure into the presidential system with a strong executive branch and changed entire parts of the previous text, the labelling itself seems to have no considerable problem. However, this labelling is a disguised identification: first, the coup was *faked* as a revolution to justify the suspension of the constitutional government and make a new constitution; and, second, an extraordinary procedure of constitution-making was employed, but it was *faked* as a legitimate procedure for amendment.

As long as an amendment is a change according to the amending rules, the Fifth Amendment cannot be called an amendment. Crucially, the military junta defied the amending rules in the existing Constitution, and instead passed the new Constitution according to a sort of emergency act that the junta had made. This means that the junta made a pretence of legality by creating the amendment procedure. Moreover, the junta masqueraded its legitimacy by holding a referendum as a final procedure of constitutional change. Overall, it was making a new constitution more than a constitutional amendment. Given this fact, although the reformers named it an 'amendment', the Fifth Amendment corresponds to 'stealth replacement', a term that Law and Whalen used to describe arbitrarily labelled replacement.[45]

Such arbitrary labelling seems easier to employ with the invisible codification model compared with other codification models.[46] As changes are neither identified at one glance nor marked in the text, the reformers can camouflage an extraordinary constitutional transformation in the name of amendment. In particular, in countries with complicated political issues or in countries that are full of dramatic events (such as coups, dictatorships or both), the reformers are more likely to do so for a political reason as identified in the Fifth Amendment in Korea. In such cases, readers can be easily deceived by the text, title and manipulated procedure of constitutional changes.

In this regard, in order to distinguish a certain constitutional change from others and properly grasp its original intention, a content-based approach is much more useful rather than a textual or procedural approach,[47] especially in relation to the invisible codification model. For example, the Fifth Amendment, albeit labelled an 'amendment', revised the constitutional preamble as well.

[45] Law and Whalen (n 1) 95.
[46] On four codification models, see Albert (n 2) ch 6.
[47] ibid 76–78.

While the preamble had remained previously untouched since its establishment, the Fifth Amendment added the text '19 April *Movement* and 16 May *Revolution*'[48] as a spiritual foundation of the *new* constitution and emphasised the new start by specifying 'in the establishment of a new Republic'. It shows that the reformers' invisible intention to break from the past constitution was visibly reflected in the text.

V. Conclusion

Let me conclude by drawing some implications from the analysis of preceding cases associated with the codification technique and its relation to *amendment politics*.

The Third Amendment in 1960, motivated by the civil revolution, aimed at the transformation of governmental structure. Such a huge change could have been a foothold for *making* a new constitution; however, constitutional reform was carried out by *amending* the existing Constitution. The Fifth Amendment in 1962 was driven by a military coup that also aimed to transform an entire form of government. Thus, the junta desired to *make* a new constitution, but nominally *amend* the existing Constitution in order to camouflage the illegality of usurpation and maintain legal continuity. These cases show some salient patterns of constitutional amendments in Korea, where the method and labelling of constitutional reform were largely affected by political context and strategies, which could be explained by amendment politics.

The amendment politics demonstrates that the reality of constitutional amendment is not fully accounted for by the general typology of constitutional change and regularly thinkable path. In Korean cases, significant constitutional changes that would otherwise require a new constitution were made through the amendment procedure. In my view, one technical factor that affected the amendment politics was the codification model. As the Korean practice adopted the 'invisible model', which is susceptible to the blurring of the distinction between constitutional change methods, the reformers were offered more available options to play politics by making use of constitutional amendments. To be clear, both the 1960 invisible replacement and the 1962 stealth replacement, be they good or bad, were possible due to the invisible model. In this way, albeit a technical factor, the codification model could be said to be a hidden decisive factor in dealing with the Korean Constitution in terms of the amendment politics.

[48] These terms were used by the drafters of the 1962 Constitution intentionally, although the common terms are the April Revolution and the 16 May military coup. The drafters intended to legitimise the coup in 1961 as a revolution, which would complete what was not achieved in the students' democratic movement in April of the previous year.

9

Crafting Amendments during Political Upheaval

Amendment Models and Constitutional Stability in Afghanistan

SHAMSHAD PASARLAY

> [Amend the Constitution] by writing in [Article 2] that Islam is the religion of Afghanistan, and its official madhhab [school of Islamic jurisprudence] is the Hanafi school. In the General Criminal Code, prescribe penalties for false madhhabs that may emerge in the future and wish to promote their credos in Afghanistan. We have prohibited integrating additional explanations [footnotes] and embedded [integrated] descriptions within our Constitution. If we allow this practice, it may become a common method of [changing the Constitution], and everyone [at the time of their choosing] will write arbitrary commentaries to each sentence of our basic laws.
>
> King Amanullah's address to the 1924 constitutional amendment Loya Jirga[1]

I. Introduction

Despite adopting eight different constitutions since 1923, only three of Afghanistan's Constitutions survived long enough to be amended before a succeeding regime replaced them. The 1923 and 1987 Constitutions were each amended during armed conflicts, and their amending choices were crafted as vehicles by which to directly incorporate the interests of armed groups excluded from the original constitutional bargain. In each case, the decision to amend the Constitution was meant to stabilise a crumbling constitutional order by incentivising the armed opposition to participate in peaceful political discourse. Conversely, amendments to the 1931 Constitution came during peacetime, sparing its authors the strain of an armed opposition rallying against certain constitutional provisions.

[1] Reported in Burhanuddin Khoshkaki, *Roedad-i Loya Jirga-ye Dar al-Sultana 1303* [*Proceedings of the Loya Jirga of the Kingdom 1924*] (Kabul, Sangi Publisher of the Ministry of War, 1925) 151, 153–54.

This chapter looks at amendments to these constitutions and how they were recorded within the original text. Not unlike constitutional amendments elsewhere around the world, certain changes to the Afghan constitutions raise thorny questions, including, for instance, the 'amendment'-'replacement' distinction and uncodified changes to formal amendment procedures. Hence, it is important at the outset to clarify one point: some changes with which this chapter will engage through the lens of 'amendments' may not, precisely, be construed as such by several scholars. Those who amended the 1923 Constitution of Afghanistan did not strictly follow the *formal* amendment procedures written in the Constitution, and the 1931 Constitution codified no specific amending procedures at all. The 1987 Constitution was amended in a manner consistent with the Constitution's formal amendment rules, but a single amendment attempt altered 35 of the Constitution's 149 *articles*. These changes ranged from simple textual mending to wholesale erasing of entire articles and even included integration of several new ones into the original document.

Comparative constitutional theorists may conceptualise these changes differently. Scholars who adopt a sternly procedural approach to distinguishing *formal* amendments from other types of constitutional alteration might recognise changes to the 1923 Constitution as constitutional 'replacement' rather than as 'amendments' per se.[2] For them, the fact that amendments were made outside of the formal rules of change may be the reason to characterise them as something demonstrably different (ie, constitutional replacement). Scholars who rely on the scope and magnitude of change, rather than on stringently formal criteria, may also not view changes to the 1923 and 1987 Constitutions as 'amendments'. Some may label such sweeping changes as 'constitutional dismemberment' because they defied the original designs of the Constitutions and took the documents in directions unforeseen at the time of constitutional founding.[3] Other scholars may view changes of the degree made to the 1923 and 1987 Constitutions as examples of 'stealth replacement' because, as I will explain, these formal amendments involved modifications of enormous scale and altered at least one of the core elements of the Constitutions.[4]

Constitutional amendments in Afghanistan are thereby inescapably linked to these debates and merit deeper scrutiny, but I do not wish here to take a position on which of these labels best describes such modifications. For the purposes of this chapter, I consider these changes 'amendments', simply because those in charge of writing these changes understood their task to be one of amending the

[2] Zachary Elkins, Tom Ginsburg, and James Melton, *The Endurance of National Constitutions* (Cambridge, Cambridge University Press, 2009) 55.

[3] Richard Albert, *Constitutional Amendments: Making, Breaking and Changing Constitutions* (Oxford, Oxford University Press, 2019) ch. 2; Richard Albert, 'Constitutional Amendment and Dismemberment' (2018) 43 *Yale Journal of International Law* 1.

[4] David Law and Ryan Whalen, 'Constitutional Amendment versus Constitutional Replacement: An Empirical Comparison' in Xenophon Contiades and Alkmene Fotiadou (eds), *Routledge Handbook of Comparative Constitutional Change* (Abingdon, Routledge, 2021).

original documents rather than replacing them or writing entirely new fundamental charters.[5] This is particularly true with respect to the 1987 Constitution, changes to which, though massive in magnitude, were made in strict adherence to its amendment procedure.[6] Similarly, those who amended the 1923 Constitution first *tacitly* altered the document's amendment rules, without a related change to the text of the original Constitution, and then made amendments according to the new, uncodified amendment procedure.

Afghan constitutions recorded their amendments in various manners. Those who amended the 1923 Constitution adopted what Richard Albert has called the 'invisible' model of amendment codification. This means that the amended constitution does not make clear 'what in the text has been altered, how it has been altered, or when precisely it was altered'.[7] By contrast, those in charge of amending the 1931 Constitution adopted the 'appendative' approach by affixing changes to the end of the Constitution. The 1987 Constitution used an alternative method of amendment codification – one that combined the 'integrative' approach, in which the amended Constitution clarifies where, when and how it was altered,[8] with the 'invisible' model. This approach allowed the 1987 Constitution to clarify in some places that certain of its articles had been removed, while other changes were not written so visibly.

At the time of constitutional creation, the architects of the Afghan constitutions did not debate how changes to the constitution should be recorded or where in the text the constitution should reflect that it had been modified. Nevertheless, at the constitutional amending conventions, framers were forced to make choices about how they desired to remember their original fundamental charter. The choice of the 1923 and 1987 Constitutions to erase their controversial texts and the choice of the 1931 Constitution to attach amendments at the end were neither accidents nor exercises in aesthetic matters. Instead, these choices were informed by pragmatic considerations – that is, enhancing the stability of the constitutional order. The 1923 and 1987 Constitutions deployed the invisible model to erase from memory the traces of constitutional norms (and text) that the architects of amendments believed were the root causes of opposition to the Constitutions. By contrast, the authors of amendments to the 1931 Constitution opted to affix changes to the end of the document, leaving intact the Constitution's original design that had proven remarkably effective in securing peace in a society whose constitutive communities had just overthrown the 1923 constitutional order.

This chapter also assesses the relative effectiveness of these amendment codification models where the goal of amendment is to create 'buy-in' from powerful stakeholders in a controversial constitutional order. In Afghanistan, peacetime

[5] As Tom Ginsburg notes, 'if those promulgating the constitution declare it to be a "new" document, we believe them. If the actors claim to be amending the constitution, we believe them'. Tom Ginsburg, 'Constitutional Endurance' in Contiades and Fotiadou (n 4) 61.

[6] Constitution of Afghanistan 1987, art 141.

[7] Albert, *Constitutional Amendments* (n 3) 238.

[8] ibid 236.

amendments tended to be minor in scale and were appended to the Constitution to perpetuate the master text – original arrangements typically hailed as useful formulations in preventing conflict in a deeply divided, conflict-prone society. By contrast, amendments engineered during periods of war or political crises were generally greater in scope and were blended within the original text in a way that entirely removed the original controversial norms. Without deploying such an approach to amendment codification, securing the constitutional order appeared untenable. To shed light on this trend in Afghanistan, section II evaluates amendments to the 1923 Constitution, the framers' choice to adopt the invisible approach, and the model's practical consequences regarding constitutional stability and endurance. Section III turns its attention to amendments affixed to the 1931 Constitution. Section IV probes the sweeping changes to the 1987 Constitution and their method of codification. Though constitutional amendments in Afghanistan have remained understudied, the country's experience has implications that may be of interest to those studying constitutional change more broadly. Hence, section V concludes by gleaning tentative insights from the case study of Afghanistan.

II. The Invisible Model: The 1923 Constitution

Afghanistan was among the first nations in the Muslim world to adopt a written constitution in the early twentieth century. Before then, the region that falls within the modern borders of Afghanistan was ruled by autocratic monarchies with no prospects of law-bound governance.[9] The area that later became Afghanistan shared numerous characteristics of a society that was deeply 'tribal' in nature – where traditional power structures were shaped by tribal arrangements.[10] In this land of diverse tribal communities, Islam wielded normative supremacy in all socio-legal and political affairs. Throughout the region's history, as Islam expanded its reach to tribal communities, it merged with local customs and generated different approaches to the faith.[11] In modern Afghanistan, these various approaches to Islam presented the moral 'frame[s] of reference' for both the rulers (the state) and for those who challenged the state's expanding power.[12] This socio-religious structure of the region vested enormous power in two notable groups: the tribal leaders and the ʿulama (clergy) – the class of people schooled in classical Islamic

[9] Vartan Gregorian, *The Emergence of Modern Afghanistan: Politics of Reform and Modernization, 1880–1946* (Stanford, Stanford University Press, 1969); Jonathan Lee, *Afghanistan: A History from 1260 to the Present* (London, Reaktion Books, 2018).

[10] William Maley, 'Political Legitimacy in Contemporary Afghanistan' (1984) 27 *Asian Survey* 705, 709; Thomas Barfield, *Afghanistan: A Cultural and Political History* (Princeton, Princeton University Press, 2010); Christine Noelle, *State and Tribe in Nineteenth-Century Afghanistan: The Reign of Amir Dost Muhammad Khan (1826–1863)* (London, Routledge, 1997).

[11] Nile Green (ed), *Afghanistan's Islam: From Conversion to the Taliban* (Berkeley, University of California Press, 2017) xiii.

[12] ibid; Asta Olesen, *Islam and Politics in Afghanistan* (London, Routledge, 1995) 36.

scriptures, law and theology. The tribal chieftains exercised political influence because the power of the Afghan monarch depended upon his ability to levy tribal warriors from these tribal communities. The ʿulama were influential because without their endorsement, the monarch's legitimacy and his ability to assemble tribal soldiers would be questioned.[13] Further, the ʿulama's power sprang from their ability to stir tribal warriors into rebellion if they believed that the state's laws and policies did not sufficiently comply with Islamic values. As such, monarchies survived as long as they had the blessings of these two camps of power.

Afghanistan's early rulers did not write a constitution because they believed that formally imposing a common set of values upon the deeply divided tribal communities might exacerbate communal conflict. They feared that the powerful leaders of the tribes and the influential members of the ʿulama might choose to rebel if they believed that a formal charter did not sufficiently respect their values or forced them to accept the state's construction of their identity.[14] These early rulers advised their successors not to rush to draft a constitution that would 'set the people against their rulers', and to instead establish a constitutional government only incrementally.[15] Even so, King Amanullah Khan (1919–29) dismissed these concerns and adopted Afghanistan's first written Constitution.[16]

A. The Making and Amending of the 1923 Constitution

In 1923, King Amanullah and his entourage drafted a constitution that mirrored 'the basic framework of what [the king] and his modernist supporters envisaged the modern Afghan nation-state to be', representing 'the ideological break with the past, the departure from the autocratic but still tribally-based' monarchies before him.[17] To ratify the Constitution, the king assembled a Loya Jirga, Afghanistan's constitutional convention, in eastern Afghanistan. The Loya Jirga approved the king's Constitution without any changes or debates on its key and divisive issues, including on the role of Islam. The constitutional drafting committee and the ratification convention included figures who were wedded to the king's version of a 'modernist' Islam, and therefore did not embrace the form of 'traditional' Islam to which the powerful tribes and the ʿulama had been profoundly devoted for centuries.[18]

[13] Agnus Hamilton, *Afghanistan* (Norwood, MA, Plimpton Press, 1910) 228–229; Donald Wilber, *Afghanistan: Its People, its Society, its Culture* (New Haven, HRAF Press, 1962) 146.

[14] Clark Lombardi and Shamshad Pasarlay, 'Constitution-Making for Divided Societies: Afghanistan' in David Law (ed), *Constitutionalism in Context* (Cambridge, Cambridge University Press, 2022) 98.

[15] Sultan Mohammad Khan, *The Life of Abdur Rahman Khan: Amir of Afghanistan*, vol 2 (London, John Murray, 1900) 187–90.

[16] Faiz Ahmed, *Afghanistan Rising: Islamic Law and Statecraft between the Ottoman and British Empires* (Cambridge, MA, Harvard University Press, 2017) ch 5; Shamshad Pasarlay, 'Making the 2004 Constitution of Afghanistan: A History and Analysis through the Lens of Coordination and Deferral Theory' (DPhil thesis, University of Washington, 2016) 63–73.

[17] Olesen (n 12) 120.

[18] Faiz Ahmed, 'In the Name of Law: Islamic Legal Modernism and the Making of Afghanistan's 1923 Constitution' (2016) 48 *International Journal of Middle East Studies* 655.

Amanullah's Constitution expanded the writ of the state over tribal aristocrats by building a centralised system of governance. It created a partially elected Council of State and a Council of Ministers that exercised legislative and executive powers, respectively. Amanullah hoped that these institutions would gradually unseat the traditional tribal councils his predecessors had created to safeguard tribal interests.[19] Further, Amanullah's Constitution was engineered to reduce the historical power of the ʿulama. It required that Islamic law be codified and applied by the state-appointed judges rather than by the members of the ʿulama who were not bound by the state's (ie, the king's) interpretation of Islamic dictates.[20] The tribal leaders and the ʿulama thus took offence to their exclusion from the drafting process and to the Constitution's provisions which they thought betrayed their values. They aired their opprobrium for the document by revolting against its author.[21] This revolt forced the king to convene a Loya Jirga in 1924 that amended the Constitution in an effort to incentivise the rebels to play by its rules.

Notably, the 1923 Constitution defined no formal role for the Loya Jirga in the amendment process. Its Article 70 stated that the 'Constitution may be amended … upon the proposal of two-thirds of the members of the State Council, approval of the Council of Ministers, and ratification of the King'.[22] However, the king knew that without concessions to the rebels, his Constitution would not survive. The southern tribes had no part in writing the Constitution in 1923, but they wanted to be part of its amendment. The ʿulama were also excluded from the original ordaining of the Constitution. Hence, the battered king had no option but to involve his opponents in the amendment process, which required the abandonment of the formal amendment rules. However, it seemed that the king and his Council of Ministers first made an uncodified change to the Constitution's amendment procedure, whereby the Loya Jirga became the principal constitutional amendment convention. This new, uncodified amendment procedure was used to make changes to the Constitution in 1924 – a formula that the king himself followed in 1928 to make further alterations to the Constitution.[23]

At the 1924 constitutional amendment Loya Jirga, delegates blasted the rules of the Constitution they felt did not honour their religious beliefs. In particular, they castigated its Article 2, which stated that 'Islam is the sacred religion of Afghanistan. The followers of other religions such as Jews and Hindus … are entitled to the full protection of the state [if] they do not disturb public peace and morals'.[24] The Loya Jirga complained that this rule was incompatible with the

[19] Gregorian (n 9) 181.

[20] Ahmed (n 16) ch 5; Rhea Tally Stewart, *Fire in Afghanistan 1914–1929: Faith, Hope and the British Empire* (New York, Doubleday, 1973).

[21] Leon Poullada, *Reform and Rebellion in Afghanistan, 1919–1929: King Amanullah's Failure to Modernize a Tribal Society* (Ithaca, NY, Cornell University Press, 1973); Stewart (n 20).

[22] Constitution of Afghanistan 1923, art 70.

[23] Mohammad Sediq Farhang, *Afghanistan dar Panj Qarn-i Ākhir* [*Afghanistan in the Past Five Centuries*] (Peshawar, Pakistan, Ariana Afst Prints, 1988) 356–57; Gregorian (n 9) 259.

[24] Constitution of Afghanistan 1923, art 2.

teachings of the *Hanafi fiqh* (Islamic law developed over the centuries by scholars associated with the *Hanafi* school) because non-Muslims were required in the classical *Hanafi* tradition to wear distinct clothing and pay the Islamic tax (*Jaziya*). Delegates also rejected Article 9, which provided that all Afghan 'subjects … are endowed with personal liberty'.[25] They protested that the 'general public has … construed liberty as if it implied the freedom of religion and a free pass to perform deeds that are prohibited in Islam … but liberty in the Constitution is subject to limitation imposed by Islam and the laws of the state'.[26] Finally, the constitutional amendment Loya Jirga criticised Article 24, which prohibited 'all types of torture' and abolished punishments, such as lashing for fornication and alcohol consumption, decreed by Islamic law.[27] The Loya Jirga wished to incorporate exceptions to this rule under which Islamic punishments would be allowed.[28]

The Constitution included no rules about how and where amendments should be recorded, but during the 1924 Loya Jirga debates, both the king and his opponents took the matter of amendment codification seriously. The king seemed less willing than the tribes and the ʿulama to affix or blend changes into the original document. He was resistant to the option of integrating changes within the Constitution and desired to lower the number of modifications that would be constitutionally codified. He strongly and passionately urged the Loya Jirga to consider writing some changes in other laws, and not necessarily in the Constitution.[29] But the tribes and the ʿulama favoured incorporating changes into the Constitution itself in a way that would erase the traces of the Constitution's controversial original norms. They wanted to own the entire constitution-building project by merging amendments into the text as though the Constitution had been written in 1924. They apparently believed that appending or integrating amendments in ways that left the original text untouched would insufficiently mirror their power, reminding them of the original betrayal.[30]

Under pressure from the rebels, the king gave in and the constitutional amendment Loya Jirga blended amendments within the original text. After five major amendments were written, the king reissued the Constitution. All these amendments are invisible and can be located only if one compares the 1923 and 1924 versions of the Constitution carefully. For instance, an amended version of Article 2 reads as follows:

> The religion of Afghanistan is the sacred religion of Islam, and its official madhhab is the sublime Hanafi [doctrine]. The followers of other religions, such as Jews and Hindus who reside in Afghanistan shall pay the special Islamic tax and wear distinctive clothing; they shall be protected so long as they do not disrupt public peace and morals.[31]

[25] ibid art 9.
[26] Khoshkaki (n 1) 136.
[27] Constitution of Afghanistan 1923, art 24.
[28] Khoshkaki (n 1) 155.
[29] ibid 153.
[30] ibid 155–59.
[31] Constitution of Afghanistan 1923, art 2, amended in 1924.

The amendment added the official *madhhab* and required non-Muslims to wear distinctive clothing and to pay special Islamic taxes. However, there is no indication within this amended text about when, where and how Article 2 was modified. Similarly, the original Article 9 endowed 'all Afghans with personal liberty which should not encroach on the liberty of others'.[32] It was amended as follows: 'all Afghans are bound by religious dictates and the laws of the state in exercising their rights and liberties'.[33] Originally, Article 9 was written to reduce the widespread discrimination against *non-Hanafi* Muslims and the followers of other religions, but the amended version eliminated that guarantee entirely. This change was blended in invisibly, meaning that the amended Constitution did not clarify where and how the alteration was made. It seemed as if the changed article had existed from the start.

Those who originally wrote the Constitution were proud of the relatively modern, 'liberal' document and were unwilling to be associated with the illiberal amended version.[34] They wished to include certain distinguishing marks within the Constitution that would separate the original text from its amendments. However, the king seemed to reject integrating amendments outright because he thought that such codifications might turn the Constitution into a hodgepodge of disjointed elements. As much as he wished to preserve the Constitution's original text and design, he was forced to insert amendments invisibly into the Constitution because the Loya Jirga wanted to remove the provisions that they thought were contentious.

B. The 1928 Amendments and the Fall of the Constitution

The invisible amendments to the 1923 Constitution did engender buy-in to the king's constitutional order, and the rebels abandoned violence and retreated to the countryside. The amendments created a new modus vivendi in which the ʿulama policed compliance with Islamic law, and the tribal aristocrats restored their political influence. For example, one of the major uncodified changes the constitutional amendment Loya Jirga made to the constitutional order was the formation of a special religious committee empowered to scrutinise the consistency of state law with the *Hanafi fiqh*.[35] This committee replaced a similar institution, the *Haiʾat-i Tamīz*, a religious review body staffed with 'modernist' Islamic jurists who had divinely ordained the Constitution in 1923.[36] The reason why the new committee was not written in the Constitution may be explained by the fact that the

[32] ibid art 9.
[33] ibid art 9, amended in 1924.
[34] Senzil Nawid, *Religious Response to Social Change in Afghanistan, 1919–29: King Aman-Allah and the Afghan Ulama* (Irvine, CA, Mazda, 2000) ch 5.
[35] ibid 111.
[36] Ahmed (n 16) ch 5.

institution it replaced was also not constitutionally reflected. This new Islamic review committee essentially granted to the ʿulama, who had incited the rebellion, a veto on religious questions. The supremacy of *Hanafi* law, which the rebellious ʿulama demanded, was thus restored.

However, the stock created by the 1924 amendments faltered when the king chose to undo them in 1928. The empowered ʿulama had hindered Amanullah's ambitious reform agenda[37] and, as a result, resentment in the king's modernist camp grew steadily. Undeterred by the shocks of the 1924 rebellion, the king convened another Loya Jirga in 1928 and proposed a corpus of new amendments to the Constitution, which effectively 'dismembered' the document.[38] These changes replaced the feudal-dominated Council of State with a popularly elected parliament, whereby the tribal notables would surrender power to the elected representatives of the people.[39] Other important amendments included the 'separation of church and state' and the 'creation of a Western-style cabinet and constitutional monarchy'.[40] These changes indeed took the constitutional order in a direction unanticipated by its original architects during the constitutional founding in 1923.

Although the Amanullah-appointed Loya Jirga rubber-stamped these far-reaching amendments, trouble brewed swiftly between the king and the clergy over these controversial changes. The king's opponents slammed the amendments as being contradictory to Islamic values and a direct attack on their historically privileged positions. Neither the clergy nor the tribal notables were ready to bow to the amended constitutional order, and before the new set of amendments could be codified, the tribes and the clergy picked up arms once again and toppled Amanullah's constitutional order in January 1929.

III. The Appendative Model: The 1931 Constitution

The groups who ousted Amanullah put Mohammad Nadir Shah on the Afghan throne in 1929. Nadir Shah was initially reluctant to accept the crown, but the tribal leaders and religious notables were adamant that he be made king.[41] They believed that he was the kind of ruler who would govern in consultation with them, as he represented the two traditional hubs of power: he had the confidence of the tribes and the ʿulama. Cognisant of the tribes' enormous support, Nadir accepted the throne, highlighting that because 'the people do designate me so,

[37] Amin Saikal, *Modern Afghanistan: A History of Struggle and Survival* (London, IB Tauris, 2004) 81.

[38] Gregorian (n 9) 259–61; Farhang (n 23) 368–69; Louis Dupree, *Afghanistan* (Princeton, Princeton University Press, 1973) 463.

[39] Gregorian (n 9) 259; Mir Ghulam Mohammad Ghubar, *Afghanistan dar Masīr-i Takrīkh* [*Afghanistan in the Course of History*], vol 2 (Qom, Iran, Nohzat Publisher, 1996) 1277.

[40] Dupree (n 38) 463.

[41] Percy Sykes, *A History of Afghanistan*, vol 2 (London, Macmillan & Co, 1940) 321.

I accept. I will not be the King but the servant of the tribes and the country'.[42] He then issued a 10-point declaration that summarised his approach to governance – principles that essentially endorsed the amendments that were imposed upon Amanullah in 1924.[43] These included, chiefly, governance in line with Islam and the *Hanafi fiqh* and strict adherence to the Qur'an.[44] Through these assurances, Nadir Shah signalled to the tribal chieftains and to the religious dignitaries that he did not intend to centralise state power at their expense, or at least not in the immediate future.

Notably, Nadir Shah assembled religious figures into a council called the Jamiʿat-i ʿUlama (Society of Islamic Jurists), which was empowered to interpret extant laws and to wield the final authority on the state's religious policies. Specifically, it was granted the power of specialised Islamic review – assessing the consistency of state law with Islam and the *Hanafi fiqh*.[45] Crucially, the Loya Jirga delegates, who had placed Nadir Shah on the throne, had also appointed 105 of its members to a 'National Council' that served as a legislative body and as a constitutional assembly.[46] Thus, tribal representatives and members of the ʿulama were directly involved in the constitutional process.

Having ensured the tribes and the ʿulama that his government would rule only based on Islam and the *Hanafi fiqh*, Nadir Shah was confident that he would avoid the ire of these powerful groups. In 1931, he adopted Afghanistan's second Constitution, taking every step to guarantee that the tribes and the ʿulama participated in drafting and ratifying the basic law.[47] He aimed to unify through his constitution all the pertinent groups who had the power to wreck a constitutional order. However, the highly inclusive constitutional drafting process suggested that agreement would be difficult, and that the 1931 Constitution would be riddled with ambiguities and contrasting provisions. Nadir Shah thus sacrificed textual consistency and methodological stringency in favour of generating incentives to sustain the political order. As Asta Olesen has noted:

> [T]he complex and inconsistent formulations of the Constitution of 1931 reflected the fact that Nadir *Shāh* was trying to placate simultaneously the modernists, the clergy and the tribes by evoking values and concepts from their respective, separate discourses. The difficulties involved [in constitution-making] were like squaring the circle, and the result naturally lacked logic or consistency – but served the purpose of securing peace [for more than three decades].[48]

[42] Gregorian (n 9) 287.

[43] Lee (n 9) 512; Sykes (n 41) 324–25.

[44] Mohammad Alam Faizad, *Jirga hai Buzarg-i Milli-ye Afghanistan, Loya Jirga ha wa Jirga hai Nam-nihad taht-i Tasalot-i Kamonist ha wa Rus ha* [*Afghanistan's Loya Jirgas and Symbolic Jirgas under the Communists and the Soviets*] (Lahore, np, 1989) 139–40.

[45] Gregorian (n 9) 299; Donald Wilber, 'The Structure and Position of Islam in Afghanistan' (1952) 6 *Middle East Journal* 41, 43; David Edwards, 'Charismatic Leadership and Political Process in Afghanistan' (1986) 5 *Central Asian Survey* 273, 292.

[46] Dupree (n 38) 463.

[47] Farhang (n 23) 407; Amin Tarzi, 'Islam and Constitutionalism in Afghanistan' (2012) 5 *Journal of Persianate Studies* 205, 215.

[48] Olesen (n 12) 178–79.

The 1931 Constitution codified no procedures for its own amendments. However, through 'unwritten law', a Loya Jirga could alter the Constitution[49] – an amendment procedure borrowed from the 1923 Constitution. In practice, 'courts could speculate and the National Council debate on any issue, [and if the monarch deemed it necessary] in very important cases', including the changing of the Constitution, the matter would be submitted to the Loya Jirga.[50] This was the core of the unwritten procedure for amending the 1931 Constitution.

The 1931 Constitution endured for 33 years and saw four changes under its uncodified amendment rules. The first of these amendments included an addendum in September 1932 which affixed two new articles to the Constitution.[51] One of these articles barred Afghan diplomats, military officers and students who pursued education overseas at the government's expense from marrying foreign nationals. The other stated that foreigners 'shall *absolutely* not have the right to own land in Afghanistan [and] embassies of other countries shall be dealt [with] based on bilateral agreements' (emphasis added).[52] In August 1938, an amendment was made to the second affixed article. It stated that foreigners should have 'no right to own land in Afghanistan; foreign embassies and consulates should be dealt [with] based on bilateral agreements'.[53] The amendment removed the word 'absolutely' from the first sentence of the article and added the word 'consulates' to the second sentence. The other amendment was made in April 1934 to Article 51, which originally stated that if the need for 'new laws is felt, the proposal is initiated by [the related ministry], and put before the National Assembly by a [m]inister or the Prime Minister, and will come into force after [the approval] of the National Assembly and the assent of … the King'.[54] Its amended version appended to the end of the Constitution read that if:

> [O]ne of the ministries or independent administrations [senses] the need for the adoption of new laws, [the said institution] shall prepare a draft and present it for review to the Council of Ministers. The law shall become effective after the approval of both houses of the National Assembly and the assent of the King.[55]

Unlike its predecessor, which blended amendments within the original text and made no indication of where and when the document was altered, the 1931 Constitution was reissued each time an amendment was made, with the date of its enactment written at the end of the original text. However, because the amendments leave the original text intact, changes to the Constitution's existing articles are only discernible when the original document is compared to the amendments attached to the end of the Constitution.

[49] Gregorian (n 9) 305; Dupree (n 38) 469.
[50] Wilber (n 13) 158.
[51] Donald Wilber, 'The Constitution of Afghanistan' (1965) 19 *Middle East Journal* 215, 215; Lee (n 9) 513.
[52] Constitution of Afghanistan 1931, Addendum 1, art 2.
[53] ibid Addendum 1, art 2, amended in 1938.
[54] ibid art 51.
[55] ibid art 51, amended in 1934.

This appendative approach adopted by the architects of the amendments to the 1931 Constitution merits closer attention. The framers of the Constitution borrowed the 1923 Constitution's unwritten amendment procedure, but they chose not to follow its method of amendment codification. One reason for this dichotomy could be the circumstances that led to amending the two constitutions. Unlike the 1923 Constitution, the authors of the amendments to the 1931 Constitution were under no strain to fend off a rebellion or an armed uprising. No debate on the method of amendment codification took place at the moment of constitutional change; the architects of amendments to the 1931 Constitution apparently took for granted that changes would be affixed to the end of the original text. Moreover, the engineers of the 1931 Constitution's amendments seemed to believe that appending changes to the original text was more productive because it left the original document untouched, preserved its original core, and avoided muddling the already vague and ambivalent document – a formula that the Constitution's designers glorified for sustaining the constitutional order for a long time.

IV. The Meeting of the Invisible and Integrative Models: The 1987 Constitution

For more than 30 years, the 1931 Constitution secured peace among Afghanistan's deeply divided and heavily armed communities. However, the 1931 Constitution was replaced in 1964, upending the status quo and creating new sources of conflict within the Royal Family. The Constitution, which was adopted in 1964, included a provision that barred members of the Royal Family from participating in the political process.[56] This rule forced King Zahir Shah's ambitious cousin and former Prime Minister, Mohammad Daoud Khan (1953–1963), to turn to violent means of political participation. In 1973, Daoud Khan joined hands with other disgruntled political dissidents and brought down the monarchy, abrogating its founding 1964 Constitution.[57]

The fall of the 1964 constitutional order inaugurated a destructive episode in Afghanistan, a period plagued by coups, counter-coups, armed uprisings, a foreign invasion and a vicious civil war towards the end of the twentieth century. A series of regimes succeeded each other in Kabul, with each trying to rule under a constitution that trumpeted its unique vision of the state. Every regime which came to power through coups or victory in a civil war failed to rally a critical mass of Afghanistan's powerful, armed factions behind a common state vision. Each fell and saw its constitution replaced by a fundamental charter that lionised the

[56] Constitution of Afghanistan 1964, art 24.

[57] Mohammad Hasan Kakar, 'The Fall of the Afghan Monarchy in 1973' (1978) 9 *International Journal of Middle East Studies* 195.

ideology of its opponents, a constitution that proved equally ineffective in addressing the root causes of the conflict.

Daoud Khan adopted a Constitution in 1977 that was removed less than a year later by the communist Peoples' Democratic Party of Afghanistan (PDPA) in a ruthless military coup. Afghanistan's Islamist movements, a nascent political grouping that had emerged in the cities in the 1960s, the PDPA's arch-rivals, responded to the communist takeover by marshalling armed uprisings throughout the countryside to overthrow the communist government.[58] When the PDPA government failed to extend its writ to the countryside and lost control of major urban centres, the Soviet Union invaded Afghanistan in 1979. The Soviet invasion reshaped and galvanised the Islamists' fight and gave their cause a sacred foundation – defeating an invading foreign army. They formed several warring factions in neighbouring Pakistan and Iran, which became known as the *mujahidin* (holy warriors).[59]

The Soviet-backed government in Kabul adopted an interim Constitution in 1980, which was effectively a restatement of the PDPA charter. In 1987, the last communist President, Mohammad Najibullah, adopted a permanent Constitution, but its content was no different from that of its predecessor. The enormous costs inflicted upon the Soviets during the Afghan war forced them to disengage from Afghanistan in 1988 under the Geneva Accords.[60] At this time, the fall of the Soviet-backed Kabul government became inevitable. President Najibullah then embarked upon a process of 'national reconciliation'. As part of this process, President Najibullah envisioned a sweeping amendment package to the 1987 Constitution aimed at enhancing the stability of the constitutional order. He also called on the *mujahidin* factions to join the political process and abandon violence, but because they were on the verge of a total victory, the *mujahidin* factions did not heed the President's call and instead increased efforts to topple the Kabul government through military means.[61]

The 1987 Constitution codified two separate, but related, procedures for its amendments. First, Article 141 stated that amendments to the Constitution shall be 'made directly' by the Loya Jirga. Second, the Constitution authorised the president, and one-third of the National Assembly, to propose amendments to the Constitution. In this case too, the president would call a Loya Jirga to approve or reject proposed changes.[62] Either procedure could be deployed to make changes to any rule of the Constitution.

[58] Gilles Dorronsoro, *Revolutions Unending: Afghanistan, 1979 to the Present* (London, Hurst & Company, 2005).

[59] Oliver Roy, *Islam and Resistance in Afghanistan* (Cambridge, Cambridge University Press, 1986, 1990) ch 8; Olesen (n 12) 284–85.

[60] Larry Goodson, *Afghanistan's Endless Wars: State Failure, Regional Politics, and the Rise of the Taliban* (Seattle, University of Washington Press, 2000) 69.

[61] ibid 72.

[62] Constitution of Afghanistan 1987, art 141.

In May 1990, President Najibullah appointed a commission to draft changes to the 1987 Constitution. He asked the commission to write amendments in light of the 'positive elements of peace, national reconciliation, and the inclusion of all social forces in the political process'.[63] The 'glorious principles of Islam' and peaceful settlement of the conflict were to form the basis of these amendments. The amendment commission changed no fewer than 35 of the Constitution's 149 articles, ranging from simple cosmetic tinkering to the complete removal of entire articles. For example, Article 77 was changed to add the word 'parliament' in brackets after National Assembly to elaborate that 'parliament' and 'National Assembly' referred to the same institution. Other amendments were not so inconsequential and did what Richard Albert may consider 'violence' to the Constitution's core identity – or, in other words, 'dismembered' the Constitution.[64] Changes to Articles 1 and 6 are exemplary in this regard. Article 1 originally noted that the 'republic of Afghanistan is an independent, unitary, and indivisible state'.[65] Its amended version stated that the 'republic of Afghanistan is an independent, unitary, indivisible, and *Islamic* state' (emphasis added).[66] Similarly, Article 6 of the Constitution was removed entirely from the original text. It stated that the 'National Republican Front, [the ruling party], as the most inclusive of the social organisations and political parties, shall urge and unify its [members] to participate in the [social and] political [processes]'.[67] These changes lightened the Constitution's single party and socialist character in favour of an open and 'Islamic' political process – outcomes originally unforeseen in the Constitution's design.

The Loya Jirga recorded these amendments by combining the integrative and the invisible models, meaning that the amended Constitution made clear in some places what changes were made and where they could be located, whereas in other places changes were imperceptible. For example, the amended version of the Constitution clarified that Articles 6, 12 and 26 were removed from the Constitution. Conversely, Article 1 is illustrative of the invisible model; originally, it stated that the 'republic of Afghanistan is an independent, unitary, and indivisible state … The people exercise sovereignty through the Loya Jirga, the National Assembly, and local councils'.[68] It was amended as follows: 'The Republic of Afghanistan is an independent, unitary, indivisible, and Islamic state … The people exercise sovereignty through the Loya Jirga and the National Assembly.'[69] The amendment added the word 'Islamic' in the first sentence and removed 'local councils' from the second sentence in Article 1. However, the amended Constitution made no

[63] Presidential Decree No 314 on the Formation of the Constitutional Amendment Commission (7 May 1990).
[64] Albert, *Constitutional Amendments* (n 3) 78.
[65] Constitution of Afghanistan 1987, art 1.
[66] ibid art 1, amended in 1990.
[67] ibid art 6.
[68] ibid art 1.
[69] ibid art 1, amended in 1990.

indication of the time and place of these changes. The amended Constitution also included two new articles (146 and 147) without visibly stating so.

Amendments to the 1987 Constitution were made under similar conditions to those that forced the amendment of the 1923 Constitution, and their goals were similar: to generate stakes in crumbling constitutional orders. The 1987 Constitution, as originally adopted, only entrenched the credos of the communist party, concentrating power in this faction and making competitive politics impossible. Most of the 35 amendments made to the document were aimed at eliminating the privileged position of the communist party and making the political process more competitive. Other important changes were made to restore the historically prominent position of Islam in the Constitution, a concession to the regime's opponents.

At a time when the regime's opponents despised certain provisions of the Constitution as fundamentally flawed, viewing them as inherently incompatible with Islamic standards, the original authors of the Constitution had no choice but to completely erase them from memory, as if they had never existed. However, the amendments and their model of codification made no difference in terms of enhancing constitutional stability. The regime's opponents, the *mujahidin*, were on the doors of Kabul and were in no mood to compromise. They toppled the Kabul regime in 1992 and abrogated the 1987 Constitution.

V. Conclusion

Many constitutional amendments in Afghanistan were enacted in the wake of political crises and armed uprisings. Constitutional amendments during periods of political unrest are not uncommon around the world. However, what is notable in Afghanistan is that amendments made during political upheaval tended to be of a larger magnitude, and the methods of their codification were at the centre of argumentation during the moment of constitutional alteration. Because the purpose of these sweeping amendments was to engender consent in weakening constitutional orders, the original writers of the constitutions, and those who participated in changing these constitutions, championed different approaches to recording amendments to the original documents. By contrast, peacetime amendments in Afghanistan were typically of a smaller scale, and their codification models were not intensely debated. In the latter scenario, designers assumed that amendments would be appended to the end of the original constitution.

In the battle of amendment codification in Afghanistan, the authors of the original constitutions preferred to append changes to the end of the documents or, in the case of the 1923 Constitution in particular, to codify them elsewhere in ordinary law. The reason for this is simple: the constitutions as originally written only glorified the ideologies of their authors and concentrated power in a single faction. These original designers appeared unwilling to completely erase the constitutional text that once praised their commitments, even if those norms were completely muted through amendments. However, because the rulers lacked the power to impose their choices on their opponents, they were forced to adopt the invisible approach – a model that the adversaries of the constitutions favoured because it mirrored their power bluntly.

The invisible model adopted by the authors of amendments to the 1923 and 1987 Constitutions had mixed consequences. In 1924, the model proved instrumental in creating stakes in the constitutional order and aiding constitutional endurance. The 1923 Constitution collapsed only when King Amanullah chose to reverse the 1924 amendments. The authors of the amendments to the 1987 Constitution knew, for all practical matters, that erasing constitutional norms that the *mujahidin* viewed as inherently incompatible with Islam would have a better chance (if one existed at all) of promoting political stability. However, because the fall of the Kabul government was inevitable, amendments and the way in which they were codified became irrelevant.

A useful insight may thereby be tentatively gleaned from the history of amendment codification in Afghanistan: those who amend constitutions in tumultuous political environments may likely adopt the invisible approach, whereas the appendative model may be more likely during peacetime amendments.

10

Codifying Secularism in the Bangladesh Constitution

SHAROWAT SHAMIN

I. Introduction

Constitutional amendment is a distinctive tool for shaping the legal construct, polity, social, economic and cultural development of a country. It often interferes with the founding principles and provisions set in the master text of the constitution by the makers, which sometimes results in 'breaking and changing'[1] the constitution. Multiple amendments to 'secularism' – one of the four core constitutional principles of the Bangladesh Constitution 'broke' the sanctity of the principle and 'changed' the succeeding constitutionalism.

This chapter critically investigates the interplay of the 'integrative' and 'invisible' models of codifying constitutional amendments in the Bangladesh Constitution, impacting social, cultural, political and constitutional stability. 'Secularism', the most debated constitutional principle that has been amended multiple times, has been selected to analyse this interplay. Section II of this chapter first briefly discusses the features of the Bangladesh Constitution and its developments, and then situates its codification model. Next, section III discusses the legal and political controversies surrounding 'secularism' and the 'state religion', while section IV draws a critical analysis of judicial reviews of the different constitutional amendments and their divergence in the 'state religion' case. Finally, section V examines the resultant impacts of the encroaching hybrid codification model in breaking and changing the original constitutional principles.

II. The Constitution and its Amendments: Situating the Codification Model

The Bangladesh Constitution was adopted on 4 November 1972 and came into effect on 16 December 1972, exactly a year after the country's victory in

[1] Richard Albert, *Constitutional Amendments: Making, Breaking and Changing Constitutions* (Oxford, Oxford University Press, 2019).

its liberation war against Pakistan. The Constitution features a unitary state, parliamentary democracy, judicially enforceable civil and political rights,[2] non-enforceable[3] socio-economic rights as basic state policy principles[4] and an independent judiciary. It stands on four core principles: nationalism, socialism, democracy and secularism.[5] The jurisdiction features constitutional supremacy[6] and the Supreme Court (SC) is equipped with the power of judicial review.[7] The amendment of the Constitution requires a two-thirds majority in the Parliament.[8] So far, 17 constitutional amendments have been made, among which five were fully or partly declared unconstitutional by the SC, igniting further amendments by the Parliament.

The Bangladesh Constitution has been subject to 17 amendments in 50 years, while the US has been subject to only 27 in 235 years. Conversely, the 105 amendments to the Indian Constitution in 72 years and at least 25 in Pakistan since 1973 demonstrates the comparative stability of the Bangladesh Constitution in South Asia. However, this stability is not as simple as it appears. The influences of military rule, the debates over one of the core founding principles ('secularism') and their socio-legal-political impacts are crucial to the constitutional stability of the country. This tension can be tracked back from Bangladesh's inception, i.e., liberation from Pakistan in 1971, to unconstitutional military rules after the liberation. Moreover, this debate has long been ingrained in the South Asian context, triggered the Partition of India in 1947 and still carries forward the legacy of a colonial hangover in the region.[9]

Before the Partition of India in 1947, Bangladesh was a British colony and following the partition became a part of Pakistan (named East Pakistan). The legislative text of the country follows the colonial legacy not only by keeping the British-made laws, but also by carrying the codification language, model and style. There was no discussion on the codification model of the Constitution in the 1972 Bangladesh Constituent Assembly (CA). An inconsequential debate regarding the grammatical formation of the constitutional amendment provision (Article 142) of the Constitution took place in the CA.[10] However, there was no discussion on *how* the amendments were to be incorporated into the Constitution. Therefore, just like all other regular laws, the First Amendment in 1973 was directly integrated into the original text with the footnote reference indicating the change.[11]

[2] Part III of the Bangladesh Constitution.
[3] ibid art 8.
[4] ibid Part II.
[5] ibid Preamble, para 2.
[6] ibid art 7.
[7] ibid art 102.
[8] ibid art 142.
[9] Shah Alam, 'The State-Religion Amendment to the Constitution of Bangladesh: A Critique' (1991) 24(2) *Verfassung und Recht in Übersee/Law and Politics in Africa, Asia and Latin America* 209.
[10] Kawser Ahmed (ed), *Proceedings of the Constituent Assembly of Bangladesh: Debates on the Making of the Constitution*, vol 2 (Pencil Publications, 2022) 244.
[11] Constitution (First Amendment) Act, 1973 (Act No XV of 1973).

Richard Albert recognises this pattern of codifying amendments as the 'integrative model'[12] and found that the purpose of such a model is to update the original master text.[13] According to him, a unique feature of this model is that it records where and how the original constitution has been changed by using notations and footnotes.[14] However, when the same provision is amended more than once, the notation and footnote markers only indicate the latest amendment. Because of this, the intermediate amendments become invisible from the main text of the constitution.

For example, secularism, one of the four founding principles of the Bangladesh Constitution was codified in the original 1972 Constitution as follows:

> [T]he high ideals of nationalism, socialism, democracy and secularism, which inspired our heroic people to dedicate themselves to, and our brave martyrs to sacrifice their lives in, the national liberation struggle, shall be the fundamental principles of the Constitution. (Preamble)
>
> The principles of nationalism, socialism, democracy and secularism … shall constitute the fundamental principles of state policy. (Article 8(1))

Secularism in the preamble and Article 8(1) were excluded by the First Martial Law Proclamations Order No 1 of 1977, which was later ratified by the 1979 Fifth Amendment Act. As a result, 'secularism' was replaced by the expression 'absolute trust and faith in the Almighty Allah' (ATFAA).[15] Also, a new sub-article (1A) was added after Article 8(1) stating: 'Absolute trust and faith in the Almighty Allah shall be the basis of all actions.'[16] However, after 33 years of incorporation, in 2010 the Supreme Court declared the Fifth Amendment to be illegal and void,[17] and 'secularism' was restored in both provisions by the 2011 Fifteenth Amendment.[18] The existing text uses the following notation and footnotes:

> *Preamble, Para 2* [3][Pledging that the high ideals of nationalism, socialism, democracy and secularism, which inspired our heroic people to dedicate themselves to, and our brave martyrs to sacrifice their lives in, the national liberation struggle, shall be the fundamental principles of the Constitution;]
>
> [3] Substituted for the former second paragraph by the Constitution (Fifteenth Amendment) Act, 2011 (Act XIV of 2011), section 3.
>
> *Article 8* [11][(1) The principles of nationalism, socialism, democracy and secularism, together with the principles derived from those as set out in this Part, shall constitute the fundamental principles of state policy.]
>
> [11] Substituted for the former clause (1) and (1A) by the Constitution (Fifteenth Amendment) Act, 2011 (Act XIV of 2011), section 8.

[12] Albert (n 1) 236.
[13] ibid.
[14] ibid.
[15] Article 2(ii) of the Proclamations (Amendment) Order 1977 (Proclamations Order No I of 1977).
[16] ibid art 3.
[17] *Bangladesh Italian Marble Works Ltd v Bangladesh* [2006] BLT (Special) HCD 1; *Khondhker Delwar Hossain v Bangladesh Italian Marble Works Ltd and Others* [2010] 62 DLR AD 298.
[18] Constitution (Fifteenth Amendment) Act, 2011.

The footnote references only record the latest changes and do not mention the intermediate changes. This is how an amendment in existence for about 34 years becomes invisible in the existing codified piece. Albert's fourth codification model investigates the Irish codification approach and finds no record, hint or reference of amendments indicated in their constitutional texts.[19] Albert terms this model 'invisible',[20] noting that the only way for the reader to know about the changes is to make a comparison between the old and new texts.[21] The Bangladesh Constitution, although a good example of 'integrative model' with its bracketed texts and footnote references marking the amendments, keeps track of only the latest amendment to a provision, and therefore any past amendment(s) to that provision become invisible.

The recent print and electronic versions of the Constitution include an 'Appendix', which contains all previous constitutional amendment Acts and military proclamations. But the authority to add the Appendix in the Constitution is unclear. However, seemingly this is an administrative decision by the law ministry followed by the Fifteenth Amendment reprints. Nonetheless, this Appendix is not part of the Constitution. The 1972 CA only approved the 'Schedule' after the main text,[22] and no subsequent parliament ratified it either. Unlike the Irish invisible model, this Appendix saves the reader from looking at previous editions in order to trace the apparently 'invisible' amendments. The inclusion of an Appendix in the newer editions seems useful for researchers and general readers; however, its legality is questionable and violates the separation of powers. The executives in the Ministry of Law do not hold any authority to decide the contents of the printed piece without the Parliament's expressed sanction. Thus, the Appendix could not be considered a tool to balance the invisible amendment texts in the Constitution.

It is thus clear that the notation and footnotes used for integrating constitutional amendments into the master text only codify the latest change. As a result, preceding amendment(s) to the same provision become invisible. In general, the codification follows Albert's 'integrative model', but multiple amendments to a particular provision no longer continue to be integrative. The invisibility of the intermediate amendments makes Bangladesh an example of a hybrid model. However, the invisible feature of the Bangladesh model is not quite like Irish invisibility. This codification model perhaps reinforces Albert's argument for the non-existence of a one-size-fits-all[23] rule for all amendments.

The next section of this chapter will investigate the amendment trails of secularism in the Bangladesh Constitution and its consequent impact on the legal, political and social construct.

[19] Albert (n 1) 238.
[20] ibid.
[21] ibid.
[22] Ahmed (n 10) 326.
[23] Albert (n 1) 260.

III. Secularism as the Fundamental Principle: Background and the Controversies

In 1971, during the nine-month Bangladesh Liberation War, Pakistan committed genocide, mass killings, rapes and inhumane atrocities against the Bengalis, and acutely targeted Hindus and other minority communities.[24] Several Bengali Islamic political groups actively aided Pakistan, which led to the mass murders of liberal Bengali intellectuals during the war.[25] This traumatic experience left no dissenting voice in the 1972 CA vis-a-vis 'secularism' as one of the four founding principles of the Constitution. The preamble acknowledges that those secular ideals 'inspired our heroic people to dedicate themselves to, and our brave martyrs to sacrifice their lives in, the national liberation struggle'.[26] Secularism is further defined in Article 12 as the elimination of all forms of communalism, religion-based politics, favours, discriminations and persecutions by the state.[27]

It is important to note that although 'secularism' was not contested in the 1972 CA, it was removed from the Constitution in 1977 by General Ziaur Rahman's first military proclamation,[28] which was later ratified by the Fifth Amendment.[29] Secularism was replaced by ATFAA in the preamble and Article 8, and Article 12 was deleted. Instead, a new Article 8A was inserted, which read 'absolute trust and faith in the almighty Allah shall be the basis of all works of the State', and 'bismillah-ar-rahman-ar-rahim [In the name of Allah, the Beneficent, the Merciful]' was inserted before the preamble as the inaugural verse of the Constitution.[30] A decade later, in 1988, the second military ruler General HM Ershad introduced 'Islam' as the 'state religion' in a new article 2A.[31] The Eighth Amendment not only added the state religion, but also interfered with the SC's autonomy by setting up circuit benches of the High Court Division (HCD) at the local level.[32] Immediately after the Eighth Amendment, multiple petitions were filed challenging its legality. The SC responded promptly to the petitions regarding its jurisdiction and autonomy, and in 1989 declared part of the Eighth Amendment to be unconstitutional for violating the unitary nature of the State. The SC also held the unitary character as the basic feature of the Constitution and thus as unamendable. However, it deliberately left the three other petitions contesting 'state religion' unheard during that time. Later in 2010, the SC further nullified the Fifth Amendment for being ultra vires.[33] Against this backdrop, in 2011 the Fifteenth Amendment reinstated

[24] Anthony Mascarenhas, *The Rape of Bangladesh* (Delhi, Vikas Publications, 1971).
[25] ibid.
[26] Bangladesh Constitution, Preamble, para 2.
[27] ibid art 12.
[28] Proclamations (Amendment) Order 1977 (Proclamations Order No I of 1977).
[29] Constitution (Fifth Amendment) Act, 1979 (Act No 1 of 1979).
[30] ibid.
[31] Constitution (Eighth Amendment) Act, 1988 (Act No 30 of 1988).
[32] ibid.
[33] See n 17.

'secularism' in the preamble and Article 8, and restored Article 12.[34] However, it neither removed the state religion nor the Qur'anic verse *bismillah* from the preamble; instead, it added an 'eternity clause' restricting future amendments to secularism and state religion, and freshly defined them as 'basic structures' of the Constitution.[35]

'Two-nation' theory played the driving force during the Partition of India and resulted in religion-based territorial demarcation.[36] The 23 years of Pakistani oppression, atrocities and the horrors of the Liberation War left no opposition to the inclusion of secularism in the 1972 CA. However, the secular features of the Constitution were gradually torn up within 16 years of independence by the two consequent *ultra vires* military regimes. The incorporation of Islam as the state religion by the military usurper Ershad marked the last nail in the coffin of the secular high ideals of the Constitution in 1988. The Eighth Amendment was challenged by several petitions. The only successful case was *Anwar Hossain Chowdhury v Bangladesh*,[37] which did not challenge the inclusion of state religion, but only challenged the provision of decentralising the High Court Division in Article 100. The petition was fruitful, and the verdict is considered as the cornerstone of developing the 'basic structure doctrine' in Bangladesh.[38]

However, the 'state religion' was contested by liberal intellectuals, women's rights activists and lawyers. At least three petitions were filed challenging its legality. The Citizens' Committee for Resisting Communalism and Autocracy (CCRCA), Naripokkha (a women's rights organisation) and the lawyer Shakti Das Goswami questioned 'state religion' in three petitions.[39] The petitions remained unheard for about 22 years. In 2011, at first, a supplementary petition and later a revised petition were filed, and the HCD issued two separate rulings against the government regarding the legality of the state religion. In March 2016, a date for a hearing was precipitously set. At that time, the country was facing extremist attacks on freethinkers. Several liberal and/or atheist writers, bloggers, publishers and activists were slaughtered by religious fanatics for allegedly harming Islamic sentiments. Moreover, following the announcement of the date of the hearing of the case, the whole country experienced violent demonstrations and protests causing a severe breach of law and order.[40] Although the date was fixed for the hearing, the HCD dismissed the case outright due to the 'petitioners lacking locus standi'

[34] Constitution (Fifteenth Amendment) Act, 2011 (Act No XIV of 2011).

[35] Section 7 of the Constitution (Fifteenth Amendment) Act 2011 introduced a new art 7B into the Constitution, which labelled specific parts and provisions as the 'basic structure' of the Constitution and thus as unamendable.

[36] See n 9.

[37] *Anwar Hossain Chowdhury v Bangladesh* [1989] BLD AD (Special) 1.

[38] ibid.

[39] Writ Petition No 1834 of 1988 (*Sirajul Islam Chowdhury and Others v Bangladesh*), WP No 1330 of 1988 (by Naripokkha), and WP No 1177 of 1988 (by Shakti Das Goswami).

[40] Maher Sattar and Ellen Barry, 'In 2 Minutes, Bangladesh Rejects 28-Year-Old Challenge to Islam's Role' *New York Times* (28 March 2016), www.nytimes.com/2016/03/29/world/asia/bangladesh-court-islam-state-religion.html.

on 28 March 2016.[41] With no hearing, no reasoning and the full judgment not yet published, it could easily be conceived that the HCD was moved by socio-political issues rather than legal arguments.

The reason behind the supplementary petition in 2011 was the enactment of the Fifteenth Amendment, the objective of which was to restore the 1972 original constitutional principles tampered with by the Fifth Amendment. In 2010, the Supreme Court confirmed the unconstitutionality of the Fifth Amendment due to it being ultra vires.[42] Ruling against the government and setting the hearing date after 28 years indicated the HCD's preparedness to adjudicate the legality of the state religion. However, the dismissal on the ground of locus standi contradicts the SC's decades of practice and established jurisprudence on judicial review.[43] Astonishingly, the SC did not even allow the petitioners to establish their arguments on the legal standing question. It was reported that on the day of the hearing, one of the Islamist groups met with the Chief Justice and entreated the rejection of the petition.[44] This morning meeting, combined with street demonstrations, perhaps highlights the reason behind the SC's instant dismissal of the case without holding any hearings. The sensitive timing of the court hearing in 2016 after 28 years surprised many, as the period was reported to be one in which the rise of Islamic fundamentalism was occurring.[45] Hoque found that this state religion case raised at least four intricate issues for adjudication:[46] first, to overcome the Parliament's deliberate collocation of 'secularism' and 'state religion', which contradicted each other; second, no resistance from the major political parties (including those who had earlier deleted secularism and added state religion) suggested an implied political approval of this contradiction; third, the new eternity clause[47] by the Fifteenth Amendment made both provisions unamendable; and, fourth, the non-existence of judicial abrogation of any state religion provision in the comparative jurisprudence.[48] Hoque believes these ensuing complexities altered the legal position of the original 1988 challenge.[49]

However, in this complex juncture, the trails of military amendments have become invisible in the constitutional text due to the subsequent amendments, and the subsequent electoral parliaments show the utmost reluctance in dealing with the military-induced state religion. Perhaps Hoque's second comment on 'implied political acceptance' played the most crucial role behind this reluctance.[50]

[41] ibid.
[42] *Khondhker Delwar Hossain* (n 17).
[43] Ridwanul Hoque, 'Constitutional Challenge to the State Religion Status of Islam in Bangladesh: Back to Square One?', *Blog of the International Journal of Constitutional Law*, 27 May 2016, www.iconnectblog.com/2016/05/islam-in-bangladesh.
[44] See n 40.
[45] ibid.
[46] Hoque (n 43).
[47] Article 7B of the Constitution.
[48] Hoque (n 43).
[49] ibid.
[50] ibid.

Some scholars do not accept the cohabitation of the state religion and secularism as a contradiction and instead argue it to be either harmonious coexistence or reflective of the majority Muslim demography, which endorses this 'political acceptance' impulse.[51] When state religion was inserted by General Ershad in 1988, all major political parties protested against it. However, none of them showed any subsequent interest in deleting it when they became the ruling power. Chowdhury termed this contrast existence 'Islamo-secular' and saw it as wiping out the constitutional safeguards of equality and dignity of the people irrespective of their beliefs, and as a tool of political legitimisation.[52] In other words, it has played and continues to play the dominant role in breaking and changing the original core principles of the Constitution. However, this conflicting existence not only cleanses the constitutional protection of equality, but also generates wider inequalities and divisions between the majority and minority beliefs.

The next section of this chapter will compare several judicial reviews of constitutional amendments and analyse their resulting impact in the codified text.

IV. Judicial Review of Constitutional Amendments and the Impacts of the Resulting Codification

Five out of 17 constitutional amendments were challenged, and the SC affirmed their illegality either fully or partly. Of these five, three were made by the military rulers and two by the electoral Parliament. The first time a constitutional amendment was legally questioned and nullified by the SC was the Eighth Amendment in *Anwar Hossain Chowdhury v Bangladesh*.[53] As mentioned earlier, the SC only responded to that part of the Eighth Amendment where its jurisdiction was significantly impacted.[54] In its verdict, the SC initiated 'basic structure doctrine' in Bangladesh, and later in 2011 the Fifteenth Amendment introduced this doctrine into the Constitution and made specific parts of the Constitution, including secularism and the state religion, unamendable.[55]

Bangladesh Italian Marble Works Ltd v Bangladesh,[56] also known as the *Fifth Amendment case*, questioned *bismillah* as the opening verse of the Constitution,

[51] SM Masum Billah, 'Bangladesh: Public Law, Religious Freedom and Regulating 'Religious Sentiment' in Li-ann Thio and Jaclyn L Neo (eds), *Religious Offences in Common Law Asia: Colonial Legacies, Constitutional Rights and Contemporary Practice* (Oxford, Hart Publishing, 2021); Jahid Hossain Bhuiyan, 'Secularism in the Constitution of Bangladesh' (2017) 49(2) *Journal of Legal Pluralism and Unofficial Law* 1.

[52] Rokeya Chowdhury, 'From "Secular" to "Islamo-secular" Bangladesh: Mapping the Constitutional Trajectories through Law, Religion, and Performing Arts' (PhD thesis, McGill University, 2021).

[53] *Anwar Hossain Chowdhury* (n 37).

[54] The Eighth Amendment altered art 100 and modified the SC's jurisdiction by setting up divisional circuit benches of the HCD.

[55] Article 7B of the Constitution.

[56] *Bangladesh Italian Marble Works* (n 17).

the inclusion of ATFAA and friendly relations with the Islamic states, the exclusion of secularism and the ban on religion-based politics, amongst others.[57] In 2005, the HCD first declared the amendment's illegality[58] and in 2010 the Appellate Division confirmed this decision. While nullifying the Fifth Amendment, the HCD assessed the original and amended preambles and held:

> The original Preamble clearly shows that one of the four fundamental bases of our nationhood and inspiration of liberation was 'secularism' but the amended Preamble, especially the second paragraph, shows that 'secularism' was omitted from the Preamble thus changing the basic character of the Constitution ... This provision of secularism explained and expounded in Article 12, is one of the most important and unique basic features of the Constitution. Secularism means both religious tolerance as well as religious freedom. It envisages equal treatment to all irrespective of caste, creed, or religion but the State must not show any form of tilt or leaning towards any particular religion either directly or even remotely. It requires maintenance of strict neutrality on part of the State in the matters of different religions professed by various communities in the State. The State must not be seen to be favouring any particular religion, rather ensure protection to the followers of all faiths without any discrimination including even to atheists. This is what it means by the principle of secularism.[59]

The Fifteenth Amendment Bill was introduced in the Parliament after this liberal jurisprudence was set by the SC. However, when it became clear that the Parliament would not drop the state religion, the 1988 petition was revived through two supplementary petitions. The first of these was filed before passing the Fifteenth Amendment. In response, the HCD issued a rule against the government asking why the state religion provision would not be illegal.[60] On 16 June 2011, the HCD suspended further hearings on the petition after getting three amicus briefs which advised it not to intervene in relation to state religion while the Parliament was in session with the Amendment Bill on the table.[61] The second supplementary petition was filed when the Fifteenth Amendment restored secularism but did not remove state religion. This time the petitioners revised their petition calling into question the slightly modified Article 2A by the Fifteenth Amendment (instead of the Eighth Amendment). The HCD in another ruling asked the government the same question about the unconstitutionality of Article 2A in December 2011. However, none of those two rules ever received any responses from the government. These two rulings against the government questioning the legality of the state religion demonstrate the SC's willingness to adjudicate the petition impugning the state religion. Therefore, on 28 March 2016, when the HCD summarily rejected the whole petition due to the petitioners' lacking locus standi, the reaction for many was one of absolute astonishment.

[57] Chowdhury (n 52).
[58] *Khondhker Delwar Hossain* (n 17).
[59] *Bangladesh Italian Marble Works* (n 57) 149.
[60] Staff Correspondent, 'HC Rejects Writ over Islam as State Religion', *Daily Star* (29 March 2016), https://www.thedailystar.net/frontpage/writ-challenging-islam-state-religion-rejected-1201132.
[61] Chowdhury (n 52).

The HCD did not hear the petitioners' arguments on their legal standing and nor did it give any reasoning for this, and the judgment was never published. The HCD did not question the legal standing of the petitioners while the case was pending for 28 years. Instead, it previously issued two rulings against the government asking the exact same question for which the petitioners were seeking relief. This summary rejection was reported as the victory of the Islamists in the domestic and international media.[62] As mentioned in the previous section, the Islamists' violent protests, the fragile state of religious freedom of expression in the preceding years, and the meeting with the Chief Justice on the hearing date conceivably played a decisive role in the fate of the 28-year-old petition.

It is important to note that when Islam was introduced as the state religion in 1988, there was no 'secularism' in the Constitution, as it was replaced with ATFAA by the Fifth Amendment and Article 12 was deleted. Therefore, the 'state religion' clause was not apparently inconsistent in the then constitutional set-up. 'Secularism' was brought back, striking out ATFAA, and Article 12 was restored by the Fifteenth Amendment in 2011. However, this kept Islam as the state religion in Article 2A and added an additional line stating: 'the State shall ensure equal status and equal right in the practice of the Hindu, Buddhist, Christian and other religions'.[63] In the *Italian Marble Works* case, the court advised against approving any specific religion and reiterated equal protections for all faiths, including atheists.[64] Earlier, in *M Saleem Ullah v Bangladesh*[65] (the Thirteenth Amendment case), the HCD also acknowledged ATFAA to be destructive to the basic structure of the Constitution.[66] Interestingly, at the time of this judicial pronouncement, ATFAA was one of the fundamental principles of the Constitution and secularism was still absent. At that time, the HCD's remark regarding ATFAA did not attract much attention as the subject matter of the petition was different.[67] However, it indeed shows the judicial willingness to address the conflicts among the state religion, ATFAA and the original 'high ideals' (one of which is secularism), which were envisioned by the makers of the Constitution in the 1972 CA.

It is quite clear that the 2011 revised state religion petition was different from the original 1988 petition, as 'secularism' was already omitted when the petition was first filed. Multiple verdicts from the apex court during the democratic regime depict the SC's initial concern about the eternally conflicted 'secularism' and 'state religion'. However, the way in which the HCD shut the door on a hearing in 2016

[62] See n 40.

[63] Article 2A.

[64] *Italian Marble Works* (n 17).

[65] *M Saleem Ullah v Bangladesh* (2005) 57 DLR (HCD) 171 (Writ Petition No 4112 of 1999).

[66] The Thirteenth Amendment introduced the non-party caretaker government system (CtG) for holding the parliamentary elections. The legality of this amendment was challenged in *M. Saleem Ullah v Bangladesh* (2005) 57 DLR (HCD) 171, and the HCD rejected the petition. However, on appeal the Appellate Division scrapped the CtG system and declared the Thirteenth Amendment to be void in *Abdul Mannan Khan v Bangladesh* (2012) 64 DLR (AD) 1.

[67] ibid.

was not even reflective of its previous responses of issuing rulings against the government questioning the legality of the state religion. As mentioned above, socio-political factors played a more significant role than the legal questions in the summary rejection of the petition. Also, the ground for rejection (ie, the lack of locus standi) contradicts the SC's decades of established jurisprudence on public interest litigation. The question of locus standi in the public interest writ petition was settled by the SC in 1996[68] and since then, hundreds of petitions have been accepted without calling into question the legal standing of the applicants. Since the SC did not give any reason for the petitioners' lack of legal standing, it set a precarious precedence for judicial review of constitutional amendments. Perhaps the petitioners' counsel Subrata Chowdhury explained it best: 'without a hearing … I've never seen anything like this, at least a proper hearing should have been taken place'.[69]

After the Fifteenth Amendment, the government claimed it had restored the original fundamental principles by bringing back secularism in the preamble and Article 12, although it retained the state religion. While the 'high ideals' of secularism were erased from the Constitution by the military rulers, the democratic Parliament also failed to restore it even after the most pragmatic observation from the apex court in *Italian Marble Works*. The sensitivity of religious issues and the enduring divisions in society have been long ingrained, and were nurtured and used by the colonial rulers and applied in the Partition of India. However, this divisiveness still plays a crucial role in postcolonial Bangladesh. The struggles and sacrifices of the 1971 Liberation War of Bangladesh and the religion-based atrocities by the Pakistani military and their Bengali perpetrators resulted in a consensus in the 1972 CA to adopt a secular constitution. In 1975, several military coup d'etats resulted in the murders of the founding leader of the country, Sheikh Mujibur Rahman, and his whole family at their residence, and four top national leaders in jail custody. This perpetually changed the political circumstances of the postcolonial and newly liberated Bangladesh.[70] Military rulers remained in power for 15 years. During that time, they replaced secularism with 'absolute trust and faith in the almighty Allah', approved religion-based political parties in the Constitution and introduced Islam as the state religion. It took another 20 years for the apex court to declare the military-made constitutional amendments (except state religion) ultra vires and void. However, the legal challenge over state religion remained live for 28 years and was finally fatally scrapped by the SC without a proper hearing even being held.

In 2011, secularism was restored after 34 years. The majority Muslim sentiment and the fear of losing elections conceivably played a vital role in the retention of the state religion. The current Prime Minister (who has held power since 2009) kept

[68] *Dr Mohiuddin Farooque v Bangladesh and Others* [1997] 17 BLD AD 1.
[69] See n 40.
[70] Alam (n 9).

emphasising religious freedom and secularism on the one hand and pronouncing sharp intolerance of anything anti-Islamic on the other hand.[71]

The 'invisible' model of codification of constitutional amendments therefore best fits this hide-and-seek game of secularism and state religion in the Bangladesh Constitution. The provisions of 'absolute trust and faith in the Almighty Allah', the approval of religion-based politics and prioritising Islam over other religions in all state actions are buried by the new footnotes generated by the latest amendment(s). The new footnotes leave no trace of the content of the amended texts. Hence, the apparent 'integrative' codification model performs 'invisibly' when one of the original constitutional principles, 'secularism', was amended multiple times and reshapes the existing 'Islamo-secular'[72] Constitution. The political implication of this 'invisibleness' is crucial. Indeed, it kept the ruling party in power for more than a decade – the same party that led the 1972 CA and adopted the original secular Constitution. It is difficult for new readers without a knowledge of the country's political history to grasp the 'Islamo-secular'[73] conflict in the Constitution. Secularism was first removed by the first military ruler and a decade later the state religion was introduced by the second military ruler. None of this could be traced back to the existing text. The Fifteenth Amendment's endeavour to equalise secularism with the state religion (in other words, balancing the original high ideals with Muslim-majority votes) perhaps best describes the politics of denial. This denial is also reflected in the amendment codification model, and consequently breaks and changes the core constitutional principles. Reiterating Albert's observation on hybrid models and beyond, a constitution not only constitutes a nation and a state, but also develops and deviates over time and accommodates political divergence. Thus, it is hard to limit its growth within selected predefined models.[74] Debates, controversies and amendments of secularism within the text show that the Bangladesh Constitution is a distinctive example of diverse codification models.

V. Concluding Remarks

Religion has long played a major role in South Asian politics. From the postcolonial Pakistan regime to 50 years after liberation, Bangladesh has experienced religion-based social and political turmoil. The constitutional supremacy has been torn up multiple times, resulting in ultra vires amendments destroying the founding principles of the original Constitution. While the amendments are generally codified as per the 'integrative' rule with notations and footnote references, only the latest amendments are integrated. As a result, the constitutional text only records

[71] 'Country to Be Run as per Madinah Charter: PM' *Daily Star* (22 March 2014), https://www.thedailystar.net/country-to-be-run-as-per-madinah-charter-pm-16759.

[72] Chowdhury (n 52).

[73] ibid.

[74] Albert (n 1).

the reference of the Fifteenth Amendment that restored 'secularism', and its abolition by the preceding Fifth Amendment becomes 'invisible'. Thus, the codification model remains a hybrid one conforming to the eternally conflicting presence of 'Islamo-secularism', which has significantly altered the original Constitution's high ideals. The recent addition of the Appendix compiling all previous Amendment Acts is ostensibly executive in nature, which is contradictory to the separation of powers. The apex court's dubious role in the summary rejection of the *State Religion* case drew a big question mark over the prospect of future judicial review(s) of any constitutional amendments. In addition, the Fifteenth Amendment went one step further by adding the 'eternity clause' and making many parts of the Constitution, including secularism and the state religion, unamendable. Electoral democracy, 'majority Muslim' sentiment, the sharp rise of religion-based social atrocities and the political use of religion have all perhaps contributed to the state religion's existence. All of these have contributed to the political denial of acknowledging the conflicts between these two provisions. Also, this denial conforms to the 'invisible' nature of the codification style. At this crossroads, it is quite clear that the conflicting presence of both 'secularism' and 'state religion' is not going to go away anytime soon. Instead, the original 'high ideals of secularism' have lost their purity in the 'Islamo-secular' Constitution.

11

The Integrative Model of Constitutional Amendments in Indonesia as Constitutional Communication

ROSA RISTAWATI AND RADIAN SALMAN

I. Introduction

Indonesia has experienced several constitutional changes: the 18 August 1945 Constitution (the 'Undang-Undang Dasar' (UUD) 1945), the Federal Constitution (the 'Konstitusi Republik Indonesia Serikat' (KRIS)), the Interim Constitution (the 'Undang-Undang Dasar Sementara' (UUDS) 1950), and the 'Undang-Undang Dasar' (UUD) 1945 after the 1959 Presidential Decree. The UUD 1945 after the 1959 Presidential Decree marked the longest period of constitutional regime in Indonesia. The text of the UUD 1945 after the 1959 Presidential Decree was taken from the first ever enactment of the UUD 1945. However, since it was first enacted, it has only been amended in 1999 after the 1998 reform movement as a result of the fall of President Soeharto's regime.

Subsequent amendments were made to the Indonesian Constitution four times: 1999, 2000, 2001 and 2002. This chapter describes how the constitutional amendments are indicated in the Indonesian Constitution. According to the decision of the constitution-maker (the People's Consultative Assembly (MPR)) during the Amendment Session of 1999, the amendments to the Indonesian Constitution are made by addendum via the addition of new sections. In this context, we may note that the amendment model of the Indonesian Constitution is appendative, meaning that the original constitution still exists as it was, but that the amendment is appended at the end of the original text. This method of making changes was chosen by the MPR to preserve the original text. However, since the appendative model was not considered particularly effective for public communication and publicity, the MPR, during the fifth annual session of 2002, decided to compile this model into a single document. In this version, the original provisions were deleted and/or replaced by the new amended provisions. In this context, the model of amendment in Indonesia may be classified as an integrative model.

The integrative model is without any additional information or comments,[1] but the amended provisions may be more easily identified by an asterisk or a star symbol, functioning as identification of the parts which have been amended. For example, if the provision is marked by one asterisk (*), it means that the provision is the result of the first amendment in 1999. This integrative model is more popular and easy to use for the public, even though the formal model of amendment in the Indonesian Constitution is in the form of an addendum, which consists of the original text of the Constitution and is appended with anew provision of the amended Constitution.

II. The Model for Amendment

Indonesia's first Constitution, which was officially promulgated on 18 August 1945, was not amended until 1999. Prior to its amendment, Article 37 of the UUD 1945 provided rules governing its amendment, but did not specifically stipulate whether the model of amendments were required to be indicated in the text or to be addressed as the amendment in the Constitution.[2] The Indonesian Amendment process is relevant to the context of promoting the reformation movement of 1998, which aimed at: (1) the elimination of the dual function of the Republic of Indonesia Army (ABRI); (2) the enforcement of the supremacy of law and respect for human rights, as well as the eradication of corruption, collusion and nepotism; (3) decentralisation and the equality of central government and local government (local autonomy); (4) freedom of the press; and (5) democracy.[3] These points were announced as fundamental changes to the Indonesian Constitution. One year after the reformation movement which brought down the New Order regime under President Soeharto, the MPR started a series of constitutional amendment processes which lasted from 1999 to 2002.[4]

The debates about what was to be amended were indeed interesting during the time of the process in 1999–2002.[5] However, the choice of model in the writing

[1] This is according to the MPR. This model was meant to integrate the original draft of the Constitution and the new draft of the Amendment.

[2] According to Asshiddiqie, art 37 of the Indonesian Constitution is silent on how the Constitution is amended as in the US constitutional tradition. However, Asshiddiqie argues that the original intent of the constitutional-drafter was that the amendments meant a new draft. See Jimly Asshiddiqie, *Pengantar Ilmu Hukum Tata Negara, Jilid* 1, *Mahkamah Konstitusi* RI, 2006, 269–71.

[3] The years after Soeharto's fall (1998) are usually referred to by Indonesians as the Era Reformasi (reform era).

[4] The New Order (Orde Baru) is the term coined by the second Indonesian President Soeharto to characterise his regime as he came to power in 1966 until his resignation in 1998. Soeharto used this term to contrast his rule with that of his predecessor Soekarno (retroactively dubbed the 'Old Order' or Orde Lama). For more on this, see 'Reformation: New Challenges & Changes for Indonesia', https://www.indonesia-investments.com/culture/politics/reformation/item181.

[5] This included the debates on the separation of powers in the presidential system, presidential impeachment and judicial review.

process of the amendment to the Constitution remained a difficult issue on which to reach a consensus amongst the constitutional-makers at the time. Before the amendment, all the factions in the MPR came to a consensus in the first session of 1999 on the following issues: (1) to make no changes in the Preamble to the Constitution of 1945; (2) to closely adhere to the unitary state as a form of the State of the Republic of Indonesia; (3) to strengthen the presidential system in Indonesia; (4) insert the explanatory draft of the UUD 1945 (the Indonesian Constitution) and accommodate the normative aspects of the explanatory draft into the provisions (the body of the Constitution); (5) to adopt the addendum model of the amended constitution.[6] The first and second issues of the consensus emphasised the inflexible nature of the clauses in the Preamble as well as the unitary state. The Preamble to the Indonesian Constitution refers to the centrality of the state ideology of *Pancasila* (the 'five principles') that include: the belief in one supreme God; humanity; national unity; guided democracy by the local wisdom of unanimity arising out of deliberations among representatives; and social justice for the people of Indonesia. The fourth consensus is about the constitutional structure, which concerns the removal of the explanatory draft. Ultimately, the final discussion was on how to indicate the amendment of the Constitution. The debate was about how to clarify the indication of the amended provisions in the Constitution. The questions mentioned above regarding the indications of the texts that have been amended in the Constitution may not seem complicated, but reality proves otherwise. According to Richard Albert, there are four models for codifying constitutional amendments: the appendative model; the integrative model; the invisible model; and the disaggregative model.[7] He emphasises that the appendative model is implemented when the amendments are appended sequentially to the end of the text,[8] which can be seen in the Amended Indonesian Constitution. As the Amendment to the Constitution comprises the First Amendment of 1999, the Second Amendment of 2000, the Third Amendment of 2001 and the Fourth Amendment of 2002, there are thus four appendative drafts as a result of the amendments.

With regard to the integrative model of amendments, the Amended Constitution indicates that the amendments are incorporated directly into the master text of the original Indonesian Constitution. The provisions resulted from the way in which amendments were integrated into the Indonesian Constitution of the UUD 1945: directly into the master text. Although there are four amendments to the Indonesian Constitution, the constitution-maker wanted to preserve the original structure of the Constitution, even though there was a series of amendments. To this end, the appendative model therefore adds a new section to the

[6] *Majelis Permusyawaratan Rakyat Republik Indonesia, Risalah Perubahan Undang-Undang Dasar Negara Republik Indonesia Tahun* 1945 1999–2002, *Tahun Sidang* 1999, *Sekretariat Jenderal MPR RI*, 2008, vi.

[7] Richard Albert, *Constitutional Amendments: Making, Breaking and Changing Constitutions* (Oxford, Oxford University Press, 2019) 230–40.

[8] ibid 231.

Indonesia constitutional structure, while the integrative model amends the existing parts of the original text. Neither 'invisible' model nor the 'disaggregative' model is reflected in the Amended Indonesian Constitution. Indeed, the original version of the Amended Constitution appends its amendments sequentially to the end of the master text (the UUD 1945).

III. From the Appendative Model to the Integrative Model

The Indonesian Constitution is silent on how amendments to the Constitution should be written. Article 37 of the Constitution only stipulates the process of proposing the amendment, the quorum and the voting mechanism for constitutional amendments. Since the Indonesian Constitution does not stipulate the required amendment model, the session of the 1945 Constitution amendment agenda discussed two points concerning an amendment process: which provisions must be prioritised for amendment and how the amendment model is to be carried out. With regard to both points, MPR member Gregorius Harianto, from the Demokrasi Kasih Bangsa Party, proposed changes to issues that were considered to be priorities and the model for changes which was to be made into an addendum.[9] The addendum at this point is to show the changes or the appendix without deleting the original provisions. The addendum model at first did not gain a consensus amongst those who participated in the process and instead stimulated debates. The rationale used in applying the model was taken from the proposal of Kesatuan Kebangsaan Indonesia Party. This was because the Constitution is the fundamental basis of the state and of national life, and because the constitutional documentation is of the utmost importance to the nation. Therefore, the addendum for amendments should reflect the purpose of the philosophical reasons in the Preamble to the Constitution, and the Constitution should be clear, transparent and well documented. Furthermore, it cannot be overlooked that the Constitution, in any event, was one of the matters that was passed down by the founding fathers. Therefore, by the addendum, the historical basis as well as the political goal will not be diminished.[10] With such considerations in mind, it is evident that the constitutional-makers intended to protect the historical foundation conveyed in the previous Constitution as a form of appreciation of the work of the Indonesian founding fathers. Preserving the historical aspects of the Constitution is part of delivering a message to future generations with the expectation that the historical journey of Indonesia will always be an inspiration for the future of Indonesia as a

[9] *Majelis Permusyawaratan Rakyat Republik Indonesia, Risalah Perubahan Undang-Undang Dasar Negara Republik Indonesia Tahun* 1945 1999–2002, *Tahun Sidang* 1999, *Sekretariat Jenderal MPR RI*, 2008, p41.

[10] ibid 670.

nation and as a state. Other than that, the addendum model contains information regarding the background of the Indonesian Constitution-making process, such as the psychological situation and political atmosphere at that time which can then be adopted by upcoming generations. Furthermore, the addendum model was chosen as it was a goal of the constitutional preamble to have a section which could not be amended.[11] With the consensus of an addendum model, the indication of amendments was attached as an appendix to the Constitution. This was affirmed by Harjono from the Indonesian Democratic Party of Struggle (PDIP) during the agenda of the amendment session which discussed the format of the constitutional text as a formal appendix.[12] Asnawi Latif from the Daulat Umat Party argued that the US model of amendment could be adopted, in which the text of the original US Constitution is still preserved and the amendments are appendices to the original text.[13] To this extent, the appendative model was widely supported after consideration of its historical features.

After the amendment of the UUD NRI 1945, the manuscript of the Indonesian constitution consisted of the original and the four amended texts. Between them, the first four amendments resulted in 75 provisions that were changed through deletion or removal, adding new provisions, or modifying each provision or previous institutions, with the following specifics:

(1) The first amendment of the UUD 1945 on 19 October 1999 successfully amended nine articles.
(2) The second amendment of the UUD 1945 on 18 August 2000 amended 25 articles.
(3) The third amendment of the UUD 1945 on 9 November 1999 amended 23 articles.
(4) The fourth amendment of the UUD 1945 on 10 August 2002 amended 13 articles as well as three articles within the Transitory Regulation and two articles within the Additional Regulation.

It is safe to say that by leaving just 16.33 per cent of the UUD 1945 unchanged, the amendment of the Indonesian Constitution in reality resulted in a new constitution. The newly revised Constitution is strengthened by its changes in substance that constitute fundamental matters, such as matters regarding sovereignty, members of representative bodies that are to be elected as a whole without an appointment, the presidential election that is to be done directly, and the formulation of the

[11] The Preamble to the Indonesian Constitution of the UUD 1945 must not be changed because it consists of the basic principles and aims of the Unitary State of the Republic of Indonesia. Article 37, section (5) of the Amendment indirectly recognised *Pancasila* (the five basic principles) as the unamendable clause. See Lutfi Widagdo Eddyono, *Quo Vadis Pancasila sebagai Norma Konstitusi yang Tidak Dapat Diubah, Jurnal Konstitusi. Jurnal Konstitusi Vol. 16 No. 3(2019), p. 587.*

[12] *Tim Penyusun Naskah Komprehensif Proses dan Hasil Perubahan UUD 1945*, Naskah Komprehensif Perubahan Undang-Undang Dasar Negara Republik Indonesia Tahuan 1945, Buku I, Latar Belakang, Proses, dan Hasil Pembahasan, 1999–2002 Sekretariat Jenderal dan Kepaniteraan Mah*kamah Konstitusi Republik Indonesia*, 2010, h. 362.

[13] ibid 128.

Constitutional Court. According to Ismail Sunny, the Chair of the Expert Team which helped the MPR in the process of amendments in 2001, the amendments were made much more broadly compared to the addendum model as they resulted in several new provisions. Thus, in other words, it was done through rewriting the Constitution. This statement has been confirmed by the Ad Hoc Committee Chairman I, Jakob Tobing, who believes that the Indonesian Constitution which resulted from the amendments is a new constitution; he considers that the term 'amendment' is not appropriate for the process of constitutional amendment in Indonesia. He also states that the appropriate term for what happened with the Constitution in Indonesia is renewal.[14] However, the amendment process has been widely implemented and the addendum reflects a political consensus that has been consequently applied in a similar manner. With regard to the addendum, Jakob Tobing asserts that he strongly believes that it would be better not to continue to debate the model of amendment. He further suggests that the process has to be continued.[15] He argues that, even though he thinks the process of amending the Constitution is a renewal process, the process must continue. He suggests that there is no need to hold a serious debate on the addendum/appendative model, since there was a consensus concluded during the first amendment; therefore, there was no need for further discussion about the model of the amendment.

Due to developments during the amendment process, it is evident that the constitution-makers did not foresee that the final result amounted to more than an amendment, resulting instead in a new constitution. Despite realising that the end result is a new constitution, the constitution-makers insisted that the amendment was to be conducted consistent with the addendum model. This was addressed by Soewarko from the PDIP so that another paragraph would be added to Article 37 which would stipulate that the rules surrounding the amendment of the Constitution follow the addendum model. A discussion ensued, but the end result of the amendment does not regulate or indicate any matters regarding how an amendment should be conducted. Consequently, this indicates that the amendment model is within the authority of the constitution-makers.

In the eyes of the constitution-makers, the appendative model provided difficulties when identifying the amended provisions. The MPR asserted that such an approach would bedifficult for readers who wish to know whether a provision within the UUD 1945 had already been amended before, hence causing them to resort to checking every amended text from the first to the fourth. To prevent difficulties and to assist public understanding of the UUD NRI 1945, a constitution which comprises both the articles of the UUD 1945 before the amendment and the four amendment texts was thus formulated. As the agreed amendment constitutes an addendum or the appendative model, this consolidated manuscript is not an official text, but instead is treated as a supplementary manuscript. The aim of this

[14] ibid 536.
[15] ibid 535.

consolidated manuscript is not only to assist the readers, but also to clarify which provisions have been changed and are valid.[16]

The consolidated manuscript indicates that the Amended Constitution no longer adopts the addendum model, but instead is 'integrative', and thus its new provisions are directly inserted into the text without separating the initial text. The integrative model is evident by the asterisk symbol at the end of the clause, which indicates to which amendment (first to fourth) the provision affects. This can be seen in the following example of Article 3 of the Indonesian Constitution:

(1) The People's Consultative Assembly has the authority to amend and to confirm the Constitution. ***)
(2) The People's Consultative Assembly inaugurates the President and/or the Vice President. ***/****)
(3) The People's Consultative Assembly can only discharge the President and/or the Vice President during his/her term of office according to the Constitution. ***/****)

*): first amendment
**): second amendment
***): third amendment
****): fourth amendment

This integrative model provides readers with a way to identify and find which part of the provision has been altered, as well as when it was officially amended. The integrative model of the Indonesian Constitution is based upon the model that has been implemented within the Indian Constitution. However, the Indian Constitution provides a description in the footnotes regarding particular provisions that were amended without providing a symbol, as in the Indonesian model. The integrative model in the Indian Constitution provides much more complex information in its footnotes compared to the Indonesian model, which functions as information to identify when the provision was amended.

Although the appendative model is the official model when it comes to amending the Indonesian Constitution, the integrative model is more popular in the community. At the law faculty, the teaching of constitutional law mostly uses constitutional manuscripts that follow the integrative model. Students are directly confronted with the new Constitution to learn how Indonesia's current constitutional law is structured. Likewise, various civic education teaching materials from elementary schools to high schools contain constitutional material after amendments to the integrative model. This is also often found in the documents of the activities of the state institutions in the context of the dissemination and socialisation of the Constitution to various target groups.

[16] The Drafting of the Indonesian Constitution of the UUD 1945 in one draft was in the beginning as the consensus among the Ad Hoc Committee I of the Working Committee in the MPR in 2001–02 session. Furthermore, the consensus was discussed and concluded by Committee A of the MPR in the annual session of the MPR in 2002 on 9 August 2002 and was delivered in the plenary session of the 5th annual session of the MPR in 2002.

After the series of four amendments, the decision to adopt an integrative model may be analysed as follows. First, the integrative model has the advantage of being a legal communication to the public. The public at large can more quickly find, recognise and understand the changed provisions. The Indonesian Constitution after the amendment is a new constitution due to the radical changes that left little of the original Constitution intact and the number of provisions, which increased by up to 300 per cent compared to the number in the earlier version. Despite these radical changes, the title of the Indonesian Constitution has only changed slightly. The initial Constitution was officially called the 1945 Constitution, while the amended Constitution is called the 'UUD NRI 1945'. The change only adds the words 'State of the Republic of Indonesia', but still uses the designation of 1945. The use of the designation title in 1945 preserves the historical journey of the struggle for independence. With a slight difference in its title, and as in practice people often refer to it only as the 1945 Constitution, it gives the impression that the Indonesian Constitution exists unchanged. For this reason, understanding the content of the changes is something that should be known quickly. Because Indonesia has a population of hundreds of millions, hundreds of regional languages and fundamental differences in sociological conditions, efforts to bring the Constitution to life more quickly have become increasingly relevant. Another prime concern was that the Constitution should not be complicated. The heavy-sounding word 'Constitution' is often addressed as if it is a 'lawyer's paradise' with complicated jargon and not easily understood. Therefore, this integrative model is part of the strategy to get people to know and understand what has become known as the 'New Basic Law'.

Second, the integrative model should be a quick way of satisfying the 'longing' of some people or groups to return to the past under the original Constitution. For Indonesia, this is important because prior to the amendment, the Soeharto regime, which ruled for more than 32 years, used the Constitution as a means to maintain its power. Soeharto always used jargon to implement the Constitution in a pure and consistent manner. This jargon was not intended to change the Constitution because changes to the Constitution are regarded as threats to the regime's power. In 2019. while the idea of a fifth amendment was being considered, Rahmawati, a politician and daughter of Soekarno (the founding father of Indonesia), wanted to return to the original text in accordance with the mandate of the proclamation. By returning to the original Constitution, she expected that the MPR would return to its former position as the highest state institution. Previously in 2015, several national figures gathered in the Coalition of the Movement to Save the Unitary State of the Republic of Indonesia, encouraging the MPR as the constitution-maker to restore the original 1945 Constitution instead of the Amendment Constitution as the basic law in Indonesia. The goal of the coalition was, as a result of the amendments, to regard democracy as liberal democracy, not representative deliberative democracy in one MPR body. Another 2006 movement initiated by former Army Chief of Staff General Tyasno Sudarno also called for a return to the original 1945 Constitution before the amendment. In his view, constitutional amendments were carried out in a hasty and anarchic manner. Substantively, the amendments are influenced by the perspective of liberal democracy, where direct elections may damage the deliberative order of Indonesia. Aspirations and movements that wish to return to the 1945 Constitution (before any amendment) are often promoted by 'old people' who were involved in the New Order regime. The aspiration is also often based on an evaluation of the influence of foreign ideology and politics on the Indonesian ideology and politics. For example, holding direct general elections which no longer reflect the principle of deliberation, as well as the issue of the economic system in the Amended Constitution, are both considered liberal-democracy ideas.

With the integrative model, the next generation of Indonesian people will be discouraged from letting their attention wander and will be encouraged to return to the arrangements before the amendment, without the need to know what the atmosphere of national life was like under the 1945 Constitution, especially under the Soeharto regime. In this context, the integrative model is of course contrary to the purpose of choosing the official amendment model, namely the appendative model intended by the constitution-makers so that the history of the Indonesian Constitution is not forgotten. The appendative model clearly has important aims and benefits, but only for the constitution-makers, the constitutional scholars, the political party leaders and the Constitutional Court.

Third, the integrative model is important for strengthening the commitment of human rights protection in Indonesia. The 1945 Constitution, before the amendments, guaranteed human rights, but was limited in certain aspects, such as freedom of association, assembly, the right to education, the right to a decent life and legal equality. The limited guarantee of human rights in the Indonesian Constitution is relevant to the debate in the process of the 1945 Constitution at the Investigating Committee for Preparatory Work for Independence (Badan Penyelidik Usaha-usaha Persiapan Kemerdekaan (BPUPKI)), especially the debate between Soepomo and Soekarno, who rejected the inclusion of human rights provisions in the Constitution. On the other hand, Hatta and Yamin insisted on having human rights provisions in the Constitution. In the history of the making of the 1945 Constitution, Maria Ulfah, a member of the BPUPKI, questioned why the constitutional draft did not include any human rights provisions, including the basic rights of citizens. This question was supported by several other BPUPKI members. According to Soekarno and Soepomo, the founding fathers, at that time the Indonesian Constitution should be based on the family principle (*asas kekeluargaan*), which is contrary to the principle of liberalism and individualism. Soepomo argued that the Indonesian constitution should be based on what he called an 'integralist state concept' (*staatsidee integralistik*) or the 'family state principle' (*negara kekeluargaan*) in which 'there would be no dualism between state and civil society. There will be no need for basic rights or human rights for the individual against the state, because individuals are organic parts of the state, each with their own position and responsibilities to contribute to the glory of the state'.[17]

[17] David Bourchier, 'Organicism in Indonesian Political Thought' in Megan Thomas, Murad Idris and Liegh Jenco (eds), *The Oxford Handbook of Comparative Political Theory* (Oxford, Oxford University Press, 2019).

Soepomo believed that the concept of human rights originated from Western values, which was assumed to have an individualistic ideology. For him, every country has its own specialities according to the history and the local wisdom of its people. Therefore, he felt, the fundamental principles of the Indonesian state should be adjusted to the social order of people and society.[18] Though Muhammad Hatta and Muhammad Yamin agreed with the family principle, both still proposed that some rights and freedoms would have to be incorporated into the 1945 Constitution in order to guarantee peaceful assembly, to ensure that the citizens would not be afraid to express opinions and to prevent the state from becoming a 'rule of power' state. Serious debates among the founding fathers eventually led to a compromise in which they inserted only seven provisions relating to human rights in the 1945 Constitution.

During the New Order era, the issue of human rights became one of the triggers for the rise of the reform movement which eventually brought down the Soeharto regime. Under the New Order's authoritarian regime, freedom of association and assembly were not protected, as shown by the policy of limiting the number of political parties to three. A new policy banned certain mass-media, including *Tempo* and two other independent mass-circulation media (*Detik* and *Editor*), in 1989 after an article criticising the government's decision to purchase 39 former East German naval warships proved to be the last straw. This marked a reduction of freedom of the press in Indonesia. The New Order government argued that the report by *Tempo* on indications of corruption in the purchase of warships from former East Germany could endanger national stability. As a result, in the 1989 incident, known as the Talangsari case, there were 130 killings, 77 people evicted from their homes, 53 imprisoned and 46 cases of torture. At the time, Indonesia's bad record of human rights violations made the constitution-makers aware of the need to regulate the recognition and guarantee of human rights in amendments. The series of four amendments shows an improvement over the previous constitution in terms of building a government system in Indonesia, and one of the four amendments mainly relates to the widespread provisions of human rights in the Constitution. From the perspective of human rights protection, the 1945 Constitution is much more comprehensive than the Constitution before the amendment. While the Constitution before the amendments contained only seven articles regarding human rights (the right to work and a decent life for humanity, freedom of association and assembly and expression of thoughts orally and in writing, guarantees of freedom of religion and belief, and the right to teaching, the right to access to natural resources), the Amended Constitution contains at least 17 articles on human rights.

[18] Soepomo argued that the state should be seen as a family in which the government serves a benevolent paternal role in guiding its children (the people) to the right choice. This is why in the integralist conception, the government is not requiring the limitation of power in regards to maintaining public order.

With the integrative model, the constitution as a document containing enumerated rights can be quickly known to the public. In the post-amendment democratic transitional situation, public understanding of human rights in the Constitution had an impact on the state's approach to human rights. The state does not readily use repressive measures against public criticism and uses legal mechanisms as a solution to human rights violations. For the public, understanding the protection of human rights is the beginning of efforts to defend their constitutional rights and therefore it will contribute to awareness of the importance of the Constitution in the democratic transition from post-authoritarian regimes.[19] This is demonstrated by the 1,539 cases of judicial review that have been registered with the Constitutional Court between 2003 and 2022.[20]

The indications of amendments to the Indonesian Constitution officially follow the appendative model, implemented as additional sections in the text of the Constitution, and not as amendments integrated into the existing text. The model was agreed upon by the constitution-makers for the following purposes. The first goal is to maintain the history of the development of the Indonesian Constitution and especially to define the Constitution as a series of long struggles in the Indonesian nation for independence. The birth of the first Indonesian Constitution was the result of the struggle to break free from colonialism and occupation, as stated in the preamble:

> Independence is the right of all nations and therefore colonialism in the world must be abolished, because it is not in accordance with humanity and justice. And the struggle for the movement towards Indonesian independence has now come to a time of joy to guide the Indonesian people safely and healthily to the threshold of the independence of the Indonesian State.

In this context, it was believed that the appendative model would not undermine the history of the Indonesian Constitution.

Moreover, the model reflects the outcome of the efforts of appreciation and reflection of the political will of the founding fathers of Indonesia. Appreciation in this case is for the makers of the Constitution as founding fathers, most of whom were freedom fighters at that time. The makers of the constitution wished to express their gratitude to the founding fathers by referencing the original title of the constitution, ie, mentioning 1945 with a slight addition of the phrase 'State of the Republic of Indonesia'. In addition to appreciation, the choice of reflection indicated in the appendative model in the Indonesian Constitution describes it as the best achievement of its time, having progressed along the way through various failures and mistakes in terms of its provisions. In this context, Richard Albert

[19] See Ran Hirschl, 'The Political Origins of Judicial Empowerment through Constitutionalization: Lessons from Four Constitutional Revolutions' (2000) 25(1) *Law and Social Inquiry* 91, 93. The constitutionality of rights is part of the development which is known as the 'zaman hak' (the age of rights). See Norberto Bobbio, 'The Age of Rights', as quoted in Martin Loughlin, *The Idea of Public Law* (New York, Oxford University Press, 2003) 2.

[20] M Laica Marzuki, 'Konstitusionalisme dan Hak Asasi Manusia' (2011) 8(4) *Jurnal Konstitusi* 479, 484.

argues that 'the supplementary model makes the constitution a public record of the many mistakes of a country, a living history lesson both from past mistakes and times when the extraordinary mobilization of people has tried to correct their failures'.[21] However, in the amendments to the 1945 Constitution, criticism and condemnation were not levelled against the previous Constitution, instead being directed more towards the ruling regime which had manipulated the Constitution in order to maintain its hold on power. The constitution-makers and the public thought that no matter how good a constitution is, it will have bad consequences because those who are called to manage it are not always honourable. The use of the appendative model for reflective purposes also sends a message to future generations, in the hope that they will not repeat the same mistakes in terms of constitutional development.

However, in the end, because the series of four amendments to the Indonesian Constitution resulted in significant changes in terms of the substance and number of provisions, the previous Constitution seems to have been deleted, except for the fundamental aspects (namely, the preamble, unitary state, flag and language). The results of this series of amendments have indeed been criticised for having fundamental weaknesses caused by the conceptual ambiguity in the basic consensus of the MPR members, as well as for shifting the paradigm from democratisation to changes in the system of government. As a result, there are many incoherent principles, rules and norms in the Amended 1945 Constitution, a situation which creates difficulties in terms of implementing the Constitution. However, for Indonesia, the results of the amendment to the 1945 Constitution are still an achievement and, more importantly, are major events in the history of the Indonesian constitutional development, considering that similar efforts in 1956–59 failed. The amendments to the 1945 Constitution have been effectively enforced, but they have not been able to create an effective government for the purpose of public welfare. In addition, several aspects of the amendments to the 1945 Constitution have strengthened the commitment to the constitutional principles in the Indonesian Constitution. Therefore, there is not much criticism regarding the choice of the appendative model as an official consensus in the constitution-making process in Indonesia, nor in regarding the integrative model as an auxiliary (unofficial) text to make it easier in terms of understanding the contents of the amendments. To this extent, the purpose of incorporating amendments into the integrative model does not cause difficulties for the constitution-makers in relation to formulating the Constitution in the integrative model.

The Indonesian case may be different from Richard Albert's view of the integrative or invisible model, where according to him 'it requires a close familiarity with the existing constitution, how it has been interpreted in court and how political actors have used it in public discourse, and also a full understanding of the amendments'.[22] In the context of the interpretation of the Constitution, particularly

[21] Albert (n 7) 244.
[22] ibid 251.

by the Constitutional Court in a judicial review, the integrative model does not present any problems in relation to the interpretive approach used by judges. Since many new provisions revoke and replace the old provisions with a new conceptual basis, this does not mean that it is relevant to trace the interpretation of a provision from the previous Constitution. The new provisions which contain human rights or constitutional rights of individuals and citizens do not require interpretation by looking at the relationship with the previous provisions. However, the interpretation of the Constitution in judicial review may lead to an informal constitutional change through the decisions of the Constitutional Court. In this context, this is not due to the problems of coherence with the previous provisions that were not amended. The informal changes may merely be based on the Constitutional Court's decision – for example, about the competence of the Constitutional Court in judicial review. As according to Article 24C, paragraph (1), the Constitutional Court has the competence to adjudicate in the first and final process, the judgment of which is final, to review laws against the Constitution, whereas in practice the constitutional judges ruled that the Court also has the competence to review the government regulations in lieu of laws (the Emergency Laws).

The integrative model, which was originally intended as a complementary text and a model for legal communication, has become more popular, not only in society, but also in legal academia and political discussions. It has also acted as a reference for the law-makers in Indonesia. Consequently, the original text has been ignored and remains as a monument.

IV. Conclusion

The challenge for the 'new Constitution' in Indonesia is the post-amendments regime, not the amendments or the renewal process. Whenever the constitution-makers find that the results of the amendments have changed the Constitution, a strategy is needed to disseminate, communicate and publicise the 'new Constitution'. In a democratic transition situation such as that experienced by Indonesia after the post-Soeharto era, the constitutionalism of human rights must be maintained by ensuring that people are aware of their human rights. The integrative model is an 'innovation' to indicate that the Indonesian amendments have been an important contribution to the constitutional development in Indonesia. The model also discourages the 'romantic' intention to return to the pre-amendments period (which nowadays is still being promoted by the older generation and those who are disappointed with the results of the amendments). However, the appendative model that has been agreed upon by the constitution-makers is still beneficial for the public in terms of learning from history, giving both a record of a state's failures, such as the failures of previous regimes, and a record of the country's successes, such as the moments when the extraordinary mobilisations of people have tried to make amends for those failures.

12

The Amalgamation of Amendment Codification Models in Ethiopia

A Move Towards an Unwritten Constitution

ZELALEM ESEHTU DEGIFIE

I. Introduction

The Ethiopian constitutional framework comprises the federal constitution and 11 state constitutions. The current Federal Democratic Republic of Ethiopia (FDRE) Constitution, adopted in 1995, contains 106 articles written in a single master text document. It has been formally amended twice in three decades. At the state level, all 11 constituent units of the Ethiopian federation have adopted their own constitutions. Most of these state constitutions have been changed more than once since 2001.[1]

The language of the state constitutions is not precise regarding the distinction between constitutional revision and amendment. All the state constitutions use the word 'revision' to indicate the 2001 constitutional changes which were substantial in their content and broad in their scale. Meanwhile, they use 'amendment' to refer to the 2005 and 2006 constitution-level changes that were relatively not extensive in terms of their scope. However, both the revision and the amendment of state constitutions have been carried out by following the same methods and procedures. In this context, therefore, the relative scale and substantiality of the constitutional changes make a distinction between revision and amendment. Similarly, throughout this chapter, I use the term 'revision' to signify the 2001 large-scale constitutional changes that brought significant alternations to the state constitutions.

[1] Nine of them were revised from 2001 to 2004 and three of these revised state constitutions have been amended more than once since 2005.

The FDRE and state constitutions record their constitutional changes in various ways. Constitutional amendments to the FDRE Constitution have not been published at all, in contrast to the various ways in which state constitutions have recorded their own constitutional changes. For instance, most state constitutions incorporate their changes by replacing the old texts with new ones, albeit without annotations in the constitutions. In addition, some of their constitutional amendments are found in separate laws that have constitutional status.

I have in the past explored the politics and operation of constitutional amendment in Ethiopia, with a focus on both federal and state constitution.[2] However, until now, legal scholars and politicians have had little concern with how and where constitutional amendments are codified. Recent amendment proposals and debates on constitutional changes pay scant attention to questions involving how to codify constitution-level changes, where to locate amendments in the constitutional text and how to keep current the constitutional texts of the Ethiopian federation. The codification of constitutional amendments, as a topic, has hardly received any attention in the Ethiopian constitutional law scholarship.

As Richard Albert has rightly observed, the problem is global. Accordingly, how and where to codify constitutional amendments is a neglected – though often pivotal – issue in constitutional design.[3] Ethiopia is no exception. The way in which the constitutions of the Ethiopian federation codify amendments has far-reaching legal, political and social consequences affecting the judiciary, the legislature and the citizenry.[4]

Against this backdrop, this chapter examines Ethiopia's approach to amendment codification and its implications for constitutional politics, the rule of law and the public accessibility of the text. The chapter is intended both as an addition to the scholarly literature on the subject and as a contribution to initiate and provoke a national debate in Ethiopia about the codification of amendments. The chapter is divided into five main sections. Following this introduction, section II discusses the amendment codification models of the federal and state constitutions in Ethiopia. In particular, it examines the FDRE Constitution and the constitutions of the regional states in light of the various codification models. Section III assesses the relevant constitution-making and legislative records in order to understand the historical foundations of Ethiopia's choice of amendment codification model at both the federal and state levels. The implications of these models for the writtenness of the constitutions, rule of law and constitutionalism are examined in section IV. Finally, section V closes with some concluding remarks.

[2] See, Zelalem Eshetu Degifie, 'The Politics of Constitutional Amendment in Ethiopia: Issues Worth Considering' (2019) 8 *Haramaya Law Review* 1.

[3] Richard Albert, *Constitutional Amendments: Making, Breaking and Changing Constitutions* (Oxford, Oxford University Press, 2019) 229–60.

[4] ibid.

II. Amendment Codification Models of the Current Federal and State Constitutions

A. The Codification Model of the FDRE Constitution

Article 98 of the FDRE Constitution previously conferred concurrent legislative power over taxation to federal and state governments. Accordingly, both levels of government would levy and collect the specified taxes jointly.[5] The first amendment has replaced this arrangement with a revenue-sharing scheme that allows the specified taxes to be determined and administered by the federal government while the regional states share the proceeds from it.[6] The actual amendment appears and reads as follows:

Article 98

Concurrent Power of Taxation

1. Profit, sales, excise, and personal income taxes on enterprises jointly established by the federal government and regional states;
2. Taxes on the profit of companies and on dividends due to shareholders; and
3. Taxes on incomes derived from large scale mining and all petroleum and gas operations and royalties on such operation shall be levied by the federal government, and the proceeds will be divided between the federal government and states in pursuance of a formula determined by the House of Federation as provided under Article 62(7) of the constitution. The federal government may delegate its power of tax collection to regional states.[7]

The second constitutional amendment changed Article 103(5) of the FDRE Constitution, which sets a 10-year periodic interval for holding a national population census. The amendment allows the original 10-year timeframe to be postponed as necessary by the joint decision of the two chambers in the bicameral national legislature, namely the House of Peoples' Representatives and the House

[5] The original text of Article 98 of the FDRE Constitution reads as follows:

Article 98

Concurrent Power of Taxation

(1) The Federal Government and the States shall jointly levy and collect profit, sales, excise, and personal income taxes on enterprises they jointly establish.
(2) They shall jointly levy and collect taxes on the profit of companies and on dividends due to shareholders.
(3) They shall jointly levy and collect taxes on incomes derived from large-scale mining and all petroleum and gas operations and royalties on such operations.

[6] The Minutes of 2nd Joint Meeting at the 2nd term of Years of the House of Peoples' Representatives and House of Federation (10 April 1997, Addis Ababa, Ethiopia, available at the Archive of HOPR).

[7] ibid.

of Federation.[8] The amendment added a new provision to Article 103(5) of the Constitution, which reads as follows:

> However, when the House of Peoples' Representatives and the House of Federation in a joint session ascertained the existence of a force majeure to conduct the National Population and Housing Census, this period of ten-year may be prolonged as necessary.[9]

Neither the first nor the second amendment has been incorporated into the text of the FDRE Constitution. The amended provisions still appear in their original form and content, meaning that the original text of the FDRE Constitution has not been changed and its original words remain untouched. What is more, the constitutional amendments have not yet been published in the *Negarit Gazeta*, which is an official newsletter for the publication of federal laws in Ethiopia.[10] In the Ethiopian context, the publication of laws in the Federal *Negarit Gazeta* is a means for the official promulgation of laws.[11] It is more a matter of practicality and judicial notice than of validity.[12] As a legal matter, publication is not necessary because amendment proposals acquire constitutional status upon their approval at the joint secession of the two Houses without further requirement of publication and official promulgation.

The first and second amendments will not lose their constitutional status and effect by the mere fact of being unpublished in the Federal *Negarit Gazeta*. They are now officially part of the FDRE Constitution, though they exist in a separate document, in this case only in the parliamentary records.[13] The two amendments are unpublished parts of the FDRE Constitution that do not appear in the single codified document known as the Constitution.

In light of this, we can describe the model of amendment codification in the FDRE Constitution as being closest to what Albert has labelled the 'disaggregative' model of amendment codification, which refers to the practice of recording constitutional changes in distinct legislative enactments or separately codified constitutional laws.[14] Yet the first and second amendments are neither ordinary legislation nor constitutional laws separately codified in the official *Negarit Gazeta*. The Ethiopian approach therefore departs from the commonly known disaggregative models evident in the UK and Italy.[15] The amendments to the FDRE Constitution do not appear either in separate law, or in detached constitutional acts, or even in the official register of laws. They are nowhere to be found as distinctly published enactments. In effect, constitutional amendments to the

[8] The 1st Joint Meeting at the 5th term of Years of the House of Peoples' Representatives and House of Federation (5 October 2004, Addis Ababa, Ethiopia, available at the Archive of the HOPR).

[9] ibid.

[10] Proclamation No 3/1995, Federal Negarit Gazeta Establishment, *Federal Negarit Gazeta*, Year 1, No 3, Addis Ababa, 22 August 1995.

[11] FDRE Constitution, art 71(2).

[12] Proclamation No 3/1995, arts 2 and 3; FDRE Constitution, art 57.

[13] See the Minutes of the 2nd Joint Meeting (n 6) and the 1st Joint Meeting (n 8).

[14] Albert (n 3).

[15] ibid.

FDRE Constitution have been decodified. Their decodification gives them a fuzzy separate existence, making them the lost parts of the FDRE Constitution. Nonetheless, they are still higher laws that enjoy legal supremacy and exert the preclusive effect of negating acts to the contrary. The decodification approach of the FDRE Constitution therefore bears some resemblances to the disaggregative model of amendment codification while also revealing unique features.

B. The Hybrid Model of Codifying the Amendments of State Constitutions

i. The Tri-modal Approach

There is an Ethiopian state constitution that uses all three major models of amendment codification. The first Constitution of the Regional State of Oromia (CRSO) was promulgated in 1995 and contained a preamble and 99 articles organised into 12 chapters.[16] It was formally amended for the first time in 1997.[17] Since then, it has been substantially revised in 2001, and then amended in 2005 and 2006.[18]

The first amendment was published as 'The Oromia Regional State Constitution (Amendment) Proclamation No 21/1997' in the *Megeleta Oromia*, which is an official newsletter for the publication of state laws in the Oromia regional state.[19] The amendment repealed Articles 78(3) and 86(3) of the CRSO and replaced them with new texts. It also added a new sub-article (4) under Articles 78 and 86 of the CRSO.[20] However, the original texts of the CRSO were not renovated accordingly. The changes had not been incorporated into the master text of the Constitution. As a result, until the 2001 revision, the CRSO remained in its original form. Readers could find and know the constitutional changes from a separate law, the Oromia Regional State Constitution (Amendment) Proclamation No 21/1997, which stands apart from the text of the ORSC. Therefore, in this way, the CRSO has adopted the dissaggregative model of codifying constitutional amendments.

The CRSO was substantially revised in 2001. The revision changed the original text and the amending Proclamation No 21/1997. It also yielded a single document, known as 'the Oromia Regional State Revised Constitution (ORSRC)

[16] Proclamation No 1/1995, Constitution of the Regional State of Oromia, *Megeleta Oromia*, 21 August 1995, Finfine.

[17] Proclamation No 21/1997, the Oromia Regional State Constitution (Amendment), *Megeleta Oromia*, 9 November 1997, Finfine.

[18] Proclamation No 46 of 2001, A Proclamation to Enforce the Oromia Regional State Revised Constitution of 2001, *Megeleta Oromia*, 12 July 2000, Finfine (hereinafter ORSRC of 2001); Proclamation No 94/2005, A Proclamation Issued to Amend Proclamation No 46/2001 the Revised Constitution of Oromia Regional State Proclamation; Proclamation No 108/2006, A Proclamation Issued to Amend the Revised Constitution of Oromia Regional State No 46/2001.

[19] Proclamation No 21/1997 (n 17).

[20] ibid art 2.

of 2001' containing 113 articles.[21] The text of the revised constitution has no annotations and marks about what has been changed in the Constitution.

For instance, Article 6 of the original CRSO text stated that 'Finfine shall be the Capital City of the Regional State of Oromia', while the revision changed the capital city to Adama by rewriting it as 'Adama shall be the Capital City of the Regional State of Oromia' in the ORSRC of 2001. The ORSRC of 2001 further contains several provisions such as Articles 3, 4, 48, 49 and 50 to name but a few, which have been renovated with additional stipulations and sub-articles, albeit without indicating the nature of the changes made to these texts. Consequently, these changes are unnoticable without a comparative reading of the original and the revised texts of the state constitution. We can therefore conclude that the ORSRC of 2001 uses the invisible model to codify the 2001 constitutional changes.

The ORSRC of 2001 was subsequently amended in 2005 and 2006. These amendments were published in the official *Gazeta* of the regional state as Proclamation No 94/2005 and Proclamation No 108/2006 respectively.[22] The 2005 amendment changed 19 lists of constitutional items ranging from the nomenclature to the relocation of the capital city of the regional state.[23] The 2006 amendment, approved as Proclamation No 108/2006, amended Articles 82(3) and 94(3) of the ORSRC of 2001. These amending proclamations were appended sequentially at the end of the Constitution without altering the internal form of the text of the Constitution.[24] In that way, the ORSRC of 2001 also replicates the appendative model. Overall, the state constitution of Oromia merges the disaggregative, invisible and appendative models for codifying its amendments.

ii. The Dual-Modal Approach

The mixed model of codifying amendments is a constitutional feature of other regional states too. All regional state constitutions incorporate the 2001–04 revisions in their texts, but without leaving any indications regarding what in the texts has been changed or where the changes appear in the constitutions. In this manner, they reflect the invisible model of codification.[25] Additionally, they codify the 2005 and 2006 amendments using the disaggregative model of codification.

For instance, the Revised Constitution of the Amhara National Regional State (Revised Constitution of the ANRS) was amended in 2005 and 2006. The first amendment was ratified by the regional state council and the lower local councils on 22 July 2005, and was later published in the *Zikre-Hig Gazeta*, which is an official newsletter for the publication of state laws in the Amhara regional

[21] Proclamation No 46 of 2001 (n 18).
[22] Proclamation No 94/2005 (n 18); Proclamation No 108/2006 (n 18).
[23] ibid.
[24] Oromia National Regional State, the Oromia Regional State Revised Constitution Proclamation No 46/2001 with its Amendment Proclamation No 94/2005 and No 108/2006, 8 September, Finfine.
[25] Albert (n 3).

state, as Proclamation No 112/2005.[26] This amendment repealed Articles 54(2), 76(3), 89(2), and 100(2) of the revised Constitution and replaced them with new provisions.[27] In the same way, the second amendment that was approved as Proclamation No 127/2006 changed Articles 89 and 100 of the revised Constitution by adding new texts.[28] However, these changes have not been incorporated into the present text of the Constitution of the ANRS. They can be found only in separate laws (Proclamation No 112/2005 and Proclamation No 127/2006) that have their own distinct existence. Therefore, the Revised Constitution of the ANRS mirrors the disaggregative model of codifying constitutional amendments.

The same trend has been followed by the Revised Constitution of Tigray National Regional State (the revised Constitution of the TNRS), which uses the invisible model to codify the 2001 constitutional revisions, and the disaggregative model for codifying the subsequent changes made through Proclamation No 105/2005 and Proclamation No 98/2006.[29] These amending proclamations exist separately and the actual text of the revised Constitution remains unchanged.

Therefore, the revised state constitutions combine the invisible and disaggregative models to codify their amendments. Unlike the ORSRC of 2001, they do not append the amending proclamations at the end of the texts.

III. The Ethiopian Choice of Codification Models: Probing the Records

A. The Model of the FDRE Constitution: Deliberate or Accidental?

The minutes of the constitutional assembly is the only official and historical record available for the creation of the FDRE Constitution. As these sources reveal, the matter of amendment codification was not discussed as an issue at the moment of constitution-making.[30] However, this fact alone does not give a blank cheque to codify amendments unsystematically. Instead, it may indicate that either the problem was not clear to the assembly at that time or it deferred the matter to be

[26] Proclamation No 112/2005, A Proclamation Issued to Approve the First Amendment of the Revised Constitution of the Amhara National Regional State, 22 July 2005, Bahir Dar.

[27] ibid art 2.

[28] Proclamation No 127/2006, A Proclamation Issued to Approve the Second Amendment of the Revised Constitution of the Amhara National Regional State, 8 April 2006, Bahir Dar, art 2.

[29] Proclamation No 45/2002, Tigray Regional State Constitution, *Negarit Gazeta National Government of Tigray*, Mekele, 2002; Proclamation No 98/2006, A Proclamation Issued to Amend the Revised Constitution of Tigray National Regional State Ratified through Proclamation 45/2002, 24 March 2006, Mekele; Proclamation No 105/2006, A Proclamation Issued to Amend the Revised Constitution of Tigray National Regional State Ratified through Proclamation No 45/2002.

[30] Minutes of Constitutional Assembly vols 1–6 (available at the Archive of the HOPR, Addis Ababa, 1994).

resolved by subsequent leaders. Whatever was in their minds, one thing that is clear from the constitutional assembly discussions is that the framers did not intend to open the door for the frequent and intrusive modification of the Constitution, whether in content or form.

The first instance where this was shown was the constitutional assembly's debate on the amending formula.[31] The assembly strongly argued for stringent amendment procedures for the purpose of preserving the Constitution across generations.[32] The main objective of these very rigorous procedures, as noted in the records, was to keep the Constitution, as much as possible, in its original state.[33] The second instance is the political outlook of the Ethiopian People's Revolutionary Democratic Front (EPRDF), the main architect of the FDRE Constitution that dominated the constitution-making process.[34] It considered the Constitution as the manifestation of the covenant of the nations, nationalities and peoples of Ethiopia, and as the symbol of the new nation.[35] The EPRDF argued for the preservation of the Constitution by any means. In light of this background, a codification model gesturing to the political community that the Constitution remains open to change could not be expected from the assembly. Therefore, the appendative model would have been chosen had the matter been debated in the constitution-making assembly.[36]

The first and second constitutional amendments are clear enough in their language and intent about the alteration of Articles 98 and 103(5) of the FDRE Constitution.[37] For instance, the first amendment proposal approved by the amending bodies stated that 'this amendment proposal is presented to repeal and replace Article 98 of the Constitution by this new provision' and further rewrote the content and form of the new texts of Article 98 that substitute the original ones.[38] In the same way, the resolution presented to the legislatures for extending the timeline of the national population census plainly stated the new text should be added at the end of the existing Article 103(5) of the Constitution.[39] All these parliamentary records confirm that the amending bodies of the time decided not only on the content of the amendments, but also on the mode of codification. Accordingly, the language of the legislatures suggests that the invisible model ought to be used to codify the amendments in the present text of the FDRE Constitution.

[31] Minutes of Constitutional Assembly vol 5 (available at the Archive of the HOPR, Addis Ababa, 1994).

[32] ibid. See also Zelalem Eshetu Degifie, 'Apprising Constitutional Amendment in Ethiopia: Vexing Questions and Qualms' (2014) 5 *Bahir Dar University Journal of Law* 314.

[33] ibid.

[34] Tsegaye Regassa, 'The Making and Legitimacy of the Ethiopian Constitution: Towards Bridging the Gap Between Constitutional Design and Constitutional Practice' (2010) 23 *Afrika Focus* 85.

[35] ibid.

[36] Albert (n 3).

[37] See the Minutes of the 2nd Joint Meeting (n 6) and the 1st Joint Meeting (n 8).

[38] ibid.

[39] ibid.

Nonetheless, the FDRE Constitution decodifies its constitutional amendments. The amendments are neither incorporated into the actual text of the constitution nor officialised through publication in the Federal *Negarit Gazeta*. The decodification of the amendments could be the result of the political views of the then-ruling party, the EPRDF. The political environment that surrounded the Constitution during the reign of EPRDF was not hospitable to the codification of amendments. During this period, constitutional reforms were not discussed seriously. For EPRDF and the ruling elites, the Constitution was regarded as 'near to perfect, untouchable and sacred'. They viewed the FDRE Constitution as the 'Ark of the Covenant' that was too sacred to be touched.[40] In effect, the EPRDF was suspicious of any attempt to change the Constitution. Given this general disposition, it is not surprising that codifying the two amendments was doomed at the outset by the EPRDF for preserving the alleged sacredness of the Constitution and the finality of the text in the eyes of the political community. As such, it did not utter a word about the amendments publicly, let alone go so far to codify them. Nevertheless, the amended provisions practically govern the affairs of the nation. For instance, the national population census has been postponed more than three times since 2005 on the basis of the second constitutional amendment.[41] The first constitutional amendment also governs the administration of concurrent sources of revenue.[42] Therefore, by decodifying these changes, the FDRE Constitution could secure the appearance of perfection in the content and finality in the form of the Constitution.

B. The Models of the State Constitutions: By Default or Design?

Almost all state constitutions contain a ratifying proclamation on their front pages.[43] It is by virtue of these proclamations that the state councils adopted the codified texts of the revised state constitutions.[44] Modern codification, as Gunther A Weiss noted, derives its authority from the exercise of the legislature.[45] In light of this, the ratification proclamations are proof of the authoritativeness of the revised constitutional texts. As these proclamations declared, the state councils adopt the revised state constitutions after examining the texts, both in content and form,

[40] See Degifie (n 2).

[41] Interview with Seifu G/Mariam, Senior Legal Advisor to the Speaker of the HOPR (Addis Ababa, Ethiopia, 2 May 2020).

[42] Tom Harris and Edris Seid, '2019/20 Survey of the Ethiopian Tax System' (Institute for Fiscal Studies, March 2021).

[43] Proclamation No 59/2001, A Proclamation Issued to Provide for the Approval of the 2001 Revised Constitution of the Amhara National Regional State; Proclamation No 46/2001, A Proclamation to Enforce the Oromia Regional State Revised Constitution of 2001.

[44] ibid art 2.

[45] Gunther A Weiss, 'The Enchantment of Codification in the Common-Law World' (2000) 25 *Yale Journal of International Law* 437, 456.

thoroughly.[46] This suggests their approval for not only what has been changed, but also the way the changes have been incorporated into the texts of the revised constitutions. In other words, they authorised the invisible model of amendment codification for revisions from 2001 to 2004.

The same invisible model was implicitly endorsed in the subsequent proclamations that amended the revised state constitutions in 2005 and 2006. These amending proclamations envisaged changing the text of the Constitution by means of substitutions and insertions.[47] The former intended to replace the existing texts of the Constitution with new texts and the latter aimed to add new texts to the end of the existing provisions of the Constitution. A careful reading of these proclamations reveals that the state councils approved the form and content of the amendments, including the wordings, placement and sequencing of the new texts in the Constitution.[48] They approved the (re)numbering and rephrasing of the new texts that repealed or replaced the old ones, and inserted or added to the existing texts of the Constitution. These amendment proclamations are suggestive of the invisible model of codification. However, the state constitutions hardly incorporate the amendments accordingly into the actual text of the constitutions. This, by default, results in the disaggregative model of codification.

C. The Virtues and Limitations of the Ethiopian Models of Codification

i. The Style of Appending Amendments: Does it Matter?

The ORSRC of 2001 appended the whole body of the amending proclamations at the end of the master text of the Constitution.[49] The internal form of the state constitution remains unaltered and its existing words are intact. Unlike the US model, the appended proclamations clearly indicate the repealed provisions of the ORSRC of 2001 and the placement of the new texts. For instance, Article 2(3) of the amending Proclamation No 94/2005 declared that Article 6 of the ORSRC of 2001 has been amended (repealed and replaced) as 'Finfine shall be the Capital City of the Regional State of Oromia'. Additionally, the appended amending legislation changes the ORSRC of 2001 by adding new texts to the existing provisions of the revised Constitution. For instance, the 2005 amendment added a new proviso on Article 57(3)(h) of the ORSRC of 2001 to grant the president of the regional state the power to 'dissolve any district council which it believes has endangered the Region's Constitution'.[50]

[46] Proclamation No 59/2001 (n 43) art 2; Proclamation No 46/2001 (n 18) art 2.

[47] Proclamation No 94/2005 (n 18); Proclamation No 108/2008 (n 18); Proclamation No 112/2005 (n 26); Proclamation No 127/2006 (n 28).

[48] ibid.

[49] Oromia National Regional State (n 24).

[50] ibid.

In effect, the amendments have changed the meaning of the existing texts of the revised Constitution directly and expressly. The appended amending proclamations clearly show the extent of the changes and the effect of the amendments on the existing constitutional provisions. They clearly indicate the repealed texts of the Constitution, and the new texts substituted and/or inserted into the Constitution. As a result, the appendative model revealed by the ORSRC of 2001 avoids the need to reconcile the meaning of the amendments with the old texts of the Constitution and thereby mitigates the problem of interpretation that has been common in the appendative model elsewhere.[51] However, the model has created its own problem of systematisation. Appending the whole body of the amending proclamations at the end of the constitutional text looks like a compilation instead of codification.[52] And while it may allow readers to access the constitutional rules as one-stop shopping, the problem of obsolescence remains unresolved, as some of the text in the existing Constitution has effectively lost legal validity as a result of the appended new texts that supersede the old constitutional rules. Consequently, the model cannot present a clearly consistent whole of constitutional rules and principles.[53] It then cannot promote the internal coherence of the text of the Constitution. Externally, the constitutional text looks like a collection of old and in some cases outdated proclamations, lacking completeness.[54]

ii. The Signposts of Constitutional Changes: Naming and Prefixes

The prefaced ratification proclamations notify readers about the revisions of the old texts of the state constitutions. Moreover, they state the justification of the constitutional revision that was to clarify the separation of powers and to ensure the accountability of regional state organs.[55] The nomenclature of the constitutional texts – for instance, 'the 2001 Revised Constitution of the Amhara National Regional State' – also tells readers about the year of revision. As such, the nomenclature of the state constitutions together with the prefaced proclamations give readers information as to the fact that the constitutions have been altered, but not in a way that enables them to identify what in the text has been changed or where those changes appear in the actual text of the constitutions. Unlike the Irish invisible model of amendment codification, the regional states' approach does not provide the list of amending acts, along with their content and purpose on the front pages of the constitution.[56] As a consequence, knowing what has been amended and where the change has been placed in the text of the constitution becomes an awkward undertaking for all, even for researchers and lawyers.

[51] Albert (n 3).
[52] Weiss (n 45).
[53] ibid.
[54] ibid.
[55] Proclamation No 59/2001 (n 43); Proclamation No 46/2001 (n 43).
[56] Albert (n 3).

The list of the revised texts and their location within the constitution cannot easily be known. The revised state constitutions demonstrate the inherent limitation of the invisible model of amendment codification.

By comparison, the ORSRC of 2001 is relatively better. The most recently codified constitutional text has a table of contents of amendments on its opening page. This contains the names (short titles) of the amending proclamations. However, the table of contents lacks detail and it is incomplete in the sense that it does not give readers sufficient clues about what has been changed in the text of the ORSRC of 2001. Additionally, the designation of the newly codified constitution, 'the Oromia Regional State Revised Constitution Proclamation No. 46/2001, with its Amendment Proclamation No. 94/2005 and No. 108/2006', is more informative relative to the designation of other state constitutions.[57] These signposts in tandem with the appended proclamations would allow readers to better identify the changes made in the Oromia state constitution.

IV. The Implications of the Ethiopian Codification Models

A. The Loss of Constitutional Writtenness

At the outset, constitutional writtenness has been the basic feature of the Ethiopian constitutional system. However, the disaggregative model diminishes this key feature of the federal and state constitutions. At present, the FDRE Constitution is not codified into a single master text. Some of its parts are found in sub-constitutional parliamentary records. The state constitutions have also witnessed the same problem of unwrittenness. Most of them are not codified into a single document. Some of their rules are found in the disaggregated amending enactments. These dispersed constitutional rules nevertheless function as sources of authority for the executive and legislative actors. For instance, the national population census has been postponed for the third time since 2017 on the basis of the second amendment.[58] The first amendment of the FDRE Constitution governs the current administration of concurrent taxation powers.[59] This disaggregative model produces a number of self-standing laws having higher law status, yet these laws have not been systematically codified into a single document. This practice has destroyed unified writtenness and pushes Ethiopia towards the tradition of British disaggregated constitutionalism, which is partly written but uncodified in a master text.

[57] Oromia National Regional State (n 24).

[58] 'Ethiopian MPs Vote to Delay National Census for Third Time' *Ethiopian Monitor* (11 June 2020), https://ethiopianmonitor.com/2020/06/11/ethiopian-mps-vote-to-delay-national-census-for-third-time.

[59] Harris and Seid (n 42).

B. The Inaccessibility of Amendments and Public Obfuscation

A systematic codification would help to make the law known by laying it down in an easily comprehensible, public and definite form.[60] This would simplify the law and make it more accessible and knowable to the citizenry, law-makers and researchers.[61] Instead, the Ethiopian approach of amendment decodification in the FDRE Constitution hinders the public accessibility of amendments. As a result, little is known about the first and second constitutional amendments even by lawyers, researchers and law students.[62] As such, some lawyers and researchers have decried the recent postponement of the national population census as unconstitutional based on the obsolete texts of the Constitution.[63] The same argument had been echoed even by some Members of Parliament.[64] Similarly, lawyers and researchers have overlooked the first constitutional amendment and have complained about the legal basis of the current tax administration of concurrent revenue sources as constitutionally unfounded.[65] This confusion is the direct result of the decodification of amendments in the FDRE Constitution.

The situation is more complicated in the case of state constitutions. From the outset, the public is not well aware of the existence of state constitutions.[66] On top of this, public and legal actors cannot readily identify the changes that have been dispersed throughout the text of the revised constitutions and the various self-standing amending laws that comprise their associated constitutions. The hybrid model that combines the invisible and the disaggregative approaches is far from accessible, and this impedes public knowledge of the higher laws that bind them. The codification models make the texts of the constitutional amendments less accessible at both the federal and state levels, and thereby undermine the fundamental constitutional principle of publicity of law.[67] This obscures not only the presence of the constitutional changes but also their scope and contents.

[60] Weiss (n 45).

[61] ibid.

[62] Recently I did a preliminary assessment. Accordingly, most of the LLB students at Wollo University, School of Law who have taken the course of constitutional law do not know about the fact that the FDRE Constitution has been amended. Most of them have no information about the last amendments of the state constitutions of the Amhara and Oromia regions. The same trend is also observed among the LLM students, most of whom are practitioner lawyers. Most of the judges and attorneys which I have consulted have no information about the fact that the federal and revised state constitutions have been amended.

[63] Yohannes Kinfu, 'In-depth Analysis: The Postponement of the 4th Ethiopian Census: Was it Justified and What Next?' *Addis Standard* (5 April 2019), https://www.facebook.com/177352718979398/posts/in-depth-analysis-the-postponement-of-the-4thethiopiancensus-was-it-justified-/2129000267147957.

[64] Interview with G/Mariam (n 41).

[65] For instance, Ghebrehiwet Tesfai Baraki, 'The Practice of Fiscal Federalism in Ethiopia: A Critical Assessment 1991–2012; An Institutional Approach' (Doctoral thesis, University of Fribourg, 2015) 230–33.

[66] Tsegaye Regassa, 'State Constitutions in Federal Ethiopia: A Preliminary Observation' (a summary for the Bellagio Conference, 22–27 March 2004).

[67] Jane Pek. 'Things Better Left Unwritten? Constitutional Text and the Rule of Law' (1980) 83 *New York University Law Review* 1979.

The government cited ethnic conflicts, political instability, logistic constraints and the recent coronavirus (COVID-19) pandemic as reasons for the successive postponements of the national census, while little is known about the conditions of postponement publicly.[68] The public must be familiar with what the Constitution sets out before it can control government actions according to such standards. The inaccessibility of the amendments would make the public scrutiny against abuses and violations unproductive.[69] In light of this, the codification models used by the federal and state constitutions may fuel the risk of arbitrary government actions and threaten the rule of law and constitutionalism in the Ethiopian context.

V. Conclusion

All models of amendment codification except the integrative model have been used in Ethiopia. The FDRE Constitution adopts the decodification approach that is closely related to the disaggregative model. The state constitutions use the mixed approach that combines the invisible and disaggregative models to codify their constitutional changes. However, the ORSRC of 2001 is unique at least on two points: first, it also uses the appendative model to codify amendments; and, second, it reflects the tri-modal approach that combines the disaggregative, invisible and appendative models to codify constitution-level changes that have been made since 1997. This chapter therefore reveals that in Ethiopia, the federal and state constitutions adopt various models to codify their amendments. It also shows that both the federal and state constitutions commonly reflect the disaggregative model, while the state constitutions further use the invisible model to codify broader-scale constitutional changes that have substantially changed their texts. This perhaps reveals that the scale and significance of the constitutional changes have some relevance to the choice of a codification model.

This chapter also explained that these codification models had not been discussed at the moment of constitution-making. However, the political and historical settings of the FDRE Constitution intimate that a model that promotes the sense of finality to the text and then discourages further constitutional modification would have been chosen to codify the amendments of the federal constitution. Therefore, I argue that the decodification approach that reflects the features of the disaggregative model has been used deliberately to preserve the alleged sanctity of the FDRE Constitution, both in form and content. It is also shown that the revised state constitutions use the disaggregative model by default to codify the 2005 and 2006 amendments, while the amending proclamations quietly suggest the invisible model for codification.

[68] Kinfu (n 63).
[69] Pek (n 67).

These models have several implications, including the erosion of the writtenness in the Ethiopian constitutional tradition. The disaggregative model, as used by the federal and state constitutions, resulted in dispersed constitutional rules found in several amending proclamations. This, together with the invisible model that lacks sufficient signposts, makes the text of constitutional amendments inaccessible to the general public. The problem of accessibility has consequences for Members of Parliament, lawyers and researchers. All in all, the models do little to ensure the principle of publicity that is central to the rule of law and constitutionalism.

Therefore, it is imperative to make the issue of amendment codification an agenda worthy of debate and scholarship in Ethiopia. Given Ethiopia's constitutional history and its modern political practices, I suggest a hybrid model of amendment codification that combines the invisible and appendative models for both federal and state constitutions. However, what is appended at the end should be framed well enough to avoid the problems of harmonisation and systematisation.

13

Amendment Codification in Switzerland

Codifying an Evolving Culture of Constitutional Pragmatism

CASPAR PFRUNDER

I. Introduction

Swiss citizens regularly vote on proposed amendments to the Swiss Constitution. The constitutional text is generally open to change, and the authority on textual change is the totality of Swiss citizens with the qualification that a majority of the cantons must assent to any amendment.[1] This chapter addresses the following questions: (1) how and where does the constitutional text indicate change?; (2) where does this put the Swiss Constitution in a comparative typology of amendment codification models around the world?; and (3) why was the model chosen? More generally, this chapter interprets the Swiss model in its relationship with temporalities of constitutional creation.

Article 67a of the Swiss Constitution stipulates in its first paragraph that 'the Confederation and Cantons shall encourage musical education, in particular that of children and young people'. Footnote 37 indicates that Article 67a was adopted by a popular vote on 23 September 2012. The third paragraph of Article 72 on 'Church and State' stipulates that 'the construction of minarets is prohibited'. Footnote 38 indicates that this constitutional norm was adopted by a popular vote on 29 November 2009.[2] While all articles of the Constitution must be adopted by the majority of Swiss citizens and the majority of cantons according to Swiss constitutional law, these two popular votes share an extraordinary point of origin: unlike other articles, they were initiated by citizens collecting signatures rather than by elected politicians serving in the Federal Assembly, the Federal Council or cantonal political offices.

[1] Swiss Federal Constitution 1999, art 140.
[2] ibid arts 67a and 72.

However, their special point of origin cannot be discerned from the footnotes. Footnotes merely indicate that there has been an amendment adopted by popular vote at a specific date. Moreover, the footnotes only trace the amendments back to the last total constitutional revision of 1999, the second since Switzerland became the first federal state in Europe in 1848. In the general consciousness, the moment of 1848 is remembered as a major event of Swiss history and the foundation of the modern state; however, the original text is forgotten.

Richard Albert has conceptualised four models of codifying constitutional amendments from the study of constitutions across the world. This chapter attempts to situate the Swiss model within this theoretical framework. The four models are extracted from distinct codification arrangements in the US Constitution, the Indian Constitution, the Irish Constitution and the British Constitution. Drawing from their rules of codification, Albert categorises these models under the four labels *appendative*, *integrative*, *invisible* and *disaggregative*. He argues that the decision about which model a constitution follows is not just a legal formality, but a choice about how a people remembers its past.[3]

This idea could be extended even further: it is not only a choice about constitutional memory, but also a choice about construing a temporal bridge between constitutional foundation and the as-yet unknown demand for constitutional principles which the future might bring. Consequently, not only do modern constitutions institutionalise and channel citizen agency, set up legitimate powers and create cyclical rhythms of political life, but they also place constitutional creation in the arc of political time. The choice of amendment rules and codification models reveals assumptions and reflections of constitutional creators about the place in time they envisage for their Constitution.

The chapter analyses Albert's typology of codification models with regard to temporalities of political legitimacy and situates the Swiss codification model within it. It argues that the Swiss case is a form of the integrative model and reflects an evolving culture of constitutional pragmatism. It also traces the historical development of this culture and the emergence of a form of citizen constitutionalism.

II. Codification Models and Temporalities of Political Legitimacy

The moment of constitutional creation raises two possibilities: it may repudiate pre-existing arrangements and replace them with something radically novel, or it may attempt to reform these arrangements. The line is not sharp: even when pre-existing arrangements are repudiated, novelty is only partial. Some practices and

[3] Richard Albert, *Constitutional Amendments: Making, Breaking and Changing Constitutions* (Oxford, Oxford University Press, 2019) 230.

normative interpretations will be carried over into the new constitutional time. While objective factors such as the amount and depth of new principles certainly influence the categorisation as a new beginning or reform, so do the demands of the political moment: do historical actors seek continuity with or distance from the past? These interpretations may already be contested in their time. In addition, future generations may change the interpretative emphasis of past events again. The choice of a model of constitutional codification is a revealing historical source for the interpretation of decisive constitutional moments in the history of polities.

The *appendative model* is motivated by the idea of keeping the original text untouched as it affords its words a foundational status bound up with the existence of the polity itself. This means that the text structures time into a pre-eminent beginning and restricts change to extra chapters added to it, which I will call 'constitutional foundationalism'. It enshrines an authoritative founding moment which cannot be entirely repudiated (although inspire repetition) without endangering the continuity of the republic. The choice of the model creates an interpretative framework that is consequential not only for constitutional law, but also for a culture of political memory and legitimacy. Amendments necessarily refer to the foundational moment to which they add something in taking up the language of foundational authority. However, unintentionally, this model also leads to open acknowledgement of breaks and renewal in the amendments.

The *disaggregative model* does not aggregate all norms of constitutional significance in a single text. The decisive aspect is the absence of a separate source of authority for constitutional norms: constitutional norms are enacted through the exact same procedure as ordinary law and are not weaved together into one text. Accordingly, constitutional change occurs through the creation or change of single legislative acts. This model of codification reflects the absence of a marked-out moment of foundation. Constitutional beginnings fade out into the mists of time. Evolving practice and commitments rather than explicit foundational authority serve as a source of legitimacy. I will call this form of political legitimacy in time constitutional historicism. In this model, no single act of foundation may outshine the prudent continuity of an old evolving history. Legal texts of very different historical moments may assume enduring fundamental constitutional significance without being integrated into one text.

Both the *appendative model* and the *disaggregative model* place interpretative obstacles in the way of non-jurists who would like to understand the valid constitutional law of the moment. The *invisible model* is clearer: the past is deleted out of the text without indication. This reflects an attitude to political legitimacy in time that may be described as constitutional presentism. There is an important foundational moment and a distinct source of constitutional authority. However, textual codification does not emphasise temporal markers, but rather continuity. It presents a fluid text: parts of the past are invisibly in the present and are integrated into the present.

Just like the *invisible model*, the *integrative model* integrates amendments into a living text. It differs in that the text includes markers that indicate the place and moment of textual change. There is a founding moment in which a coherent original text is produced. There is a distinct source of constitutional authority that may amend the text. Yet the act of integration is made visible and the text demonstrates its character as a dynamic and temporal document. Parts of the relatively short constitutional present are integrated into the extended constitutional past from which the stability of the whole derives. This attitude to political legitimacy in time may be called constitutional pragmatism as it is focused on the action of textual integration of past and present. The text introduces its potential amenders to its history since its adoption and may be read like an encouragement to make new suggestions rather than to shy away from touching the Constitution short of activism for foundational new principles.

III. The Place of the Swiss Constitution

The Swiss Constitution creates two procedures of partial revision: partial revision may be proposed by 100,000 Swiss citizens, or it may be decreed by the Federal Assembly (both chambers of the Parliament). Both procedures trigger a mandatory vote of the people and the cantons.[4] Amendments are integrated into the original text and the moments of the popular votes are indicated by footnotes. However, the indication of integrated amendments only extends back to the last total revision – currently the Swiss Federal Constitution of 1999. Older amendments have become invisible. Yet constitutional life has already produced a rich array of new amendments. The totally revised Federal Constitution of 1999 now contains added articles such as Article 139b and it also contains article numbers without any corresponding text such as Article 139a.[5] Footnotes indicate when these articles have been introduced, altered, replaced or repealed by popular vote, but they do not say anything about the previous version of the text.

Two features differentiate the Swiss model from the type of integrative model that Albert has identified in the Indian Constitution: the absence of old text and the fact that indications do not extend beyond the last total constitutional revision, although the latter may simply be the result of the fact that the Indian Constitution has never undergone a complete revision. Notwithstanding these differences, the Swiss case may be regarded as a moderate form of the integrative model of codification. Swiss citizens may always attempt to amend the Constitution, but are challenged to integrate their present demands with the text that history has bequeathed them through the action of placing their amendment in it. In the event that their proposal finds popular and cantonal approval, their agency on the text leaves a footnote for the future.

Constitutional pragmatism of the Swiss type is not only marked by the visible integration of constitutional past and present in an ever-unfinished text; it also

[4] Swiss Federal Constitution 1999, arts 140, 192 and 194.

[5] ibid arts 139a and 139b.

stands for an ongoing practice rather than a theory of citizen sovereignty as the source of constitutional principle. Constitutional amendment became not an act of rare meaning, but a relatively frequent occurrence of political life.

IV. From Treaty to Constitutional Federalism: The Foundation of a New Power

The Swiss Confederation adopted its Federal Constitution in 1848, the year of revolutionary upheavals across Europe. Unlike the other revolutionary movements which rose up against old established monarchies, Swiss liberals and radicals did not have to stage a revolution against a power to assert the democratic nation. Switzerland had not participated in the development towards enlightened absolutism in the early modern period: no standing army, no centralised tax collection and no rational bureaucracy. The short attempt to modernise and centralise Switzerland during the unitary Helvetic Republic that lasted from 1798 to 1803 introduced wide-ranging equalising changes in the relationship between the cantons, but it failed to establish a lasting central power. Cooperation of instructed delegates remained the way of communal political life. The radicals did not want to replace an old sovereignty around which a state had been built up, but to erect a new national sovereignty with its own state by political voluntarism building on the experience of a common history.

The fact that the Constitution had not been the result of resistance against governmental authority shaped its text: it was not a list of liberties and rights won against a defeated power, but rather a textual statement of a political project to be realised through a new power. This power was democratically bound to the new collectivity of equal Swiss citizens. One way to create a new power rather than to reorganise one would have been to elect a foundationalist national constitutional convention. This would have bypassed the existing institutional forms. Instead, the old Swiss confederate assembly managed to stay on top of radical demands by establishing a commission, the Revisionskommission, out of the existing confederate assembly with representatives of most cantons to draft a liberal constitution corresponding to the spirit which fuelled 1848. It was an extraordinary fusion of popular sovereigntist radicalism with its discourse of supra-positive natural rights to constitute national self-government and a legalist moderate liberalism with its insistence on positivist legal means to achieve the shared goal of national integration. The international political moment contributed decisively to this alliance.[6]

How did liberals and radicals gain their position to become constitutional legislators for a new form of political union? In the early 1830s, 11 cantons

[6] Historian Oliver Zimmer argues that without this temporary ideological convergence of moderate liberalism and democratic radicalism, the nation-state of 1848 would hardly have come about: Oliver Zimmer, *A Contested Nation: History, Memory and Nationalism in Switzerland, 1761–1891* (Cambridge, Cambridge University Press, 2003) 132.

had undergone substantial constitutional change – in some places universal male suffrage was introduced, often as a result of popular pressure. However, attempts to integrate the Swiss cantons into a national state rather than mere military collaboration and a common foreign policy failed.[7] The goal was fiercely contested: conservative governments were opposed to national integration, which was synonymous with secular modernisation (particularly state education) and liberal rights. In the 1840s, these governments formed a separate military alliance to protect themselves from attacks by liberal revolutionaries. By 1847, liberals and radicals had achieved power in a narrow majority of cantonal governments. They used this majority to engage the Confederate Assembly in a new project of constitutional revision and soon decided to start the Sonderbundskrieg, a short war to dissolve the separate military alliance that was deemed an illegal breach of the Federal Treaty of 1815.[8]

The crushed resistance paved the way for the Federal Constitution. The Revisionskommission, which had already been formed before the war, was now complemented with liberal representatives from the defeated cantons. The constitutional project envisioned a dynamic federal state with a liberal economic union with a common coin, a mobile society with freedom of movement and settlement, powers to establish federal public works, a postal service, a better coordinated military defence structure and new national universities. Moreover, the Constitution set up an institutional arrangement of public powers as the main political actors: a national citizenry with constitutional agency and electoral power, a bicameral Federal Assembly, an executive Federal Council elected by the Federal Assembly and a Federal Court.[9]

V. Legitimating the Constitution: A Hidden Revolution?

A popular referendum was the radical path to legitimate the new Constitution. It was not the first referendum held on a nationwide basis; during the unitary Helvetic Republic, there had been a very first constitutional referendum in 1802. However, it was this one that definitively impressed on the public mind the idea of a sovereign national citizenry ultimately responsible for federal constitutional matters. The referendum was conducted by the cantons. The cantons asked all male Swiss citizens – a legal status created by the new Constitution – whether they consented to the adoption of the new Constitution. This inaugurated the principle of political

[7] Andreas Kley, *Verfassungsgeschichte der Neuzeit: Grossbritannien, die USA, Frankreich und die Schweiz* (Bern, Stämpfli Verlag, 2020) 239.

[8] Historisches Lexikon der Schweiz, René Roca, 'Sonderbundskrieg' (2012), https://hls-dhs-dss.ch/de/articles/017241/2012-12-20.

[9] Federal Constitution 1848.

nationality, though the historically evolved principle of sovereign cantonal particularity remained tangible in the stipulation of a consenting cantonal majority.

The Sonderbundskrieg which preceded the Constitution had not been legitimated in revolutionary language, but had drawn on a historically and legally legitimated discourse of military unity and common purpose to justify military intervention. The gradualist historical rhetoric allowed the impression of a legal and smooth transition to a new federation. The language of continuity and the considerable autonomy that remained with the cantons made the new arrangements more palatable. This links the Swiss case to constitutional historicism: there was reluctance to regard the Constitution as a foundationalist text since the idea was not to liberate the political project from the past for a new beginning, but to build on the past and renew it, while adapting to the needs of the time.

Yet while revolutionary rhetoric was largely absent from the centre of constitutional action, in legal substance it was a proper revolution: it created the first federal state on the European continent, it institutionalised the national citizenry as the new sovereign with a right to constitutional revision at any time, it carved out new areas of common policy and it proclaimed a list of liberal rights to protect certain activities from state interference. The right to constitutional revision at popular request resulted from a democratic theory of constitutionalism that differed from universalist liberal constitutionalism.[10] This radical conception of constitutionalism regarded the Constitution as the direct expression of the wishes and concerns of the citizens. According to this theory, the Constitution was not conceptualised as a binding contract rooted in enlightened reason guaranteeing a set of universally rational and just principles, but rather as state purposes, rights and limits to power legitimated by practical citizen mobilisation.

The Swiss fusion of elements of constitutional historicism and elements of constitutional foundationalism was the easiest solution to bridge the habitual local liberty and the desire for modernisation and national representation. Constitutional historicism emphasised a homegrown tradition of political liberty and consensus in the absence of a strong power and the ways in which the Constitution left these traditions in place. Constitutional foundationalism emphasised that it did not draw its inspiration from the French revolutionary constitutions with their rationalist centralism, but from American federalism.[11] Notwithstanding the strong tendency to downplay foundationalism in a historicist language, in essence the outcome was a foundationalist constitutional text which set up a new democratic republic on the European continent.

[10] Zimmer (n 6) 119.

[11] An influential example is the treatise by the Swiss philosopher Ignaz Troxler on Swiss constitutional reform: Ignaz Paul Troxler, *Die Verfassung der Vereinigten Staaten Nordamerikas als Musterbild der Schweizerischen Bundesreform* (Basel, Verlag der Brodtmann'schen Buchhandlung, 1848) 9.

VI. Debating Revision and Codification in 1848

How did the Revisionskommission debate the possibility of revision and the form of codification of such revisions? The question of revision was an important topic on the agenda. The participants had the previous Federal Treaty of 1815 as a comparison on their minds – a treaty that did not regulate revision at all. In particular, the radical President of the commission, Ulrich Ochsenbein, spoke out in favour of providing a clear channel to constitutional revision at any time in line with his position of democratic constitutionalism. Moreover, such a provision was seen as a means to avoid revolutions by providing a legal channel for change. The commission followed him on this matter. It also decided that regular revision would happen in the same way as ordinary federal laws.[12] This had effects on the codification model: the form of codification was to be analogous to ordinary law. An *appendative model* of codification was out of the question.

This decision stayed true to the practice of using historical continuity to legitimate novelty. The Revisionskommission was itself a product of this practice that was now also adapted for future revision: no constitutional convention had to be elected to do so, the initiative could simply be taken by any member of the Federal Assembly and had to be ratified by the majority of citizens and cantons. The Federal Assembly and the national citizenry – both of which had come into existence simultaneously in 1848 – were perceived as closely related political actors. The Federal Assembly played the leading part, while the citizenry (and the cantons) followed with the sovereign right to refuse undesired steps.

However, the question whether the right of initiative for revision was to be restricted to Members of Parliament or opened up to citizens was the subject of intense debate. Ultimately, the stipulation that 50,000 citizens could demand a revision and request a popular vote on this question was accepted. If the majority of the Swiss citizens and cantons voted for such a revision, a general re-election of the members of the two chambers was to follow to proceed with the task. The report written in the name of the Revisionskommission to the confederate assembly stated that it was a consequence of popular sovereignty that the people could revise its Constitution at any time and that most revolutions in history had happened in circumstances in which constitutional amendment had been made too difficult to achieve.[13] The result was a mix produced by three forces: a desire for historical continuity, a project of substantial foundationalism and pragmatic thinking about policy areas suited for centralisation.

[12] Rolf Holenstein, *Stunde Null: Die Neuerfindung der Schweiz im Jahr 1848, Die Privatprotokolle und Geheimberichte der Erfinder* (Zurich, Echtzeitverlag, 2018) 818.

[13] H Druey and JC Kern, 'Bericht über den Entwurf einer Bundesverfassung' (8 April 1848) 76, https://www.e-rara.ch/zut/content/titleinfo/7530617.

VII. The Journey from a Foundationalism of Principles to Constitutional Pragmatism

The difference between partial revision and complete revision, which was to play an important role in Swiss constitutional history, was not yet clearly conceptualised in 1848. In practice, the codified rules meant that the power of partial revision was restricted to the Federal Assembly, while a popularly accepted citizen initiative against its will would effectively subject the whole Constitution to an examination for revision by a re-elected Parliament. Hence, the citizens' vote on constitutional change was essentially a sovereign's right to veto. The Constitution was considered a foundationalist document to be amended only for acts of rare significance for which a popular vote was considered necessary. The citizen right to initiate revision against the will of the Parliament was not an invitation to do so, but an emergency provision where an alienated citizenry had lost confidence that elected politicians would take their wishes and concerns seriously.

For 18 years the Constitution produced by the alliance of 1848 had remained untouched, but in January 1866, the sovereign citizenry gained the first chance to use its right to veto constitutional change and it did so. Out of nine proposed constitutional amendments, eight were rejected. This weakened the assumption that the discourses and decisions of the Federal Assembly reflected the wishes and concerns of the citizenry. It was the beginning of a decoupling process between citizen confidence in politicians and citizen expression on constitutional matters. Over time, the citizens came to consider it their practical task to shape the Constitution and separated this task intellectually from electing suited politicians.

The first attempt at constitutional amendment from above necessitated a concrete suggestion of codification within the text. As was to be expected from the decision to treat constitutional law technically like ordinary law, a form of textual integration was proposed. New articles would be integrated by adding a letter to the number of the existing article next to which the new article was to be placed (for example, Article 54a).

During the 1860s, several Swiss cantons experienced strong democratic movements that demanded more popular participation in legislation and these demands produced several new cantonal constitutions. In response to the Federal Council's proposal for the first constitutional revision, these demands were also voiced in the Federal Assembly. One parliamentary motion demanded the introduction of a popular referendum on ordinary laws at citizens' request.[14] One line of argument was that private material interests had proven very influential on federal policies and that it was important not to forget to think about developing citizens'

[14] Alfred Kölz, *Neuere Schweizerische Verfassungsgeschichte II: Ihre Grundlinien in Bund und Kantonen seit 1848* (Bern Stämpfli Verlag, 2004) 504.

participatory possibilities when amending the Constitution for the first time. Yet the prominent entrepreneur and politician Alfred Escher was finally able to rally support against this proposal by insisting that a referendum on laws would destroy the highest constitutional principle of the Swiss Federation, namely 'representative democracy'.[15] Supporters of this position added that such a right would be used to obstruct progress and that the citizens would lack the necessary education. The motion was subsequently rejected, and the constitutional revision was put to the vote without any proposition to expand the possibilities of popular participation.

For some citizens, the reaction to the vote on the revision without any chance to decide on new forms of popular participation to compensate for more centralisation was to start to organise for a complete constitutional revision. While many accepted more centralisation, a proclaimed goal was to gain more participative power so that centralisation would not make the federally constituted powers too powerful.[16] In these years, the democratic movement for more popular participation on the cantonal level peaked in Zurich. A new Constitution was adopted with overwhelming majorities which turned the leadership between representatives and citizens on its head: it stated that the people would exercise the right of legislation with the collaboration of the (legislative) Cantonal Council.[17]

During these years, direct democracy gained support in popular consciousness. As the democrats and radicals also won more seats in the National Council, they started to push for a constitutional revision. They charged the Federal Council with the task to examine which parts of the Constitution should be revised to bring it into concordance with the requirements of the times, 20 years after its first adoption. Soon after its proposal, demands created by the military situation around 1870 made clear that a total rather than just a partial revision would be necessary.[18] Subsequently, the two chambers elected separate Revisionskommissionen. There, many politicians supported the introduction of new elements for popular participation in legislation and lively discussions on different possibilities took place.

While a first attempt at legitimating a revised Constitution at the polls failed to secure both a popular and a cantonal majority in 1872, the citizens and cantons accepted a second proposition for revision with less centralisation and more anticlericalism in 1874. Unlike the draft of 1872, it did not include a right for citizens to initiate legislation or challenge legislation after a prescribed time limit to do so has passed by. Yet it did include a new possibility for citizens to challenge federal legislation after the law had passed the Parliament and to demand a popular referendum. This weakened the theory that the Constitution was a foundationalist text of fundamental principles to be amended only in extraordinary moments of citizen mobilisation.

[15] ibid 505.
[16] ibid 508.
[17] Zurich Cantonal Constitution 1869, art 28.
[18] Kley (n 7) 270.

VIII. Voting on Laws

The expansion of popular participation in legislation of the 1874 Constitution changed the relationship between constitutional law and ordinary legislation. The original arrangements had expressed a clear difference between the sovereign of the Constitution, the citizenry and the cantons, and the ultimate source of authority on ordinary federal laws, the two chambers of the Parliament. The new set-up diluted this clear distinction in the source of legitimacy and made it possible to regard the Constitution less as a supreme law of utmost significance and more as an important channel of citizen expression among others. Parliamentary concretisation could take a pragmatic and reconciliatory approach rather than a strictly principled form sustained by an external institution. After all, the citizenry could intervene again with referenda if it did not approve of the parliamentary decisions.

As a consequence of the revision of 1874, the Constitution was no longer the only channel of direct popular political expression other than the election of persons. The frequent votes on both constitutional law and ordinary law engraved a strong sense of political participation on the public mind that turned on the perceived importance of the issue rather than the juristic categorisation as constitutional or legislative. This helped to bring about a pragmatic rather than a symbolically charged attitude to the Constitution. Winning a campaign for a constitutional norm meant to exert a significant effect on political attention and resources: the Constitution became a contested text that assumed a different role than simply setting up fundamental principles for the polity which were to be defended against the politics of the day.

The possibility of referenda on laws left the option open to mobilise the citizenry whenever opposed groups believed that they stood a significant chance to win against the Parliament. Thus, rather than becoming more removed from access by daily politics and subjected to elaborate juristic dogmatisation, the text of the Constitution became more involved in daily politics – contemporaneously with the expansion of the powers of the citizenry. Frequent citizen voting practice on both fundamental constitutional norms and regular laws complemented the written principles of the Constitution and its professional interpreters, and came to act as a main source of legitimate power. The citizens had become the guardians of the living Constitution by reserving the right to block anything they regarded as stepping beyond the legitimate power of the Parliament, which they had accepted in the Constitution.

IX. Constitutional Text Written by Citizens

The referendum on ordinary laws was important for shaping a new public attitude towards the Constitution. It was not decisive for establishing constitutional codification, which had already been set on its path in practice with the first propositions for constitutional revision in 1866. The integrative model was suited to the exclusive access of Members of Parliament to constitutional text. The Parliament was an institution where educated lawyers usually played a significant role, and they would attempt to integrate new amendments well into the text.

Yet the development of participatory rights for the national citizenry did not stop with the referendum on federal laws introduced in 1874. In 1879, one Member of Parliament failed to gain support for a motion to centralise the right to issue banknotes at the federal level. In response, he started to collect signatures to demonstrate popular support for his idea. During the public discussion, dissatisfaction with the restriction of popular initiative to total constitutional revision came to the fore and a subsequent petition by the 'society of the people' demanded that the Constitution should be complemented with an article on banknotes, but should also be amended to allow popular initiatives for partial revision. Yet the Federal Council turned this into the simple question: 'Should there be a revision of the Federal Constitution?', which was negated by the citizenry.[19]

Five years later, three conservative Members of Parliament drafted a parliamentary motion which included the request to make the constitutional text accessible to partial revision by popular initiative. The democrats supported the idea and five years later, the Federal Council supported a specific version of the request. It pushed the idea that popular initiatives should be introduced only in the form of suggestions. The final amendment of the constitutional text would remain in the hands of the Parliament and the citizenry would subsequently only be able to have a vote on that proposition. However, the Parliament changed the proposition and allowed the possibility that organised citizens could propose the precise textual reform themselves, but had to stick to one matter at a time. In 1891, the citizenry and the cantons accepted this new popular right, although the campaign was contested. The reform was pushed by conservative and democratic forces, while liberals and radicals were sceptical as it weakened the power of the Federal Parliament, which they considered to be a progressive force. Yet the Federal Council – and subsequently the Parliament with a rather narrow majority – ultimately supported the revision as it deemed the restriction of popular initiative to total constitutional revision an obstacle to the detection of actual popular will.[20]

The opening of the constitutional text to citizen initiative furthered the attitude of dynamic constitutionalism. While some parts of the Constitution remained stable and well accepted, the text had become a work in progress rather than a venerated reference text. The initiative proved to be a popular political device. However, in contrast to obstructive referenda that stood considerable chances of success, initiatives were insecure campaigns. They bypassed the parliamentary chambers not to block a law, but to introduce constitutional principle. It was a form of popular empowerment against the representatives, but was also open to use

[19] Kölz (n 14) 638.
[20] ibid 643.

by parliamentary minority forces to pressure majorities by threatening a popular vote on a matter which they refused to discuss.

For these reasons, the idea of the initiative had originally been treated as necessitating a re-election of Parliament. The process of decoupling popular expression on constitutional matters from political elections only really came to an end with an introduction of the popular initiative on constitutional text. The integrative model required organising citizens to study the existing text and integrate their demand pragmatically with the Constitution arising out of history. Since 1891, the Swiss citizens have voted on 225 initiatives and accepted only 24. Of those 225 initiatives, 189 initiatives were voted on after 1950 and only 36 (of which seven were accepted) in the period between 1891 and 1950.[21] Nevertheless, initiatives have led to momentous constitutional revisions, such as the introduction of a system of proportional election of the National Council (1918) and the decision to join the United Nations (2002).

X. Conclusion

Switzerland has opted for a form of the integrative model of codification. This model has not developed as the outcome of a contested debate, but was adapted from the codification models of ordinary laws. It reflects a constitutional culture of pragmatism. Three elements are decisive in terms of understanding this constitutional culture. The first is the radical theory that the Constitution is to be understood as the practical expression of considered collective will of equal citizens; practice would habituate the citizens to consider themselves as the legitimate authority on constitutional matters. The text was not lauded as the creation of enlightened founders whose theories and intentions would become the object of extended interpretative disputes. Instead, it was considered as the creation of pragmatic men combining the widespread demands for democratic sovereignty on a national scale and the historically evolved political structures and habits in a federal structure. Although there was a downplayed foundationalist dimension to the original text of 1848, the political culture ended up not enshrining the moment of constitutional foundation and declared principles, but encouraging further pragmatism in constitutional development by normalising the idea of a frequently mobilised citizenry as the ultimate source of law.

This process took first place through the dissolution of clearly separate sources of legitimacy for constitutional as opposed to ordinary legislation. The distinction between extraordinary constitutional politics in rare moments of collective mobilisation about fundamental principles and regular ordinary politics largely disappeared. Although rare moments of breakthrough were not excluded, the

[21] Swiss Federal Chancellery, https://www.bk.admin.ch/ch/d/pore/vi/vis_2_2_5_9.html.

focus of constitutional development lay on incremental change resulting from the regular consultation of the wishes and concerns of the citizenry. The vote on concrete laws rather than simply on abstract constitutional principles contributed to this culture of pragmatism and permanent dialogue.

This evolving culture of participation on laws facilitated the introduction of the popular initiative to amend constitutional text. It was this shift that completed pragmatic constitutionalism and became an invitation for citizens to become co-authors of an evolving constitutional text. The integrative model of codification required that organised citizens had to study the text in considerable depth in order to place and make their proposed changes. Nevertheless, the political culture that evolved sacrificed constitutional purity and simplicity for a palimpsestic work in progress. Pragmatic integration of past and present became the hallmark of Swiss constitutional culture.

14

Between Accessibility and Oblivion

Strengths and Weaknesses of the 'Invisible' Dutch Constitutional Amendment Model

GERT-JAN LEENKNEGT AND REIJER PASSCHIER

I. Introduction

In the definitive account of constitutional amendments, Richard Albert distinguishes four models for codifying constitutional amendments.[1] First, constitutions may follow an *appendative* model. Here, amendments are appended sequentially to the end of the text; the US Constitution is probably the most important example of this. Second, constitutions may reflect the *integrative* model, whereby amendments are incorporated directly into the master text of the original constitution; the Indian Constitution, among others, illustrates this model. Third, constitutions may adopt an *invisible* model, in which the constitution does not indicate where the amendments have been codified; Albert uses the Irish Constitution as an example. Finally, constitutions may adhere to a model that Albert describes as *dissaggregative*: 'a form of codification characteristic of uncodified constitutions that situate their constitutive rules and principles in different sites of constitutional importance'.[2]

As Albert posits, the 'choices involved in recording alterations to the constitutional text entail implications for how interpreters of constitutional meaning will read the constitution in the course of adjudication, whether the constitution will become a focal point of reference in constitutional politics, and how intensely citizens may come to venerate their constitutional text'.[3] According to him, choosing how and where to codify an amendment is 'ultimately a choice about how and whether a people chooses to remember its past'.[4]

[1] Richard Albert, *Constitutional Amendments: Making, Breaking and Changing Constitutions* (Oxford, Oxford University Press, 2019) ch 6.

[2] ibid 230.

[3] ibid.

[4] ibid.

In this chapter, we seek to fit the Dutch Constitution into Albert's theoretical framework. We believe that the Dutch case has a lot to add. As we will show in section II, the Dutch Constitution is paradigmatic of Albert's 'invisible' model: 'it inserts, removes and changes the constitutional text without any clear indication of what in the text has been altered, how it has been altered, or when precisely it has been altered'.[5] In section III, we will explain that this model was never deliberatively chosen – or, at least, we have no proof of any careful consideration or discussion of this choice. Nevertheless, as Albert hypothesises, the model used for amendment codification seems to have important legal, political and sociological consequences. Suggesting that the invisible approach taken by the Dutch Constitution shows several important strengths and weaknesses, we will argue that the 'clean pages' produced by the Dutch way of codifying constitutional amendments may indeed be connected to a collective forgetfulness of constitutional history and a common disregard of the historical character of the constitutional order. We call this phenomenon 'constitutional oblivion' and discuss why it may be considered a loss.

The chapter continues in section IV by describing and explaining a few ways in which the negative consequences of amendment invisibility in the Netherlands have been countered. These practices may be of interest to invisible-approach constitutional orders around the world. In conclusion, in section V, we suggest some questions for further research.

II. The 'Invisible' Dutch Amendment Model

Like the Irish Constitution, the Constitution of the Kingdom of the Netherlands (or the 'Dutch Constitution') takes what can be described as an 'invisible' approach to codifying amendments. In accordance with Article 137, formal amendments to the Dutch constitutional text require two legislative readings, with intervening general elections for the Lower House of Parliament (Tweede Kamer). In the first reading, a proposal for constitutional amendment requires a simple majority in both Houses. Before the second reading, which requires a qualified two-thirds majority in both houses, a general election must be held to ensure that the electorate is consulted on any proposed constitutional amendment.[6] If it is adopted at the second reading, the proposal is then formally ratified by the king. Article 139 stipulates that 'amendments to the Constitution passed by the States General

[5] ibid 238.

[6] The adoption of a proposal at the first reading does not automatically trigger a general election. For at least a century, Dutch constitutional actors waited for the regular general Lower House election to take place. Therefore, constitutional issues are commonly overshadowed by ordinary political debates during elections. In fact, the average voter does commonly not realise that his or her 'ordinary' vote might also be relevant to a proposal for constitutional amendment. See EA Alkema, 'Constitutional Law' in JMJ Chorus et al (eds), *Introduction to Dutch Law*, 3rd edn (Dordrecht, Kluwer, 1999) 293.

and ratified by the King shall enter into force immediately after they have been published'. The last relevant rule appears in Article 141: 'The text of the revised Constitution shall be published by Royal Decree in which the chapters, sections and articles may be renumbered and references to them altered accordingly.'

Articles 139 and 141 therefore outline a 'double publication practice'. The first part of this double practice, governed by Article 139, concerns the publication of an individual amendment. Article 139 does not stipulate a specific constitutional regime for the publication of any amendment. This implies that constitutional amendments should be published only as ordinary statutes; that is, by publication in the Official Gazette (*Staatsblad*).[7] Prior to the constitutional reform of 1983, constitutional amendments were published by solemn proclamation. However, the government thought this part of the amendment procedure was out of date and Parliament remained silent on the matter.[8] According to Article 139, amendments to the Constitution enter into force 'immediately after' they have been published in the *Official Gazette*. As the *Official Gazette* has only a date of issue and not a specific time, 'immediately after' should arguably be interpreted as 'from the day after the date of issue of the *Official Gazette* in which they are published'.[9]

After the publication of the individual amendments, the text of the entire Constitution (as amended) is to be published as a continuous, consolidated text in accordance with Article 141. This is the second part of the Dutch double publication practice for constitutional amendments. As van der Meulen noted, Article 141 embodies 'a fundamentally different approach to that of the United States, where changes are not incorporated into the Constitution text, but are added as amendments'.[10] The incorporation into the document may take some additional time, but is often done within a few years. Sometimes the Constitution, or parts of it, is renumbered. In those instances, the new text does not give away any sign that it has been changed. On other occasions, letters are used to make space for a textual addition. One example is Article 57a ('The temporary replacement of a member of the States General during pregnancy and maternity leave or during illness shall be regulated by Act of Parliament'). Indeed, apart from a few articles that have been inserted without renumbering, the Dutch way of codifying constitutional amendments is perfectly consistent with Albert's description of the invisible model:

> [I]t inserts, removes, and changes the constitutional text without any clear indication of what in the text has been altered, how it has been altered, or when precisely it was altered. All that appears in the main text are clean pages with no accompanying notes,

[7] See Article 3 Bekendmakingswet.

[8] BMJ van der Meulen, 'Artikel 139 – Bekendmaking en inwerkingtreding' ['Article 139 – Publication and Entry into Force'], https://www.nederlandrechtsstaat.nl/grondwet/inleiding-hoofdstuk-8-herziening-van-de-grondwet/artikel-139-bekendmaking-en-inwerkingtreding.

[9] AK Koekkoek, 'Beantwoording van rechtsvraag (145) staatsrecht/strafrecht' (1984) *Ars Aequi* 169.

[10] BMJ van der Meulen, 'Artikel 141 – Bekendmaking herziene Grondwet' ['Article 141 – Publication Amended Constitution'], https://www.nederlandrechtsstaat.nl/grondwet/inleiding-hoofdstuk-8-herziening-van-de-grondwet/artikel-141-bekendmaking-herziene-grondwet.

no references, and no other details that could quite readily alert readers that something new may have inserted, something old may have been removed, or that anything at all may have been changed.[11]

III. Consequences: Strengths and Weaknesses

The present invisible amendment model of the Dutch Constitution has been more or less conventional since the beginning, when the Constitution was created in 1814. We have not been able to trace whether the Dutch way of codifying constitutional amendments has been a deliberate choice between alternative amendment models or merely an accident of history. Between 1814 and 1983, the articles concerning constitutional amendments used the words 'changes' ('verandering') or 'additions' ('bijvoegingen').[12] The current Article 141 of the Dutch Constitution was added only in 1887 and 1922. So, purely in light of the text of the Constitution, constitutional actors of the nineteenth century might have also adopted the US way of codifying constitutional change.

Referring to the French translation of the 1814 Constitution, the 'classic' Dutch constitutionalist and statesman JR Thorbecke commented in 1840 that constitutional amendments should be inserted in the original text, while the parts that have been replaced should be deleted.[13] After all, as Thorbecke argued, the French translation of the 1814 Constitution did not say 'ajoutés' (added), but 'joints' (seal). Although we have no direct proof, it could be the case that the French translation of the Dutch Constitution to which Thorbecke referred reflected the French revolutionary way of presenting legislation – namely, not as historical products, but as the command of a sovereign body shaping the political life of its nation independent of traditions and the institutional context of the past. In that light, providing only clean constitutional pages was only logical and modern. This may explain the wording of the French translation. However, we are unsure whether the Dutch adopted the invisible amendment model for the same reason; they could just as well have adopted it without really thinking about alternatives at all.

The Dutch way of codifying constitutional amendments itself has never been controversial. The only questions that were raised concerned its exact source of authority.[14] On what bases had the invisible amendment model been adopted? The debate was less about what the Constitution prescribed – the legality of double publication scheme was uncontroversial – than about its exact source.

[11] Albert (n 1) 238.

[12] 'Artikel 137: Eerste en tweede lezing; splitsing van voorstellen; kamerontbinding' ['Article 137: First and Second Reading; Splitting Proposals; Dissolution of Parliament'] https://www.denederlandsegrondwet.nl/id/vkugbqve0yzk/artikel_137_eerste_en_tweede_lezing.

[13] JR Thorbecke, *Aantekingen op de Grondwet II* [*Notes on the Constitution*] (Leiden, Martinus Nijhoff, 1906 [1843]) 315.

[14] PJ Oud, *Het constitutioneel recht van het Koninkrijk der Nederlanden Deel II* [*The Constitutional Law of the Kingdom of the Netherlands Part II*] (Haarlem, Tjeenk Willink, 1947) 50.

As noted above, Thorbecke based his argument on the French translation of the 1814 Constitution, which left less room for interpretation. However, Kranenburg, another 'classic' constitutionalist, claimed that the wording of the 1814 Constitution could in fact be explained in multiple ways. As Kranenburg argued, the term 'additions' (*bijvoegingen*) could be read both as prescribing the American way (adding amendments to the text) or the Dutch invisible method.[15] Struycken, yet another authoritative commentator, agreed with Thorbecke that the fact that the French translation of the 1815 version of the Constitution used the term 'joints' should be considered an important indication that the invisible model for codifying constitutional changes is indeed the right one.[16] With the adoption of what is now Article 141 (in 1887 and in 1922), these debates became largely irrelevant, as the text of the Constitution itself now explicitly stipulates how amendments should be codified.

The strengths and weaknesses of the Dutch model for codifying amendments have been discussed only briefly in the constitutional literature. To our knowledge, the subject has not been discussed in separate publications. Only a few textbooks have briefly addressed its advantages and disadvantages, usually compared to the way in which the US Constitution codifies amendments. For example, PJ Oud, author of a 1947 textbook, noted that while the US amendment model secures the visibility of the historical character of the Constitution, it would have important disadvantages in the Dutch context.[17] If amendments to the Constitution become relatively numerous and extensive (as they did in the Netherlands),[18] the US model of codifying amendments would make it utterly obscure. After a while, it would become impossible to tell which parts of the text would still be in force and which would not. Conversely, if the text of the Constitution itself were to be adapted immediately upon amendment, it would always be up to date. Today in the Netherlands, in order to find out what constitutional rule is currently applicable, one can simply consult the latest version of the document on the government's portal for legislation.[19]

Accessibility and actuality may be considered some of the strengths of the Dutch model.[20] But have these strengths – deliberately or subconsciously – been

[15] AAH Struycken, *Het Staatsrecht van het Koninkrijk der Nederlanden* [*The Constitutional Law of the Kingdom of the Netherlands*] (Arnhem, Gouda Quint, 1915 and 1917) 75, cited by Oud (n 14).

[16] R Kranenburg, *Het Nederlandse Staatsrecht Deel II* [*Dutch Constitutional Law Part II*] (Haarlem, HD Tjeenk Willink & Zoon, 1938) 524, cited by Oud (n 14).

[17] ibid.

[18] Since the Constitution of the Netherlands was adopted in 1814, its text has been formally revised 21 times: in 1815, 1840, 1848, 1884, 1887, 1917, 1922, 1938, 1946, 1948, 1953, 1956, 1963, 1972, 1983, 1987, 1995, 1999–2000, 2002, 2005–06 and 2008. Most of these revisions consist of several individual amendments. See WJM Voermans, 'The Constitutional Revision Process in the Netherlands; Sensible Security Valve or Cause of Constitutional Paralysis?' in X Contiades (ed). *Engineering Constitutional Change: A Comparative Perspective on Europe, Canada and the USA* (New York, Routledge, 2012) 263.

[19] This version can be found here: https://wetten.overheid.nl/BWBR0001840/2018-12-21.

[20] For example, at 8,739 words, the Dutch Constitution is certainly not the shortest constitution in the world, but it is also not very long. See 'Constitution Rankings' https://comparativeconstitutionsproject.org/ccp-rankings.

at the expense of making the historical character of the Constitution obvious? As Allott put it, every constitutional norm is 'the fruit of a society's contemplation of itself in time and space'.[21] A constitution like that of the US clearly reflects this with, for example, its provisions on the temporal unamendability of slavery in Article V and the Fourteenth Amendment, added in 1868, addressing citizenship rights and equal protection under the law. Of course, a reader of the US Constitution still requires *some* context in order to fully appreciate (and indeed to put in perspective) this remarkable development. At the same time, its tracks are right there, visible on the face of the document itself, reminding the reader of the fact that a constitution neither originates nor operates in a vacuum and is much more than a legal scheme framed at some point in time.

The Dutch constitutional document shows much less history. From the almost 'clean pages' of the Dutch constitutional document, it does not show, for example, that the parliamentary system is not self-evident, but rather the result of an important constitutional 'moment' that occurred around 1848.[22] In around this year, the powers of the king were significantly reduced, the principle of ministerial responsibility and the duty of ministers to inform Parliament were introduced, and the lower House of Parliament was turned into a directly elected body. The structures that were implemented in 1848 still belong to the core of Dutch constitutional law, anchoring the principles of democratic constitutionalism and the parliamentary system. However, the changes, as well as the previous system, are not immediately apparent from the constitutional text. Reading the current text, a layperson or hasty professional might think that the current order has always been as it is, missing the important history that that the current system has evolved over time from a very different one.

Another example is the Dutch colonial past. Until 1953, Article 1 of the Dutch Constitution provided that 'The Kingdom of the Netherlands includes the territories of Indonesia, Surinam and the Dutch Antilles' (although Indonesia had become an independent nation in 1949). Until 1983, the same article provided that 'The Kingdom of the Netherlands includes the territories of Surinam and the Dutch Antilles' (although Surinam had become an independent nation in 1975). In 1983, the phrase was erased completely. The new Article 1 states that: 'All persons in the Netherlands shall be treated equally in equal circumstances. Discrimination on the grounds of religion, belief, political opinion, race or sex or on any other grounds whatsoever shall not be permitted.' Short of a preamble, ever since it has been adopted, the new Article 1 almost functions as one. It appears on sidewalks, in police stations and government buildings. It is often cited by progressive political leaders and emancipatory movements. Over the past few decades, it has increasingly been presented as the fundamental norm of the present Dutch constitutional order.[23]

[21] P Allott, *The Health of Nations* (Cambridge, Cambridge University Press, 2002) 132.

[22] CAJM Kortmann and PPT Bovend'Eert, *Dutch Constitutional Law* (Dordrecht, Kluwer Law International, 2000) 29.

[23] See, eg, EMH Hirsch Ballin, *Artikel 1 van de Grondwet als fundamentele constitutionele norm* [*Article 1 of the Constitution as Fundamental Norm*] (Haarlem, WEJ Tjeenk Willink, 1988).

The way in which the old, colonial Article 1 has been replaced by the new, emancipatory Article 1 has erased some of the most important traces of the Dutch colonial past in the Dutch constitutional document. A news broadcast on 18 March 2014 illustrates how this could lead to a certain historical forgetfulness. On that day, a newsreader from the (usually quite reliable) state broadcaster NOS reported with a certain pride, if not a touch of nationalism, that Article 1 of the Dutch Constitution has stipulated since 1814(!) that 'All persons in the Netherlands shall be treated equally in equal circumstances. Discrimination on the grounds of religion, belief, political opinion, race or sex or on any other grounds whatsoever shall not be permitted'.[24] If the old phrase had still been in place, such a mistake would never have been made and people would have been reminded earlier that the institutional order in which they live is not self-evident and should not be taken for granted.

Another important observation is that the Dutch way of codifying constitutional amendments allows for what Dutch constitutionalists refer to as 'deconstitutionalisation'. Over time, various topics have been *deconstitutionalised*. Although these topics were of a constitutional nature, they have been taken out of the Constitution and left to the ordinary legislature to regulate. In some cases, this was motivated by what we could call 'constitutional hygiene': the text of the Constitution should not be burdened with unnecessary details about issues that the legislature can deal with easily. For example, the forms containing the texts that are spoken when ministers or Members of Parliament swear an oath or make an affirmation and promise to accept their responsibilities used to be in the Constitution itself until 1983. With the major revision in that year, these rather extensive forms were taken out and are now laid down in an Act of Parliament.[25]

In other cases, *deconstitutionalisation* is based on more opportunistic motives. A constitutional provision may be outdated or may hamper legal development. However, while there may be general agreement on the need for change, there may not be a broad consensus on the desirable way forward. As we have seen, amendment of the Constitution requires two parliamentary readings separated by general elections for the Lower House, and a two-thirds majority in both Houses of Parliament at the second reading. A solution may then be to agree on the *deconstitutionalisation* of that particular provision, which leaves the issue to the legislature to decide by a simple majority. Until 2018, Article 131 stated that mayors and provincial governors were appointed by Royal Decree (a government decision). While a majority in Parliament supported the idea of elected mayors, the two-thirds majority needed to amend the Constitution could not be reached. As a political compromise, parties agreed on an amendment stating that the method

[24] 'Geschiedvervalsing bij de NOS over Artikel 1 van de Grondwet' [Falsification of History at the NOS about Article 1 of the Constitution'], https://www.youtube.com/watch?v=1vQwsE6wUqU&t=30s.

[25] Wet beëdiging ministers en leden Staten-Generaal ['Act on Swearing in Ministers and Members of the States General'] arts 2 and 3 respectively. The Act can be found at: https://wetten.overheid.nl/BWBR0005430/1992-03-25.

of appointment will be determined by law. Consequently, the method of appointment of mayors is no longer found in the Constitution itself. A risk of this kind of operation is that we may forget that certain topics are constitutional by nature, even when they are no longer in the Constitution.

In summary, one disadvantage of the invisible amendment model of the Dutch Constitution is that the mistakes and achievements from the past are not obvious from the constitutional text. Another related disadvantage of the Dutch way of codifying constitutional amendment is that it has de facto allowed political actors to *deconstitutionalise* issues that are actually constitutional and arguably require constitutional protection. Moreover, as a result of its way of codifying constitutional amendment, the Dutch constitutional text does not remind the reader of the important fact that the constitutional text, as well as the context in which it operates and generates meaning, is the product of long-term processes of legal, political and social development. In other words, it fails to convey that the constitutional document, in all its different parts, is constructed historically, over time, and that the nature and prospects of any single part will be best understood within the long course of political formation.[26]

A lot more research would be required in order to reveal causal relationships. However, the fact is that Dutch citizens know very little about their constitution,[27] let alone the way in which it has come into being and how its meaning has changed over time. The historical-institutional character of the constitutional order is often disregarded. We propose calling this phenomenon 'constitutional oblivion' – a phenomenon to which the Dutch 'invisible' way of codifying constitutional amendment may well have contributed.

IV. Making Invisible Amendments Visible

Constitutional oblivion, which was probably partly caused by the invisible way in which the Dutch Constitution is amended, may risk undermining the legitimacy of the political order. If too few people are aware that the Constitution is a historical construct and that its success in promoting and anchoring fundamental values is not self-evident, fundamental values may be placed in jeopardy. In that respect, awareness of the historical context of constitutional rules and of the dynamics of those rules is crucial.

[26] *cf* K Orren and S Skowronek, *The Search for American Political Development* (Cambridge, Cambridge University Press, 2004) 1.

[27] TNO/Nipo, *De Grondwet: Wat weet en vindt de Nederlander?* [*The Constitution: What Does the Dutchman Know and Find?*] (np. 2008). See also W Voermans, 'A 200-Year-Old Constitution: Relic or Enigma?' in G Franco Ferrari, R Passchier and WJM Voermans (eds), *The Dutch Constitution beyond 200 Years: Tradition and Innovation in a Multilevel Legal Order* (The Hague, Eleven International Publishing, 2018) 153–68.

How can we remedy constitutional oblivion? Several websites function as a portal to the constitutional history of the Netherlands, providing access to previous versions of the text of the current Constitution and to the historical context of its current meaning.

Wetten.overheid.nl contains coordinated and consolidated texts of all legislation at the national level (including the Constitution) and at the regional and local levels, as well as the texts of all treaties signed and ratified by the Netherlands.[28] Every provision (and even every title) has a series of buttons, each giving access to additional (mostly technical) information. One button links to older versions of that particular provision or title. Using this function, one can trace the evolution of the wordings of every single provision of any Dutch law over time. The buttons also give access to the underlying Parliamentary Papers explaining the aims and considerations for each amendment. An important limitation is that versions of national legislation (including the Constitution) only date back to 2002, while the Dutch Constitution has historical continuity over more than 200 years. Basically, this database provides primary sources for consecutive versions of the Constitution, dating back to 2002. Its main objective is not a communicative one; it is aimed mostly at legal professionals.

Denederlandsegrondwet.nl contains the texts of the current Constitution and of older versions that have marked major revisions, back to the original 1814 version, and even to older constitutions or 'Staatsregelingen' of the Batavian Republic (between 1798 and 1805).[29] In all versions, short explanatory notes on the meaning of each provision are added. As the notes are brief, not very technical and easily understandable, they are aimed at a broad public, providing access to the general historical context of the Dutch Constitution.

NederlandRechtsstaat.nl is an online platform founded by a small group of constitutionalists.[30] In collaboration with about 40 academic authors, it publishes elaborate comments on the Dutch constitutional text, including its chapters and individual articles. On the same platform, a forum is maintained in which topical political and legal developments are discussed in relation to the Dutch Constitution and to the doctrine of democratic constitutionalism it arguably seeks to anchor. This important initiative may be of particularly interest to invisible-approach constitutional orders around the world.

Nederlandrechtsstaat.nl is not *explicitly* meant to be a remedy to the risk of constitutional oblivion associated with the invisible amendment approach, but it may partly *function* as one. As one of the founders of nederlandrechtsstaat.nl, Ernst Hirsch Ballin explained, 'the authors of this commentary are part of a tradition that understands the Dutch Constitution as an attempt to improve upon the

[28] Wetten.overheid.nl is an initiative of the Ministry of the Interior and of Kingdom Relations; it is produced and managed by the Kennis- en Exploitatiecentrum Officiële Overheidspublicaties (KOOP), an agency responsible for publishing official government information.

[29] This website is administered by the Ministry of the Interior and of Kingdom Relations.

[30] NederlandRechtsstaat.nl is currently managed and edited jointly by a group of constitutional scholars from Tilburg University and the Open University.

ideals of the democratic constitutional state'.[31] This means, among other things, that the contributors to the commentary tend to place the different elements of the constitution in their historical and institutional context, and try to ascertain to what extent they have managed to anchor fundamental values.

The constitutional commentary on Nederlandrechtsstaat.nl is structured around the eight chapters and 142 articles of the Dutch Constitution. Each chapter has a general introduction, which is usually historical and theoretical in nature. It introduces the subject of the articles of the chapter by outlining historical developments, placing the Constitution in context, and reflecting on democratic and constitutional values. For example, Voermans' chapter on legislation and governance discusses the principle of legality and its development in detail.[32] Partly because of the invisible way in which the Dutch Constitution codifies its changes, it is impossible to read those developments from the constitutional text. However, with the extensive and clear explanation of the commentator, it remains alive.

The general commentaries on each chapter precede specific commentaries on the individual articles. Most commentaries follow a similar outline: (1) they introduce the article and describe its historical development and current meaning; (2) they situate the article within the entire Constitution and the constitutional order; (3) they explain the different elements of the article; (4) if relevant, they situate the article within the European and international legal order; (5) and they discuss, if applicable, recent developments and controversies surrounding the article. Some of the commentators also critically reflect on the question whether the article concerned is (still) doing its job – that is, the extent to which it really anchors the fundamental values it is supposed to anchor.

Although Nederlandrechtsstaat.nl is intended to be a comprehensive commentary on the Constitution, it does leave several gaps. It does not discuss provisions or subjects that have been deleted from the Constitution entirely at some point in history. For example, the issue of colonialism and the colonial history of the Constitution associated with the old version of Article 1 (as discussed above) is not discussed anywhere.

Despite their respective limitations, these three websites deliver an important contribution in terms of combating constitutional oblivion. Although they hardly have any role in legal practice – at least not in courts, partly due to the lack of constitutional review of legislation in the Netherlands – they do play a role in other ways. Legal scholars, policy-makers and mainstream media all make use of these sources. In particular, the blog posts on Nederlandrechtsstaat.nl fuel academic and political debate from a constitutional perspective on a wide range of topical issues.

[31] EMH Hirsch Ballin, 'De Grondwet uitleggen. Algemene inleiding' ['Explaining the Constitution. General Introduction'], https://www.nederlandrechtsstaat.nl/grondwet/#algemene-inleiding.

[32] WJM Voermans, 'Inleiding hoofdstuk 5 – Wetgeving en Bestuur' ['Introduction to Chapter 5 – Legislation and Administration'], https://www.nederlandrechtsstaat.nl/grondwet/inleiding-hoofdstuk-5-wetgeving-en-bestuur/#het-legaliteitsbeginsel.

V. Conclusion

Denederlandsegrondwet.nl, wetten.nl and nederlandrechtsstaat.nl may be of interest to invisible-approach constitutional orders around the world, as such initiatives partly remedy the collective constitutional forgetfulness that may result from only keeping 'clean' constitutional pages. However, a lot more research is needed in order to fully substantiate this claim. We have hardly any empirical proof of a causal relationship between the Dutch way of codifying constitutional amendments and the phenomenon of constitutional oblivion that may be observed in the Dutch constitutional order. We only have good reasons to believe that a causal relationship might exist.

The Dutch invisible amendment model is in any case certainly not the only cause of the collective constitutional forgetfulness – constitutional oblivion – that is afflicting the Netherlands. The fact that the Dutch Constitution explicitly forbids constitutional review of Acts of Parliament by the courts is also important in relation to constitutional oblivion.[33] First of all, there is relatively little constitutional debate in Dutch legal practice, and with the constitutional ban on constitutional review of Acts of Parliament, there are no famous or landmark cases on the interpretation of current or historical constitutional provisions. There is no Dutch equivalent of famous American cases, like *Marbury v Madison*, *Roe v Wade* or *Brown v Board of Education*. This may also be an important explanation of why constitutional questions are not in the public conscience or memory either. Second, because there is no authoritative interpretation of constitutional norms by the courts, any discussion on the desired meaning and application of constitutional norms is a parliamentary one in the end. A re-interpretation of the existing Constitution can only be really anchored by codifying it as a constitutional amendment, rendering previous versions invisible and historical.

Further research might also examine how and whether constitutional oblivion can be remedied. Civic education is often suggested as a very important remedy against constitutional oblivion, although its effects have hardly been researched. The Netherlands has also experimented with introducing a 'Constitution Day' in order to generate more attention for the Dutch Constitution, constitutional democracy and history. However, to date, festivities have been of such a small scale that hardly anything can be said about their effects.

We do not believe that the Dutch way amending its constitution should be changed. As we have indicated, the sober and accessible constitutional document that results from it has major advantages too. However, we do believe that the historical character of the Constitution is of such importance that constitutionalists should put much more effort into bringing it up and communicating it to political and juridical leaders as well as the people as a whole.

[33] See art 120 of the Dutch Constitution.

15

Codification of Constitutional Amendments as a Symbol for Transitions

A Case Study from Hungary

ESZTER BODNÁR

I. Introduction

If all provisions of a constitution are amended at the same time, is it old or new? What if a newly adopted constitution retains 80 per cent of the former text? Can two constitutional texts be in force concurrently? The recent three decades of the history of the Hungarian Constitution raised (and partly answered) these unexpected questions that will serve as the leading thoughts of this chapter.

Hungary follows the integrative model of constitutional amendments in which new provisions are integrated into the text, but with identifiable changes.[1] However, these formal requirements have led to constitutional and political debates well beyond legal scholarship. During the 1989–90 democratic transition, the content of the 1949 Constitution was entirely changed, but the number, date and structure of the Soviet-type text were kept. The ultimate aim was to have a new constitution adopted by a democratically elected parliament. While the Constitutional Court developed a modern constitutional system on this basis, the symbolic hiatus led to the adoption of a new constitution in 2011, which was primarily based on the previous text. While the Constitutional Court averted an attempt to shift to the appendative amendments model, the current Constitution has been amended 11 times.

[1] On the models of constitutional amendments, see Richard Albert, *Constitutional Amendments: Making, Breaking and Changing Constitutions* (Oxford, Oxford University Press, 2019) 229–39.

This chapter provides an analysis of the Constitution's eventful history, focusing on the legal and symbolic aspects of the amendment process.[2] First, it presents a brief historical overview to understand the road to Hungary's first constitutional charter (the 1949 Constitution) and its amendments. Second, it offers an analysis of the 1989–90 constitutional amendments, which essentially created a new constitutional system, along with amending the text. Third, it shares the background of the 2011 Constitution, its amendments and the failed attempt to change Hungary's constitutional amendments model. Finally, the closing remarks reflect on whether the integrative model has any significant legal, political or other consequences.

II. New But Old: The 1949 Constitution and its Amendments

Hungary did not have a constitutional charter until the mid-twentieth century. Before that, similar to its British counterpart, the Hungarian Constitution was composed of several statutes, doctrines and customs. Together, they formed the so-called 'historical constitution'. The elements of this constitution were not fixed; they were defined flexibly, taking into account the given features of the historical period.[3]

There have been two attempts in Hungary to establish a codified constitution. The first occurred after the First World War during the short period of the Hungarian Soviet Republic. Two constitutional charters were adopted then – one by a decree of the Revolutionary Governing Committee and the other as an act of the National Assembly of Soviets. However, these attempts did not influence the subsequent constitution-making processes.[4] The second attempt was made after the Second World War when the foundations of a new democratic and republican

[2] This chapter focuses on the formal amendments; however, the informal amendments are also part of the Hungarian constitutional system. See Tímea Drinóczi, Fruzsina Gárdos-Orosz and Zoltán Pozsár-Szentmiklósy, 'Formal and Informal Constitutional Amendment in Hungary' (2019) 8 MTA Law Working Papers, https://jog.tk.hu/uploads/files/2019_18_Drinoczi_GardosOrosz_PozsarSzentmiklosy.pdf.

[3] Regarding the historical constitution, see Zoltán Szente, 'A Historizáló Alkotmányozás Problémái – A Történeti Alkotmány és a Szent Korona az Új Alaptörvényben' [Problem of the Historicism in Constitution-Making – The Historical Constitution and the Holy Crown in the New Basic Law] (2011) 3 *Közjogi Szemle* 1; Kálmán Pózca, 'Is a Revival Possible? Theoretical Reflections on the Historical Constitution' in Ferenc Horkay Hörcher and Thomas Lorman (eds), *A History of the Hungarian Constitution: Law, Government and Political Culture in Central Europe* (New York, IB Tauris, 2019) 181; Fruzsina Gárdos-Orosz, 'The Reference to Constitutional Traditions in Populist Constitutionalism: The Case of Hungary' (2021) 1 *Hungarian Journal of Legal Studies* 23.

[4] See Thomas Lormann, 'The Use and Abuse of Flexibility: Hungary's Historical Constitution 1867–1919' in Hörcher and Lorman (n 3) 126, 136; Gábor Schweitzer, 'Közjogi provizórium, jogfolytonosság, új közjogi irány – Az 1919/1920–1944 közötti magyarországi alkotmányjog-tudomány vázlata, II. rész' [Temporary Legal Order, Legal Continuity, the New Direction in Public Law – Sketch on the Hungarian Public Legal Science between 1919 and 1944, Part II] (2014) 2 *Közjogi Szemle* 8.

regime were regulated by Act I of 1946 on the Form of the State of Hungary. This was a more influential text that affected the drafting of the 1989–90 and 2011 Constitutions. However, the 1946 Act cannot be considered a true constitution. It only regulated a few state-related matters, and fundamental rights were only mentioned in its preamble, without any detailed regulatory guidance. Very soon after the Act entered into force, the Hungarian constitutional system slid into a Soviet-style socialist dictatorship.[5]

Paradoxically, Hungary's first written constitution was adopted during the non-democratic, non-liberal era. Act XX of 1949 on the Constitution of the Hungarian People's Republic was a Soviet-influenced constitution, based almost entirely on the translation of Stalin's 1936 Constitution. The government submitted the associated bill on 10 August 1949 and, after a two-day debate, the Members of Parliament (MPs) adopted it unanimously. Act XX entered into force on 20 August 1949.[6]

The 1949 Constitution represented a clear break from any previous constitutional traditions. Basic constitutional principles including the separation of powers, the rule of law and democracy were missing from the text, being replaced by a constitutional system based on the unity of power, governing by decrees and a dearth of human rights protections.

The Constitution was adopted in the form of a statute: the number (twentieth in 1949) was one of a series, the form and structure being the same as other statutes (divided into paragraphs). While it was a constitution in name, it lacked a hierarchy of norms and any real treatment of constitutional review.[7] The 1949 Constitution stipulated that it could be amended by a two-thirds majority of MPs. Still, formally, the Constitution was amended as if it were a statute, using the same procedure. According to Hungarian constitutional traditions, all legal acts, including statutes, follow the integrative model – that is, the modifications are integrated into the original text. There are also examples where a simple statute has amended the constitutional text.[8]

Before the 1989–90 democratic transition, the 1949 Constitution was amended 23 times. This was a relatively high number of amendments over the course of 40 years, especially when considering the governing power was the same throughout the entire period due to the one-party system. The explanation for this

[5] For more on Act I of 1946, see Balázs Fekete, 'Law I of 1946 and Law XX of 1949: Continuity or Discontinuity in the Traditional Hungarian Constitutionalism?' in Hörcher and Lorman (n 3) 159, 161–69.

[6] For a detailed analysis of the 1949 Constitution, see ibid 169–73.

[7] The Constitution granted power to the Presidential Council (a collective institution functioning as head of state) (§ 20(4)) and the Council of Ministers (the government) (§ 25(4)) to annul unconstitutional administrative acts, but established no institutions to execute and protect the Constitution from the legislative branch. There were some proposals in the scholarship favouring some form of constitutional review, and a first attempt to introduce something similar occurred in 1984 when a Constitutional Council was established as a committee of the Parliament.

[8] Act III of 1970 on the amendment of Act III of 1966 on the election of Members of Parliament and members of local councils contained a constitutional amendment in § 21(2): 'The provisions on the election of the council members in the Act XX of 1949 are amended accordingly.'

can partly be found in § 24 of the 1949 Constitution. This provision provided an exhaustive list of government ministries and had to be amended every time there was any restructuring of the state administration; indeed, seven of the amendments exclusively concerned this provision.[9]

An amendment with a more significant scope was added in 1972. At that time, the Soviet Union and other socialist countries had already 'built the basis of socialism' and wanted to emphasise this by creating new constitutions (or amending old ones) and enshrining the social and political changes of the previous decades.[10] In Hungary, this process resulted in a constitutional amendment. However, Act I of 1972 did not take the usual form of an amendment; instead, it contained the entire codified constitutional text, including the oldest and newest amendments.

The last constitutional amendments incorporated before the democratic change were clearly part of the socialist government's attempts to slowly reform the system from the inside. However, these were only small steps; the amendments did not serve as tools for fuelling fundamental change. For example, a Parliament-created Constitutional Council tried to install a form of constitutional review, but the Council was only a parliamentary committee and was therefore not entitled to suspend statutes (only lower-level regulations).[11]

III. Old But New: The 1989–90 Constitution and its Amendments (Albeit Flawed)

The political transition in 1989 was paired with constitutional changes. As a result of the so-called 'National Roundtable' talks in which negotiations between new democratic movements and the state party, as well as organisations such as trade unions took place, Act XXXI of 1989 on the Amendment of the Constitution was adopted and promulgated on 23 October 1989, along with the Proclamation of the Republic.[12] The amendment was adopted based on the amendments rule of the 1949 Constitution that required a two-thirds parliamentary majority, and the amended provisions were incorporated into the text, following the integrative model.

Act XXXI of 1989 was formally a constitutional amendment, not a new constitution. It was incorporated into Act XX of 1949, though the name was changed from the Constitution of the Hungarian People's Republic to the Hungarian

[9] eg, Act I of 1952, Act IV of 1953, Act III of 1954 and Act IV of 1955.

[10] Barna Attila, Horváth Attila, Máthé Gábor and Tóth Zoltán József, *Magyar Állam- és Jogtörténet* [State and Legal History of Hungary] (Budapest, Nemzeti Közszolgálati Egyetem Közigazgatás-tudományi Kar, 2014) 330–31.

[11] Act II of 1983.

[12] The 1989 democratic transition is described in numerous works. See, eg, András Bozóki, András Körösényi and George Schöpflin (eds), *Post-communist Transition: Emerging Pluralism in Hungary* (New York, St Martin's Press, 1992).

Republic. The rationale for this change is clear from the amended preamble to the Constitution: 'To enable the peaceful political transition to the rule of law with a multiparty system, a parliamentary democracy and a social market economy, the Parliament – until the adoption of our homeland's new constitution – adopts the text of the Constitution of Hungary as follows.' The last socialist Parliament adopted this constitutional amendment, and the plan was to have the first freely elected Parliament adopt an entirely new constitution.

Although its assigned number was a remnant of socialist times, the content of the 1989 Constitution was primarily derived from Western European constitutions (especially from the German Basic Law). The constitutional foundations were those of a liberal democracy – the separation of powers, the rule of law, democracy and fundamental rights as central pillars of the text – and a constitutional court was established as the foremost institution of constitutional review.[13]

The 1989 Constitution remained consistent regarding the constitutional amendment procedure: the Constitution could be amended by a two-thirds majority of MPs.[14] And while there were no special provisions for adopting a new constitution, there was a consensus that the same majority was necessary to do so.

After the first free elections in Hungary in 1990, it soon became evident that the plans for a new constitution were implausible. The parties of the former democratic opposition were divided and there was no chance of a two-thirds majority consensus. Even between 1994 and 1998, when the government parties had the necessary majority, the coalition parties disagreed, and the idea of adopting a new constitution was abandoned.[15]

However, the lack of consensus on a new constitution did not hinder the promulgation of amendments. Between 1989 and 2009, the Constitution was amended 25 times. Some of these amendments were minor and technical, but others were more comprehensive. Act XL of 1990 contained the results of a post-election agreement between the two largest parties. The legislation ensured that some of the questions pertaining to state organisations and fundamental rights could only be regulated by a two-thirds majority of the MPs through the adoption of organic statutes.[16] Act LXI of 2002 rewrote several provisions

[13] The Constitutional Court became an important actor in the transition to a democracy governed by the rule of law. On its beginnings, see, eg, Gábor Halmai, 'The Hungarian Approach to Constitutional Review: The End of Activism? The First Decade of the Hungarian Constitutional Court' in Wojciech Sadurski (ed), *Constitutional Justice East and West* (Dordrecht, Kluwer Law International, 2002) 189; Catherine Dupré, *Importing the Law in Post-communist Transitions: The Hungarian Constitutional Court and the Right to Human Dignity* (Oxford, Hart Publishing, 2003); László Sólyom, *Az alkotmánybíráskodás kezdetei Magyarországon* [*The Beginnings of Constitutional Adjudication in Hungary*] (Budapest, Osiris, 2001).

[14] § 24(3).

[15] The preparatory process of the 1994–95 (failed) attempt to promulgate a new constitution is well documented as the Ministry of Justice published all of the related documents. See *A Magyar Köztársaság Alkotmányának szabályozási koncepciója* [*Concept of the New Constitution of the Republic of Hungary*] (Budapest, Igazságügyi Minisztérium, 1995).

[16] István Kukorelli, *Közjogi tűnődések* [*Reflections on Public Law*] (Budapest, Triorg, 1991) 44–49.

relating to basic principles, the organisation of the state and fundamental rights to make the Constitution compatible with the law of the European Union (EU) by 1 May 2004, the date of Hungary's accession.[17] Like the 1989 Constitution, both of these amendments had significant symbolic value, opening up a new phase in the country's history and introducing a new constitutional system without adopting a new constitution.

These amendments followed the integrative model, which seemed to work seamlessly – with one major exception. Specifically, a technical question emerged in 2010 when the new government parties, finally having the necessary majority, intended to adopt a new constitution.

On 4 June 1995, a new provision was added to the Constitution: '[A] majority of four-fifths of the votes of the Members of the Parliament is required to pass the parliamentary resolution specifying the detailed regulations for the preparation of the new Constitution.'[18] The governing coalition drafted this rule as a mechanism of self-restraint, since they had the necessary two-thirds majority, but did not want to draft a new constitution without a broader consensus. The provision was inserted into the Constitution via § 1 of Act XIV of 1995. § 2 of the same amendment provided that the entire Act should cease to be in force the day the 1994 Parliament's mandate ended. The intention was to adopt a new constitution during this parliamentary period. However, a technical question asked whether the amendment would definitively be incorporated into the Constitution's text, and the amending Act's expiration would not change the force of the incorporated provision, or whether it was only temporarily incorporated and lapsed on the same date as the amending act. Before 2009, the consensus was that the second option was valid and that the four-fifths majority was not part of the constitutional text.[19]

On the twentieth anniversary of the 1989 Constitution, the official government gazette, *Magyar Közlöny*, published the codified text of the Constitution along with the original text of the 1949 Constitution and its amendments. This codified text contained § 24(5), indicating that it was still in force, much to everyone's surprise. The supporting argument for this was primarily based on a Constitutional Court decision which ruled that amending laws become part of the amended law. Therefore, the *ex nunc* nullification of the amending law did not affect the validity of the amended legislation.[20] However, this decision was issued in 2006, years after the constitutional amendment in question, so it was uncertain whether the Court's holding could actually be applied.

[17] András Sajó, 'Az EU-csatlakozás alkotmányosságára gyakorolt hatása az új tagállamokban' [The Effect of the EU Accession on the Constitutionalism in the New Member States] (2003) 2 *Fundamentum* 14.

[18] § 24(5).

[19] See, eg, the leading commentary on the Hungarian Constitution: András Jakab (ed), *Az Alkotmány Kommentárja* [*A Commentary to the Constitution*] (Budapest, Századvég, 2009) 64. The constitutional text in most of the legal databases (there were only commercial ones at that time) also did not contain the provision.

[20] 4/2006 (II 15) CC decision, paras 101, 115.

The conservative government coalition, which came into power in 2010, decided to end this legal quagmire by abrogating the provision using one of its first constitutional amendments after the election.[21] This shifted the debate to whether a provision with a four-fifths majority requirement for a new constitution could be amended by a two-thirds majority.[22] We agree with the opinion that there was no legal obstacle.[23] The entire situation points out how technical questions concerning the integrative model can still cause a constitutional crisis.

While the 1989 Constitution met its requirement to create a basis for the democratic transition, the attempts in 2010 to replace it can be partly traced back to the vulnerability of the 1989 Constitution itself. This vulnerability was derived both from the instrument's failure to symbolise the democratic transition by choosing the path of an amendment as opposed to a new constitution and its desire to garner public attachment to the document.[24]

IV. New But Old But New: The 2011 Constitution, its Amendments and an Attempted Model Change

After winning the election with more than two-thirds of the mandate in 2010, the governing coalition of two conservative parties announced that it would use its majority position to adopt a new constitution.[25] However, before that, the coalition amended the 1989 Constitution 12 times. In adopting these amendments, the coalition used them as a tool to realise political goals, including adding a 98 per cent tax on severance payments to dismissed public servants and packing the Constitutional Court with additional members.[26]

[21] Amendment of the Constitution of 5 July 2010.

[22] See, eg, János Kis, 'From the 1989 Constitution to the 2011 Fundamental Law' in Gábor Attila Tóth (ed), *Constitution for a Disunited Nation* (Budapest, CEU Press, 2012) 4; Andrew Arato, 'Arato on Constitution Making in Hungary and the 4/5 Rule', *ICONnect blog*, 6 April 2011, www.iconnectblog.com/2011/04/arato-on-constitution-making-in-hungary-and-the-45-rule.

[23] See a more detailed analysis of the question in Pál Sonnevend, András Jakab and Lóránt Csink, 'The Constitution as an Instrument of Everyday Party Politics: The Basic Law of Hungary' in Armin von Bogdandy and Pál Sonnevend (eds), *Constitutional Crisis in the European Constitutional Area* (Oxford, Hart Publishing/Beck, 2015) 43.

[24] ibid 42.

[25] This section of the chapter is partly based on a previous publication: András Jakab and Eszter Bodnár, 'The Rule of Law, Democracy and Human Rights in Hungary: Tendencies from 1989 until 2019' in Tímea Drinóczi and Agnieszka Bień-Kacała (eds), *Rule of Law, Common Values, and Illiberal Constitutionalism: Poland and Hungary within the European Union* (Abingdon, Routledge, 2020) 105–18.

[26] For a detailed analysis of these amendments, see Fruzsina Gárdos-Orosz, 'Why Does a Constitutional Change Emerge and Who Has a Say in it? Constitution-Making, Constitutional Amendments and Their Constitutional Review in Hungary between 2010 and 2018' in Martin Belov (ed), *Revolution, Transition, Memory, and Oblivion. Reflections on Constitutional Change* (Cheltenham, Edward Elgar, 2020) 183, 187–92; Tímea Drinóczi, 'Constitutional Politics in Contemporary Hungary' (2016) 10(1) *Vienna Journal on International Constitutional Law* 69.

The draft of a new Hungarian Constitution was prepared behind closed doors in a non-transparent process. Neither the members of the opposition parties nor civil society organisations were involved. Members of the governing coalition submitted the bill on 14 March 2011, and the Parliament adopted it barely a month later, on 18 April 2011. None of the opposition parties voted in favour of the new Constitution: some did not participate in the parliamentary debates, which were already partisan, and the rest voted no. The President of the Republic promulgated the new Constitution, called the 'Basic Law', on 25 April 2011, and it entered into force on 1 January 2012.[27]

Several formal elements, especially political rhetoric, emphasised a new beginning, a discontinuity with the 1949 Constitution, and the 1989 democratic transition. For example, the instrument was entitled 'Basic Law' (Alaptörvény) instead of 'constitution', which would have referred to a single document.[28] The preamble also contained several political statements that reflected the lack of continuity.[29]

Contrary to the political rhetoric, and from a legal point of view, the 2011 Constitution highlighted that its adoption was based on the previous Constitution's provisions applicable to constitutional amendments.[30] More importantly, about 80 per cent of the text was derived from the 1989 Constitution.[31] However, amendments later changed this, as described below.

The 2011 Basic Law regulates its own status in the chapter entitled 'Foundation'. According to Article R) (1)–(2): 'The Basic Law shall be the foundation of the legal system of Hungary. The Basic Law and the legal acts shall be binding on everyone.' With this rule, the text made it unequivocal that the Basic Law was not a legal act (ie, a statute or decree), but rather a *sui generis* source of law with supremacy over the other elements of the legal system. This is also expressed in its name ('Basic Law'); its title (there is no number or year indicated as in the case of statutes); its structure (it is not numbered by paragraphs

[27] See also Kriszta Kovács and Gábor Attila Tóth, 'Hungary's Constitutional Transformation' (2011) 4 *European Constitutional Law Review* 183. European institutions followed the constitution-making process in Hungary with great interest. The Council of Europe's Venice Commission issued two opinions during the process. The European Parliament adopted a resolution on the Hungarian Basic Law, holding a debate on the new document a few months later (18 January 2012). None of these actions had any real impact on the constitution-making process or the Constitution's text (except for a few technical details).

[28] Herbert Küpper, *Einführung in das ungarische Recht* [*Introduction to Hungarian Law*] (Munich, Beck, 2011) 295; Attila Vincze and Márton Varju, 'Hungary: The New Fundamental Law' (2012) 18 *European Public Law* 437.

[29], eg, 'We do not recognise the communist constitution of 1949, since it was the basis for tyrannical rule; we therefore proclaim it to be invalid' or 'We date the restoration of our country's self-determination, lost on the nineteenth day of March 1944, from the second day of May 1990, when the first freely elected organ of popular representation was formed. We shall consider this date to be the beginning of our country's new democracy and constitutional order'.

[30] Point 2 of the Final Provisions to the Basic Law.

[31] Sonnevend, Jakab and Csink (n 23) 65–70.

and instead uses three different systems – letters, Roman numerals and Arabic numbers); and its unique regulatory scheme. The *sui generis* feature is expressed, for example, in Article S), which only describes the amendment procedure for the Fundamental Law, separated from the amendment procedure of statutes. This is different from the 1949 Constitution, which was titled, numbered and structured like other statutes.

The original text of the Basic Law of March 2011 contained no transitional provisions. However, Point 3 of the Final Provisions of the Basic Law referred to the Transitional Provisions, which had to be adopted using the same procedure as the Basic Law's amendments. On 30 December 2011, the Parliament, acting as a constituent power, adopted the Transitional Provisions collectively as a kind of appendix to the Basic Law. The Transitional Provisions entered into force two days later, on 1 January 2012, together with the Basic Law.

Contrary to their title, and in addition to regulating the transitional period between the old and the new constitutions, the Transitional Provisions contained several substantive measures, for example, the cut on the pensions of the former leaders of the communist dictatorship (Article 1) or the competence of the President of the National Judicial Office and the Supreme Prosecutor to move court cases from one court to another (Article 11(3)–(4)). Some of the substantive measures included specific restrictions on fundamental rights, and others were seemingly designed to undermine the Constitutional Court's jurisprudence.[32]

The adoption of the Transitional Provisions may have been a first attempt to switch to the appendative amending model by adopting supplementary documents that were hierarchically at the same level as the Constitution instead of replacing the text with an amendment. However, the Commissioner for Fundamental Rights turned to the Constitutional Court, challenging the Transitional Provisions. The Commissioner continued his challenge even after the adoption of the First Amendment to the Basic Law that reinforced the constitutional level of the Transitional Provisions.[33]

In the pivotal decision of 45/2012 (XII 29), the Constitutional Court opined that the Parliament had exceeded its constitutional power by adding rules to the Transitional Provisions, which did not possess the transitional character. The Court affirmed its previous case law, claiming that it lacked the power to review the Constitution on the merits, but it was empowered to ensure that procedural requirements were satisfied. Since Point 3 of the Final Provision of the Basic Law authorised the Parliament to adopt actual transitional provisions, which was regarded as a procedural rule that the Constitutional Court could enforce.

[32] Sonnevend, Jakab and Csink called the Transitional Provisions 'The Source of Evil'. ibid 49–51.

[33] Article 1(1) of the First Amendment to the Basic Law stipulated that 'the Transitional Provisions adopted according to Point 3 [of the Final Provisions of the Basic Law] are part of the Basic Law'.

Consequently, the Court held that the Parliament was operating outside the scope of the entitlement in Point 3. Therefore, the non-transitional provisions could be annulled without overstepping the limits of constitutional review. This decision ended the attempt to change the constitutional amendments model and consolidated the use of the integrative model.

The 2011 Constitution retained the amendment formula that makes it relatively easy to change the text – particularly with a governing coalition having more than two-thirds of the mandate. According to Article S), the President of the Republic, the government, any parliamentary committee or any MP may submit a proposal for the adoption of a Basic Law or an amendment to it. The new constitution or the amendment shall be adopted by a two-thirds majority of MPs. However, the President may veto the amendment and send it to the Constitutional Court for review if the formal requirements are seemingly not met. There are no other formal or substantive limitations on amendments. The form of the title of amendments is also regulated in the Constitution; they should include the name, the chronological number of the amendment and the date of promulgation.[34]

After the entry into force of the 2011 Constitution, the Prime Minister declared the Basic Law to be 'solid as granite'.[35] However, at the time of writing, the Basic Law has been amended 11 times. Formally, these amendments have several features that reveal they are not ordinary statutes, but rather amendments to the Basic Law, including their titles and structures.[36] These amendments follow the tradition of the integrative model, and their content has been incorporated into the Constitution's text. Indeed, looking at their substance, almost every amendment has taken a step further away from the heritage of the 1989 Constitution. The most significant amendments to the 2011 Constitution have been the Fourth, Seventh and Ninth.

The principal part of the Fourth Amendment, which was adopted in 2013, intended to reverse the above-mentioned 2012 Constitutional Court decision by annulling the non-transitional sections of the Transitional Provisions. In turn, the Parliament opted to unify the two parts of the Constitution's text. This amalgamation clarified that Hungary would continue to use the integrative model of constitutional amendments after the short interim with the Transitional Provisions. The Fourth Amendment added the Transitional Provisions to the text of the Basic Law. These reinstated rules included substantive provisions, such as the President of the National Judicial Office's competence to re-allocate court cases,[37] and the suspension of the statute of limitations for criminal offences not prosecuted during the communist regime for political reasons.[38] Apart from these,

[34] Article S)(4) of the Basic Law.

[35] 'Orbán: Gránitszilárdságú az alaptörvény' [Orbán: The Basic Law is Solid as Granite] *Mandiner* (2 January 2012), www.mandiner.hu/cikk/20120102_orban_granitszilardsagu_az_alaptorveny.

[36] The title of each amendment follows this form: 'First Amendment to the Basic Law of Hungary (18 June 2012)'. The structure has articles instead of paragraphs, which are used in statutes.

[37] Article 27(4).

[38] Article U)(6).

the Fourth Amendment reversed virtually all of the Constitutional Court's politically sensitive decisions handed down after the 2010 elections. This was achieved by incorporating the content of the statutes repealed by the Constitutional Court into the constitutional text itself, thus making it constitutional law.[39] The amendment resulted in a Basic Law with many specific exceptions to fundamental rights, as well as numerous topics generally regulated at the level of an ordinary statute. These changes reduced the level of protection of fundamental rights and diminished the possibility of constitutional review. Finally, the Fourth Amendment 'overruled' the Constitutional Court decisions made before the entry into force of the Basic Law.[40] The amendment also specified that the Court could review constitutional amendments on formal grounds, but not on substance, thus eliminating any potential for judicial activism.[41] The Venice Commission criticised the Fourth Amendment,[42] and law-makers took some of the criticisms into account when drafting the Fifth Amendment that addressed unrealistically tight deadlines for some Constitutional Court procedures and the President of the Regional Court's ability to re-allocate cases.[43]

The Seventh Amendment, adopted in June 2018, must be viewed in light of the government's anti-migration propaganda campaign and its refusal to consider relevant EU policies. The amendment's main topic was indeed migration, but it also obligated all state institutions to protect constitutional self-identity and the Christian culture of Hungary[44] and to set limits on EU participation, stating that it 'shall be consistent with the fundamental rights and freedoms laid down in the Basic Law, and shall not limit Hungary's inalienable right to determine its territorial integrity, population, form of government and governmental organisation'.[45] The Seventh Amendment's other two elements overruled previous Constitutional Court decisions, including the prohibition of 'using a public space as a habitual dwelling'[46] and a restriction on the freedom of assembly such that it 'shall not impair the private and family life and home of others'.[47]

[39] See, eg, art L(1) about the definition of family; art VII(2) and (3) about the recognition of churches.

[40] Point 4 of the Closing and Miscellaneous Provisions.

[41] Based on this new provision, the Constitutional Court rejected the initiatives to review the Fourth Amendment (12/2013 (V 24) CC decision). See an analysis of this in Attila Vincze, 'Az Alkotmánybíróság határozata az Alaptörvény negyedik módosításáról. Az alkotmánymódosítás alkotmánybírósági kontrollja' [The Constitutional Court's Decision on the Fourth Amendment to the Basic Law] (2013) 3 *Jogesetek Magyarázata* 3.

[42] European Commission for Democracy through Law (Venice Commission), Opinion on the Fourth Amendment of the Fundamental Law of Hungary (No 720/2013, 14 June 2013).

[43] For analysis of the Fourth Amendment, see Judit Zeller, 'Nichts ist so beständig … Die jüngsten Novellen des Grundgesetzes Ungarns im Kontext der Entscheidungen des Verfassungsgerichts' [Nothing is So Permanent … The Newest Amendments to the Basic Law of Hungary in the Context of the Constitutional Court Decisions] (2013) 3 *Osteuropa-Recht* 307; Imre Vörös, 'The Constitutional Landscape after the Fourth and Fifth Amendments of Hungarian Fundamental Law' (2014) 1 *Acta Juridica Hungarica* 1.

[44] Article R)(4).

[45] Article E)(2).

[46] Article XXII(3).

[47] Article VI(1).

The Ninth Amendment, adopted in December 2020, added more controversial language to the constitutional text. Specifically, it declared that 'the mother is a woman, and the father is a man', and marriage is the foundation of family relations.[48] Furthermore, it complemented the provisions on the protection of children, adding language defending the right of children to identify with their birth gender. Finally, the Ninth Amendment introduced the definition of public finance and redesigned the categories of emergency powers.[49]

V. Concluding Remarks

Constitutional amendments have different aims, including formal (eg, correcting the text), functional (eg, checking the judiciary, promoting democracy) and symbolic (enshrining national values) ones.[50] In the case of Hungary, the most important constitutional amendments have served functional goals, but many have also been clearly symbolic.

The 1989 Constitution created a line of demarcation between the socialist, non-democratic, non-liberal system and a Western-style liberal democracy. The document also acted as the first step towards fulfilling the dream of an entirely new constitution. However, the drafters were unaware that the choice of adopting amendments instead of a new constitution would make the 1989 Constitution vulnerable and open the doors to a largely opaque process of creating a new instrument.

Clearly, the 2011 Constitution was crafted to highlight its discontinuity with the 1949 and 1989 versions. This detachment was manifested in the formal features of the text and in political rhetoric, but not the actual content. However, subsequent amendments confirmed this detachment by adding exceptions to fundamental rights, overriding various Constitutional Court decisions and using the text as a tool to serve political interests.

With regard to form, Hungary has followed the integrative constitutional amendments model. This model was based on a historical tradition emanating from the era before the constitutional charters when statutes were amended in the same way. There was only one attempt to change the model's use in Hungary,

[48] Article L)(1).

[49] See more about the Seventh and Ninth Amendments in Eszter Bodnár, Johanna Fröhlich, Fruzsina Gárdos-Orosz and Zoltán Pozsár-Szentmiklósy, 'Hungary' in Roberto Barroso Luís and Richard Albert (eds), *The International Review of Constitutional Reform* (Program on Constitutional Studies at the University of Texas at Austin and the International Forum on the Future of Constitutionalism, 2021) 136; Eszter Polgári and Tamás Dombos, 'A New Chapter in the Hungarian Government's Crusade against LGBTQI People', *Verfassungsblog*, 18 November 2020, https://verfassungsblog.de/a-new-chapter-in-the-hungarian-governments-crusade-against-lgbtqi-people; Viktor Z. Kazai, 'Power Grab in Times of Emergency', *Verfassungsblog*, 12 November 2020, verfassungsblog.de/power-grab-in-times-of-emergency.

[50] Albert (n 1) 39–48.

but the Constitutional Court prevented this by annulling specific passages of the Transitional Provisions, a document with previously unknown placement among the hierarchy of norms.

The use of the integrative model has generally been straightforward, although this chapter has described a circumstance when the question of the incorporation of constitutional amendments led to both academic and political debates. This example demonstrates that technical questions associated with the constitutional amendment models can lead to constitutional crises. Therefore, understanding the features, advantages, disadvantages and risks of these models is a crucial component of the academic discourse on the Hungarian constitutional system.

16

One Constitution, Two Models of Codification

Between Trust and Distrust Towards Constitutional Interpretations in Albania

ARTA VORPSI

I. Introduction

It is well known that constitutions generally provide formal rules for adopting amendments to themselves. These formal rules routinely specify the parties entitled to initiate or propose amendments, time periods and quorum(s) necessary for the proposals, as well as the steps required for final approval. These rules commonly differ from those required to pass an ordinary law. This difference suggests that formal amendment rules and ordinary amendment rules serve different functions in relation to constitutional values and the rule of law.[1]

Formal rules for amending the constitution are particularly necessary to channel the popular will into the institutional dialogue, so that it can then be transformed further into constitutional change. Because of their nature, the formal rules for amending a constitution simultaneously reflect both trust and distrust in political stakeholders: on the one hand, they authorise political actors to improve the constitution, while on the other hand, they limit the manner, procedure and timing of their actions to that end. Given the essential functions embodied in the formal rules for adopting a constitutional amendment, it is to be expected that the constitution itself will provide for it in the most exhaustive manner, and in fact most of them follow this line.[2]

[1] Richard Albert, 'The Expressive Function of Constitutional Amendment Rules' (2013) 29 *McGill Law Review* 225.

[2] Bjørn Erik Rasch and Roger D Congleton, 'Amendment Procedures and Constitutional Stability' in Roger D Congleton and Birgitta Swedenborg (eds), *Democratic Constitutional Design and Public Policy: Analysis and Evidence* (Cambridge, MA, MIT Press, 2006) 319–25.

When it was approved in 1998, the Albanian Constitution could be best described as a 'framework' text that avoided the prolixity of statutory constitution. Yet with time and after several constitutional amendments, the Constitution grew more detailed, and in some cases created tensions with other parts of the constitutional text. In at least two cases when constitutional amendments were introduced, specifically in 2008 and 2016, one of the most debated topics among drafting experts was the length of the proposed amendments. The discussions focused on whether detailed specificity was appropriate for a constitutional text. In the end, the country chose the path of specificity, a reflection of the lack of trust in politicians and also concern about how the Constitutional Court would interpret a text that was written broadly rather than narrowly. Following the logic of that approach, this model of codification would guarantee the implementation of the constitutional provisions while constraining the possibility of easy modification through constitutional interpretation.

This chapter will focus on the model of codification of constitutional amendments in Albania. I will explain its origins and effects on the country's political and legal environment. I will draw from my experience as a member of the expert group in charge of drafting the constitutional amendments related to the justice reform in 2016. In this experience, I was involved in determining the best legal formulations for amendments while also seeking political consensus, without losing the focus from the ultimate aim of the amendments: to reform the justice system in order to ensure the professionalism, independence, and integrity of judges and prosecutors. It proved to be anything but a simple task.

II. Constitutional Amendment in Albania

The Albanian Constitution is now almost 25 years old[3] and has been amended six times.[4] With the exception of the amendments in 2016, which introduced the deepest justice reform in Albania since 1990, the rest were focused on purely political objectives, without bringing any significant positive effect on state building aspects. Some of these amendments still continue today to negatively impact the relationship between state powers. For example, the amendments introduced with respect to the election of the President of Republic or the no-confidence vote both eliminated the political consensus in Parliament,[5] resulting in a

[3] Adopted by Law no 8417, dated 21 October 1998.

[4] Amended by Law nos 9675/2007, 9904/2008, 88/2012, 137/2015, 76/2016 and 115/2020.

[5] For more on this, see 'Analysis of the Justice System', parliamentary document drafted by the Ad Hoc Commission for the Justice Reform www.nchb.al/wp-content/uploads/2015/06/Analiza-e-Sistemit-t%C3%AB-Drejt%C3%ABsis%C3%AB.pdf, 19, 22, 23. See also the interview of Aurela Anastasi, one of the prominent professors of constitutional law, on this subject: https://www.osfa.al/publikime/aurela-anastasi-kushtetuten-se-ndryshon-vetem-klasa-politike-revista-java.

strong politicisation of the President's office and in giving more power to the party leadership.[6] In this section, I will summarise the six amendments to the Albanian Constitution, with attention to their content, their aim and their model of codification.

A. The First Amendments

The first amendments to the 1998 Constitution extended the mandate of local government units from three years to four.[7] It remains unclear why the mandate of these organs was originally codified in the Constitution, since such details are usually regulated by ordinary laws. This constitutional revision introduced only a minor and insignificant change. With regard to the form of its codification, the amendment to Article 109 contains a note with information about what has been amended and by which particular law.[8]

B. The Second Amendments

Soon afterwards, another set of amendments was introduced, this time significantly changing the political landscape in Albania. The first of these changed the electoral system from a mixed majoritarian-proportional system into a regional proportional system with multi-name constituencies in accordance with one of the administrative units of the territorial division of the Republic of Albania.[9] As a result, the two major political parties grew in power, while the smaller parties effectively lost all chance to win by running alone. In order to have any hope of representation, the smaller parties had to enter into a coalition with the bigger parties. The constitutional changes also affected the timeframe for parliamentary mandate,[10] the election procedure for the President of the Republic,[11] and the motion of no-confidence vote against the prime minister. These changes were introduced as a preventive measure by the majority to discourage any possible initiative against the majority leader.

[6] Arta Vorpsi, 'Country Report on Constitutional Developments in Albania 2019, 2020' in Richard Albert,David Landau, Pietro Faraguna and Šimon Drugda, *The I·CONnect-Clough Center 2020 Global Review of Constitutional Law*. ISBN: 978-0-692-15916-3. Published by the Clough Center for the Study of Constitutional Democracy: https://ssrn.com/abstract=3942876.

[7] Article 109(1), as amended by Law no 9675/2007.

[8] Article 109, as noted: 'Paragraph 1, as amended by Law no 9675, dated 13.1.2007.'

[9] Articles 64 and 68 of the Constitution, as amended by Law no 9904/2008.

[10] Articles 65 and 67 of the Constitution.

[11] ibid arts 87 and 88.

C. The Third Amendment

The third amendment was introduced in 2012 due to the pressure from the international partners (the EU and the US) to undertake measures against corruption mostly among the politicians and the judiciary. Prior to the amendment, investigations could not be initiated without the prior consent of the Parliament (for Members of Parliament) or of the High Judicial Council (for judges). This often resulted in blocking investigations into wrongdoing. The amendment abolished immunity from criminal investigation (including from arrest) for judges,[12] but did not to remove immunity from arrest or search warrants for legislators and executives.[13]

D. The Fourth Amendment

The fourth amendment sought to limit the right to be elected where a candidate had been sentenced to imprisonment for committing a crime. In exceptional and justified cases, the law may provide for restrictions of the right to be elected for citizens serving a prison sentence or the right to be elected prior to a final decision being rendered, or where citizens have been deported in connection with a crime or a very serious and grave breach of public security.[14] This amendment was added to the Constitution's section on Constitutional Principles, though perhaps it might have been better situated in the section on Political Rights and Freedoms.[15] The amendment was also added to Article 45, which would have been sufficient on its own. This double codification reflects the lack of trust political actors had in future interpretations of these new constitutional rules.

E. The Fifth Amendments

The year 2016 saw the codification of the most significant set of constitutional amendments, resulting in changes to one-third of the Constitution, not to mention the addition of a temporary annex to the Constitution consisting of 10 additional articles. The main reason for this major reform was to reform the justice system with a focus on professionalism and integrity. The amendments affected virtually all justice institutions directly or indirectly related to judicial power, and established new rules for how to exercise judicial authority and how to ensure its accountability. The key part of these amendments was a new vetting process for all

[12] ibid arts 126 (for judges of the Constitutional Court) and 137 for all judges, as amended by Law no 88/2012.

[13] ibid art 73 of the Constitution, as amended by Law no 88/2012.

[14] Article 6/1 in conjunction with art 45 of the Constitution, as amended by Law no 137/2015.

[15] Chapter III, Political Rights and Freedoms (arts 45–48).

judges, prosecutors and legal advisers, requiring each to be scrutinised for their assets, integrity and professional background.[16]

The Albanian Constitution of 1998 had been drafted in close cooperation with the Venice Commission.[17] At the time, it was thought that the constitutional arrangements were sufficient to guarantee judicial independence and accountability. Yet in Albania, as well as in some other post-communist countries, constitutionalising the standards on the independence of the judiciary resulted in a paradox: constitutional guarantees had been bestowed upon judges who were not yet independent and impartial in practice. As a result, in the opinion of Albanian politicians and the public, many members of the judiciary developed corporatist attitudes (supporting, promoting and protecting each other's interests) which led to widespread corruption and lack of professionalism, integrity and efficiency in the justice system. In light of these circumstances, the initiative to revise the constitutional provisions on the judiciary was seen as perfectly understandable.[18]

The constitutional amendments of 2016 were intended to introduce a permanent reform of the judicial system by introducing temporary provisions relating to the extraordinary measures intended to vet the suitability of the existing judges and prosecutors and cleansing the system from those found incompetent, corrupt or linked to organised crime. With regard to the extraordinary measures to vet judges and prosecutors, the Venice Commission was of the opinion that such measures were not only justified but also necessary for Albania to protect itself from the scourge of corruption which, if not addressed, could completely destroy its judicial system.[19]

One of the distinguishing features of the 2016 constitutional amendments was their detailed text. Although the expert group proposed leaving most regulations on the legislative level though an organic or simple law, in the end the text was codified in the Constitution. There was a strong need to inform the public that this was not just a normal political reform and that corruption was being taken very seriously. Putting this reform into the Constitution was therefore seen as a political imperative.

Comparing the Constitution before and after the 2016 reforms reveals an enormous difference in the number of words in the constitutional text. For example, Article 147 contained 206 words prior to the reform, but 755 afterwards, not including the three additional articles on dealing with termination of mandates,[20] disciplinary proceedings[21] and incompatibility,[22] which amount

[16] Article G of the Annex.

[17] CDL-INF(1998)009, the Venice Commission Opinion on Recent Amendments to the Law on Major Constitutional Provisions of the Republic of Albania.

[18] CDL(2015)052, the Venice Commission Draft Interim Opinion on the Draft Constitutional Amendments on the Judiciary in Albania, para 8.

[19] CDL(2016)002, Final Draft Constitutional Amendments on the Judiciary in Albania, para 54.

[20] Article 147/b of the Constitution as amended in 2016.

[21] ibid art 147/c.

[22] ibid.

to an additional 279 words. This pattern reveals itself throughout the entire text of the Constitution. The original text of 1998 contained 13,185 words, but today it contains nearly 23,000 words. The annex outlining the new vetting process contains 3,210 words, though it will lose its legal effect in 2026.[23]

F. The Sixth Amendments

Recently in 2020, the sixth constitutional change altered the system in relation to the allocation of mandates, through the introduction of some elements which would ensure a better representation of the people. The constitutional amendment had the effect of abolishing the pre-election coalitions of political parties and the possibility of running as such, and it also imposed a requirement of gender balance.[24]

III. The Incorporation of Amendments

When drafting provisions on constitutional amendment, there is a need for awareness of the potential effects of such rules; this requires both general and comparative analysis, as well as a good knowledge of the national constitutional and political context. Rules and procedures on constitutional amendment should be as clear and simple as possible so as not to give rise to problems and disputes of their own. Unfortunately, there are no rules on how to incorporate the amendments. Therefore, there is a strong need for constitutional lawyers who have extensive knowledge on where and how to incorporate amendments.

Incorporating amendments take time and requires a deep knowledge of the existing constitution, how it has been interpreted in court, how political actors refer to it in political debate and most of all an understanding of the intent of the new amendments. In an ideal situation, there would be time to deliberate carefully and without pressure about where and how to incorporate an amendment.

The Albanian Constitution has chosen a hybrid invisible-integrative model for amendment codification,[25] meaning that there is a note explaining which provision

[23] ibid art 179/b, as added in 2016. The Assembly shall decide on repealing this Annex after the last re-evaluation decision becomes final, following a report submitted by the Chairperson of the Appeal Chamber on the state of affairs of the pending cases or at the end of the mandate of the Special Qualification Chamber.

[24] Aurela Anastasi and Arta Vorpsi, 'The 2020 International Review of Constitutional Reform, Country report- Albania', www.cleveadvogados.com.br/wp-content/uploads/2021/09/SSRN-id3917596.pdf, 11–15.

[25] Richard Albert, *Constitutional Amendments: Making, Breaking and Changing Constitutions* (Oxford, Oxford University Press, 2019) 250.

was amended and when it occurred, but without any further details with regard to the content of the provision. Therefore, the reader is informed about the fact that there has been a change to the constitutional text, but there is no trace of the old or original text. One should go back to the older versions of the text to get more information about the changes or maybe to study the parliamentary documents such as the report to introduce the amendments or discussion in parliamentary commission.

Whether or not the incorporation of an amendment has been done properly also depends on its complexity. If the amendment aims to change specific provisions, such as timeframes, numbers or even institutions, the risk of unclarities or uncertainties remains low. If there is a need to change the whole branch of government (including the relations between the executive and legislative, or the head of state's competences, or even the whole judicial power as in the 2016 reform), the process becomes more complex and difficult because the drafters need to check all the existing provisions to be affected by proposed amendments and afterwards to cross-check any possible conflict among provisions. Referring to the process of 2016, I reveal that the whole incorporation procedure was quite complex and time-consuming. Although most provisions on judicial power are included in a separate part of the Constitution, there were still some other aspects to be reviewed in the light of limitations introduced due to the vetting process (for example, the right to challenge a judicial decision in a higher court).[26]

Another issue was how to introduce a whole new process which was planned to be temporary, namely the vetting process. The general idea was to introduce an extraordinary and temporary process for all judges and prosecutors. After the time limit of nine years, these regulations would no longer be in force. Therefore, the best solution was to include all provisions in relation to the vetting process in a separate annex, while the final and transitory provisions of the constitution was foreseen in the effect and correlation of the Annex's provisions with the 'old' constitutional text.[27]

It is a fact that successful integration requires careful deliberation on how and where to incorporate the new rules by Members of Parliament before they adopt them.[28] Referring to the last constitutional and legal reform of 2016, the formal integration of constitutional amendments introduced suggests a positive cooperation (although imposed by external factors) between political and legal actors in incorporating the amendments in the right place. One could argue about the substance of the amendments in terms of length and detailed contents, which came as a result of mutual political distrust in the Parliament.

[26] Article 43 was amended in terms of limiting the right to challenge a judicial decision in minor civil cases.

[27] Article 179, 179/a and 179/b of the Constitution.

[28] Albert (n 25) 254.

IV. The Political and Legal Consequences of the Albanian Model

As noted above, all six amendment processes have had their own characteristics in terms of initiative, objectives and political, social and legal effects. The first political effect was the minimal consultation process before the approval of constitutional amendments. Although there is a requirement of a qualified majority (two-thirds) to approve the amendments, it has been almost sufficient for the majority to ensure the rest of the votes without any prior consultation or at least not following the formal consultation in the Parliament. It came as a surprise that the 2016 amendments were not only approved unanimously by all 140 Members of Parliament, but also went through a very long and wide consultation process both within and outside the Parliament, among politicians, lawyers, non-governmental organisations (NGOs) and other interested groups, which is not common for the Albanian legislative power This uncharacteristic unanimity can be explained by the well-coordinated diplomatic pressure exerted by the EU and the US, which were both involved from the beginning in the political and technical process of drafting the constitutional amendments.[29] Albania took care to heed this pressure because the country's desire to join the EU would not become a reality without taking concrete measures to fight corruption – the very ones reflected in the enormous 2016 reform.[30] Because of that pressure, there were some last-minute changes to the text of amendments, just a few hours before the final votes in the Parliament, which would not comply with previous legal analysis prepared and proposed by the experts.[31] Therefore, some explanations based on presumptions need to be made in the event of an interpretation by the Constitutional Court or even the legislature. The sense of urgency often helps to overcome resistance that in ordinary times would be sufficient to block change; it conveys the perception of a truly constitutional moment so that influential actors and decision-makers set aside at least some of their concerns in pursuit of the necessary consensus.[32] Yet, on the other hand, it leaves constitutional lawyers without any convincing reason to understand the rationale behind it.

A democratic elected parliament normally should not be put under such pressure to enact the necessary reforms. The parliament is the most appropriate arena for constitutional amendment, in line with a modern idea of democracy. Therefore, a normal, wide-ranging consultation process among the political stakeholders and

[29] Decision No 3, dated 22 December 2014 of the Ad Hoc Parliamentary Committee, 'On representation of international organizations with their experts for the purpose of contributing in the reform of justice system'.

[30] Albania Progress Report 2014, 1, https://neighbourhood-enlargement.ec.europa.eu/albania-progress-report-2014_en. See also Report from the Commission to the Council and the European Parliament on Albania's Progress in the Fight against Corruption and Organised Crime and in the Judicial Reform', COM (2014) 331 final, 4 June 2014.

[31] The amendments were approved around 2 am, during the last session before the summer holidays!

[32] For example, in Germany after the Second World War and in Spain after the death of Franco.

NGOs, and other parties given an adequate timeframe, should take place before the amendment of the fundamental texts.[33] During the past 25 years of the life of the Albanian Constitution, the several constitutional amending processes have led to: (i) a new model of codification (more detailed provisions, including an annex, which are not typically for a constitution); (ii) a reduced frequency in terms of introducing constitutional amendments; and (iii) a majority initiative to amend the Constitution without securing a political consensus in Parliament, not to mention public support. This is an example of how the fundamental law, which is presumed to ensure good governance through trust and respect for politics and state institutions towards the rule of law and democracy, formally became a mirror of mistrust among the political parties, which is reflected in the public demanding to have a voice as a constituent power.

A duly open, informed and timely involvement of all political forces and civil society in the process of reform can strongly contribute to achieving consensus and securing the success of the constitutional revision even if this inevitably takes time and effort.[34]

V. Conclusion

Albania has chosen a hybrid model of codification when it comes to the constitutional amendment procedure. There is no official document which could explain why this model of amendment codification has prevailed. There is also no specific elaboration by the Constitutional Court or scholars on the model of codifying constitutional amendments. One could imply that taking into consideration the young age of the Albanian Constitution, it is easy to recall what has been changed, where and why over the course of the last two-and-a-half decades, so the historical factor is not of much an influence.

The age of a given constitutional document may influence amendment in different ways. On the one hand, it can be argued that the older the text, the more it will be in need of flexible amendment procedures in order to adjust to fundamental transformations in politics and society. On the other hand, very old constitutional texts may over time obtain a particular symbolic value, creating a constitutional culture in which amendment is very difficult. If this is the case, then

[33] Venice Commission Opinion CDL-AD(2020)036 on the Amendments to the Constitution of 30 July 2020 and to the Electoral Code of 5 OCTOBER 2020 in Albania, dated 11 December 2020, para 11.

[34] See, eg, CDL-AD(2007)045, Opinion on the Constitutional Situation in the Kyrgyz Republic, § 57; CDLINF(2001)023, Interim Report on the Constitutional Situation of the Federal Republic of Yugoslavia, § 5; CDLAD(2009)010, Opinion on the Draft Amendments to the Constitution of the Republic of Azerbaijan, § 6; CDLAD(2004)029, Opinion on the Referendum of 17 October 2004 in Belarus, § 14; CDL-AD(2007)004, Opinion on the Constitution of Serbia, §§ 103–04; CDL-AD(2005)016, Second Interim Opinion on Constitutional Reforms in the Republic of Armenia, § 31; CDL-INF(2001)015, Opinion on the Amendments of 9 November 2000 and 28 March 2001 of the Constitution of Croatia, item 4 and conclusions.

the substantive contents of the constitutional system may nevertheless be expected to develop through judicial interpretation and political convention.

Albania is a new democracy and therefore will need time to develop its own constitutional culture and tradition. Furthermore, the transformation process into a consolidated rule of law democracy will require constitutional adjustment for many years to come. This should be done politically, through democratic amendment procedures, rather than through judicial interpretation or other more informal ways. A new democracy should therefore aim for an amendment formula designed to last for a while. New democracies are not only in special need of flexibility, but are arguably also in more need of constitutional stability and rigidity than established democratic systems.

As for the practical aspect, the reader of the constitution would be more interested in knowing the actual, present meaning of their constitution rather than knowing the peculiar history and evolution of a given constitutional provision. For instance, the 2016 constitutional reform of the judiciary was perhaps the only one that was enthusiastically welcomed and well received by the public. The reason for this is because of the negative perception of judges and prosecutors. The Constitution is a political document as much as a legal one and, as such, it should provide for limitations of state power to ensure a better level of protection of fundamental rights. If this cannot be achieved, from the public perspective it is not of much interest to know the frequency and model of amendment codification.

Although one could research the parliamentary documents (*travaux préparatoires*) in order to understand the goal of an amendment, it is not possible to obtain this information from reading the constitutional text. The hybrid model of the Albanian Constitution does not give much guidance in terms of understanding the content of the old provision and the aim of the new one. In cases where a considerable number of provisions have been introduced (such as in the 2016 reform), it could be confusing if one wishes to understand why a part of the constitution is much broader and detailed than the rest of it. Perhaps an explanatory note attached to the Constitution could be helpful to give some guidance on the historical, political and legal background of the introduced amendments. This could prevent any attempt to interpret them more widely or narrowly by the judges, which remains a concern of the legislator justifying the detailed provisions. But, as Rosalind Dixon states, no amount of specificity in constitutional language can ever hope to be entirely complete, or exhaustive, in setting out the aims and understandings of drafters. Even if it could be, it would also still need to be interpreted by judges in order to have effect. In this sense, processes of constitutional drafting based on distrust will largely be doomed to failure from the outset: they will attempt to respond to a distrust of judges by imposing legal constraints on judges that can never actually be broad or strong enough to overcome the reasons for their ongoing distrust.[35]

[35] Rosalind Dixon, 'Constitutional Drafting and Distrust' (2016) 13 *International Journal of Constitutional Law* 819.

17

Georgia's Model of Constitutional Amendment Codification

MALKHAZ NAKASHIDZE

I. Introduction

How does the Republic of Georgia codify amendments in its Constitution? The answer to this question is more closely tied to historical practice and context than intentional constitutional design, as is often the case with constitutions worldwide.[1] The choice among models of amendment codification has significant consequences for the course of constitutionalism in any country, as I will demonstrate in the example of Georgia. In this chapter, I analyse the Georgian model of amendment codification, the historical background, and the legal and political preconditions for selecting this codification model. I also examine the consequences of the selected model, including the challenges in terms of accessibility, harmonisation and its incorporation.

II. The Constitution of Georgia: A Single Codified Constitutional Document?

When analysing the implications of the Georgian model of codifying constitutional amendments, it is important to answer one main question: what type of constitution is the Georgian Constitution? The Constitution of Georgia was adopted in 1995 as a single codified document. It is important to note that before the adoption of the Constitution, Georgia had lost control over its two regions (the Autonomous Republic of Abkhazia and the Tskhinvali Region) due to the armed conflict between these two separatist regions and the central government of Georgia with the active instigation and support of the Russian Federation.

[1] See Richard Albert, *Constitutional Amendments: Making, Breaking and Changing Constitutions* (Oxford, Oxford University Press, 2019) 231–40.

Therefore, the Constitution mentions that constitutional law shall determine the territorial state structure of Georgia based on the principle of delimitation of powers after the complete restoration of jurisdiction of Georgia over the whole territory of the country.[2]

During the same period, the status of another autonomy – the Autonomous Republic of Adjara – was not defined by the Constitution of Georgia, and it was ruled by the 1978 Soviet Constitution of Autonomy. In 2000 the Constitution of Georgia was amended with the following article: 'The status of the Autonomous Republic of Adjara is defined by the Constitutional Law of Georgia on the status of the Autonomous Republic of Adjara.'[3] Later on, the same article about the Autonomous Republic of Abkhazia was added to the Constitution.[4] Based on these constitutional amendments, the Constitutional Law on the Status of the Autonomous Republic of Adjara was adopted in 2004,[5] but the Constitutional Law on the Autonomous Republic of Abkhazia has not yet been adopted. The Constitution of Georgia and these constitutional laws have equal legal force.

Therefore, it can be assumed that the Constitution of Georgia is not a single codified document. As Georgian scholars working on the amendments to the Constitution believe, the Constitution of Georgia since 2004 consists of two normative documents.[6] According to the criteria for classification of constitutions, the current Constitution of Georgia can be characterised as partially codified. The Constitution of Georgia consists of two normative documents: the main text of the Constitution of Georgia and the Constitutional Law on the Autonomous Republic of Adjara.[7] Scholars consider that the Constitutional Law on the Autonomous Republic of Adjara is an integral part of the Constitution of Georgia, and though it has not been incorporated into the main text of the Constitution,[8] the Constitution includes this constitutional law.[9] Thus, we can say that the Constitution of Georgia is not a single codified document, as it consists of two different constitutional documents. In addition, adoption of the constitutional law on territorial arrangement of the country and about the status of the Autonomous Republic of Abkhazia is foreseen in future. The adoption of this type of constitution led to the selection

[2] Constitution of Georgia, 24 August 1995, 'Sakartvelos Parlamentis Uckebebi' (1995), 31–33.

[3] Constitutional Law of Georgia, 20 April 2000 (25 April 25 2000), Legislative Herald of Georgia, 15, art 36, https://bit.ly/3NLMnRk.

[4] Constitutional Law of Georgia, 10 October 2002 (28 October 2002), Legislative Herald of Georgia, 28, art 128, https://bit.ly/3z8P37D.

[5] Constitutional Law of Georgia on the Status of the Autonomous Republic of Adjara, 1 July 2004, Legislative Herald of Georgia, (2004) 16, https://bit.ly/3NcAG6b.

[6] Irakli Kobakhidze, *Constitutional Law, Law of State Arrangement* (Tbilisi, Favority Stili, 2019) 30.

[7] ibid 33.

[8] Avtandil Demetrashvili and Giorgi Gogiashvili, *Constitutional Law* (Tbilisi, Iuristebis Samkaro, 2016) 22.

[9] Didmitri Gegenava (ed), *Introduction to the Constitutional Law of Georgia* (Tbilisi, Sulkhan-Saba Orbeliani University Press, 2019) 13.

of a specific model for the codification of constitutional amendments, which will be discussed in more detail in the following section.

III. The History of Constitutional Amendment Codification in Georgia

Georgia's first democratic constitution was adopted on 21 February 1921, but was suspended on 25 February due to the Soviet occupation. Four constitutions (1922, 1927, 1937 and 1978) were adopted in Georgia during the Soviet period. The current Constitution of Georgia was adopted on 24 August 1995. Thus, Georgia has gained experience in codifying constitutional amendments both during the Soviet period and after the adoption of the current Constitution of Georgia.

A. The Model of Constitutional Codification in the Georgian Soviet Constitutions

In the Soviet Georgian constitutions, the integrative and invisible models of constitutional amendment codification were used. For example, the 1932 Soviet Constitution of Georgia uses square brackets at the bottom of the relevant article of constitutional amendments. Article 23 of the Constitution, which deals with the all-Georgian Soviet Congress, is amended as follows: '[Resolution of all-Georgian Soviet Congress of Georgian SSR, February 19, 1931 (Law Volume, 1931, #9, Art. 92)].'[10] The Constitution also includes special notes under a particular amended article which interprets the content of the article (eg, paragraph 6 of the 1922 Constitution on the State Language).[11] The same kind of notes appear in the 1927 Constitution. The text in both constitutions was structured into chapters, and instead of articles, there were paragraphs without titles.[12] The model of such a codification was applied to the constitutional amendments adopted on 18 November 1989, completely revising the Soviet Constitution.[13] Thus, an integrative model of constitutional amendment codification was used in the Soviet Constitutions of Georgia.

[10] Constitution of the Socialist Soviet Republic of Georgia (Basic Law) (Tbilisi, 1932) 11–12, https://bit.ly/3wYWBHq.

[11] Constitution of the Socialist Soviet Republic of Georgia (Tbilissi, 1922), 5, https://bit.ly/3t5bAOP.

[12] Constitution of the Socialist Soviet Republic of Georgia (Basic Law) (Tbilissi, 1927) 24, https://bit.ly/3GJ9PMY.

[13] Law of the Soviet Socialist Republic of Georgia on Amendments to the Constitution (Basic Law) of the Georgian SSR, 'Utskebebi of the Supreme Soviet of the Georgian Socialist Soviet Republic' (November 1989, N11 (592), 15–34; https://bit.ly/3adD9if; ibid 115, https://bit.ly/3x84knL.

B. The Model of Amendment Codification during the Transition Period (1991–92)

On 28 October 1990, in the first multi-party elections in Georgia since the defeat of the Communists, the Supreme Council amended the 1978 Soviet Constitution of the Republic of Georgia (the Basic Law).[14] For the first time since the end of communist rule in 1990, the still-valid 1978 Soviet Constitution was published in Georgia. Both the integrative and the invisible models of codification were used in this case. For example, the text of the Constitution states 'Article 3 (removed)'.[15] This article described the principles of the Soviet socialist state, which were removed. There are similar references to other articles that have been removed, although elsewhere, where the norms have changed, the text was completely updated according to the invisible model, which did not include any note about amendment. However, in 1990 the same text was published in Russian without any reference to amendments. Only the first page of the Constitution indicates that the text includes amendments from 1984, 1986, 1989 and 1990.[16] In this case, the invisible model of codification was purely used as it was impossible to determine where and what was amended specifically in the text.

Why were the integrative and invisible models used during the last amendments to the Soviet Constitution? It should be noted that the Soviet Constitution was entirely based on the ideology of the Communist Party and did not recognise the fundamental principles of constitutionalism. The Constitution explicitly stated that the Communist Party was the sole ruling party in Georgia and the country was the Soviet Socialist Republic. After the declaration of independence, the adoption of a new constitution did not happen swiftly. The government planned to draft a new constitution based on the first Constitution of Georgia of 21 February 1921.[17] Prior to the adoption of the new constitution, the main goal of amendments to the Soviet Constitution was to remove all the communist and socialist provisions, and replace them with democratic principles.

The invisible model was chosen for this purpose, and though a Soviet tradition, the model fell into line with the goal of democratic development in Georgia – to erase the Soviet legacy, to reflect on the development of democratic constitutionalism and to make this change accessible and understandable to the general public. The invisible model of constitutional amendment codification, which was first used in Georgia to amend the Soviet Constitution, proved highly instrumental for specific purposes.

[14] ibid 17–18, https://bit.ly/3Man6PE.

[15] Constitution of the Republic of Georgia Constitution (Basic Law) (Samshoblo, 1990) 5.

[16] Constitution of the Soviet Socialist Republic of Georgia (in Russian) (Sakartvelo, 1990) 3–61.

[17] Law of the Republic of Georgia on the Annoucement of the Transition Period in the Republic of Georgia, 11 November 1990 (1990), 'Sakartvelos Parlamentis Utskebebi', 11, https://bit.ly/3PUGAL9.

C. The Model of Amendment Codification Used after the 1991–92 Georgian Coup d'etat

Following the collapse of the Soviet Union, an internal armed conflict developed in the newly independent Georgia from 22 December 1991 to 6 January 1992. The coup ended with the first democratically elected President of Georgia, Zviad Gamsakhurdia, being exiled. Eduard Shevardnadze, the last Soviet Foreign Affairs Minister, was invited by the military council that was formed after the coup to take power as the Chairman of the State Council. The Soviet Constitution amended by Gamsakhurdia's government was not recognised by the new government. They needed a new constitution, but it could not possibly have been adopted immediately. That is why the Law on 'State Power'[18] was adopted on 6 November 1992, which scholars call the 'Small Constitution'. This law was amended on 30 March 1994 and used an integrative model, which provided for the renaming of a single state body and its reflection in the main text of the law.[19] The choice of the codification model in this case was also affected by rapid changes, which was supposed to become the basis for the adoption of new laws for the operation of this entity. At that time, there were no laws in the country at all, a hierarchy of normative acts and a 'Small Constitution' was the only law that gave legitimacy to the government.

D. The Codification Model in the Constitution-Making Process (1993–95)

The current Constitution of Georgia was adopted on 24 August 1995. The draft constitution was prepared by the Constitutional Commission from 1993 to 1995 and was then adopted by the Parliament. Were models of codification of constitutional amendments discussed in the Constitutional Commission? Yes, both the European (for example, the French and German) and the US Constitutions were used as guiding principles while drafting the constitution in Georgia, although the appendative model was not chosen as an example, as no one at the time thought it was important to leave the original document untouched. It was decided that the Constitution would exist in the future in the form of several acts with equal legal force. Therefore, in the future, this could have been seen as a prospect of the disaggregative codification model. Everyone knew from the beginning that this was not the final and complete constitution of Georgia and it would be impossible to keep its original text untouched. Moreover, it is possible that the creation of a completely new constitution would have been necessary if the territorial

[18] Law of the Republic of Georgia on State Power (1992), 'Sakartvelos Parlamentis Utskebebi' 1, https://bit.ly/3mbBxrT.

[19] Law on Amendments to the 'Law of Republic of Georgia on the State Power' (1994), 'Sakartvelos Parlamentis Utskebebi', 16–17, 78–79, https://bit.ly/3t1GlUL.

integrity of the country had been restored. For these reasons, Georgia adopted a 'temporary' constitution.[20] It was thought that the Constitution would take effect for a period of 10 years in transition and then it might be changed again.[21] For example, Professor Hermann Schwartz, who was an advising expert, thought that Georgia should have considered a mandatory revision of the Constitution after seven or 10 years.[22] We must therefore assume that the establishment of an integrative and invisible model of codification was caused by the temporary, imperfect structure of the Constitution established during the drafting process. After the adoption of the Constitution, these models responded well to the task of eliminating the gaps in the text (for example, territorial arrangement) and made the constitutional amendments more accessible to the public.

The choice of the model of constitutional amendments is also indicated in the discussions over the constitutional law that took place during the drafting process of the Constitution. Some, like Professor Avtandil Demetrashvili, assumed that constitutional amendments were equal to constitutional law. Others, however, thought that constitutional law was not equivalent to a constitutional amendment. Vakhtang Khmaladze, another member of the commission, considered 'constitutional law' as a norm *sui generis*. In his view, the notion of 'constitutional law' means that such laws should become an integral part of the Constitution. Levan Aleksidze, a professor of international law, shared the same view, arguing that 'constitutional law has the same meaning as the constitution, but it deals only with specific issues. These laws become part of the Constitution. Professor Ninidze believed that the constitutional law would have been a separate law, but without it the constitution would have been meaningless'.[23] On the other hand, Professor Ugrekhelidze[24] said that constitutional law could be part of the Constitution, just like the Bill of Rights. The drafters thought that the Constitution would change when the country became united and established peace.[25] Based on Ugrekhelidze's argument, it is possible that the creators of the Constitution also considered the possibility of an appendative model of constitutional amendments regarding the territorial arrangement of the country in the future. However, at that time, it was important to immediately hold the first elections. Therefore, the Constitution designers were forced to accept the so-called a 'flexible constitution' that would include several constitutional laws.[26]

[20] Wolfgang Babeck, *Adoption and Elaboration of Constitution in Georgia (1993–1995)* (Tbilisi, GIZ, 2002) 288

[21] ibid 167.

[22] ibid 140.

[23] ibid 99–101.

[24] After the adoption of the Constitution, he was Chairman of the Supreme Court of Georgia and later a judge at the European Court of Human Rights.

[25] Babeck (n 20) 100.

[26] ibid 81.

According to Professor Demetrashvili,[27] codification was not a crucial issue during the drafting of the Constitution, as there were other more important topics that had to be discussed and other laws that had to be written. Because of this, the codification issue was not thought through comprehensively.[28] Thus, the discussions that took place during the process of drafting the Constitution and the viewpoints of the participants indicate that, in those particular conditions, it was natural to use the integrative and invisible model of codification established in the Soviet period, the main purpose of which was to make constitutional amendments easily accessible to the public.

E. The Codification Model for the First Constitutional Amendment (1999)

The first amendment to the Constitution of Georgia was adopted on 20 July 1999, which increased the electoral threshold for parliamentary elections from 5 per cent to 7 per cent.[29] This amendment was implemented using the same model of codification as in the Soviet period. Was the codification model examined during the first constitutional amendment? What determined the final choice? Based on the available information, it should be noted that discussions over this issue had not taken place by that time. The first amendment was a purely political decision that served to strengthen the parliamentary majority, being passed in a fast manner before the parliamentary elections. This threshold was changed to 5 per cent again in 2008,[30] and even then the government argued that lowering the threshold would strengthen political pluralism.

As already discussed above, during the first constitutional amendments, the integrative and invisible codification models established from the Soviet period were already used in Georgia. However, one of the authors of the drafted Constitution of Georgia, Vakhtang Khmaladze,[31] associated the use of the integrative model of codification of constitutional amendments with the adoption of the 'Law of Georgia on Normative Acts' in 1996, which defined the rules for preparing,

[27] In 1993–95 he was the Secretary of the Constitutional Commission and subsequently the First Chairman of the Constitutional Court of Georgia, in 2009–10 he was the Chairman of the State Constitutional Commission.

[28] Avtandil Demetrashvili, personal Interview with Malkhaz Nakashidze, 19 May 2022, Tbilisi.

[29] Constitutional Law of Georgia on Amendments to the Constitution of Georgia (20 July 1999), Legislative Herald of Georgia, 35 (42).

[30] Constitutional Law of Georgia on Amendments to the Constitution of Georgia (12 March 2008), https://bit.ly/38QgmZI.

[31] In 1992–95 he was a Member of the Parliament of Georgia, and from 1993 to 1995 was the Deputy Chairman of the State Constitutional Commission. He was also a member of the Constitutional Commission and the Organizing Commission for the Public Discussion of Constitutional Amendments from 1995 to 2022.

adopting and amending all types of normative acts.[32] According to Khmaladze, the main purpose of selecting this model was to make the changes clear and understandable for the citizens, so that readers could detect and read the changes. At that time, the requirement of this law was also extended to the constitutional amendments; therefore, they did not think of adopting a different model for the constitutional amendments.[33]

Tengiz Sharmanashvili[34] shares the same view, saying that the integrative model of codification was reflected in the first law on normative acts in 1996 and has not changed much since then, and as no one has argued against this issue, the Parliament continued to use it. He believes that this model was inherited by Georgia from the Soviet period, and the Soviet tradition of legislative technique was very much similar to the German one. He confirms that this issue has not been discussed in any of the constitutional commissions. Only in 2017, when a new version of the Constitution was adopted, with numerous changes made and many more to be introduced, was a new edition of the Constitution prepared and convened into one article, otherwise it would have been very difficult to understand the changes. Such an approach simplified the discussion of the draft constitutional amendments in the Parliament because the amendments were provided as one article. It was the first case in which such a model was used; however, it was used in compliance with the existing legislative techniques. Sharmanashvili says that another model of codification can be used, but in the Georgian tradition, which is defined in the Law on Normative Acts, the legislative technique of a constitutional law is not different from the legislative technique of other laws, so this issue should be considered and reflected in the legislation.[35] In addition, Professor Vasil Gonashvili[36] says that the model of codification of constitutional amendments has not been discussed in the constitutional commissions and it was considered as a matter of pure legislative technique, which followed established practice.[37]

Thus, it seems that an integrative-invisible hybrid model of constitutional amendment codification was initially established in Georgia in accordance with the Soviet tradition, and in 1996 in accordance with the principles of legislative technique defined by the Law on Normative Acts.

[32] Law of Georgia on Normative Acts, 29 October 1996 (1996), 'Sakartvelos Parlamentis Utskebebi', https://bit.ly/3NehXHy.

[33] Vakhtang Khmaladze, interview with Malkhaz Nakashidze, 25 May 2022, Tbilisi.

[34] In 1995–99 he was a Member of the Parliament of Georgia and Deputy Chairman of the Legal Committee. In 2009–10 and 2016 he was the Secretary of the State Constitutional Commission. Since 2016, he has been Advisor to the Chairman of the Parliament of Georgia. At various times, he was also a member of the Organizing Committee for the Public Discussion of Constitutional Amendments.

[35] Tengiz Sharmanashvili, written interview with Malkhaz Nakashidze, 27 May 2022, Tbilisi.

[36] He was a member of the Constitutional Commission and the Organizing Committee for the General Public Review of Constitutional Amendments at various times.

[37] Vasil Gonashvili, interview with Malkhaz Nakashidze, 24 May 2022, Tbilisi.

IV. The Constitutional Amendments Codification in the Current Constitution

The Constitution of Georgia does not specify which model of codification of constitutional amendments should be used. In addition, the Constitution no longer has unamendable provisions and any part of it can be amended. There is no official type, format or standard for publishing the text of the Constitution in Georgia. The Constitution is officially published by the Ministry of Justice online as an official text, but a hard copy could be published by any private company, publisher, law firm or university using different models of codification. Since the adoption of the Constitution in 1995, 36 constitutional amendments have been implemented in Georgia. The constitutional changes were mainly based on the integrative model; however, due to various circumstances, the invisible, aggregative and appendative models were also used, which will be discussed below.

A. The Integrative Model of Codification of Constitutional Amendments

In Georgia the integrative model is mainly used for the codification of constitutional amendments. In the Georgian model, the old text of the Constitution does not indicate a new text, nor does it have a footnote, and basically no new text is inserted in square brackets. The text of the constitution simply indicates amendment, the date, and the number of the law by which the amendment was made to the entire article.[38] In some editions it is also acceptable to indicate notes in parentheses (i.e., 20.04.2000 N260).[39] The numbers in parentheses indicate the day, month, year and number of the constitutional law.[40] I consider the practice of codifying the constitutional amendments used in the current Constitution of Georgia as an integrative model, although this does not take into account the inclusion of new amendments and the old text in the Constitution, as Albert has considered in the example of India.[41] As a result of the constitutional amendments in 2009, when the location of Parliament was changed, and during a fundamental constitutional reform on 15 October 2010,[42] the published text of the Constitution included both the current norms and new amendments in yellow on the official

[38] Constitution of Georgia, 24 August 1995, Legislative Herald of Georgia (Consolidated versions, 13 October 2017–23 March 2018).

[39] Constitution of Georgia, 24 August 1995 (Center for Crime Research and Forecasting, Tbilisi, 2007) 6.

[40] Constitution of Georgia, 24 August 1995 (last amended 25 November 2013, Regional Center for Research and Promotion of Constitutionalism, Tbilisi, 2013) 5.

[41] Albert (n 1) 236–38.

[42] Constitutional Law of Georgia of 15 October 2010, №3710-SSM I, №62, 5 November 2010, art 379.

website[43] and in some print editions using italic and parentheses.[44] Thus, it is an integrative model that does not contain detailed instructions for new changes as it does in India, but still contains reference to changes in the text.

B. The Disaggregative Model of Codification of Constitutional Amendments

The disaggregative model of constitutional amendments is also used in Georgia. According to Richard Albert, in the disaggregative model of constitutional amendment, changes of constitutional importance do not appear in a single codified constitutional document, nor are they necessarily always formalised in a text – for instance, in the case of changes to and by constitutional convention.[45] If we evaluate the Constitution of Georgia according to this definition, we can say that the existence of constitutional laws on autonomous republics of Georgia indicates that the disaggregative model of constitutional amendment is used in Georgia because constitutional amendments do not appear in the main text of the Constitution, but they are provided in the form of a constitutional law or amendment. If we follow the logic of codification of the Constitution, any amendments to the Constitutional Law on the Autonomous Republic of Adjara can be considered as an amendment to the Constitution of Georgia.

The choice to use this model, as mentioned above, was made due to the given political situation. The dissaggregative model was the most suitable model for the purpose of resolving relationships between the central government and autonomies after the Soviet past. In that particular political context, the integrative model would not have been able to fully address this political challenge. This model will be used to define the powers of the Autonomous Republic of Abkhazia by the constitutional laws of Georgia, which still remain to be adopted today.

C. The Appendative Model of Codification of Constitutional Amendments

Since the constitutional amendments came into force on 16 December 2018,[46] the fully updated text of the Constitution was amended once again on 23 March 2018.

[43] Constitutional Law of Georgia on Amendment to the Constitution of Georgia, 24 September 2009, Legislative Herald of Georgia, I, №29, 12 October 2009, art 157, https://bit.ly/3NcUAy1.

[44] Constitution of Georgia, adopted on 24 August 1995, last amended 15 February 2011, RCRPC, Publication #3, Batumi, 2011, art 72, 100; Constitution of Georgia, adopted on 24 August 1995 (Tbilisi, 2013), last amended 1 June 2013, RCRPC, CIPDD, art 72, 102.

[45] Albert (n 1) 234.

[46] Salome Zurabishvili's inauguration was held on 16 December.

As a result, the updated text of the Constitution was published without the transitional provisions of the December Law, which was in force and regulated important issues in the next transitional period. As a solution to this issue, the published text of the Constitution was accompanied by transitional provisions entitled: 'Transitional Provisions of the Constitutional Law of Georgia of 13 October 2017 (Article 2).'[47] The Constitution was printed and published on the official website of the President of Georgia, including transitional provisions and the Constitutional Law on the Autonomous Republic of Adjara.[48] I consider the practice of such codification of constitutional amendments as an appendative and disaggregative model; when the constitutional amendment is not published together with the main text, it has equal legal force of the Constitution and is enclosed to the main text of the Constitution.

D. The Invisible Model of Constitutional Amendment Codification

The invisible model is rarely used in the current Constitution of Georgia; however, in some editions prepared by the Parliament, nothing is specified and the full text is updated using the invisible model.[49] A special model of codification of constitutional amendments was used in Georgia in 2017, which I consider to be an invisible model. At that time, the entire text of the Constitution was completely updated and the note at the bottom of each article indicated the same law, date and number of the constitutional amendment. In my opinion, it does not make much difference if the law of the constitutional amendment, the date and number are mentioned only once on the first page of the Constitution, as it is in the invisible model, or next to each article, as in both cases it is unclear where and what was amended exactly. This particular choice was driven by the fact that the text of the Constitution, which was fully revised in October 2017, was updated once again in March 2018, with the aim of reflecting the recommendations made by the Venice Commission in the new version of the Constitution.[50] Following the revision of the entire text of the Constitution, both constitutional laws on constitutional amendments were referenced at the end of each article of the Constitution. The Venice Commission had a few recommendations, but Parliament wrongly chose to fully revise the Constitution. We do not know exactly where and what was amended.

[47] Constitution of Georgia (Parliament of Georgia (GIZ), Tbilisi, 2018) 77–78.

[48] Constitution of Georgia, 24 August 1995, Administration of the President of Georgia, https://bit.ly/3gIK0QD.

[49] Constitution of Georgia, 24 August 1995 (Parliament of Georgia Edition (GIZ), Tbilisi, 2018) 77–78.

[50] Resolution of the Parliament of Georgia (2 November 2017), N1326-I, https://bit.ly/3m8t5tH.

V. Popular Accessibility of the Text of the Constitutional Amendments

Constitutional amendments are accessible to different degrees in the appendative, disaggregative, integrative and invisible models of constitutional amendment codification respectively. In Georgia, public access to constitutional amendments is often restricted. For example, on 13 October 2017, an entirely new version of the Constitution was approved, and although it is formally called a constitutional amendment, it should be considered a dismemberment as defined by Richard Albert.[51] This law consists of three articles. The first states that the Constitution of Georgia should be drafted in a new edition and provides a new 78-article text, the second contains 10 paragraphs, mainly transitional provisions, which are not written in the codified, updated main text of the Constitution, and, finally, the third sets the deadline for the enactment of the constitutional amendment.[52] In the new version of the Constitution, only the date of the adoption of the Constitution (1995) and the name of the President (Mr Shevardnadze) remained unchanged. But in March 2018, the new law on the full revision of the Constitution did not contain the transitional provisions adopted in 2017. Thus, this amendment can be considered lost and no longer available to the public. As a result, lawyers, scholars and citizens may not be aware that such norms exist.

The accessibility of constitutional amendments is directly linked to the practices of 2009 and 2010. According to these practices, both the old and the new text were published together for a limited time after the adoption of the constitutional amendments. After the enactment of the constitutional amendments, the old, invalid norms were deleted from the text of the Constitution. These changes were significant and far-reaching as two terms of government had expired, the governance model was changed to a parliamentary system, and the timing coincided with the preparations for the 2012 elections. In order to make the changes understandable for people, it was decided to jointly reflect them in the Constitution using an integrative model, a practice that had not existed in Georgia before. Due to the form of publication, it was not clear to the public which text was valid.

VI. Judicial Interpretation of Constitutional Amendments

In constitutional law, the problem of incorporation has serious consequences in terms of how to interpret the text in the face of a dispute about its meaning.[53]

[51] Albert (n 1) 92.

[52] The Constitutional Law of Georgia on Amendments to the Constitution of Georgia (19 October 2017), Legislative Herald of Georgia, 1324-RS, https://bit.ly/3GNDPY0.

[53] Albert (n 1) 254.

The definition of constitutional norms in Georgia is provided by the Constitutional Court of Georgia in its decisions on human rights. The Constitutional Court rejects the exercise of constitutional control over the constitutional amendments themselves on the basis of a purely formalistic approach.[54]

The issue of codification and interpretation of constitutional amendments has always been the subject of special attention in the process of 2017 constitutional amendments. It is written in the Constitutional Law that the amendments made to the second chapter of the Constitution of Georgia cause the change of the normative grounds for admissibility of lawsuits, if necessary, in accordance with the amendments made to the second chapter of the Constitution.[55] After the constitutional amendments, the court made the following interpretation: 'the Constitution of Georgia was drafted with a new wording. Consequently, the named constitutional provisions are invalid. Based on the above, the Constitutional Court of Georgia will assess the constitutionality of the disputed norm in relation to the provisions of the current Constitution, which have identical/similar content'.[56] The court today uses such an interpretation and determines which norms are identical to the old norms and how the content should be interpreted.

There have been cases in Georgia where it has become necessary to explain constitutional amendments due to different understandings of their powers by different branches of authorities. The practice is in place in Georgia, according to which preference is given to amendments to the Constitution rather than to the interpretations of the courts. This is due to the established political system in which a one-party majority could very easily amend the Constitution and it was an easy and fast method for the government to implement constitutional reforms.

Interpretation of the constitutional amendments became especially important, for example, in 2014, when the issue arose as to who should sign the Association Agreement with the EU – the President or the Prime Minister. The Prime Minister eventually signed the treaty, although the President issued an act delegating signing authority, which the Prime Minister did not recognise as necessary. The second case was in 2022 when the President of Georgia visited the EU during the Ukrainian-Russian war. The government claimed that according to the latest constitutional amendments, the President cannot make visits without the consent of the government, so the President had violated the Constitution and the government would ask the Constitutional Court to interpret the Constitution on this point. The government was against the visit of the President because she might have a different position from the government at this particular moment

[54] Richard Albert, Malkhaz Nakashidze and Tarik Olcay. 'The Formalist Resistance to Unconstitutional Constitutional Amendments' (2019) 70(3) *Hastings Law Journal* 639.

[55] The Constitutional Law of Georgia on Amendments to the Constitution of Georgia (19 October 2017), Legislative Herald of Georgia, 1324-RS, https://bit.ly/3GNDPY0.

[56] *Tiflis 777 Ltd v Parliament of Georgia*, N1/2/1250 (18 April 2019) I, II; *Irakli Khvedelidze v Parliament of Georgia*, N1/3/1263 (18 April 2019) I.

regarding relations with the EU and Ukraine. Today, one party does not have a majority in Parliament to change the Constitution, In the near future, it will become clear whether or not the government will apply to the Constitutional Court for interpretation.

VII. The Harmonisation and Incorporation of the Constitutional Amendments

The harmonisation of constitutional amendments in Georgia mainly arises before the codification of constitutional amendments, when designers choose where to codify constitutional amendments and in what form. Incorporating changes to the Constitution in Georgia has not always occurred in the right place. The Constitution had many shortcomings in this regard. For example, at the time of the adoption of the Constitution, the prosecutor's office was defined as an institution of the judiciary, and though it then became part of the executive branch, today it is still placed in Chapter 6, 'Judiciary and the Prosecutor's Office'. Also since the Constitution was adopted, the structure of Parliament was divided between Article 4 and Article 49. In 2017 the provision on Georgia's accession to the EU and the North Atlantic Treaty Organization (NATO) was defined in Article 78 of the Constitution in the Transitional Provisions of the Constitution, although it was considered that it should be specified in the preamble or in the first chapter. It should be noted that one of the goals of the constitutional amendments in 2017 was to correct the legal deficiency of the Constitution,[57] and this task was partially fulfilled. The structure of the Constitution was completely changed, the articles were retitled and the volume of the text was reduced. Eventually, better harmonisation was achieved, many norms were thematically incorporated into articles, and the Constitution was structurally much improved and made more accessible.

The incorporation of constitutional amendments is related to the further amendment of once-adopted constitutional amendments, which is often caused by rapid changes. For example, as mentioned above, in 2018,[58] an amendment was made to the Law on Constitutional Amendments adopted on 19 October 2017 and the full text of the Constitution was amended, although the amendment did not apply to Article 2 of the same law, which defined elections, judiciary, taxes and other issues. The same constitutional amendments in 2020 included another constitutional amendment regarding the 2020 and 2024 parliamentary elections.

[57] Explanatory Card on the Draft Constitutional Law of Georgia on Amendments to the Constitution of Georgia, Resolution of the Parliament of Georgia, N742-II (3 May 2017), Legislative Herald of Georgia.

[58] Constitutional Law of Georgia on Amendments to the Constitution of Georgia on Amendments to the Constitutional Law of Georgia, 23 March 2018, Legislative Herald of Georgia, 2 April 2018.

Thus, the transitional provisions today exist separately and are not reflected in the main text of the Constitution.[59] Incorporation into the Constitution through the use of transitional provisions can be considered malpractice created in Georgia due to frequent and rapid constitutional reforms. Because of this model of harmonisation, these norms are lost, and constitutional changes are not available.

VIII. Conclusions

In conclusion, Georgia mainly uses the integrative model of constitutional amendments, which is a Soviet legacy, and this tradition has been maintained. This model is mainly considered in Georgia as a legislative technique regulated by a separate law, and its advantage is considered to be the public accessibility of constitutional amendments. This model was also more suitable for Georgia, which has been closer to the continental European legal system since the Soviet period. The appropriateness of the integrative model has therefore almost never become controversial. The invisible model was also used in Georgia, mainly during the fundamental revision of the initial period of transition from the Soviet system, when Soviet socialist norms were completely removed from the text of the Constitution.

Georgia also uses the disaggregative model of constitutional changes, which was defined from the very beginning when the Constitution was adopted, which meant the adoption of constitutional laws on the territorial arrangement of the country in the future, as well as the constitutional status of the Autonomous Republic of Abkhazia. Adopted due to the violation of the territorial integrity of the country, this model was not a good choice.

Rapid, frequent and fundamental constitutional changes are characteristic of Georgia, due to which many changes in the Constitution are defined by transitional provisions and are valid for a certain period. After their adoption, these transitional provisions are not reflected in the updated text according to the integrative model and are not accessible publicly. These constitutional amendments can be considered an appendative model of constitutional amendment codification because amendments are appended to the end of the original text in various editions of the Constitution for a certain period of time. This model of codification of constitutional changes is often considered to be dismemberment as defined by Albert.

Another peculiarity of the Georgian model is the simultaneous inclusion of new constitutional amendments and old text in the master text of the Constitution using the integrative model, but only for a certain period of time before the new amendments come into force. This is a special model of constitutional amendments unique to Georgia.

[59] Constitutional Law of Georgia on Amendments to the Constitutional Law of Georgia on Amendments to the Constitutional Law of Georgia (29 June 2020), https://bit.ly/38StkWA.

The role of the Constitutional Court of Georgia in the interpretation of constitutional amendments is limited and it generally refuses to consider the constitutionality of constitutional amendments from a purely formalist point of view. However, it interprets the norms of the new constitutional amendments when considering constitutional claims relating to human rights.

Today, Georgia has not considered a better model than the integrative model for codifying constitutional amendments. First, Georgian constitutional designers consider that the integrative model is the best in terms of public accessibility of the constitutional amendments. Second, the current Constitution is not even considered as a final document and it has been suggested that after a transitionary period, a new constitution may be adopted. This could be, for example, the restoration of territorial integrity and Georgia's integration into the EU. If in the future after the adoption of the Constitution, it is deemed necessary to keep the original document untouched, another method of codification may be considered.

INDEX

www.ingramcontent.com/pod-product-compliance
Ingram Content Group UK Ltd.
Pitfield, Milton Keynes, MK11 3LW, UK
UKHW020250290926
15470UKWH00002B/847